APPLIED
GENEALOGY

APPLIED GENEALOGY

By Eugene Aubrey Stratton

Library of Congress Cataloging-in-Publication Data

Stratton, Eugene Aubrey.
  Applied Genealogy

  Includes index.
  1. Genealogy. I. Title.
CS16.S854 1988   929'.1   88-70336
ISBN 0-916489-32-9

Robert J. Welsh, Managing Editor
Design and Production by Robb Barr
Cover Design by Newman Passey Design, Inc.

First Printing 1988
10 9 8 7 6 5 4 3 2 1

Printed in the United States of America.

Contents

Introduction vii

1. Background and Purposes of Genealogy 1
2. Genealogical Potpourri 15
3. The Scholarly Journals .29
4. Standards and Documentation 41
5. Whole-Family Genealogy .61
6. Onomastic Evidence vs.
   the Name's the Same Game 75
7. Analyzing Evidence 89
8. Indirect Evidence 107
9. Forgivable Sins 127
10. Pride of Ancestry – Hereditary Societies 137
11. Royal Genealogy – Case Studies 157
12. Royal Genealogy – Ways and Means 171
13. Academia and Genealogy 191
14. Computers and Genealogy 209
15. The Organization of Genealogy 223

Appendix A. The Validity of Genealogical
             Evidence 241
Appendix B. Essay on Medieval English
             Land Tenure .263
Appendix C. An Interesting Medieval Document . .285
Appendix D. A New Royal Line:
             John Harleston of South Carolina 301
Index 317

Introduction

With all the genealogical "how-to" books on the market, anyone presuming to write another had better have a good reason. "What," the writer should ask, "can I give the reader of value not readily obtainable elsewhere?"

Perhaps then I should first introduce myself, describe my purpose, and name my intended audience. As historian general of the General Society of Mayflower Descendants, as herald/genealogist for the Descendants of the Illegitimate Sons and Daughters of the Kings of Britain, and as the approving genealogist for other hereditary societies, I have had the occasion over the past eight years of examining and passing upon literally thousands of membership applications giving the generation-by-generation descents of applicants from Revolutionary War soldiers, colonial American clergymen, the Pilgrim fathers (and mothers), and medieval British kings. These applications were required to be accompanied by documentation "proving" the validity of every generation, and it was my job to make sure that the documentation people submitted was sufficient.

Being blessed with great curiosity, I was not content just to say that a line was false or unproven, but I often conducted additional research to see how an insufficiently supported line could be proven, or, if it could not, to see if there might be a good alternative line. During this time, I lectured at and otherwise participated in national genealogical conferences, taught genealogical classes, sometimes did research for clients with particular genealogical problems to be solved, and wrote the book *Plymouth Colony: Its History & People, 1620-1691*. I have had articles published in all the national genealogical journals, and I am a contributing editor for *The American Genealogist*. In 1987 I was given the National Genealogical Society Award of Merit. Prior to my work for the Society of Mayflower Descendants, I had spent one year in England doing genealogical research. After I left the society, I spent more than three years in Salt Lake City using the world's largest genealogical library, the Family History Library of the Church of Jesus Christ of Latter-day Saints. Beyond this, and more important than all my other experience put together, I have had the good fortune of having frequent and meaningful contact and interaction, in person and by correspondence, with some of the most accomplished genealogists in this country as well as a few from abroad.

Thus I have had first hand acquaintance with a lot of genealogical problems and a good number of genealogical answers. Moreover, I have seen the way thousands of other people, from beginners through intermediates to the advanced, have confronted genealogy in its many facets. To see the many different views on sources, evidence, standards, documentation, authorities, and other aspects of genealogy, is a rich experience, showing, among other things, the vast diversity in the genealogical public. It is also a sad experience, though, to see the tremendous amount of misunderstanding that exists in the field of genealogy.

In spite of large numbers of practitioners (I have read, without seeing statistics on it, that genealogy is America's fastest, or one of its fastest, growing hobbies), genealogy is not well understood. There is much confusion about the requirements of hereditary societies, the value of genealogical publications, the feeling of some people that genealogy is a frightening occult science, and the contempt of many others that genealogy is so easy to master that it would be a waste of time to study principles. There is also confusion among academicians who have been brought up to think of genealogy as something less than scientific, but who make use, to support some of their studies, of genealogical materials that good genealogists would never cite. Although there are many good "how-to" books on the market, a large number of them concentrate on where to find genealogical evidence. Very few attempt to explain what genealogy is, or show people what to do with information once it is found. There would seem to be a need for something new to show how genealogy can be applied to meet human needs. That is the purpose of this book.

This book then is intended for genealogists on all levels. It is further intended for intelligent non-genealogists (people in the university, media, and business worlds, etc.) who might have occasion to wonder what genealogy is all about, what it encompasses, what its methods are, who its practitioners are, how scientific it is, how it is evaluated, or how it is organized. Above all, this book is concerned with helping people understand what is good genealogy and what is bad genealogy.

I have naturally drawn on my personal involvement and experience. The nature of the coverage lends itself to personal views, and thus, far more than in other writings, I have resorted to the personal pronoun in this book. My acquaintance with medieval English and colonial New England genealogy will of course show through in the many examples I give; however, there are many universal aspects of genealogy, and the examples often provide insights that would be equally true in conducting genealogical research in other areas. The examples are merely an educational technique used to make material more easily understandable, but the real concern of the book is whole genealogy, not regional genealogy. Though intended primarily for the individual reader, this book may also be used as a textbook on genealogy, as I myself will be using it in a university class I will be teaching. I know that there are many people with an interest in German, French, Mexican, Amerindian, Afro-American, Asian, and numerous other branches of genealogy, and there are many techniques and processes described in this book which would apply to them, even though the examples take place in the areas I know the best.

Books like this are never written by a single person. I have drawn upon the experience of many people in general, and some in particular. The latter are those who generously looked over all or part of the book in draft stage and offered helpful suggestions. I especially want to thank Professor David L. Greene, F.A.S.G., and Ruth Wilder Sherman, F.A.S.G., co-editors of *The American Genealogist*, and George Ely Russell, F.A.S.G., former editor of the *National Genealogical Society Quarterly*, for reading a draft of all chapters and graciously offering suggestions and comments. Their help has been as invaluable as their company has always been pleasurable.

A number of other people kindly offered to read individual chapters, and I am no less grateful to them. Michael Altschul, author of *A Baronial Family in Medieval England: The Clares*, took time out of a very busy schedule as a professor of history at Case Western Reserve University to read and offer comments on appendix B, "Essay on Medieval English Land Tenure," as did Professor C. Warren Hollister of the Medieval Studies Department of the University of California at Santa Barbara.

Thomas Roderick, C.G., Ph.D., a career geneticist, patiently answered my many questions about genetics, and some of my understanding of his answers on this complicated and rapidly changing science are found in chapter 13. Milton Rubincam, F.A.S.G., Walter Lee Sheppard, Jr., F.A.S.G.; Rabbi Malcolm Stern, F.A.S.G.; Robert Charles Anderson, F.A.S.G.; Lynn C. McMillion, C.A.I.L.S; and Marcia Wiswall Lindburg, President of the Essex Society of Genealogists, read one or more chapters and gave me helpful suggestions for improvement.

Neil D. Thompson, F.A.S.G., read the manuscript on behalf of the publisher and offered a number of helpful suggestions for which I am grateful. I am also grateful to Robb Barr, who edited the book for the publisher. I am thankful to John Sittner, Publisher; Robert J. Welsh, Managing Editor; and the others at Ancestry, Inc., for their parts in publishing this book. It would be fitting also to note Bob Welsh's great patience in dealing with writers such as myself. My wife, Ginger K. W. Stratton, helps me in innumerable ways on everything I write, and her role is an indispensable one. There are many other people not mentioned here who deserve much gratitude for their help over the years in my continuing education as a genealogist. I alone bear responsibility for the way the ideas in this book are interpreted and presented, but I certainly had a lot of wonderful expertise to draw on in making my decisions.

Chapter 1

Background and Purposes of Genealogy

> *Do we really write for our own family? If that is so, then I think it is absolutely amazing...the number of books written by genealogists who are just writing for their own family...that end up on library shelves. There they are not only being used by other genealogists, but also by the new breed of historian, cultural geographer, demographer, or medical researcher, who recognizes the potential genealogy has to offer to the academic world.*
>
> —Elizabeth Shown Mills

Noel C. Stevenson in his book *Genealogical Evidence* points out that ultimately the law is the arbiter of genealogy.[1] I agree up to a point but must believe that higher than the law are common sense and conscience.

The Warming-pan Baby

My case in point is the warming-pan baby, James Francis Edward Stuart, son of King James II of England and his queen, Mary of Modena. Or was he their son? The facts are that Queen Mary was visibly pregnant, and on 10 June 1688 (Old Style), she was delivered of a son in her bedchamber, which was full of doctors, ladies-in-waiting, servants, and others. Queens did not have their babies in private.[2]

But the birth of a son for the king, if the son survived, was a political matter. The king and queen were Catholic in an England where Catholics were no longer wanted by a sizeable majority. If the king died without a male heir, his Protestant daughter Mary, by his first wife, would be his heir to the throne. But a son by the second wife would be brought up Catholic and perpetuate the strife and division accompanying the reign of James.

At some point during the momentous birth of James Francis Edward, a servant brought a warming-pan into the room – England can be cool in June and drafty in palaces. The opposition to King James had already determined that the queen's pregnancy was a fake, even though she had given birth four times previously (to children who did not live). How convenient that warming-pan was! The king's opponents quickly spread the story that the queen had padded herself to look pregnant, and a newborn baby not of royal blood had been smuggled into the bedchamber in the warming-pan. Naturally all believed what they wanted to believe. Not long after, King James was deposed by his daughter and her Dutch prince husband, and thus began the reign of the Protestant William and Mary. James's son survived, lived in exile, and eventually became known as the Old Pretender. Much blood was shed on such matters, especially during the 1745 uprising of the Old Pretender's son, Bonnie Prince Charles.

The English Parliament, the highest law of the land, by its acceptance of William and Mary was effectively accepting the allegations that James Francis Edward was not the son of the king. It could be construed as treason for anyone to assert the right of the self-styled James III to the throne. According to the highest law in the land, he was nothing but a pretender.[3] But common sense and conscience would seem to indicate that James III was in fact the son and legitimate heir of King James II.[4]

The Origin of Genealogy

This story illustrates what genealogy is all about. Every human being has a father and a mother. The heart of genealogy is merely determining as correctly as possible who the father and the mother of any given person were. I suspect that genealogy began with the concept of inheritance.[5] A primitive tribe owning all in common had no need for genealogy. Once it was determined that crowns (and other titles) or property should remain in the family, it became necessary to determine who were the members of a family.

In the United States we have been primarily concerned with American colonial and English genealogy. In recent times, though, we have seen increasing emphasis on ethnic and black genealogy. This is a good thing, and those such as myself who mainly research Anglo lines have no right to be smug. I understand that recognized genealogical experts in a number of lands can trace lines back further than English lines. This is said of Japan and Ethiopia, among others, and certainly Moslems have maintained continuous trace on many of the descendants of the Prophet Mohammed.

Purposes of Genealogy

Although genealogy originated to serve the aims of an aristocracy, its scope has broadened over the years to serve religious purposes, medical purposes, sociological purposes, demographic purposes, and others. However, judging by the number of practitioners alone, its main purpose today is that of a hobby, much like stamp or coin collecting. Genealogy has much appeal for those who like to solve mysteries, enjoy understanding history, possess analytical minds, and have a keen desire to know more about themselves via a study of their ancestors and their ancestors' times.

Genealogy and History

When we learn about our ancestors, we learn about ourselves. We also learn about history in a most immediate way, as we could not otherwise learn it. The immortality of humans on earth consists of chromosomes passed from parents to child. In a sense, we were there back in history as a part of our ancestors. There are some people who believe that environmental changes (history) can, over a long period of time, be passed from generation to generation (heredity), and, if true, then we are not only a product of our ancestors but also of the times they lived in, but this is probably wishful thinking.[6] History and genealogy are inseparable. The historian who neglects genealogy sees only the forest but not the trees – can any historian today have a good understanding of the forces that brought about the Magna Charta in England in 1215 without having read Michael Altschul's study showing that thirteen or fourteen of the twenty-five Magna Charta sureties were of or related to the Clare family?[7] On the other hand, the genealogist who neglects history has only a list of names that are really ciphers, and genealogy becomes a void.

3

The best genealogists stress how important a knowledge of history is to facilitate research in genealogy. Milton Rubincam, for example, mentions the need to know changing state and county lines, which ethnic groups settled in which areas, migration patterns, and other historical facts, and he concludes that "History and genealogy are so intertwined that one cannot do without the other."[8] Donald Lines Jacobus points out that "One of the chief delights of genealogical research is the insight it gives us into the motives, the customs, the daily manner of life of people who lived in a different epoch."[9] The reverse of course is also true. A knowledge of the motives, customs, and daily manner of life of our ancestors can help us identify who they were. An idea of the norms of the times – average ages on marrying, life expectancy, how accurate ages given at death are, the age when a child becomes officially an adult, inheritance customs, social class distinctions, the possibility of early death because of epidemic or war at certain periods, average education – all can help determine if a given John Doe was our John Doe.

In a very important *Mayflower* case, Robert C. Anderson and Ruth Wilder Sherman drew heavily on their knowledge of the law of inheritance in seventeenth-century Massachusetts:

> The most telling evidence for or against the inclusion of daughters in the family of Nathaniel Soule comes from the records disposing of his estate, and they are especially important because Nathaniel died intestate. The intestacy laws of the times required distribution of both personal and real estate to all children surviving, and not just to sons....Since there is no indication of any [division during the father's lifetime, nor legal suit after his death] by the purported daughters of Nathaniel, we must conclude that these three women do not belong in this family.[10]

In another article, Mr. Anderson uses a knowledge of land records in both Plymouth Colony and New Jersey to determine the most likely facts in another disputed case involving early descendants of *Mayflower* passenger George Soule.[11] This is applied genealogy: knowing not just where to look, but equally important what to do with information once it is found. If for this purpose alone, a knowledge of history is indispensable.

The History of Genealogy

Even the history of genealogy itself can be interesting. Genealogy developed over the centuries in a topsy-turvy way. In Greek, Roman, and post-Roman European times, noble houses traced their descent from gods. Following the Norman conquest of England, it became desirable to be descended from one of the warrior companions of William the Conqueror. The Battle Abbey Roll, originally compiled at the abbey as a memorial to the companions of William, became worthless as a reliable source for knowing who was at the Battle of Hastings as "monks were always found willing to oblige a liberal patron by inserting his name."[12] In the late Middle Ages in England as the established old noble families died out (or were killed off) and were replaced by new families, who usually had more money than recorded ancestry, there was much inventiveness in extending lines backwards. The College of Heralds had to be given the function of making "visitations" to inquire who had the right to bear coats of arms and who bore them anyway without the right.

The Beginning of Modern Genealogy

In a sense modern English genealogy can be said to have started with William Dugdale (1605-1686), of the College of Arms, who, in compiling genealogies of the noble houses, became virtually the first person to cite references for his identifications. He was not always right, but his relatively high attainment of accuracy stands out far beyond that of anyone prior to his time and for years after. In the nineteenth century, amid all the people writing undocumented family histories, some fair and some horrid, a few people became known for good documented work, but they were the exception. Robert E. C. Waters in England made extensive use of documentation to show where he got his facts. In the United States, the New England Historic Genealogical Society began publishing *The New England Historical and Genealogical Register* (*NEHGR*) in 1847 and has continued without lapse to the present date. Though not all articles were documented, and some contained considerable errors, *NEHGR* gave a forum to a number of genealogists who were ahead of their times, such as Henry F. Waters, Joseph Lemuel Chester, and Lothrop Withington.

But the real father of modern scientific genealogy was J. Horace Round of England (1854-1928), whose writings were numerous.[13] Round used a technique of "destroy and reconstruct" to show up the pretenders, posers, and fabricators who had so filled the pages of English genealogy with myths and lies. In language that was sometimes vicious,[14] Round tore down the elaborate and illustrious family trees rich and famous men had concocted for themselves, and then he proceeded step-by-step to build new pedigrees so thoroughly documented with contemporary evidence that they would be impervious to antagonistic investigation. More than anyone before his time, he recognized the role that history played in genealogical research, and many of his writings are as much or more historical treatises as genealogical discoveries. He haunted the Public Record Office and other repositories of ancient manuscripts, pouring over the documents with a purpose which drove him to take infinite pains to prove his points. He took on for battle some of the most fearsome academics of his times such as Professor Edward Freeman, who virtually ruled the world of English history. He became the advocate and the yeoman worker of the *Victoria History of the Counties of England.* By the time he died his name was interwoven for all time with the study of genealogy.

American Genealogists

Among the American greats in the field of genealogy of the nineteenth and early twentieth centuries were William Sumner Appleton, Charles Edward Banks, Joseph Gardner Bartlett, George Ernest Bowman, Joseph Lemuel Chester, Walter Goodwin Davis, Elizabeth French, J. Henry Lea, George Andrews Moriarty, Henry F. Waters, W. H. Whitmore, Lothrop Withington, and quite a good number of others. But the man generally recognized by all as the father of American scientific genealogy was Donald Lines Jacobus (1887-1970). The founder of one of the country's leading genealogical journals (see chapter 3), Jacobus was a professional genealogist who depended in good part on his fees from clients to support himself. Milton Rubincam describes him as a complete master of his subject, one who "considered genealogy in all of its phases – the use of source materials, the evaluation of evidence, the cultural and sociological aspects, the origin of the American colonists, conditions in the genealogical profession, and the compilation of a family history." David L. Greene refers to Jacobus's "marvelous acumen in using the raw material."[15] Above all, Jacobus served as an example to his contemporaries and all those who came after him. There were many good American genealogists before Jacobus, but of him it can uniquely be said that after him the study could never be the same as it was before his time.

Making a Living in Genealogy

When we think of people like Jacobus, it helps remind us that one of the purposes of genealogy is as a means to make a living. Jacobus lived off his fees as a professional genealogical researcher. While a good number of the genealogical greats before Jacobus did the same, it almost seems, with but a few exceptions, that this is another era that has ended with Jacobus. Wealthy people in the past (a good number of them) were quite willing to pay substantial fees for genealogical work – not outrageous fees but money in proportion to the work and the preparation necessary for the worker to be able to do it. There are a few people today who get paid good fees, but in general clients, who do not balk at paying $100 an hour to a lawyer or $50 for a brief visit to a doctor, seem to feel that a person (with two or three academic degrees) doing genealogy should be satisfied with $5 an hour. When I lived in Salt Lake City I saw many professional genealogists who started the day when the Family History Library of the Church of Jesus Christ of Latter-day Saints (Mormon) – hereinafter referred to as LDS – opened at 7:30 A.M., and they were still there in the evening. They had rushed through the day making every minute count in order to earn the money which would provide them with modest support. I do not think any group of professionals works harder for the money they get. Marry for money if you must, but become a genealogist for love.

Genealogical Resources of the Church of Jesus Christ of Latter-day Saints

Among other purposes served by genealogy is a religious one, and today when one thinks of genealogy in religion probably the LDS church comes to mind. There can be few serious genealogists who have not benefitted, even if only indirectly, from the LDS interest in genealogy. The Family History Library is the best collection of genealogical material in the world, stored mainly in the form of books and other documents, microfilm, and microfiche. Through Family History Centers (branch libraries) scattered throughout the United States and in many foreign countries, much of the material available in Salt Lake City can be ordered and made available at relatively short distances from wherever one might reside. These tremendous resources can be used most effectively if non-LDS users understand something about why and how the materials exist. LDS support of genealogy is in furtherance of a religious belief that it is necessary to baptize and perform other ordinances for all people who ever lived, regardless of how long ago they might have died, and that these people then have the right in the afterworld to accept or reject such ordinances. Such people are "sealed" together in families, but first data on them such as parentage, spouse, and children, together with dates and places, are necessary. Thus the church devotes substantial resources toward discovering this type of genealogical information.[16]

Information available at the Family History Library consists of all the types of primary and secondary source material discussed elsewhere in this book. The primary sources – probate, land, vital, census, and other records – are of the highest importance to genealogists. The number of U.S. county clerks' offices, registries of probate and deeds, foreign parishes, and other jurisdictional record holders that have had their records microfilmed by the LDS church is staggering to contemplate. Library users at Salt Lake City can, for example, spend all morning researching their father's side of the family in Massachusetts records and then all afternoon researching their mother's side in Georgia records, and in both cases they can skip from county to county at will.

Secondary source information at the library ranges from the scholarly to the routine. The International Genealogical Index (IGI) is one of the more useful secondary sources, though its limitations should be understood. Volunteers transcribe vital records obtained from all over the world, and these are computerized and put on microfiche.[17] Information is sequenced by geographic area – by state for the United States – and then by name in alphabetical order. Birth information gives the person's name, date and place of birth, and parents' names, while marriage information appears under both the bride's and groom's names, together with date and place of marriage, and spouses's name. Death records are not contained in the IGI (though they would be a boon to genealogists) because such information is not required for the LDS ordinances. A warning about IGI information should be kept in mind. Such information should be used for leads but not taken as absolute fact just because it appears in the IGI. There are transcription errors, and I have noticed some grievous ones. Also, the sources that go into the IGI are a mixture of primary and secondary. As I have been told by library officials, about 80 percent of the information is from primary records, but about 20 percent comes from family group records (see below). In all cases, a column on the microfiche gives a number that can lead back to the source, and all information obtained from the IGI should be checked in the original source, which can both give an idea of the reliability and at times show additional valuable information. For genealogists, the IGI is an aid to finding sources, not a substitute for the sources themselves.[18]

A word on family group sheets is in order. These are not only the sources for about one out of every five IGI records, but they are readily available to be copied at the Family History Library in Salt Lake City (information from them has been widely used by some inexperienced people as sources for articles and books). Family group sheets are made by LDS church members at the request of their leaders for religious purposes. Although it is desired that the submitted sheets be as accurate as possible (and there *is* space on them for documentation), the majority of the sheets are prepared by inexperienced people. Documentation, when given at all, is apt to be "Virkus," or "Davis," or *Six Hundred Years of the Doe Family.* As Jacobus has pointed out a number of times, genealogical records prepared by people on their immediate ancestors (their parents, their grandparents if they had not died long before, and, under the right circumstances, perhaps one more generation) are apt to be correct, though some error may creep in. The further back the generations, the more likely the records will contain significant error. Once again, the rule has to be that such records cannot be accepted beyond their documentation, and then the documents should be cited as support, not the family group sheets. The most valuable information on these sheets is the very recent information, and if you have interest in someone that recent, you are quite likely to be related to the person making the sheet and should establish direct contact.

One more thought in case you should plan to visit the Family History Library in Salt Lake City: Be prepared! It is a huge library, and even learning to use the index system (on microfiche and called the Family History Library Catalog – FHLC) can take a bit of time. It is sometimes crowded, especially in summer, and library attendants are not always immediately available to answer your questions. To learn how to make the best use of the library, invest a little of your time and perhaps a bit of money before you make the trip. For a thorough treatment of the collections and services of the library, see Johni Cerny and Wendy Elliott, eds., *The Library: A Guide to the LDS Family History Library* (Salt Lake City, 1988). Some information on the library can be obtained from the library itself by writing to the LDS Family History Library, 35 North West Temple, Salt Lake City, UT 84150, and asking for their free guide pamphlet.

Other Purposes

Genealogy even finds its way into governmental operations. The U.S. Bureau of Indian Affairs provides a variety of programs and services to tribes that are recognized to have a government-to-government relationship with the United States. Not all tribes are recognized to have such a relationship, however, and many of those who are not presently recognized have petitioned the United States for acknowledgment of their status as American Indian tribes. Because the decision to acknowledge a tribe establishes a perpetual relationship between the Federal Government and the Indian tribe, the Bureau of Indian Affairs employs two full-time genealogists to help make these decisions.

Another purpose that draws people to genealogy, sometimes reluctantly, is a desire to join hereditary societies. (A lot of people who want fervently to join a hereditary society cannot understand why some societies insist that they have a valid genealogical line back to one of the qualifying ancestors.) Chapter 10 is devoted to that subject, and so it will only be noted in passing here. Even people not interested in hereditary societies for membership may find some of the published material of such societies helpful for clues. Again, however, it should be noted here as elsewhere that only the documentation, if of an acceptable type, not the mere fact of a lineage being printed, should be considered support for your research conclusions.[19]

Finally, we should note, along with Elizabeth Shown Mills in the quotation given at the beginning of this chapter, that the academic world *is* paying more attention to genealogy, both in the world of physical science, where heredity studies can contribute much to the advancement of medicine, and in the world of social science, where "micro" studies are made for their own sake as well as to support general conclusions.[20] There are many manifestations here, too, of the symbiotic connection between academia and genealogy, for if knowledge of the minutiae of genealogy allows academicians to draw broad, sweeping conclusions, so does knowledge of those conclusions aid the genealogist in making correct identifications of ancestors in a given line. The connection between academic pursuits and genealogy will be examined in greater detail in chapter 13.

However, the question implicit in the Mills quotation should be asked here in the beginning: Do academicians, trained to take painstakingly critical care in their acceptance of other materials, realize what they are getting when they use the countless number of books that end up on library shelves even though they were just written "for family members"? Are they aware of how cautious and wary recognized genealogical authorities themselves are of these "just for family" publications? Do academicians have any real concept of both the strengths and the perils of genealogical material in print or of what differentiates the reliable from the much more available mediocre? One of the most important purposes of this present book is to examine this differentiation and note the processes, as distinct from the sources, that are used in good genealogy.

Notes

1. Noel C. Stevenson, *Genealogical Evidence: A Guide to the Standard of Proof Relating to Pedigrees, Ancestry, Heirship and Family History* (Laguna Hills, Calif., 1979).

2. This is well known history, and much of it can be found in such places as David Ogg, *England in the Reigns of James II and William III* (Oxford, 1955; reprinted in paperback, 1969), 201ff. Ogg points out, "Now the warming-pan story was grossly unfair to James and his Queen, who, whatever may have been their faults, were incapable of such deception." I would have expected to find something on the subject also in my edition of the *Encyclopedia Britannica* (Chicago, 1971). However, though I have not always agreed with some statements in this authoritative reference work, I never knew just how prejudiced some of its writers could be until I looked for information on the son of James II. This prejudice takes the form of both omission of much information and deliberate slanting of the few words deemed sufficient. These forms are found in articles on James II and Mary of Modena, both written by a professor of the University of Hull, England. Apparently some taboo still attaches to the affair.

3. Parliament later passed an act of attainder against the "pretended" Prince of Wales (Ogg, *James II and William III*, 484).

4. That was, of course, long ago, and no rational person today can use these old events to challenge the royal rights of the current reigning family in England, whose legitimacy has been hallowed over the centuries by descent from a long line of kings and queens.

5. One knowledgeable genealogist points out that genealogy was also used quite early as a form of identification (e.g., Edward, son of John, son of William, etc.). The best single volume on the history of genealogy is Otto Forst-Battaglia, *Wissenschaftliche Genealogie* (Bern, 1948), available in German and French but unfortunately not at this time in English.

6. The role of environment in heredity is quite controversial (see chapter 13), and current scientific consensus holds it not significant. However, today's world of future shock so rapidly overturns the most widely held theories of yesterday that even the most seemingly confirmable hypotheses are better expressed in qualified terms.

7. Michael Altschul, *A Baronial Family in England: The Clares* (Baltimore, 1965).

8. *Pitfalls in Genealogical Research* (Salt Lake City, 1987), chapter 12.

9. Donald Lines Jacobus, *Genealogy as Pastime and Profession*, 2d ed., rev. (Baltimore, 1986) 11.

10. "The Mythical Daughters of Nathaniel[2] Soule," *The American Genealogist* 57 (1981):193-203.

11. "Elizabeth Soule, Wife of Francis Walker, and their Posterity," *Mayflower Quarterly* 50 (1984):31-40.

12. Quoted from the Dutchess of Cleveland by L. G. Pine, *Sons of the Conqueror* (Rutland, Vt., 1973), 164.

13. Round's book published posthumously, *Family Origins and Other Studies,* edited by William Page (London, 1930; reprinted Baltimore, 1970), contains a memoir of his life and a bibliography of his works, which should be of interest to any genealogist, not to mention indispensable to those with a more than a passing interest in English genealogy.

14. In his "Memoir" in *Family Origins,* Page, though an ardent admirer of Round, explains, in terms of the prejudices of his upbringing, that Round's "bitterness in controversy was largely the result of his health and upbringing. He had been a delicate child, missing the formation of character which a public school gives and for which a university career was no substitute."

15. Rubincam's remarks are from his introduction to Jacobus's *Genealogy as Pastime and Profession.* Professor Greene's comment is from a personal letter.

16. Members of the LDS church have been accused at times of being poor genealogists because some individual members have claimed generation-by-generation descent from Adam and Eve (many non-LDS church members, too, have suffered from the same credulity). It is interesting, therefore, to note that Robert C. Gunderson, Senior Royalty Research Specialist in the LDS Family Department, wrote in the official LDS publication, *The Ensign* (February 1984), "In thirty-five years of genealogical research, I have yet to see a pedigree back to Adam that can be documented. By assignment, I have reviewed hundreds of pedigrees over the years. I have not found one where each connection on the

pedigree can be justified by evidence from contemporary documents. In my opinion it is not even possible to verify historically a connected European pedigree earlier than the time of the Merovingian Kings (ca. A.D. 450-752)."

17. The IGI on microfiche can also be found in various non-LDS genealogical libraries and is available to the public at a cost of ten cents per fiche for the 1984 edition (as an example of cost, the 1984 IGI for Massachusetts consists of 116 fiches). The 1988 IGI contains more items per fiche, and each fiche costs fifteen cents.

18. More detailed information on the IGI can be found in Elizabeth L. Nichols, "The International Genealogical Index," *The New England Historical and Genealogical Register* 137 (1983):193-217, and Kory L. Meyerink, "Genealogical Tools and Indexes," *The Source: A Guidebook of American Genealogy* (Salt Lake City, 1984), 432-33.

19. A good source of bibliographic information on ancestors from American colonial times (sometimes including their origins) is available in Meredith B. Colket, Jr., *Founders of Early American Families* (Cleveland, 1975).

20. Just to mention a few such academic studies, see John Demos, *A Little Commonwealth – Family Life in Plymouth Colony* (New York, 1970); Sumner Chilton Powell, *Puritan Village – The Formation of a New England Town* (Middletown, Conn., 1963; reprinted in paperback, 1975); David Grayson Allen, *In English Ways* (1981; reprinted in paperback, New York, 1982); Kenneth Lockridge, *A New England Town – The First Hundred Years* (1970; expanded edition in paperback, New York, 1985); and Roger Thompson, *Sex in Middlesex – Popular Mores in a Massachusetts County, 1649-1699* (Amherst, Mass., 1986).

Chapter 2

Genealogical Potpourri

And his sisters and his cousins, whom he numbers by the dozens, and his aunts.
                                                    —Gilbert and Sullivan

No one human is unrelated to me.
                                        —Variation on a theme by Terence

British labor leader Neil Kinnock asked rhetorically, "Why am I the first Kinnock in a thousand generations to get a university education." That is a lot of generations. Were there Kinnocks, not to mention universities, thirty thousand years ago? What is a generation anyway? How many ancestors are included in ten generations? About how many years would it take to make ten generations? If the further I go back, the more ancestors I have, don't I reach a point where I have more ancestors than there were people on this earth? Do some people have more ancestors than others? I heard of a man who claimed to have forty distinct lines back to John Alden of the *Mayflower* – is this possible? Why do genealogists favor umbilical lines? Is genealogy worthwhile? Before we go any further, let's answer a few questions.

Generations

A generation has several definitions. A generation can be a person in someone's ancestral line. My fourth generation back would be my great-grandparent, that is, any one or all of my eight great-grandparents, depending on the context of what I was talking about. If talking about a single line from me back to my namesake ancestor, Samuel Stratton of Watertown, Massachusetts, of the 1640s, then my fourth generation back would be Joseph Stratton. If talking about the surnames in my fourth generation back, that generation would consist of the surnames Stratton, Mann, Mann, Luce, Holmes, Atkins, Chamberlain, and Sherman. In case anyone wonders why the surname Mann occurs twice, an explanation will be given below.

But a generation can also be the average number of years between parents and children in an ancestral line. For any given family line there can be long generations, short generations, or medium generations. Queen Elizabeth II has short generations, at least in her main line, for as the heir to the throne she goes back to many firstborn children in her line. There are eleven generations between Elizabeth, who was born in 1926, and her ninth great-grandfather, King George I, who was born in 1660; thus, in this one of her lines, an average generation would be 266 years divided by eleven, or about twenty-four years per generation. There are 335 years in the nine generations between me and my seventh great-grandfather, Samuel Stratton; thus, in this one of my lines, an average generation is more than thirty-seven years – more than 50 percent longer than Queen Elizabeth's average generations. Since I have a royal line, just think, if I had had shorter generations, I might now be king of England.

But what would an average generation be? Well, it would depend in great part on the ages people started and stopped having children. Obviously, the youngest child of the youngest child of the youngest child would have longer generations than the oldest child of the oldest child of the oldest child. An average then would be the middle child. If a couple started having children when the man and wife were about twenty-four and stopped when the man and wife were about forty-four, then the middle child would be born when the couple were roughly about thirty-four. More likely it would be somewhat less because as the wife grew older there would be a longer gap between children. Thirty years has often been considered the average time between generations.

The Power of Two

Aside from the fact that it takes the power of two people to make a new generation, the power of two is also highly significant in genealogy because for each generation back the number of your ancestors doubles.

You have two parents; and two times two, or four, grandparents; two times four, or eight, great-grandparents; and two times eight, or sixteen, great, great-grandparents. Let's stretch this back ten generations:

```
GENERATIONS: 1   2   3   4   5   6    7    8    9   10
ANCESTORS:   2   4   8  16  32  64  128  256  512 1024
```

Here, with your parents as the first generation back, we can see that your tenth generation back would consist of 1,024 ancestors. But how many ancestors would you have all total in ten generations, that is, including the tenth, the ninth, the eighth generations, and so on? Add the numbers 2 + 4 + 8 + 16 + 32 + 64 + 128 + 256 + 512 + 1,024, and you will get a total of 2,046 ancestors. You can take a shortcut in adding by doubling the last figure in the string (1024) and subtracting the first number (2). This short cut works for any string of numbers where each consecutive number is the double of the previous one.

It is convenient to say that for ten generations back a person has about 1,000 ancestors. Consider this, if you take each of those 1,000 ancestors back ten generations, then each one of them would have about 1,000 ancestors. Thus going back twenty generations from yourself, you would have, in the twentieth generation, 1,000 times 1,000, or one million ancestors. That is just the twentieth generation *alone*. When you add *all* of your ancestors in twenty generations (that is, include the nineteenth, the eighteenth, the seventeenth, etc.), you have about twice the number that was in the twentieth generation alone, or some two million ancestors. Since each ten generations back multiplies the starting point by a factor of roughly one thousand, your thirtieth generation back would have about one billion ancestors, and your fortieth generation back would have about one trillion ancestors.

One Septillion Ancestors

How many years would be represented in ten generations, twenty generations, thirty generations, or forty generations? If we figure thirty years to the average generation, then ten generations would represent 300 years, twenty would be 600 years, thirty would be 900 years, and forty would be 1,200 years. Thus forty generations ago would take one back to about A.D. 800, about the time of Charlemagne. Another forty generations (that is, eighty generations back of a person living today) would take one back to the time of Socrates, a time when each of us would have over one septillion ancestral lines. Let's take a look at that number: 1,000,000,000,000,000,000,000,000!

Pedigree Collapse

Obviously there were never one septillion people on this earth, and there never will be – the number is just too huge to contemplate. What happened? Do I have all those ancestors or don't I? The answer is in the marriage of cousins. We all have marriages between cousins in our genealogies, and usually we do not have to go too far back to find them. My father and mother never knew it while they were living, but they were ninth cousins. A Thomas Trowbridge came to Massachusetts Bay Colony around 1636 with three sons. Son James stayed in Dorchester, Massachusetts, and became the ancestor of my father. Son Thomas moved to New Haven, Connecticut, and became the ancestor of my mother. The father, Thomas Trowbridge, Sr., was my eighth great-grandfather – twice! On my overall genealogy chart, where the tenth generation has 1,024 lines to represent 1,024 ancestors, Thomas Trowbridge, Sr., occupies two lines, and his wife, Elizabeth Marshall occupies two more. So, though I have 1,024 lines in the tenth generation, the number of possible different people (ancestors) has already been cut down to 1,022, and, as we shall see, it will be cut down further.

Now you may say, "But that's an oddball occurrence." But it is not. It is a very common occurrence – for a very scientific reason. As Peter Laslett observes, we in the twentieth century are very different from all our ancestors. In fact, in many respects, all our ancestors from the nineteenth century backwards had much more in common with each other than with us.[1] The choice of marriage partner is one such difference. I was born in Massachusetts, my wife was born in Georgia, and we met in Washington, D.C. I had originally arrived in Washington D.C. by train, and my wife arrived by car. Had I been born in some prior century, I would have been much more dependent on my feet, and perhaps (with some luxury) on a horse. Let's see how my parents met and particularly how they got from the original two Trowbridge brothers to where they were in a position to meet.

My father's Trowbridge line, starting with James Trowbridge in Dorchester, Massachusetts, continued in Newton and then went to Petersham, Athol, and Greenfield, Massachusetts, where my father was born. On my mother's side, the line from Thomas Trowbridge of New Haven continued there for several generations, and then a descendant moved to Saratoga County, New York. The family then moved to upper Ontario, Canada, where my mother's grandmother married and had my mother's mother, who later moved with her father to Boston, Massachusetts. My mother's mother left home and went to Fitchburg, where she married and had my mother, and then the family moved to Greenfield, where my mother met my father. Now what were the chances that a man and woman meeting in Greenfield, Massachusetts, some years prior to World War II would be distant cousins? Actually the chances were rather high. Although both families had moved around a bit from the time of the two Trowbridge brothers, they were in the same general wide area. Both my mother and father were of families that had been in that general area for some generations. It is not really surprising that they were related. It did not have to be that way, but it was not an unusual occurrence.

As we go back in time we see on the average less movement on the part of people who were to get married, and even in great migrations there was a tendency to marry within the group, just as, at least until very recently, a Greek American tended to marry another Greek American, a Jewish American tended to marry a Jewish American, a Chinese American tended to marry a Chinese American, and so on. My mother's family moved perhaps more often than average for the times. My father's family took three-and-one-half centuries and nine generations to move the one hundred miles from the Boston area to Greenfield. Perhaps that is why we see more marriage between cousins on my father's side. Young men did not tend to look far for their wives. My studies of Plymouth Colony show that frequently a man had to go no further than his own back yard to meet the girl who would become his wife: the daughter of his family's next-door neighbor. Young people did not have the chance to meet a lot of eligible members of the opposite sex before marriage. When such meetings did take place, they frequently involved relatives. If the boy did not marry the next-door girl, he frequently married the daughter of one of his parent's siblings or cousins. It was the most natural thing in the world for siblings, after their respective marriages, to get together with their families. These broad family occasions very often created the pool from which future marriage partners chose each other. And the further back in history we go, the more such cousin marriages were likely to occur; in past centuries remaining in one village for a lifetime was common, and over the centuries there was a tendency in small villages for almost everyone to be related to almost everyone else.

How Does It Happen?

Going back to my father's family, his father, Horace Stratton, married his second cousin, Helen Abbie Mann. Helen was the daughter of Samuel Mann, Jr., whose first cousin, Alice Whitney Mann, married Joseph Stratton, and Joseph and Alice became the parents of Horace Stratton. But it does not stop there. Helen's mother was Marie Antoinette Luce, whose father, James Madison Luce, was the brother of Sarah Luce, who married Samuel Mann, Sr., and became the mother of Samuel Mann, Jr. If this seems complicated to figure out, it is easier, I assure you, to see the results when you put down the names on my genealogy chart (see chart 1). Since my great, great-grandfather, Samuel Mann, Sr., and my great, great-grandfather, Thomas Mann (father of Alice Whitney Mann), had the same parents, when I carry their lines to my ninth generation I find that 62 of my ancestors along the way duplicate sixty-two other ancestors. Since my great, great-grandfather, James Madison Luce, and my great, great-grandmother, Sarah Luce, had the same parents, I lose another sixty-two people from my ancestral lines that way. Going back further, but still within the nine generations, I find that my fourth great-grandfather, John Stratton, Jr., not only was the father of my third great-grandfather, Jabez Stratton, but was also the father of Abigail Stratton, my fifth great-grandmother, for she had married John Stone, and her great-granddaughter, Esther Stone, was the mother of the above-mentioned Alice Whitney Mann. Further, Abigail (Stratton) Stone's son, Jonas Stone, married his second cousin, Anne Stone, and still further, Anne Stone's mother was Hepzibah Coolidge, who was the aunt of Tabitha Coolidge, who married the above-mentioned Jabez Stratton. My sweet wife refers to this as the "blithering idiot" factor in genealogy.[2]

I cannot find the ancestry of my great-grandfather, Nathaniel Chamberlain, who migrated from England to Canada and then to Massachusetts. Thus one-eighth of my ancestry is lost to me. Of the 1,024 unique ancestral lines I have in my first nine generations, I can account for about 684 of them (that is, I have not been able to identify 340 of

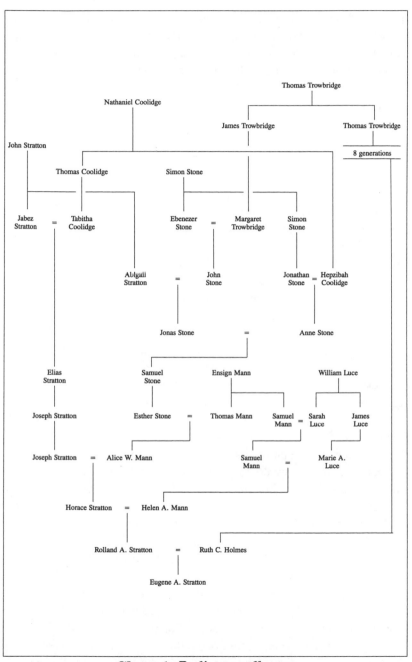

Chart 1. *Pedigree collapse.*

them). Of the 684 ancestral positions that I can identify on my charts, 157 of them are duplicates of others. Thus, only 527 out of 684 ancestors are unique ancestors, and so far in going back nine generations I lose about 23 percent of my total possible ancestors – almost one in four. This percentage would undoubtedly increase considerably as I go further back in my ancestry, if I were able to identify enough people, and this is true for virtually every person on earth.

My first wife was of Ukrainian ancestry, and there was not much possibility of our being able to find ancestors in common. But all of our children have the same duplicates in their ancestry that I have in mine. Since I have contributed only 50 percent to their ancestry, my duplicates of 23 percent would be more like 12 percent for them, but if we could have traced their mother's ancestry back beyond the little village on the Vistula River from where her parents emigrated, it is certain that we would have found a significant percentage of duplicate ancestors for her, too (perhaps 20 percent, perhaps 40 percent or more in nine generations), and when half of this percentage is added to the 12 percent my children get from me, their percentage, too, gets very high. The bulk, though far from all, of my duplicate ancestors came from my father's side, and so we see that the percentage is not going to be the same for every person. The percentage of duplicate ancestors can vary considerably for any given person, especially in the early generations back from that person. But as we go from ten generations back to twenty generations back to thirty generations back to forty generations back, we find the percentage has to increase considerably for everyone. This is called pedigree collapse. This is the reason why, though we double our ancestral lines with each succeeding generation back, we do not get into such ridiculous figures as one septillion, or even one trillion, unique ancestors. It is also apparent that we all have a tremendous number of cousins out there in this world of ours.

Let us look at the question another way. Population figures for past centuries vary considerably depending on which expert you rely on. However, no expert gives the population of the earth as exceeding one billion in either A.D. 800 or 400 B.C. Thus, if we use one billion as the world's population in both these years, we are very safely on the extremely conservative side. If you have at least one trillion ancestral lines in A.D. 800, but there were less than one billion people alive at the time, then on the average each one of those one billion people must represent 1,000 lines (one trillion divided by one billion). But we are not dealing with

22

averages when we consider that large percentages of a given person's ancestors would be concentrated in one or a few geographic areas, and thus it is not unreasonable for one person of A.D. 800 to represent thousands and thousands of your ancestral lines. When we get to 400 B.C., on the average one person could represent much more than a quadrillion ancestral lines! Let's take a look at this number: A given person in 400 B.C. could be your ancestor more than 1,000,000,000,000,000 times. Since Socrates was survived by children, he was probably one of my ancestors and probably one of yours, too.

Ancestral Lines

As with generations, we can define ancestral lines more than one way. If we consider our 1,024 ancestors (including duplicates) that we have ten generations back and think of each line going back to them as an ancestral line, then we have 1,024 ancestral lines in ten generations. We can also, however, think of an ancestral line as the connection between ourselves and any given ancestor. From myself to my father would be one ancestral line, and from myself to my father's father would be another ancestral line, for a total of two. Since we have 2,046 ancestors in ten generations, we can have 2,046 ancestral lines, and this is the way I mean it here. Though some lines will contain many duplicate ancestors, each line will be unique in the sense that no line will be a perfect duplicate of any other line. Consider then the man with forty ancestral lines to John Alden in some ten to twelve generations – is it possible?

Certainly it is possible for my father and my mother both to have one or more lines back to John Alden (in fact, my mother does have one, but my father does not). It is also possible for each of their parents to have one or more lines back to John Alden, and that would make four lines. If each of their parents had a line back to John Alden, we now have at least eight lines, and we have only covered three generations back. Four generations could yield us at least sixteen lines, five generations could yield us at least thirty-two lines, and so we can see that it is in fact possible to have forty lines back to one man in some ten generations. Even though we obviously are involved with the marriage of cousins, the cousins do not have to be all near cousins – they could be fourth, fifth, or sixth cousins in some cases.

I like the study of Plymouth Colony because so much can be done with it. There are so many records available, and it opens up so many possibilities for genealogical discoveries. We can compile very comprehensive genealogies, learn much about norms and averages, and calculate very helpful statistics. There are some twenty-five families of those who came over on the *Mayflower* in 1620 to whom we can trace descent, and literally millions (perhaps twenty-five million) Americans today descend from these people. My research in *Mayflower* genealogy has shown me a number of interesting things, and I have met people with many, many lines back to the *Mayflower* passengers. One general rule I can formulate is this: On the average, the longer a family stayed in Plymouth or the general Plymouth area, the more *Mayflower* ancestors any given member of that family has today. I know people who go back to just one *Mayflower* family, and almost invariably we find that some ancestor in their *Mayflower* line left the Plymouth area in the very early times. I go back to nine *Mayflower* families in a total of fifteen lines (that is, some of my lines are duplicates). It should not be surprising then that my family left the Plymouth area in the early 1800s, about midway between 1620 and now. There are people living in the Plymouth area today whose families have never moved out of the Plymouth area. These people go back to fifteen, seventeen, twenty, or in some cases all twenty-five of the *Mayflower* passenger families, and they have scores and scores of lines.

As a general rule then we can say that the longer a family stays in a small area, the greater the chances are for duplicate ancestors and significant pedigree collapse. The perfect place to test the accuracy of this statement is to look into the genealogies of islanders. Martha's Vineyard, Nantucket, and, although not an island but close to it, Cape Cod are easily studied in genealogy, because so many vital and other records exist, and we can easily see how true the statement is. There is a small island off Cape Cod where the Massachusetts legislature recently had to change the state law prohibiting local officials from awarding contracts to relatives because not enough people could be found in that island who were not related in one way or another.

Umbilical Lines

My wife was obviously just joking when she referred to the various cousin marriages in my ancestry as the blithering idiot factor. I say obviously because if it were true, then most of us would be blithering idiots –

the number of duplicate ancestors in my first ten generations is not unusual. But other people have posed a much more serious problem for genealogists, which we might call the bastardy factor but more correctly is the infidelity factor. Someone wrote that genealogy depends on a concept of chastity in women that history has shown to be not justified. Someone else gave rise to the saying "It's a wise child who knows its own father." When we make detailed studies of morals in other times and places we find that fornication and adultery have been common pastimes throughout the ages, and indeed we need look no further than the Bible to see the truth of this.

Many genealogists feel that umbilical (also known as matrilineal) lines are more apt to be correct over long generations than either agnate or mixed lines. An umbilical line is one that goes from any given person, male or female, to that person's mother, and then to the mother's mother, and the next mother, and so on back as far as possible. An agnate line is easier to visualize because ordinarily the surnames are all the same. My agnate line goes back to my father Rolland Stratton to his father Horace Stratton; to Joseph Stratton, Jr.; to Joseph Stratton, Sr.; and so on. My umbilical line goes back to my mother Ruth Holmes, to her mother Henrietta Chamberlain, to her mother Myra Ann Sherman, to her mother Susan Wilcox, to her mother Hannah Andrus, to her mother Hannah Baker, and so on.

Some genealogists have been able to take umbilical lines back fifteen generations or more, but to be able to go back just ten is considered an accomplishment. Umbilical lines are of course much more challenging since record keepers of the past tended to record the male in more detail than the female. However, the main reason genealogists prefer umbilical lines is that they are apt to be more reliable. We usually can be certain as to the mother of the child. Paternity is more subject to question. That being the case, is it worthwhile to engage in genealogical research in the first place? Each person must answer that question individually.

False Pedigrees

A knowledge of such things as geographic areas, times, prevalent morals, and fashions, is helpful. Thomas H. Roderick has prepared a chart showing the statistical chances for any given line being wrong based on the number of male generations involved in it and the estimated percentage of children who are not the natural children of their putative father.[3] The first factor, the number of male generations, is based on the assumption that the recorded mother of a child is the natural mother in virtually all cases, but the recorded father may not be the natural father. Thus, in an average line going back ten generations, I would go through five males and five females. My agnate line for ten generations would have ten males, and my umbilical line for ten generations would have no males.

The second factor is a percentage applied by whoever is making the estimate, and Roderick gives tables for 5 percent, 1 percent, and 0.1 percent. The 5 percent, of course, would indicate the estimator's guess that wives were not overly faithful to their husbands in the community involved. Such a community might, in my estimate, be the higher social class in Victorian England for children born during the last half of a given marriage. There was a strong feeling then that a wife owed it to her husband to give him an heir of his body (with a backup or two), but that after this was accomplished she might be more promiscuous if she did so with some discretion. At the other end of the scale, the 0.1 percent would indicate a community where adultery was very infrequent, and a case in point might be colonial New England where fornication before marriage was common enough, but adultery, though it occurred, did so infrequently.

In using the table, if I took one hundred of my lines back ten generations with half of them, five, going through the male line, a 5 percent infidelity factor would mean that 23 percent of those lines would, on the average, be false. However, using 0.1 percent as the factor would mean that only 0.5 percent of the lines would be false. Of course, no one can apply a perfectly accurate factor for any given case, but the lesson to be learned from this exercise is that the further we go back in our lines, the greater the chance that some putative father was not be the real one, thus breaking the male part of the line at this point. No wonder umbilical lines are in much demand.

Is Genealogy Worth the Candle?

Is it all worth it? There is a lot of self delusion in genealogy. Most people do not play by the rules, and they claim all kinds of ancestors that are not really theirs. But even those who do play by the rules must confront the infidelity factor. Anyone claiming a line back to Charlemagne must realize that it cannot be guaranteed 100 percent correct. Jacobus points out that "much more in genealogy is tentative than is generally recognized."[4] This lack of complete certainty should keep us from displaying too much pride in our ancestry. It is also a good reason for engaging in genealogy for something other than just indulging our vanity. Jacobus writes that "one of the nice things about genealogy, as vocation or hobby, is that many times it opens the door to various related subjects of interest. The primary one is doubtless history."[5] Genealogy is indeed the handmaid of history when it leads us into a greater appreciation of what the generations of the earth have accomplished before us. Add to that the thrill of the chase, the satisfaction of solving puzzles, the delight in making new discoveries, and, not least significant, the association with many fine people – for genealogy seems to attract people who are far more than just ordinarily interesting – and, yes, it is worth the candle. With but a little effort, one will get out of genealogy much more than one puts into it.

Notes

1. People who relied on horses for transportation and simple tools for work in some respects had more in common with each other, regardless if they were born in nineteenth-century America or first-century Rome, than with people like you and me who ride in cars and airplanes, watch television, microwave our meals, and consume newly compounded chemicals in our food.

2. See chapter 13 for comments on inbreeding.

3. "Estimations of the Percentage of Genetically False Pedigrees," *The American Genealogist* 37 (1961):241.

4. "Preponderance of Evidence," *The American Genealogist* 38 (1962):189.

5. "Genealogy and Related Subjects with My Swan Song Appended," *The American Genealogist* 37 (1961):243.

Chapter 3

The Scholarly Journals

They know enough who know how to learn.
—Henry Adams

Grace is given of God, but knowledge is bought in the market.
—Arthur Hugh Clough

If I had my way, every person calling himself or herself a genealogist would be required to subscribe to at least one (but preferably more) of the current genealogical journals and in addition be familiar with using the others in a library.

Why does a person spend years of time and hundreds, if not thousands, of dollars looking for one more ancestor, when that particular ancestor, and perhaps others, were identified and documented in a genealogical journal article ten or thirty years ago? No, not every ancestor you are looking for will turn out to have been included in a journal article. No, your grandfather probably will not appear in a journal article unless your cousin wrote about him. Yes, the families of recent immigrants will probably be less covered in the genealogical journals than those of the older immigrants, though that picture is gradually changing. Then what will genealogical journals do for you?

Why Subscribe to a Genealogical Journal?

Depending on definition, there are some half a dozen high-quality national genealogical journals in this country. These are supplemented by hundreds of local geographic area and family association publications, whose quality ranges from excellent to less than fair. The number of good, well-documented articles published annually is quite high, and the resulting number of genealogical connections (that is, identifying parent-child relationships) is probably in the thousands. The oldest journal, *The New England Historical and Genealogical Register* (*NEHGR*) started publication in 1847 and has published four issues each year continuously now for some 140 years. The *National Genealogical Society Quarterly* (*NGSQ*) began in 1912, and *The American Genealogist* (*TAG*) started (under the original name *New Haven Genealogical Magazine*) in 1922. Some of the articles published in these journals, indeed a surprisingly large number, published fifty years ago or even 100 years ago are pertinent and helpful to genealogists today. A more recently established journal, *The Genealogist* (*TG*), has rapidly become accepted by genealogical authorities as containing some of the finest articles being written today.

I think a good acquaintance with the journals is indispensable to becoming a good genealogist. There are at least six areas where the journals can be of great help:

Information. First and foremost, of course, the journals contain articles giving you genealogical information. You will find family histories sometimes covering many generations. For example, *NEHGR* had a series of twenty-six articles between 1974 and 1984 giving a complete five-generation history in the male line of the Gifford family that started in southeastern Massachusetts.[1] Anyone doing research on a Gifford surname in the seventeenth, eighteenth, and nineteenth centuries would be most negligent to ignore this finely documented series. You will also find individual genealogies; for example, if you were curious to see if you had any ancestors in common with the presidents of the United States, you could find journal articles giving their various ancestral families. You will find the solution to many a difficult genealogical problem, including corrections of erroneous information that has been perpetuated from book to book; for example, several books, including the widely-used *The Doty-Doten Family in America,* repeat the old error that Joseph Doty, son of immigrant Edward Doty of Plymouth Colony, married Deborah Hatch, but you will find it correctly shown in *TAG* and *NEHGR* that his wife was Deborah Ellis.[2]

Education. For those people interested in being self-taught, there is nothing like frequent study of the best journals to learn how to be a good genealogist. All the techniques are there, shown in plain language in articles written by the best scholars and reiterated over and over by their colleagues. One learns how to find material, how to use and evaluate sources, how to analyze evidence, how to avoid the common pitfalls of genealogy, how to be thorough, how to determine when an identification is adequately supported, how to use chronology, and so many, many more things. Though not all articles and writers are equally instructive or authoritative, one quickly learns how to be selective, for with time the best models become readily recognizable. The educational value of the leading journals is alone worth the subscription price.

Book Reviews. Genealogists use books, and books are certainly abundant in genealogy. And newer ones are appearing on the market all the time. The journals have both regular reviews of new books in each issue (quite a few of them in some) and contain intermittent special evaluations of frequently used references. For many genealogists this is the only way they will ever have of learning what new books are worth buying, why some sources are better than others, what information of interest has been updated, where some hard-to-find sources may be obtained, or what is the extent of literature on a given family (some reviews are really bibliographic essays).

Writing. Not every person will want to write genealogical articles or books on a regular basis, but it would be the rare genealogist who is not tempted to share some important new find with others in the form of an article, or who does not harbor a desire to publish a number of generations of the history of a favorite family.[3] It is a very human trait to want to leave our discoveries or our compilations behind for others, but so many people who would otherwise be inclined to write, vacillate for lack of experience or knowledge of how to go about it, how to begin. Again, it is all there in the journals. A little study will show one the different styles, (e.g., the formal *NEHGR* and *NGSQ* styles or the less rigid *TAG* and *TG* styles). A little more study will show that there are conventions in genealogy, that are most helpful in getting thoughts across to others. The way to start out, the way to achieve that all-important unity in an article, the way to cite references – all are available in many models in the journals.

Bulletin Boards. The journals are the communication system in genealogy – the way to keep everyone abreast of what is going on. They publish genealogical queries, ancestor tables, announcements, solutions to common problems, warnings (such as on fraudulent pedigree peddlers), and a host of other helpful genealogical notices.[4]

Reference. Throw away or sell your old magazines when you no longer have the space to store them, but, as long as you maintain any interest at all in genealogy, hold on to your back issues of the genealogical journals. They say that nothing is more stale than yesterday's newspaper. However, genealogical journals from past years can seem as fresh today as ever, especially when they contain an article that was of no more than passing interest when it first came out, but, as you discover new ancestors, can subsequently become important. Your interests in genealogy, by its nature, constantly grow. Take out the old journals every now and then when you are looking for casual reading material and scan the table of contents to see if some article might now have new meaning for you. Or, as you document your notes, and then want to refer to some article you cited, how nice it is to have it conveniently nearby where you store your old copies of the journals.

Evaluating the Journals

Donald Lines Jacobus published in an early issue of *TAG* his evaluation of the leading scholarly journals, and David L. Greene in 1985 published an updated evaluation.[5] Greene's definition of a scholarly genealogical journal is worth emphasizing. He and George Ely Russell reached the same conclusion that the highest function of the genealogical journal is to publish compiled genealogies and he went on to say:

> Journals that publish only source material or articles on methodology do valuable service, but in the strictest sense they are neither genealogical nor scholarly, since genealogy must involve the demonstration of family relationships and since scholarship is the drawing of careful (and carefully documented) conclusions from raw data.

Including *TAG* itself, Greene found five journals that he considered sufficiently scholarly for his purpose, the others being *NEHGR, NGSQ, TG,* and the *Genealogical Journal.* The number can vary from time to time. Dr. Neil D. Thompson's *The Genealogist* just began in 1980 and so is a recent addition to the field. Some journals reflect the interests of their editors and so vary considerably from time to time. Greene found that *NGSQ* has been much more important under its most recent editors than under its earlier ones. The *Genealogical Journal* might have remained just one more journal published by a local area genealogical society until, under the editorship of Kip Sperry, in recent years it grew to be of national importance; now that Sperry has left the editorship, it remains to be seen if it will continue his high standards. Some specialized journals have had editors who want to meet the highest standards for genealogical articles but have been restricted by their respective societies to publishing more society news than genealogical material.

As Greene pointed out also, *NEHGR* in the mid-1970s had an identity crisis, its administration being "uncertain about whether the future of the society and its journal belonged in the realm of colonial and local history or in genealogy." In the case of *NEHGR,* it has since leaned toward genealogy, and this trend will probably continue under its current editor, Jane F. Fiske. The opposite result came about in the *Essex Institute Historical Collections,* which at one time published much excellent genealogical material on the northeastern area of Massachusetts, but has since, unfortunately for genealogists, decided to publish no genealogy at all. For genealogical information on families of Essex County, Massachusetts (an area of interest to many genealogists because it became settled almost as early as Plymouth Colony), one must now refer to *The Essex Genealogist.* This journal, which publishes some compiled genealogies (see chapter 7), is sponsored by the Essex Society of Genealogists under the leadership of its editor, Marcia Wiswall Lindberg.

The New York Genealogical and Biographical Record (*NYGBR*), published since 1870 and currently under the direction of Henry B. Hoff and Harry Macy, Jr., is mainly a regional journal today, giving exemplary coverage of New York and New Jersey subjects. At times in its past it has been more general, and, as Greene points out in part 2 of his article on scholarly genealogical journals, its cumulative subject index should be checked in any thorough search of published genealogical literature. Other regional or specialized journals of note would include *The Virginia Genealogist,* founded and edited by John Frederick Dorman, and the newly established *Western Maryland Genealogy,* founded and edited by Donna Valley Russell. There are many others. The *Mayflower Descendant,* published by the Massachusetts Society of Mayflower Descendants, and originally edited by George Ernest Bowman, has been resurrected in recent years under the editorship of Alicia Crane Williams, and it is especially noted, as was the original, for its considerable emphasis of original source material. *The Mayflower Quarterly,* published by the General

Society of Mayflower Descendants, featured a good number of significant genealogical articles when it was edited by Ruth Wilder Sherman and then Elizabeth Pearson White, and it is hoped that this will continue under its new editor, Richard L. Husband, Sr.

All of the above journals publish (or have published at some time in the past), compiled genealogies among their offerings, that is, detailed information linking two or more generations, such as giving all the first three or four generations of a given person. There are other types of genealogical publications featuring specialized information other than compiled genealogies, such as society newsletters. The very popular *The Genealogical Helper,* edited by Valarie N. Chambers, is especially noted for publishing current news and queries from readers wishing to get further information on ancestors; it is also the place where many professional genealogists advertise their services. The *Ancestry Newsletter,* edited by Robb Barr and published by Ancestry, Inc., has presented some excellent short articles giving readers helpful familiarization into sources and techniques not frequently covered by the national journals; its continuing feature of describing the genealogical collections of important libraries throughout the country should be particularly noted.

The journals have unique personalities. *NGSQ* reflects the desire of its organization to be truly national in scope, and it seldom publishes anything on genealogy outside the United States, other than those articles that pertain to pre-American origins and research. *NEHGR* not only specializes in New England but is known also for its many articles on the English origins of New England settlers. *The Genealogist* serves a most important purpose of providing an outlet for long or esoteric articles that might not get published elsewhere because of size and other restrictions. This journal, which has a rather broad range of genealogical content including medieval, colonial, foreign, and nineteenth-century American articles, both long and short, has achieved a remarkable reputation for scholarly content, reflecting a deliberate effort by Dr. Thompson, who tells his writers "I don't care if you submit articles to other journals, just as long as you give me your best ones." However, some of the best ones do get to the other magazines, too, and it is not possible to classify any one journal as "best" without the qualification "best for what purpose?"

TAG has maintained a distinctive "*TAG* style," originated by Donald Lines Jacobus and continued through the four editors who succeeded him including the current co-editors Ruth Wilder Sherman and David L.

Greene. Its articles are usually short, concentrating on a particular problem or aspect of a family's genealogy rather than on many-generation family histories, and it has a lively style with in-text documentation, frequent continuing attention to a given problem, and a readiness to correct errors appearing in both itself and other journals. Though it publishes more New England colonial genealogy than anything else, it has a considerable number of other topics such as foreign origins of American colonists and wide-ranging discussions of terminology, statistics, trends, customs, patterns, and interesting developments in genealogy. One thing to be kept in mind is that the earlier the period a journal specializes in, the more readers it should appeal to in general. A seventeenth-century ancestor will on the average have far more descendants living today than an eighteenth-century one, who in turn will have far more descendants than a nineteenth-century one. It is much easier to be (though not necessarily to document it) a descendant of Charlemagne than of a signer of the Declaration of Independence, if only because the descendants of the former number in the millions and millions, while those of the latter would number in the thousands at most.[6]

Journal Contents

If I had to advise a genealogist who could subscribe to one and only one journal, in most cases I would recommend a subscription to *TAG,* at least as a starting point. There are good reasons for this, including the fact that other journals ordinarily publish only a few articles in each issue, and thus it is possible to look at the table of contents for a given issue and see nothing of particular current interest. It would be most difficult to look at *TAG,* which has two or three times as many articles as most journals, usually of a carefully chosen mix, and not be able to spot something interesting. Two typical *TAG* stories are these: In *TAG* 61 (1985):79-82 there appeared an article entitled "Was Tobias Makin an Ancestor of the New England Shermans?" by Myrtle Stevens Hyde and Douglas Richardson. Many Americans today descend from the seventeenth-century Shermans who emigrated to New England from Dedham, Essex, England. As the article points out, it had long been held that Grace, who married (1) John Sherman, (2) Thomas Rogers, and (3) Roger Porter, and Joan, who married Edmund Sherman, were the daughters of Tobias

35

Makin of Fingrinhoe, Essex, England. The Hyde and Richardson article proved by examination of several wills that this was not the case; whoever Grace and Joan were, they were not the daughters of Tobias Makin.

TAG 62 (1987):65-77, 161-70 contained an article "The English Origin of Grace (Ravens) (Sherman) (Rogers) Porter, and Mary (Ravens) Coolidge of Watertown, Mass.," by Michael J. Wood of England. Though he began his research before he knew of the Hyde and Richardson article, Wood's article furthered the story by taking it an important step further and showing that the Grace in question was the daughter of the Reverend Richard Ravens of Dedham, Essex, England, and that Ravens had another daughter, Mary, who had married emigrant John Coolidge, but whose surname and parentage had not previously been known. Part of the editors' note which preceded the article is worth quoting:

> The article which follows is an outgrowth of Mr. Wood's systematic study of all records relating to Dedham, Co. Essex, and provides an excellent example of how studying an entire community can provide the answers to problems that seemed unsolvable.[7] This article is also noteworthy for the variety of sources utilized, especially manorial court rolls, which, even though they are second in genealogical importance in England only to parish registers and probate records, are often ignored by both English and American researchers.

I might note also that this is a rare example of an article in *TAG* so long that it had to be split over two issues, but editors of genealogical journals who can recognize a really good article when they see it are almost always willing to bend the rules. The sad thing is that twenty years from now there will still be untrained (and seemingly untrainable) genealogists publishing family histories showing their descent from John Sherman of Essex, who will still call John Sherman's wife, Grace, the daughter of Tobias Makin.

One of the most interesting series of articles, particularly to anyone with an interest in *Mayflower* genealogy, began with one entitled "English Ancestry of Seven *Mayflower* Passengers," by Robert Leigh Ward in *TAG* 52 (1976):198-208. There had previously been published several possibilities for the origins of *Mayflower* passenger brothers John and Edward Tilley, which, though far from supported by convincing evidence, were accepted by noncritical genealogists and perpetuated. But Ward produced an abundance of evidence from parish registers and probate records to show that beyond any doubt he had discovered their true parents and their origin in Henlow, Bedford, England, and his article included information on related *Mayflower* passengers such as Henry Sampson, who was known from Governor William Bradford's writings to be a relative to Edward Tilley. Ward then followed this remarkable discovery up with "Henry Sampson's Maternal Grandfather" in *TAG* 56 (1980):141-43, to give one generation earlier back and also to show that later Plymouth settler, Abraham Sampson, who until then had been thought to be Henry's brother, was more likely his cousin. In *TAG* 60 (1984):171-73, Ward wrote another article entitled "Further Traces of John Tilley of the *Mayflower*," in which he presented still more information. Most recently in *TG* 6 (1985):166-86, in an article entitled "The Baronial Ancestry of Henry Sampson, Humility Cooper, and Ann (Cooper) Tilley," he has produced what I would call a blockbuster article giving much new information, too much to summarize here. All of these articles should be read if only for the education of seeing how much can be accomplished by going about things in a time-proven way. Still, again I guess there will be people writing in the future on the old, thoroughly discredited claims of ancestry of the Tilley brothers as if these claims were the last word, just because they feel they can be genealogists without bothering to read the genealogical periodicals.

As the last example indicates, noteworthy articles may appear in any of the national journals. *TG,* for example, has had and will be continuing for years a most ambitious series of articles on "A Medieval Heritage: The Ancestry of Charles II, King of England," by Neil D. Thompson and Colonel Charles M. Hansen, carrying the king's ancestry back through the nobility of Europe as far as it can be traced. Another article of note is in *TG* 6 (1985):4-84, "(de) Mezi'eres-Trichel-Grappe: A Study of a Tricaste Lineage in the Old South," by Elizabeth Shown Mills, in which she demonstrates what can be accomplished in non-Anglo genealogy in the South. *TG's* widespread interests can be seen in such articles as Eric Beerman, "An Aztec Emperor's Descendant, General Jeronimo Giron y Moctezuma: Spanish Commander at the Battle of Mobile, 1780," *TG* 5 (1984):172-87; Kip Sperry, "The Harrison Family: Manx Immigrants to the Western Reserve in Ohio," *TG* 5 (1984):240-55; Robert Charles Anderson, "Seventeenth Century New England Research: A Review Essay and Status Report," *TG* 6 (1985):251-58; and Sir Iain Moncreiffe of that Ilk, Bt., Albany Herald, "The Descendants of Chaucer," *TG* 3 (1983):131-36.

Elizabeth Shown Mills and her husband, Dr. Gary B. Mills, are the new editors of *NGSQ,* succeeding George Ely Russell, who gave the journal sixteen excellent years. Ms. Mills has written some important articles for *NGSQ,* most notably in recent years "Academia vs. Genealogy: Prospects for Reconciliation and Progress," *NGSQ* 71 (1983):99-106, and jointly with Gary B. Mills, "The Genealogist's Assessment of Alex Haley's *Roots,*" *NGSQ* 72 (1984):35-49. These are articles that go far beyond a simple list of begets; they show the interaction of the genealogical discipline with other disciplines. Other articles of more than purely genealogical interest are Mary Smith Fay, "Genealogy of Howard Robard Hughes, Jr.," *NGSQ* 71 (1983):3-12, in which the author shows another aspect of applied genealogy, for she had been appointed the genealogist in the famous Howard Hughes probate case to investigate "who were the heirs and only heirs of Howard Robard Hughes, Jr., under the laws of the state of Texas;" and Johni Cerny, "From Maria to Bill Cosby: A Case Study in Tracing Black Slave Ancestry," *NGSQ* 75 (1987):5-14, in which the author gives the results of her research commissioned by celebrity Bill Cosby as a Christmas present for his mother and aunt. Virginia Steele Wood, "Georgia's Colonial and Public Land Records, 1732-1832," *NGSQ* 72 (1984):113-31, is an example of this journal's contributions to genealogical education, just as my own "Descendants of Mr. John Holmes, Messenger of the Plymouth Court," *NGSQ* 74 (1986):83-110, 203-23, is an example of the multi-generation compiled genealogy (in this case four generations plus the children of the fourth) found in this journal from time to time (appendix A contains an example of another type of article, this time on genealogical evidence).

The genealogist who fails to read the journals is to be pitied. Matthew Henry expressed it best when he said there are "none so blind as those who will not see."

Notes

1. Almon E. Daniels and Maclean W. McLean, "William Gifford of Sandwich, Mass. (D. 1687)," *The New England Historical and Genealogical Register,* ed. Anne Borden Harding, vols. 128-38.

2. Mrs. John E. Barclay, "Notes on the Dotey and Churchill Families," *The American Genealogist* 36 (1960):9-11; and Lydia B. (Phinney) Brownson and

Maclean W. McLean, "Lt. John[1] and Elizabeth (Freeman) Ellis of Sandwich, Mass.," *The New England Historical and Genealogical Register* 119 (1965):173. The Deborah Hatch error is found in Ethan A. Doty, *The Doty-Doten Family in America. Descendants of Edward Doty, an Emigrant by the Mayflower, 1620,* 2 vols. (Brooklyn, 1897), 626-628. It is interesting to see how our preconceived notions blind us to the evidence in front of our eyes. On page 626, the Doty-Doten book states that Joseph Doty "remained on very friendly terms with the widow Ellis and her family, for though there is no apparent connection by marriage, one of his sons born about this time is named Ellis Doty."

3. Anyone doubting that the urge to write is among the most basic of human motivations need only look at all the genealogical and family history books that have been published, usually at the expense of the compilers.

4. The bulletin board utility is best realized in journals such as *The Genealogical Helper* and newsletters published by some of the societies that sponsor genealogical journals; for example, The New England Historical and Genealogical Society not only publishes *NEHGR* but also a newsletter called *Nexus;* and the National Genealogy Society, in addition to *NGSQ,* also publishes the *NGS Newsletter.* These newsletters usually go further than most journals in giving details on dates, places, and programs of genealogical conferences and many other events.

5. David L. Greene, "Scholarly Genealogical Journals in America," *The American Genealogist* 61 (1985):116-20. This was part 1. Part 2, covering a number of the regional and local journals, was published in *The American Genealogist* 63 (1988):138-44.

6. There are some forty or so generations between us and Charlemagne but only some seven or eight between us and a signer of the Declaration of Independence. Though (in general) families are smaller in this century than in other centuries, we may disregard this, since there would only be a few generations in the twentieth century. Allowing for the high infant and child mortality rates of the past and for the fact that some families die out for various reasons (people not getting married, early death of either spouse, epidemics, etc.), we might reasonably postulate an average of four children per generation to perpetuate the line. Charlemagne then would represent four to the fortieth power, while a signer of the Declaration of Independence would represent four to the eighth power. Though this is a vast oversimplification, it will serve to show us the differences between many generations and just a few generations. Charlemagne might thus have one septillion descendant-lines (that is, there are not that many people, but a given person might have many lines of descent from Charlemagne), while our signer might have sixty-five thousand descendant-lines.

7. Wood thus expands on the concept of whole-family genealogy. See chapter 5.

Chapter 4

Standards and Documentation

Equity is according to the conscience of him that is Chancellor, and as that is larger or narrower, so is Equity. 'Tis all one as if they should make the standard for the measure we call a "foot" a Chancellor's foot; what an uncertain measure that would be. One Chancellor has a long foot, another a short foot, a third an indifferent foot. It's the same thing in the Chancellor's conscience.

—John Selden

"When I say a word," Humpty Dumpty said, "it means just what I choose it to mean – neither more nor less."

—Lewis Carroll

Not long ago I received an interesting letter in which a woman wrote the following:

> Persons like Eugene Aubrey Stratton should not be a Registrar or Genealogist to verify papers. I sent the above information when I joined [a certain hereditary society], and he accepted it for that society. I will never join another society if he is the one to check my papers. I thought that the various societies wanted members, but with him checking papers, they will get very few.

She also wrote, "Can he not read?...This is documented proof as there are footnotes," but we can discuss documentation later.

I must plead guilty to maintaining two standards. For most societies, I believe that a simple preponderance of evidence is sufficient. The injustice of accepting an invalid line should be weighed against the injustice of rejecting a valid one. But one of the societies for which I was the approving genealogist – the Descendants of the Illegitimate Sons and Daughters of the Kings of Britain, commonly called the Royal Bastards (RBs) – was created specifically to encourage scholarship in genealogy, and for this society it was necessary to require higher standards, for such standards were the very raison d'être of the RBs.[1] On more than one occasion I received an application for membership in the Royal Bastards based on the same line that I had previously approved for membership in one of the other societies but found that the standards of the Royal Bastards required additional evidence. I was not always successful in getting that concept across, such as to the woman who wrote the above words.

A Double Standard

Did you know that the law has at least two standards? If you are sued by your neighbor who fell and injured himself on the sidewalk you failed to clear of snow, the judge will instruct the jury to decide in favor of the party that has a simple preponderance of evidence: that is, more than fifty percent. But if your neighbor accuses you of robbing him at gunpoint, the state will become the prosecutor, and the judge will instruct the jury that they can find you guilty only if the evidence is beyond any reasonable doubt – which is more than a simple preponderance. The law requires a higher standard of evidence to take away your freedom than your money.

What are standards in genealogy, and why should the average genealogist be concerned about them in the first place? Well, knowingly or not, everyone uses standards; they are unavoidable. There is perhaps one exception. The closet genealogist – I mean literally the one who keeps the results of his or her genealogical work locked up in a closet so no one else can see them – might not need to know anything more about standards. Such a person could get away with it, just as he or she could get away with thinking that he is Napoleon, or she Josephine (or vice versa), as long as that person did not go around broadcasting his or her oddities.

Perhaps there is another exception. The closet might be big enough to hold two, three, or more like-minded people, and they could demonstrate their genealogical ignorance to each other and not do any harm outside the closet. But this case exists more in theory than in practice. What starts out to be the case of a person insisting on a right to practice genealogy as he or she sees fit, often later results in disappointment, embarrassment, or even harm when the closet door almost invariably is opened. Let me show you the two sides of this coin:

Scene One. At the *Mayflower* office in Plymouth, a woman telephones me and asks for information about one of the *Mayflower* passengers. I answer her questions, and then she volunteers that she needs the information for a family history she is writing. "If you are writing a family history," I say, "be sure that you put down the source for each fact you give." "Oh, no," she replies, "that would be too much trouble, and besides this is just for family." "In that case," I suggest, "you should put a warning in the front of your book that it is just for family and is not intended to be used to support an application for membership in an hereditary society."

Scene Two. At the same office some time later I receive a very angry letter from a man who is upset because I will not approve an application for membership for his daughter without additional evidence. How dare I refuse approval in the face of the proof she submitted? The "proof" for several generations consisted of pages from an undocumented family history written by someone related to the applicant's family. I remember the letter and the book quite well, because later I noticed a review of the book by George E. McCracken in *TAG* which included such typical Mc-Crackeniana as:

> at various points...there are doubtless instances in which a child is correctly shown with his actual father, but this does not validate the whole line. It is exceedingly difficult to compile a book in which there is not a single true statement, but the reader would be unwise who did not question every statement in this book.

I am not saying that the woman from the first scene was the compiler of the book in the second. The connection between the two scenes is not so direct. But it is so typical that we get the disclaimer from the person writing a book that "I am writing it according to my own standards, not yours," and then later someone insists that the book has to be accepted universally as absolute fact. The truth is that once the book (or some other result of genealogical research) comes out of the closet, it must undergo a comparison in confrontation with someone else's standards. Thus this chapter is written to aid the reader in understanding some commonly encountered standards and to give the reader the opportunity to develop standards appropriate to one's needs.

Standards are Ultimately Subjective

Even in the case of the genealogist who claims to use no standards, we could say that the lack of a standard is a standard in itself. The paradox about standards is that the word implies objectivity, when in fact standards in genealogy (and in some other aspects of human endeavor, such as writing employee efficiency reports) are essentially subjective. I have seen so many cases of people trying to quantify genealogical standards. The LDS Family History Department considered a rule about which family group sheets would be used when there was conflict between information submitted by two or more people. In this case the rule was to use the information supported by the largest number of references.[2] A state Mayflower Society compiled a list of rules for people submitting applications, and one rule specified that a single primary source was sufficient, but at least two sources would be required if they were secondary. They were trying to quantify quality, but it cannot be done.

Truly objective standards could be expressed in an algorithm for computer determination, without reference to case-by-case human judgment. But genealogy is not like a manufacturer buying parts according to written specifications. We can say in genealogy that the biological connection between parent and child must be supported by a direct statement in official records, and many times this would be sufficient but not always. Sometimes vital records are in error. Sometimes a man in his will implies that an adopted son is a biological son. And sometimes a relationship can be established only by indirect evidence or by an affidavit. And in fact official records themselves are usually created by affidavit-like statements. A birth record can be created by a doctor. Suppose it is burned in a fire: May we not accept an affidavit by the same doctor twenty years later? Thus our standard must be broader than just a direct statement in official records.

How about using "a direct statement by someone in a position to know"? In modern times this ignores the fact that the government itself lies when it amends birth certificates to show an adopted father as the biological father. In earlier times such a definition fails to cover the many cases where there are no direct statements: for example, census records.

We would ordinarily accept a census record showing a head of family John Doe, age thirty-two, living with a Mary Doe, age twenty-nine, and Richard Doe, age eight, and Charles Doe, age seven, as adequate evidence in itself that Richard and Charles Doe were the sons of John and Mary Doe. But suppose other primary records showed Richard Doe to be born in April 1852 and Charles Doe to be born in July 1852, obviously not twins, and a woman does not ordinarily have two children born three months apart.[3] We could program a computer to catch this one, but suppose Richard and Charles were born seven months apart: Could the younger have been premature? How about six months apart? At some point a human would ask if Richard and Charles were really brothers. Could one be a cousin? To program a computer to raise all possible questions like this and then to make the additional analysis necessary to attempt a resolution of the apparent conflict would be far more difficult than programming a computer to play chess or translate foreign languages.

A computer could determine genealogical relationships if all evidence were direct, contemporary, substantial, and unambiguous. But in a genealogy of one thousand ancestors, how many are going to be supported by this kind of evidence? In this sense, genealogical evidence is no different from evidence used in legal cases. It will be a long time before juries are abolished in favor of computers. And just as jury verdicts are subjective, so ultimately are genealogical determinations. But just as juries can be aided by general guidelines (such as instructions from judges), so can the person making a genealogical determination be aided by a knowledge of the general standards used by genealogical authorities.

Knowledge and Common Sense

In the final analysis, good standards come down to an admixture of common sense and a decent knowledge of the specialized subject matter. In genealogy it is important to know not just what was said, but who said it. And then we must ask: How did the person saying it know? This is a seemingly simple concept, but there are many people who have a mental block when it comes to accepting it. That is usually because they have been brought up to believe that if it is in print, it must be true. Therefore they see no need to go behind any assertion that appears in print. Until this concept of believing in the inviolability of the printed word can be demolished, the person so stricken with the belief will not be able to understand what genealogy is all about.

Let's take as an example William T. Davis's well-known *Ancient Landmarks of Plymouth,*[4] in which he lists Plymouth residents from the earliest time first by surname then by adult male first name. He identifies the father of that male and then gives the man's marriage(s) and children. Thus whole genealogies can be constructed, up or down. Davis was born in 1822, and obviously he did not have personal knowledge of the parents, spouses, and children of men who were born in the seventeenth and eighteenth centuries. So the question arises: Where did he get his information? Well, we know the answer to that – he had access to and did much research in Plymouth records that were contemporary with the people he was studying. His sources included vital records, probate records, land records, Bible records, private papers, and others, and he would also have learned much orally from the town's old-timers. These are all good sources, but Davis failed to cite them for his individual entries. He used them for his research, he drew conclusions from them, and then he set down his bare conclusions without showing how he arrived at them. Some of his conclusions are based on good primary evidence, but some are obviously conjecture; and when we look at given cases, we cannot tell per se which are sound and which are erroneous guesswork.

We find in Davis results such as this: Under the first John Holmes, for example, Davis shows children, including John. Under the second John Holmes, whom Davis calls son of the first John, Davis shows Joseph. Davis has the first Joseph, whom he calls the son of the second John, marrying a Mary and having children Joseph, Ephraim, Mary, Sarah, Abigail, Jonathan, Micah, and Keziah. There is a probate record showing that the second John had a Joseph. There is another probate record, a will, showing that a Joseph Holmes was survived by a wife Mary and all the children named above, but Davis apparently did not use this will, for it also names a son John. Modern research shows that Davis erroneously attributed Joseph to the second John Holmes of Plymouth when in fact he belonged to a different Holmes family, being the son of the Reverend John Holmes of nearby Duxbury. Davis was aware of another Joseph Holmes in Plymouth because he names him in his book but without showing parentage. He has confused the Joseph Holmes born in Plymouth with the Joseph Holmes who was born in Duxbury and later moved to Plymouth. And while he correctly gives part of the family of the Joseph born in Duxbury, he names only his second wife, Mary, and fails to show a first wife and a son John by that first wife.[5] A careful study of Davis's book shows errors of judgment on his part and an incompleteness in researching all the material known to have been available to him. On the other hand, it is possible, even probable, that in some cases Davis used authoritative information unfortunately no longer available to us.

Like so many undocumented county and town genealogies compiled in the nineteenth century by writers with access to varying amounts of good contemporary information, Davis's book contains many errors. While an individual reader may find this or that error in Davis, only someone making frequent and general use of his book can get an idea of just how good or how bad it is. Experienced genealogists do not rely on his conclusions, but some go too far when they use words such as "infamous" to describe his book. As I mention elsewhere in this book, Davis is much more correct than wrong, but the question becomes one of how much error can we tolerate? The answer is that for Plymouth genealogical research, Davis is almost indispensable for clues but should never be relied on as a sole source to make a genealogical determination.

For the reader who still has a mental block when it comes to information appearing in print, I suggest a strong dose of critical evaluation of some family histories and other genealogical books. Read appendix A, for example, especially the section entitled "Errors in Typical Printed Sources." Read what Jacobus says about printed sources in *Genealogy as Pastime and Profession*. Read what Milton Rubincam says in *Pitfalls in Genealogical Research*, especially chapter 1, entitled "The Sanctity of the Printed Word." In the very first sentence, Rubincam quotes Dr. Jean Stephenson as saying "I don't believe a thing I see in print." Jacobus ends one of his chapters with a quotation called the Favorite Proverb of Morons, "It must be true. I seen it in print." See what Noel Stevenson has to say on printed sources in *Genealogical Evidence*. One cannot even begin to understand or develop standards in genealogy without first throwing away the preconceived notion that what appears in print must be true.

Documentation

Developing good genealogical standards then can start with unlearning some bad habits or attitudes. The next step involves documentation, which goes hand in hand with standards, but the two concepts are not the same. One can have standards without even realizing it, but documentation involves a positive effort. In its simplest expression, documentation is merely specifying a source for information. At this point some definitions can be helpful, though the reader is cautioned that some authorities might not accept every precise detail of the following:

Primary Sources. We might jokingly say that everyone talks about primary evidence, but no one does anything about it. In genealogy especially, there is much confusion over what may be considered a primary source. Primary sources are essentially firsthand sources, though a number of things we ordinarily think of as being firsthand may on analysis seem more to be second hand. Information comes from the senses, in genealogy usually eyes and ears. A primary source in general is a person who directly saw or heard something that aids in making a genealogical determination. It seems like an easy concept, but when we push it a bit it can get tricky. Take the case where a woman in a hospital has a baby. The doctor delivers it and hands it to a nurse for cleaning and protection. The doctor has another delivery in the next room, and so he leaves. The nurse must go with him, and so she gives the baby to another nurse, who has just entered the room. In a few minutes the first nurse returns with a second baby. Then a nurse gives a baby to the first mother. The doctor signs a birth report. The mother fondles her baby; she did not have her eyes on it continuously from the moment of delivery to the moment it was handed to her, but she would certainly think of herself as a primary source for the fact that the baby was hers. But, under the described circumstances, is there really any primary source at all to prove that the baby in the mother's arms is in fact hers? Can we consider a statement by the mother that this is her child a primary source? Is the entry in the city's vital records, made by a clerk who was not present at the birth but based on the doctor's report, a primary source? Is the father, who years later names that child in his will as his own child, a primary source? Is a letter from the mother's sister, who was in the hospital waiting room, to her aunt a primary source? The father, who was away on business, later observes with pride that the baby has the same weirdly deformed little toe that he has – is the father a primary source? (His testimony about the toes might be the only acceptable answer to a question of how do we know the nurses did not get the babies mixed up.)

We can quibble around the edges to doomsday, but as a practical matter I would call all the above examples primary sources. Any single one of them could be wrong, but if we start dismissing one, we are on a trail that will end by dismissing all. And if we say these are not primary sources, we will come to a logical conclusion that there is no such thing as a primary source in genealogy. But if everything becomes a secondary source, we will have lost a very valuable and helpful distinction in evaluating genealogical information. We should not lose that distinction through philosophical hair-splitting.

I frankly do not know if we could ever come up with an all-inclusive definition of a primary source, but we as genealogists must come up with some kind of definition if we are to make any pretense at all to scientific objectivity, and we must be able to draw lines between our different concepts. I define a primary source as a contemporary one that either has first-hand knowledge about a genealogical event or has learned of that event directly and immediately from someone with first hand knowledge. I would make a further distinction: We identify a primary source, but we identify and document a secondary source. Since we have to draw the line someplace, I would say that a letter from Little Sis to her aunt saying that she was at the hospital when Big Sis had a baby is a primary source, and we identify it as a letter from one who was, in the broad sense, in a position to know. If the aunt then writes to a friend that she heard from Little Sis that Big Sis had a baby, that letter is a secondary source, identified as a letter from the aunt, and documented by giving Little Sis as the aunt's source. Little Sis is a primary source because she can truthfully say "I was there (sort of), and I know it to be true," while the aunt is a secondary source who can only say "I heard it from Little Sis, who wouldn't lie." I would say that the father, even though he was away on business, was a primary source because there would have been an immediacy to his learning of the event. He would not have left his wife that long ago. He would have been on the telephone to her at the earliest moment. He would have had a certainty about the event. If we accept the vital record of the birth (based on the clerk's learning it from the doctor, or more likely from the doctor's receptionist who was not even in the hospital), then I think we must accept the husband's statement (based on his hearing it from his wife) as a primary source, too. On the other hand, if we say that the vital record made by the clerk is not a primary source, then we should do away with the distinction between primary and secondary sources entirely because all that we have left as primary sources would occur so infrequently as to be of negligible value to genealogists.

49

There are problems with my definition, just as there can be with any all-embracing definition, but in cases like this we must adopt definitions on the basis of need. We can, for example, ask about the case of a soldier who has been overseas for six months and learns of his wife's giving birth when he receives a letter a week later. How immediate is immediacy? But the definition should serve a useful end in most cases. If we do not allow the father who has been away for a short while on business to be a primary source, then we face greater difficulties, not the least of which is that we are back to such a strict definition that we have eliminated the primary source concept again: there was no one who saw the baby being delivered and also saw the baby every moment between delivery and being put in its mother's arms. If the father cannot (under the circumstances described above) know that the baby is his, then no man can ever know that any given child is his unless he has his wife continuously in his presence or locked in a chastity belt when she is not in his presence. If the husband cannot accept the recently pregnant wife's statement that she just gave birth to a particular baby, then surely he cannot presume that he was the only one to have sexual relations with his wife at the time of conception.[6] Somewhere we have to be willing to make stipulations.

I am sure that there are highly respected expert genealogists who will find fault with my definition, but I am equally sure that some of them will have claimed to have solved genealogical problems, especially those of many centuries ago, on the basis of evidence that they call primary but which is founded on the author of the evidence knowing the facts more indirectly than I have allowed in my definition. Do keep in mind that it is on this issue of birth that the definition will be most troublesome, as well it might be in genealogy – for genealogy in its essence is concerned with two simple little facts: A man impregnates a woman who later gives birth to a child. The whole of genealogy is based on identifying with as much certainty as possible that man and that woman and that child. Those two facts, (the impregnating of a woman with a particular seed, and the delivery of the resultant child), which must be jointly considered, are very often recorded by people other than those who have the most certain and direct knowledge of the truth.

Primary sources usually come to us as written records, and of course contain much information of use to the genealogist other than recording the fact of birth. In many cases there is no recorded fact of birth, and we must deduce it from other records. Some primary records, on analysis, are more like affidavits. A land record in which Julius Brown sells land he describes as "which I inherited from my beloved father Augustus Brown," is tantamount to saying, "Within my entire memory, Augustus Brown and the woman calling herself my mother and everyone else having contact with my family have always talked and acted as if Augustus Brown was my father, and I have always believed that he was." We commonly call such a land record primary evidence; we make it fit the definition by saying that the seller was told (or otherwise given to understand) his parentage by people who were in a position to know (the parents themselves), and there was an element of immediacy in the circumstances of his becoming so convinced (the tender loving care he recalls from his earliest memories). However, he could have been adopted, but if the parents took elaborate means about keeping the fact from him, they might also have succeeded in faking records to fool future genealogists. His mother might have had an affair with the hired hand. Same thing. If she kept it from her husband, she would not likely reveal it in a way for future genealogists to discover – we would still have primary sources (almost universally considered acceptable) testifying to a lie. Anyone who fails to realize that in genealogy we are dealing more with probabilities than absolute certainties should change fields.

Few genealogists have attempted to define primary sources, but I think Jacobus would agree with my definition. In 1938 he wrote, "The original letters of people no longer living, containing their genealogical data, are primary documents which, once destroyed, can never be replaced....The dependence which many genealogists, particularly, society genealogists, place on secondary printed sources and their reluctance to accept direct statements made by living members of the family can be explained only as due to ignorance of the real nature of evidence."[7]

Examples of records we commonly think of as primary evidence are the following: vital records, probate records, land records, church records, military records, census records, Bible records, contemporary letters, diaries, gravestone records, court records, and many others. Some qualification is required here, for these are primary records of what they say even though we might infer other things from them. A census record can be primary evidence of a number of people with the same surname being recorded together in the same household; we must put our genealogical experience and skill to work to determine that the woman was in fact the man's wife and the children's mother because it is also conceivable that the wife could be dead and the woman could be the husband's unmarried sister (among other possibilities). A gravestone records the fact that the people erecting it probably believed the inscription was correct; it does not prove that the inscription is correct. A death certificate is a primary record of the fact of an individual's death, but it is not primary evidence that the age, date and place of birth, and parentage are necessarily correct because the people giving the information might not have known the true details.

Secondary Sources. Secondary sources are secondhand sources. Such sources invariably are people who learned the information from some other person or some other record, or they are using guesswork. They can be immediate, a few years after the fact, or centuries after the fact. In genealogy the value of secondary sources can range from being virtually worthless to being virtually indisputable, but in any case for them to be accepted by the genealogist as sufficient evidence by themselves to establish genealogical relationships, they must have one indispensable element: they must be documented![8] Secondary sources must provide an audit trail to show where the ultimate information came from. Some secondary sources cite other secondary sources and so on back, but ultimately there must be some primary source at the end of the trail. There must be some discoverable firsthand, or reasonably close to firsthand, source to back up the claimed fact. This does not mean that, aside from being used as clues (undocumented or insufficiently documented), secondary sources cannot be useful in establishing genealogical relationships, but they cannot establish the relationship per se, as can a primary source. Chapter 8 entitled "Indirect Evidence" shows how such undocumented secondary information may be useful in conjunction with other information.

Contemporary Evidence. The closer the evidence is to the event, the more believable in general it is. I would accept for even the strictest hereditary society (that is, the Royal Bastards) a letter from Aunt Suzy that she had heard from Little Sis that Big Sis had just had a baby named Napoleon Bonaparte Doe as adequate evidence of the mother-son relationship. Aunt Suzy is a secondary source, but she documents her assertion by giving Little Sis as the source, and she is contemporary to the event. I would not accept as sufficient in itself a letter from the same Aunt Suzy that she had been told by her mother that her great grandfather was Tom Jones (in a case like this, I would give the letter some weight, but I would want to see some additional evidence). The difference between the two cases is mainly that the assertion in the second letter is not contemporary to the event. Jacobus even allowed for acceptance of the first type of case, the contemporary one, in instances where the documentation was more implied than stated. In 1958 he wrote, "The accounts published years ago by the family itself are not subject to such possible mistakes of interpretation. I cannot see why records which were recent [that is, contemporary to the people whose relationships were being stated] when the county histories and other such books were published and which were supplied by the families concerned should be considered unacceptable."[9] Contemporary evidence then can be primary or secondary, and, in the case of secondary, the contemporary factor gives the evidence much more strength than it would have were it not contemporary.

Original vs. Transcription. A primary source may be original, or it may be transcribed. A secondary source may be original, or it may be transcribed. In either case, the original document is preferable, though genealogists more often find themselves working with transcribed documents. More often than seeing the original vital record, probate record, or land record, we see a clerk's copy of the original record.[10] Experience has shown that each time a document is copied (transcribed), there is more chance for error to be made. How many times has a clerk, in copying a record, written "Daniel" for "David?" How many times has a line been dropped in copying census records? Virtually everything in printed form is a transcription. A probate record may be copied once from an original will to the clerk's official records and then copied a second time when someone collects and publishes the probate records of this or that county. And further, a genealogist in writing an article for a learned journal may copy, once again, verbatim sections of that will from the published book.

The rule in genealogy is very simple: Get as close to the original document as you can. The more important the case, the more important it is to follow this rule. To err is human – and if proof is needed, one need look no further than in transcriptions of genealogical records.

Good genealogical standards always revolve around the matter of documentation. How well is an assertion documented? Keep in mind that even original primary documents can contain errors: typographical errors, errors of memory, errors of the senses (the town clerk recording a birth might have heard the father say "Martha" when he really said "Bertha"),[11] errors of judgment, and even malicious errors.

A Documentation Checklist

Experienced genealogists almost without thinking about it ask themselves a number of routine questions about the evidence supporting any claim:

Is this primary evidence? If secondary, can it be traced back to primary?

Is the evidence direct? Does it make a positive statement that A and B are the parents of C? If the statement is not direct, can it be very easily inferred (such as William Roe being shown as the brother of Thomas Roe, who has already been shown to be the son of Richard Roe)?

Is the evidence indirect and piecemeal? Does it require extensive analysis and logical deduction to add up to just one, and only one, reasonable conclusion?

Is the chronology reasonable? Such a question is second nature to the experienced genealogist, and alien to the point of being a dead giveaway to those lacking experience. People did not get married years before their parents were born. There is an upper age limit for a woman to have a baby (I use fifty years of age as the practical limit, though I know of doctors who say there have been cases of women giving birth in their fifties). At various times there have been varying customary ages for men and women getting married. In medieval times a woman might get married at age four, though such a marriage was usually not consummated until after puberty, but in American colonial times it was very rare for a woman to get married at fifteen or younger, or a man to marry at age seventeen or younger.[12] It would be a rare woman who had fifteen children in ten or even fifteen years, rare enough so that I would look very closely into any such claimed case.

Are the claimed facts from the evidence consistent with the other facts in the case? I was about to reject an application for Mayflower Society membership based on a line from a Lydia (Delano) (Wormall) Delano as a Henry Sampson descendant because Lydia was not in her claimed father's will. However, the late Robert M. Sherman, who was working on Sampson descendants, showed me that the bequest in the father's will to daughter Elizabeth, wife of Ebenezer Delano, had to be a contemporary typographical error, and that the preponderance of contemporary evidence showed that the daughter who married Ebenezer Delano was a Lydia, who had earlier been married to Ichabod Wormall.

Is the evidence solid that it is referring to the person in whom we have interest and not to just another person with the same name? There will be a good number of examples in this book to show that "the-name's-the-same" is one of the greatest dangers in genealogy.

Is there anything ambiguous or odd in the evidence? For example, after seeing so many wills of a given time and place, genealogists get a feel for customary terminology. We know, for example, that in a colonial New England will the phrase "my now wife" does not necessarily mean that the testator had an earlier wife. On the other hand, if I see a phrase "my wife's son," I am alerted to the possibility that that son might be (not necessarily has to be) the testator's stepson instead of biological son.

Levels of Documentation

My frustrated applicant wrote "Can he not read?...This is documented proof as there are footnotes." I remember another person who obviously misunderstood the concept when he submitted an application for Mayflower Society membership. The form called for each generation in the lineage back to a *Mayflower* passenger to be identified as the child of the next preceding generation by name, spouse, date and place of birth, marriage, and death, together with spaces for references showing the source of each item of identifying information. The applicant wrote, probably quite truthfully, under the reference space for each of the twelve or so of his ancestors in the *Mayflower* line, "My father told me." Make no mistake. This was documentation. The difficulty was that it was not adequate documentation. So with footnotes, it is not the fact of their existence that counts, rather it is what they say − their substance.[13]

Different types of documentation may be distinguished by format and substance. Substance is a very broad topic and in fact is what this whole book is about. Assuming then that the documentation will be of adequate substance, we can identify several levels of format as follow:

Basic Format. If a genealogist can be certain that his or her work will never be used by anyone else (and it is very difficult to be that certain), anything that will call to mind the source for a given fact is in a sufficient format to document that fact. It can be a personal shorthand or can even be in code. Volume, page numbers, and date of publication should be given for books and periodicals. The whole purpose of documentation on this level is merely to serve as a reminder of where the information was obtained in case of future need. There might be a need in the future – for example, in the case of someone who later planned to write an article – to look up the sources solely to get the information necessary to give a higher level of documentation. Obviously, if there is any real possibility of needing a higher level in the future, it would save time and effort to use a higher level from the beginning.

Standard Format. If your friend records a video cassette on a VCR using the VHS system, you cannot expect to play back the same cassette on your VCR that uses the Beta system. Standards exist so that people can understand each other with ease and profit, such as you driving your car on your right side of the road and oncoming cars driving on your left side of the road. In genealogy, standards of documentation have been developed for commonly used references. As a case in point, not long ago the editor of one of the genealogical journals asked me to look over an article submitted to him by a university professor. Of course, the professor understood good documentation, but he did not understand some of the standards regularly used in genealogy. He gave a short-form reference to the recently published *Plymouth Court Records* as *PCR,* which would certainly seem descriptive. However, the much more commonly used *Records of the Colony of New Plymouth in New England,* published in the last century, has long and standardly also been referenced by genealogists writing about Plymouth as *PCR.* The established genealogists did not own a copyright on those initials, but in the interest of having a common understanding between writers and readers it was better to use some other way to refer to *Plymouth Court Records.*

Standard format calls for a book to be identified by author, title, city, publisher, and year of publication, and finally by volume and page number. A journal article is identified by author, title of the article, name of the journal, volume, year, and page number.[14] There are all kinds of embellishments, particularly with books, to show revisions, reprints, editors, series, and such. Some commonly used manuscripts have been given standard ways of being referenced. Other manuscripts and documents may be identified in some commonsensical way that will have meaning for readers, such as "Bible record from a 1752 Bible bought by James Johnson, kept continuously in his family, and now in the possession of Mrs. Charles Johnson, of Rapid City, South Dakota"; or "letter dated 17 January 1742 (Old Style) from Dr. Erasmus Doe to his brother Mr. Nicodemus Doe, now in the author's possession"; or "Affidavit dated 20 March 1924 by Jane Thompson, found in the Thompson Collection stored at the Roaring City Public Library."

Ordinarily a full identification of a source need be given only once, the first time used, and thereafter may be referred to by a short title: for example *PCR*, with volume and page numbers, for *Records of the Colony of New Plymouth in New England*, edited by Nathaniel B. Shurtleff and David Pulsifer, 12 volumes (Boston, 1855-61). I found it convenient to maintain records on 4 X 6 cards, keeping a section in the card file for a bibliographic card for each new book or frequently used document. On this card I give all the bibliographic data plus a short title and then add from time to time any comments of my own or of others on the reliability of the source. I try to make the short title start with the same initials or first word of the full title so that I can easily find the full title when I need it; if I cannot do this (e.g., with *Records of the Colony of New Plymouth in New England*), then I also make a cross-reference card under *PCR* to show where I can find the full title.

There are a number of helpful guides available. Certainly anyone who intends to write a book or journal article should use standard bibliographic references. The late Richard S. Lackey wrote one such guide.[15] Probably the best guide to follow, though, because it is so universally used, is *The Chicago Manual of Style*,[16] which also has the advantage of being readily available in most public libraries. *NEGHR* has its own style sheet that it will make available to inquirers. Most genealogical journals use *The Chicago Manual of Style*, though some supplement it with guides to their own special needs. It is best when writing an article to have a particular journal in mind, and write to the editors first to see if they have their have special style requirements. It can be most bothersome (though writing with a computer may alleviate some of the pain) to prepare an article with one journal's style in mind and then have to re-do many parts of it because for one reason or another it ultimately gets to another journal.

Professional Format. I mean professional here in the sense of accomplished performer, not necessarily one who earns a living from genealogy. My father used to say that "Figures don't lie, but liars figure." Perhaps something like that can be said about unaccomplished genealogists, the ones who do not lie, but certainly try to give erroneous impressions. Specifically, the way you document your work shows a lot about how good you are as a genealogist. Be specific and be adequate. You do not have to copy whole pages from books to give your readers enough information so that the readers can draw their own conclusions, but you should selectively give them all that is needed. The genealogist who writes, "The relationship is well proven by the wills and deeds of Newcome County," is either very sloppy or is trying to give an impression that may not be borne out by the actual facts. Far preferable is something like, "The relationship is shown in several documents given in the footnotes below, and especially in the [footnoted] will of John B. Doe, dated 17 November 1810, in which he leaves money to 'my dear daughter Jennifer and her husband Claude D. Rockefeller.'" In other words, quote the most crucial part of the evidence that backs up your conclusions. If the evidence is good, it will speak for itself. If you do not let it speak for itself, your more sophisticated readers may think that there is some nefarious reason for it, as well might there be.[17]

The difference between what I would call standard format and professional format, is simply this: Standard format follows the recognized format guides, while professional format includes standard format, but also gives adequate verbatim excerpts from documents to allow readers to draw intelligent conclusions from the material presented.

Language, spoken and written, is the way human beings pass the learned experience of one generation on to the next generation. Maintaining good standards and good documentation practices is the way genealogists pass on the bona fide results of their labors to benefit other genealogists. People calling themselves genealogists who are too stubborn, inexperienced, or lazy to use these good practices should do the genealogical world a favor and keep their conclusions to themselves.

Notes

1. For more details on the Royal Bastards, see Eugene A. Stratton, "Royal, er, ahem...Bounders?" *Ancestry Newsletter* 5(1987).

2. This rule was proposed during a six-day seminar I attended as an invited outsider to consider the department's direction over the next ten-year period, and I do not know if it is in effect today.

3. It has been pointed out to me that there have occurred rare cases of a woman carrying two fetuses of different ages. I understand such events have invariably led to the death of at least one fetus, and so there would not be two living children born several months apart from the same womb – at least not until the twentieth century, when transfers from one womb to another have become possible. Future genealogists will no doubt bless the twentieth century for its abundant record-keeping and curse it for its "future-shock" ambiguities.

4. William T. Davis, *Ancient Landmarks of Plymouth,* 2d ed. (Boston, 1899). Part 1 is a valuable historical reconstruction of land ownership and usage in Plymouth. Part 2 contains the genealogical family data and has been republished as *Genealogical Register of Plymouth Families* (Baltimore, 1985).

5. For further information on this Holmes family, including other errors on the family made by Davis, see Eugene A. Stratton, "Descendants of Mr. John Holmes, Messenger of the Plymouth Court," *NGSQ* 74 (1986):83-110, 203-223.

6. The mere fact of having intercourse with a woman at the right time does not prove to a man, or even to the woman, with absolute certainty that he had to be the father of the child. *Plymouth Court Records 1686-1859,* edited by David Thomas Konig (Wilmington, Del., 1978), 2:117, shows that Mercy Hayford complained in 1731 that Isaac Lambert fathered a bastard child on her. However, when asked if she would take oath and swear that Lambert was the father and no one else, she responded that "she believed he was but would not swear to it." (Lambert was dismissed.)

7. "On the Nature of Genealogical Evidence," *NEHGR* 92 (1938):220.

8. Documented (in its simplest terms) means that the next previous source must be identified – whether or not that source is sufficient depends on other things. Further definition will be given later in this chapter.

9. "Confessions of a Genealogical Heretic: Society Regulations and Hearsay Evidence," *NEHGR* 112 (1958):81-87.

10. Although we ordinarily think of a clerk's copy as being made contemporarily with the event, sometimes even the first-time copies no longer exist, and all we have are a later clerk's copies of an earlier clerk's copies, or sometimes only a later clerk's attempt to reconstruct records that might never have existed in that form. See, for example, Robert S. Wakefield, "Little Compton R.I. Marriages: An Analysis," *TAG* 61 (1986):133-40, in which Wakefield comments that James N. Arnold's book, *Vital Records of Rhode Island 1636-1850,* "was prepared from an annotated copy and should be used with care. The annotated copy was probably prepared by Otis Wilbur, town clerk around 1850, and includes information that he could not possibly have obtained first-hand."

11. Ruth Wilder Sherman reminds me that in early records Martha's Vineyard was often written as Martin's Vineyard.

12. See Donald L. Jacobus, "Age of Girls at Marriage in Colonial New England," *TAG* 27 (1951):116-18. I am aware that every now and then we see news items such as an undated United Press International story (probably from about 1982) that "a 10-year old East Texas [Houston] girl gave birth to a premature but normal baby girl last week, a Hermann Hospital spokeswoman said Monday," or the story in the Boston Globe of 10 September 1987 that "a 55-year-old grandmother delivered a healthy boy yesterday, becoming the oldest woman to give birth in Britain....According to the *Guinness Book of World Records,* the oldest mother...was [an American] 57 years and 129 days old." However, world records are seldom useful for general guidelines, which give a normal range. If in genealogy something appears far outside that range, it is not necessarily rejected, but it does call for careful investigation and a very strong level of support.

13. Professor David L. Greene stresses that as important as documentation is, the Jacobus revolution in genealogy was not directed primarily at the level of documentation but more toward making critical use of material and basing conclusions on primary sources. Jacobus and his colleagues were not perfect models of citing documentation, and in many cases by today's standards their cited documentation was inadequate. But what they wrote was based on a very skillful interpretation of primary source materials and would be documentable by a modern scholar aware of the sources. As Jacobus himself said of others, at some point we must give more weight to the ability and reliability of the compiler than to the extensiveness of documentation – and certainly in the case of Jacobus and some others we do give additional weight to the impressiveness of their credentials, while not necessarily accepting their undocumented conclusions as the last word. Today's genealogist, though, must both document and show acumen in treating genealogical materials.

14. Not all good genealogists or all good genealogical journals insist on all these bibliographic elements; frequently publisher is left out of references to books, and year of publication is left out of references to articles.

15. See endnote 26 of appendix A.

16. *The Chicago Manual of Style,* 13th ed., rev. ed. of *A Manual of Style* (Chicago, first published 1906, frequently revised and reprinted).

17. See, for example, my remarks on Mary, wife of Nathaniel Atwood, under the heading "Mayflower Society Examples" in appendix A.

Chapter 5

Whole-Family Genealogy

Time was when the whole of life went forward in the family, in a circle of loved, familiar faces, known and fondled objects, all to human size. That time has gone for ever. It makes us very different from our ancestors.
—Peter Laslett

The plain truth is that many problems cannot be properly solved nor can we be reasonably certain of many lines of descent, unless a family is studied as a whole.
—Donald Lines Jacobus

Some problems in genealogy are really tough. You can research an ancestor for years without ever finding his or her parents. You can search for wills, deeds, vital records, church records, passenger lists, censuses, Bible records, newspapers, and so on, but all in vain. You just cannot get any more identifying information on your John or Mary Doe. It is most discouraging. But, if it is worth the effort to you, there is something else you can do. It might work or it might not in any given case, but it will certainly work in some cases. This is to take the "whole-family" approach.

Some parts of this approach will probably be familiar to you. You have done research on whole families before. Essentially you collect data and sources on the time and place of birth, death, and marriage of an individual. Then do the same for the spouse and each of their children. You continue by going back to each of the individual's two parents and try to identify their parentage. When and if you do learn who their parents were, you start the process all over again. You collect data and sources on the time and place of birth, death, and marriage of each parent, and then do the same on each of their children. On at least one child, you will already have the information, for that is where you started.

However, even experienced genealogists seldom go beyond the immediate family approach unless they are writing a family history. Most genealogists are content to start with themselves and their siblings, go back to their parents and their parents' siblings, and continue further back to their grandparents and their grandparents' siblings. Once, for example, they have identified their grandparents' siblings or their great grandparents' siblings, they seldom spend additional research time on the families of those siblings. They seldom carry each collateral sibling forward and give him or her the same treatment they reserve for the sibling who is in their direct line.

But for that difficult ancestor, when all else has failed, it can at times be profitable to keep researching all the collateral lines as if they were direct lines, especially the male collateral lines, which carry on the surname. In effect, to learn the antecedents of John Doe, study every Doe family in the area just as if you were writing a Doe family history, which is what it can amount to. There are two reasons for this. First, you never know just which relative of your ancestor might have left records which name or give clues to identify that ancestor. And, second, like doing a jigsaw puzzle, the more you have completed, the easier it is, by the process of elimination, to fill in the remaining pieces (or reject ones that do not belong).

Some Case Studies

Let's look in more detail at these two aspects, and start with an easy case. Suppose you go back to John Washburn, who was born in Plymouth Colony and married ca. 1698 a Lydia. The time and place, seventeenth- and eighteenth-century Plymouth, will tell an experienced genealogist to look in the *Mayflower Descendant,* where much primary and secondary material on Plymouth can be found. The index can pinpoint those pages where both a John Washburn and a Lydia Washburn appear. Looking up those pages will lead you to an article in volume 15, page 247 by George Ernest Bowman entitled "Washburn Notes." Bowman will inform you that printed accounts of the Washburn family have been very incomplete and inaccurate. He also mentions that the John Washburn you are interested in married Lydia Billington, daughter of Isaac Billington and granddaughter of Francis Billington of the *Mayflower*. So there you have it, all that you want to know.

Not quite, for Bowman, contrary to his usual practice, does not cite references for this conclusion. He tells you that the total information on the Washburn family is too voluminous to be given at once, and he will parcel it out in later articles. In the case of Lydia Billington, however, he never got around to it. So you check the records for the family of Lydia's claimed father, Isaac Billington. He was born in Plymouth Colony ca. 1644, died at Middleborough 11 December 1709 in his 66th year, and married before 1675 Hannah Glass, daughter of James and Mary (Pontus) Glass. Isaac did not record the births of his children, and he left no will. Probate records contain an inventory of property, but without identifying his heirs. Land records contain no mention of a daughter Lydia, though one record does mention a son Seth.

Seth Billington is not in your direct line of ancestry – dare I say that he is not a direct ancestor?[1] However, being a practitioner of whole-family genealogy, you know exactly what to do. You treat Seth as if he were in your direct line, and you make every effort to learn as much about him as possible. Do probate or other land records mention Seth? Yes, there is a Plymouth County probate record 4:100 that contains a settlement of his estate. Seth, it turns out, died unmarried (and from your point of view that is the best way for a sibling of any troublesome ancestors you may have), and thus his estate, settled on 20 June 1718, had to go to his siblings. They are all named there: his brother Isaac Billington; his brother-in-law Samuel Warren; and his sisters Elinor Warren, Desire Bonney, Mary Wood, and, though deceased at the time, Lydia Washburn, who is named for the sake of her children. Now you have documentary proof. You were not interested in Seth, but only in Lydia; however, you found nothing on Lydia by looking for her by name, but found good evidence on her when you looked for Seth by name. Whole-family genealogy also eliminated the faint possibility that there could have been a second Lydia Billington.[2]

As I said, that was an easy one. Sometimes you must recreate the families for several generations of every person in the area having the surname of your interest before you start getting results. I have had to do this on several families, such as the Luce family, which goes back to Henry Luce of Scituate in Plymouth Colony and Martha's Vineyard. This was a very prolific family, and thus by the time it got to the fifth, sixth, and seventh generations from Henry Luce, the family members were numerous and spread out all over. Some went into areas where good records were kept, some into places were few records were kept, and some into areas where the records were spotty, sometimes good and sometimes bad. My particular Luce problem was difficult, and for years I kept following false leads. When I finally solved the particular problem, I wrote an article "The Elusive Luces,"[3] the title of which expresses some of my frustration. In this particular case, very little of my whole-family research appeared in the article because once the approach had taken me where I wanted to go, it was not necessary to show all the preliminary research (which is not always the case). However, I could not have resolved this Luce family matter without having made initial use of this technique.

Sometimes in taking the whole-family approach, you can save much time and effort if you have the good fortune to latch onto a family history in book or article form already published by someone else interested in the same family.[4] Of course the person you want will not be in that family history or at least will not be accurately presented in that family history – or if accurately presented, the information will not be sufficiently documented, for otherwise you would have no need to take the whole-family approach. In the case of the Luce family, because of its early association with Martha's Vineyard, I found Banks's genealogies of Martha's Vineyard families a good start.[5] But Banks and anything else I found already published on Luce families were only a start. I had traced my Luce line back to a William Luce who appeared in eighteenth-century records of New Salem, Massachusetts, but where did he come from? To solve the problem, I researched Luce families all over New England, but I will not give a case study here, for only those families along one particular migratory path were really of interest. Thus, although I used a whole-family approach, it was perhaps too broad a study to illustrate the complete lesson I want to emerge from this chapter.

A Wilcox Example

The research I conducted over many years to find the ancestry of Tyle Wilcox of Dartmouth, Massachusetts, and upstate New York, is a more visible example of the whole-family approach, and, though a bit compli-

Chart 2. *The Wilcox family.*

cated because it involves so many individuals, the highlights can still be presented in a meaningful form (see chart 2). Tyle Wilcox of Dartmouth, Massachusetts, married Deborah Russell in 1760. They had several children in Dartmouth, and he served in the Revolutionary War from Dartmouth. Sometime during the war he and his family migrated to Easton, New York, and he also served in the wartime militia there.[6] There is no record of his birth in Dartmouth or the surrounding area. Probate and land records gave no clue to his parentage. Though the Dartmouth area at this time was full of Wilcoxes, virtually all of the same original family, the family was prolific enough to have many branches, and Tyle could not be traced to any of these. Neither could the name Tyle or Tyler be associated with any Wilcox family to give an onomastic clue.

The progenitor of this Wilcox clan was said to be Edward Wilcox, a seventeenth-century settler of Rhode Island, who was believed to be the father of Stephen and Daniel Wilcox. Stephen Wilcox moved to western Rhode Island and became in turn the progenitor of a large Wilcox family there.[7] Daniel Wilcox and his children remained in the area of southeastern Massachusetts and adjoining Rhode Island, becoming particularly associated with Dartmouth. A tremendous amount of error has been perpetuated on the descendants of Daniel Wilcox. As George Andrews Moriarty, a great genealogist, wrote, "The early Rhode Island Wilcoxes are a rather mysterious lot."[8] Daniel Wilcox married Elizabeth Cooke, the granddaughter of two *Mayflower* passengers, and for years the Mayflower Society accepted descent from any of his children as a valid *Mayflower* line. It was later shown (by contemporary evidence) that he had had an earlier, unidentified wife, and that most likely his older children were by her.[9] To complicate matters a bit more, a 1904 article presented a marriage intention for a Jerry Wilcox and a Deborah Russell.[10] Dartmouth vital records show a 1760 marriage intention for Tyle Wilcox (erroneously recorded as Iyle) and Deborah Russell, and Tiverton vital records show the 1760 marriage of Tila Wilcox and Deborah Russell. The Deborah Russell associated with Jerry and the one associated with Tyle were two different women who just happened to have the same name. The only person of the time with a name similar to Jerry, a Jireh Wilcox, later married a Bathsheba Lapham. However, these facts notwithstanding, the Mayflower Society was soon accepting applicants on a line from Tyle Wilcox (whose ancestry had not really yet been determined), who was equated with Jireh Wilcox (whose known ancestry went through one of Daniel Wilcox's older sons who was considered to be by Daniel's first, unknown, wife and therefore was not a valid *Mayflower* line).

My problem was to find the real ancestry of Tyle Wilcox. Though I was able to find a published family history on the Wilcox family of the Dartmouth/Tiverton/Little Compton area, I soon discovered it to be so riddled with error and omission as to be virtually useless.[11] Thus I decided to recreate as much of the Wilcox family genealogy as necessary to see where Tyle might fit in. I started by making a data sheet for each of Daniel Wilcox's five sons.[12] I then researched the families of each of the sons of Daniel's five sons, again making a data sheet on each. On each data sheet, I recorded all the information I could get from vital records, wills, deeds, other court documents, published articles, gravestone records, Bible records, and so on. By this time I was beginning to pick up duplicate names, as the same names were used over and over in the various families (e.g., Daniel, Stephen, William, etc.). It became apparent that I would have to keep records on the daughters, too, and also on some of the other families in the area which intermarried with the Wilcoxes (such as Russells, Allens, Howlands, and Smiths) so as to distinguish between all the characters now being researched. It was necessary, for example, to examine whether Jireh Wilcox and Tyle Wilcox were identical as others had claimed, and for this purpose it was necessary to determine who was the Deborah Russell associated with each. If Tyle married in 1760, and he might have married at an age as early as seventeen, then I needed to compile the family of each Wilcox who could have been having children as late as 1743.

Gradually I was able to eliminate some families (and eventually quite a few more) until it appeared virtually certain that Tyle had to be the son either of Stephen and Mary (Thomas) Wilcox or of Stephen and Mary (Ricketson) Wilcox. In determining which of the two couples it was, I was aided considerably by two people. Mr. John H. Schulz of New York was a descendant of Tyle Wilcox who had also spent years in researching Tyle's ancestry, and many of his efforts involved correspondence with others who had a mutual interest. Tyle's descendants in New York state were numerous, and John Schultz made contact with several who had an interest in genealogy. He also researched libraries and county offices in the places where Tyle had been known to live. Through his efforts I obtained information from wills of several people in New York contemporary to Tyle, the most important being a Micajah Wilcox.

Micajah Wilcox named in his will of 1820 his nephew Stephen Wilcox; Micajah, the son of Stephen Wilcox (so worded that this Micajah could be either nephew or grandnephew of the testator); Tylee Dunham, the son of Jonathan Dunham; and his nephew Tylee Wilcox. The 1817 will of a Stephen Wilcox was reported in a secondary source, though in this case we could not find any official record of it, and in this will Stephen was said to have named his brother Micajah Wilcox, sons Micajah and Stephen, and nephews Micajah and Tyler. Here the onomastic clue helped, for the Tyle Wilcox of our interest appeared to be the first person of this rather unusual name, but his descendants picked up the name, and later generations included several Tyle Wilcoxes, a Tyle Gray, a Tyle Beach, and a Tyle Dunham – daughter of Jonathan and Mary (Wilcox) Dunham, Mary being a daughter of the original Tyle Wilcox. It looked then as if Tyle Wilcox, Micajah Wilcox, and Stephen Wilcox of New York were brothers. Alas, my family data records showed no one named Micajah Wilcox, and though there was a Stephen Wilcox of the right age, he seemed to be in the wrong family and he apparently married, lived, and died in Dartmouth.

There was no Micajah Wilcox in the probate or vital records of the Dartmouth area. But a search through my files of land records showed a Micajah Wilcox whom I had not been able to place in any family earlier. Later I received some help from a second person, Jane F. Fiske, F.A.S.G., who had come across the name of Tyle Wilcox while looking at some contemporary Dartmouth Quaker records. He had been disowned by the Quakers for having a child born too soon after his marriage to Deborah Russell, and for not showing repentance, and the records called Tyle the son of Stephen and Mary Wilcox. Now for the first time we had proof of the names of Tyle's parents, which before was only a guess, but it still did not show which of the two sets of Stephen and Mary Wilcoxes was the correct one.[13]

However, since Dartmouth Quaker records had been so helpful, I checked them now for mention of Micajah Wilcox and found that he, too, had been disowned by the Quakers, and that earlier he had visited the Quaker settlement at the Oblong, in Dutchess County, New York. Putting this together with what we had previously had on Micajah, we could built a circumstantial case to show him to be the son of Stephen and Mary (Thomas) Wilcox. Micajah's birth was not recorded, as Tyle's was not, and the last-mentioned Stephen Wilcox more often did not record the names of his children with the town clerk, while the other Stephen (who married Mary Ricketson) did. From deeds we knew that Micajah had lived on the west side of the eastern branch of the Accoxet River, the same side as Stephen who married Mary Thomas, while the other Stephen lived on the east side of the eastern branch. Micajah was a Quaker, as Tyle and Tyle's father, Stephen, were, while there was no record of the other Stephen being a Quaker. Micajah was a tailor by occupation, as was Stephen who married Mary Thomas. Micajah had visited relatives in the Oblong, and Stephen and Mary (Thomas) Wilcox were known to have had relatives in the Oblong. Finally, neither Micajah nor Tyle Wilcox, nor for that matter the Stephen Wilcox of Tyle and Micajah's generation, were mentioned in the will of the Stephen Wilcox who married Mary Ricketson. Since they had outlived this Stephen, this was presumptive, not absolute, evidence that they were not his sons. No will was found for the Stephen Wilcox who had married Mary Thomas. The argument could have been made that perhaps the Stephen leaving a will (who had married Mary Rickectson) left out one son, Tyle, because Tyle had been disowned by the Quaker community. But Stephen who married Mary Thomas seemed more to be a Quaker, and to leave out three sons would take a lot of explaining (actually four sons, for there was a William Wilcox born to one of the Stephens and Marys, but no William Wilcox was in the one will we had – that of Stephen who had married Mary Ricketson – even though there were good indications that this William had outlived the testator Stephen).

There is a lot of indirect evidence in this case, much more than I have set down here. The purpose of this rather long example, though, is not so much to prove the parentage of Tyle Wilcox but much more to show how it was necessary to study so many members of the Wilcox and other families in order to come up with even an indirect evidence case. The case illustrates many of the techniques which are so valuable to genealogists: use of vital records, wills and deeds; onomastic evidence;[14] whole-family genealogy; getting help from others with common interest problems; use of church records; analyzing indirect evidence; and others. But notice the importance of the whole-family approach, especially in the analysis of data on Tyle and Micajah. Tyle is proven via Quaker records to be the son of a Stephen and Mary Wilcox, but which Stephen and Mary Wilcox? Micajah is not proven directly to be the son of either Stephen and Mary Wilcox, but, given the fact emerging from his will that he is Tyle's brother, he accordingly appears to be a son of a Stephen and Mary Wilcox also.

There are not as many indications in Tyle's case to distinguish between the two sets of Stephens and Marys as there are in Micajah's case. Once we see, thanks to the analysis of data on Tyle, that Micajah is the son of a Stephen and Mary, then we can see, thanks to analysis of the data on Micajah, that the Stephen who married Mary Thomas is the more likely to be the right one of the two Stephens. Tyle and Micajah hang together – each is indispensable to proving the parentage of the other.

Disproving a Line

A whole-family approach can also help disprove a line as well as prove it. Let us take, for example, the claimed royal line of William Leete, seventeenth-century governor of Connecticut. The royal line was set forth by Frederick Lewis Weis,[15] and it later appeared with one small change in Weis's *Magna Charta Sureties*.[16] From this published line, many people including myself, have traced their ancestry back not only to Charlemagne but also to King Henry I and Magna Charta Surety Robert de Vere, and many have been accepted into various hereditary societies on the basis of Weis's work.

When relying on a published line, it is always prudent to check the references personally to verify the line. Do not take someone else's word for it. Draw your own conclusions from the ultimate contemporary evidence, especially in cases where reference is made to documentary evidence but with pertinent quotations or abstracts from the documents left out. In the case of William Leete's ancestry, I began systematically checking the references given by Weis. Quite a few generations seem to rely substantially on Waters's *Chester of Chicheley*.[17] Now, as references go, that is a good one. Waters was far ahead of his time when he compiled his Chester genealogy, and he documented his work with copious footnotes citing both primary and secondary sources. It is a paradox that sometimes a good work can be more dangerous than a bad one, for people (even experts) are less likely to question an established good source such as Waters.

As I plodded along, trying insofar as possible to find the sources given in Waters's footnotes, I was able to confirm to my satisfaction a number of the generations in the Leete line. But I found a stumbling block in generation 25 of the article *Magna Charta Sureties* line 128:11): Rose Peyton (this surname is found as both Peyton and Payton), the wife of

Robert Freville, who was claimed to be a daughter of Sir Thomas and Margaret (Franceys) de Peyton. Waters gave two references for this generation.[18] The first reference led to the will of Rose's husband, Robert de Freville, in which the testator mentioned lands for the jointure of his wife Rose "according to the indenture between me and Sir Robert Payton, Knight, and other friends and kinsmen of the said Rose my wife, dated 27th April [1513]." The Robert Peyton named in Robert de Freville's will could have been one of the mentioned "friends," or one of the mentioned "kinsmen," and if a kinsman, it still would not prove that Rose's surname was Peyton, for he could have been on her mother's or even grandmother's side. Even if she were a Peyton, that would not prove her to be a daughter of Thomas and Margaret de Peyton. Robert could not have been her brother, for Thomas Peyton, who died in 1484, did not have a son Robert.

The second reference was a documented secondary source, and it called a George Freville the son of Robert Freville and "Rose (Peyton) his wife." Citations were lumped together for the entire item on George Peyton, and, though I have not been able to locate each document, from their titles they do not seem to be such as would prove Rose's surname. Indeed, one of the sources is the first reference, and so we have the possibility that the second reference inferred it from the first, with Waters going one step further and placing Rose in Sir Thomas Peyton's immediate family. *The Visitations of Cambridgeshire of 1575 and 1619*[19] show the children of Thomas Payton by his two wives, but no Rose is included. Only those by his second wife, Margaret Franceys, would be pertinent, for she was the one through whom the royal line passed. By Margaret Franceys, Payton is shown as having two sons, Francis Payton and Christopher Payton, and no daughter. It is of interest that by his first wife he had a son Thomas Payton, who had a son Robert Payton, who also had a son Robert Payton, and it is possible that one of these was the Robert Peyton mentioned in Freville's will, but if so he could lead back to other possibilities than Thomas Peyton (and Margaret Franceys) for the parents of Rose.

Thus there is no direct evidence to say that Rose was the daughter of Thomas and Margaret (Franceys) Peyton. If we stopped there, we would have something quite inconclusive. We have not proved it, but we have not disproved it either. While there should be no need to disprove it, in a case like this, where the line has been accepted by good authority for many years and where people have something to lose if the line is declared invalid, it is neater if the iconoclast who cuts the line can produce some evidence to prove the negative. This is often not easy or even possible to do, but if it can be done, it should be done. In the present case, whole-family genealogy was of help. Waters wrote that Thomas Peyton had Christopher, Francis, and Rose. He showed that Christopher married, but left no issue.

Though Waters does not cite any will for Christopher, I made a routine check and found that Christopher Peyton died in 1507 and left a will. In it he named his wife, Elizabeth; his nephew, Sir Robert Peyton; his brother, Francis Peyton; Francis's wife; Francis's son, Christopher; his godson, John Peyton; his nephew, Edward Peyton; Sir Christopher Green; Sir William [illegible]; William Smith, and his wife, and sons, John and Christopher; and Robert Glover. A childless man, he seemed quite generous to relatives and friends, but he did not mention any Rose Peyton or Rose de Freville. Considering the context of the times (family ties were strong, men died for religion, and men believed unequivocally that the status of their life after death depended in part on prayers being said for them after their departure from this earth – Christopher in his will leaves money for masses to be said for him and for the high altar at church, and he bids his wife to find a good priest to pray for him), the failure to mention a claimed sister is a good indication that the testator had no such sister. This added to the fact that no contemporary reference has been cited anywhere to prove the existence of a sister is good evidence that we cannot at this time take William Leete's line back further than Robert de Freville and his wife Rose, of unknown surname.[20]

How Far to Go?

As can be seen from the various cases given above, whole-family genealogy does not necessarily mean that you should in every case compile an entire book to include all members of a given family in order to identify one otherwise undetermined member. It really means simply going outside your direct line to investigate some of the relatives of the person who is of immediate concern. How many relatives should be investigated depends on the individual case – as many as necessary. The more you add relatives without getting a positive result, the more you should continue adding relatives, as long as you feel it is still worth the time and effort to solve that particular gap in your genealogy. Sometimes you do not need to go further than just one sibling of an ancestor, while other times you virtually would be compiling enough material to make a large family history book.

How do you go about this? What information should be obtained? This, too, depends on the case. The basic categories of desirable information are known: date and place of birth, death, and marriage for each individual; probate and pertinent land record information; occupation; military service; and as much more as it takes to differentiate that individual from other people. You are trying to make each individual as unique as possible. If each of two Stephen Wilcoxes had a wife named Mary, they are not very well distinguished from each other. But if you can identify one as a tailor and the other as a yeoman, you have started the differentiation process. You want to continue the process as much as you feel is worth the time and effort, always of course in the context of using good genealogical techniques, emphasizing contemporary sources, and documenting each and every fact.

Notes

1. Many purist genealogists quarrel with the expression "direct ancestor," asking if there is such a thing as an indirect one. I think there is, only we refer to such a person as a collateral ancestor. It serves a need to be able to refer to direct ancestors and collateral ancestors, as in writing about qualifying ancestors for hereditary societies (some societies allow membership on the basis of collateral as well as direct ancestry). Donald Lines Jacobus would agree with me, for in *TAG* 38 (1962):190, he wrote, "Too many of those interested in tracing their personal ancestral lines limit their attention to the direct ancestors and fail to realize the importance of studying entire family groups." There are so many evils committed in the name of genealogy that I think responsible genealogists should not carp on matters such as this but should save their bullets for the really important battles.

2. The Lydia (Billington) Washburn case is given as an example of how to use a technique. Since I first became aware of this case, an article on the Billington family was published that includes identification of Lydia – see Robert S. Wakefield, "Some Descendants of Francis[2] Billington of the *Mayflower*," *The Genealogist* 3 (1982):238. The early Billingtons have been well studied.

3. *Mayflower Quarterly* 47 (1981):23.

4. See the Habakkuk Lindsay example in chapter 7

5. Charles Edward Banks, *History of Martha's Vineyard, Dukes County, Massachusetts,* vol. 3, *Family Genealogies* (Boston, 1925). Martha F. McCourt, *The American Descendants of Henry Luce* (privately published), was also consulted, but this book did not at the time include the particular Luce line in which I was

interested. Since then McCourt has done considerable revision of her book, most recently with Thomas R. Luce as co-compiler, and she has included my Luce line with reference to my research.

6. The evidence showing that Tyle Wilcox of Dartmouth and Tyle Wilcox of upstate New York were identical is given in my article "Tyle Wilcox of Upstate New York," *The American Genealogist* 62 (1987):23-24.

7. For more information on some of the descendants of Stephen[2] Wilcox, see Alden G. Beaman, "A Line of Descent from Edward Wilcox of Portsmouth," *Rhode Island Genealogical Register* 2 (1979):91ff.

8. "One Branch of the Rhode Island Wilcox Family," *The American Genealogist* 24 (1948):23-31, with correction in *The American Genealogist* 24:260. As if to show just how mysterious these Wilcoxes could be, Moriarty, ordinarily a most meticulous researcher, perpetuates some errors in his article.

9. For confusion regarding another descendant of the early Wilcoxes, Winston Churchill, see chapter 10.

10. Barrett Beard Russell, "The Descendants of John Russell of Dartmouth, Mass.," *New England Historical and Genealogical Register* 58 (1904):366.

11. Herbert A. Wilcox, *Daniel Wilcox of Puncatest and the Genealogy of some of his Descendants* (South Pasadena, Calif., 1943).

12. If I had had a computer, and had the software been in existence at the time, I would have used one of the genealogical family processing systems, such as Personal Ancestral File (PAF) or Roots.

13. Jane Fletcher Fiske, "Tyle Wilcox Discovered," *The American Genealogist* 62 (1987):21-2.

14. The next chapter is devoted to explaining onomastic evidence, which in essence means the analysis of names.

15. "Descent of William Leete, Governor of Connecticut, from the Emperor Charlemagne," *The American Genealogist* 31 (1955):114-17.

16. Frederick L. Weis and Arthur Adams, *Magna Charta Sureties,* with additions and corrections by Walter Lee Sheppard, Jr., 3d ed. (Baltimore, 1979), line 128.

17. Robert Edmond Chester Waters, *Genealogical Memoirs of the Extinct Family of Chester of Chicheley; their Ancestors and Descendants,* 2 vols. (London, 1878).

18. Nicholas Harris Nicholas, *Testamenta Vetusta* (London, 1826), 2:574; Charles H. and Thomson Cooper, *Athenae Cantabrigienses* (Cambridge,1858), 1:407.

19. Harleian Society Publications (London) 41:3-4.

20. It is quite likely that William Leete has one or more royal lines that have not been discovered yet, for he has the kind of family connections that so frequently lead to royal lines.

Chapter 6

Onomastic Evidence vs. the Name's the Same Game

What's in a name? A rose by any other name would smell as sweet.

—Shakespeare

A rose is a rose is a rose.

—Gertrude Stein

Onomastic evidence, as everyone of course knows, is evidence based on the sameness or similarity of names. Here we will discuss three of the forms it may take. First, sometimes when there are two people with the same name and they are about a generation apart in age, some genealogists might assume that they are father and son, depending of course on a number of other factors. Or second, when we find someone with a somewhat unusual name such as in the case of having a surname for a first name, some genealogists might assume that that surname runs in the family, especially on the female side, such as being the maiden name of the mother, or grandmother. Third, genealogists sometimes detect naming patterns in certain families, which might help add to other evidence that a family of otherwise unknown origin belongs to a known family of the same surname.

Onomastic evidence may lead to valid conclusions or invalid conclusions. It is helpful in genealogy to know under what circumstances a valid conclusion is most likely and vice versa. Experienced genealogists are very cautious with onomastic evidence, but they do not ignore it. Some genealogists refer to the tendency of novices to jump too quickly to conclusions on names as "the name's the same game." In its simplest form this tendency leads an inexperienced person finding a Robert Smith, Sr., and a Robert Smith, Jr., in the same colonial town to assume that they must be father and son. It is well known that in colonial times the use of "Sr." and "Jr." was to distinguish between two people with the same name living in the same town, not necessarily father and son. As an example, in the settlement of the estate of Josiah Holmes of Kingston, Massachusetts, on 17 March 1792, reference was made to one of his sons as Jeremiah Holmes, Jr.[1] It is surprising how much some people can stretch credulity to the utmost on similarity of names. In appendix A, I mention a case where an applicant for membership in an hereditary society claimed that an Ann Dodge was identical with an Amee Dodge; it is not difficult to believe that an Ann may call herself Amee (however, it is also a common mistake for people to misread one for the other in the records), but in this case Amee was recorded as getting married thirty-one years before Ann was born.

Onomastics and Chronology

In a similar case, an application for Mayflower Society membership was based on a Joseph Barrows being the son of Peleg and Jemima (Drew) Barrows – Jemima being a fifth generation descendant of *Mayflower* passenger John Alden. Many dates were left out of the application, but a little research to find the missing dates showed that this Joseph Barrows and his wife Sarah Atwood had married at Plympton, Massachusetts, 3 April 1755, while Peleg Barrows and Jemima Drew had married at nearby Halifax 4 May 1775. Son Joseph was married twenty years before his parents married? Further research showed that another Peleg Barrows who lived in Plympton had married Hopestill Darling there 26 November 1733, and they of course were more likely to be the parents of the Joseph Barrows who was married in 1755. Peleg and Jemima (Drew) Barrows did have a son Joseph, but he was not born until 8 November 1792.[2] In this case – and in many, many other cases – a close attention to chronology can prevent future disappointment and embarrassment.

Naming Patterns

As will be shown further in this chapter, there clearly were naming patterns in colonial New England as well as elsewhere. These naming patterns can be helpful in conducting genealogical research and in assembling evidence. They can also, if not understood properly, be harmful. As an example of the prevalence of naming patterns, it will be helpful to go back to medieval England where we will be dealing mostly with families of the nobility. In the Braose family, you will find first names such as William and Giles, but you will not find a Humphrey, while in the Bohun family the name Humphrey predominates. The Toenys liked to alternate between Ralph and Roger, while the Mortimers alternated between Roger and Edmund. The Percys favored the name Henry, the Veres Aubrey, the Stricklands Walter, and the Clares Richard and Gilbert. Interestingly, we find the name Alexander in both the families of Captain Myles Standish of Plymouth and of the noble Standishes of Standish in England, though this does not of itself prove that the former came from the latter.

It is a paradox of genealogy that we frequently find names favored by families of a given surname in a given area also used by other unrelated families of the same surname in the same area. In an article I wrote on a Plymouth family named Holmes, for example, I pointed out that there were several unrelated families with the surname Holmes living in the Plymouth area. The family I was writing about frequently used the names John, Nathaniel, and Joseph, but, almost as if it were done with malicious intent, these names were found in one of the other Holmes families, too. It was mentioned in chapter 4 that Davis, in particular, made some grievous mistakes in trying to identify two Joseph Holmeses. As an example of the kind of difficulty frequently encountered, in a footnote I pointed out the existence of four men named John Holmes born within a dozen years and a few miles of each other.[3]

Keeping in mind that there are family naming patterns, it is helpful to appreciate just how fast families can multiply with each increasing generation. Take a pioneer ancestor named Jonathan Doe as a fictional illustration. Jonathan could have had five sons and named one of them Jonathan after himself. In the next generation, each of those five sons could have named a son Jonathan, in honor of the grandfather, for a total of five Jonathans plus many other males, who, by the fourth generation, could have been naming, say, twenty-five of their sons Jonathan. In real life the proliferation of the same name does not expand that fast, but it is still fast enough to supply fuel for the confusion of genealogists. The original John Holmes of my article had two sons, John and Nathaniel. Three generations later there were six cousins named Nathaniel Holmes.

Not all people of the same name are necessarily cousins. The great English statesman Winston Churchill, born in 1874, was not related to the well-known American writer Winston Churchill, born in 1871. I descend from a Massachusetts Stratton family and am not related, as far as I can learn, to the famous author of dog and boy stories, Gene Stratton Porter, who was female (Porter being her married name) and who descended from a New Jersey Stratton family.[4] Frequently children are named after unrelated famous people or sometimes after friends (several examples will be given below). There are also trends in names, which sometimes account for like names by unrelated people. Horace Stratton, the name of my grandfather, would not seem to be a common name, but Harriet Russell Stratton in her *A Book of Strattons* (which traces lines in many unrelated Stratton families), shows a fair number of unrelated Horace Strattons. Incidentally, one would expect to find Horace as a name much more in eighteenth- or nineteenth-century America than in the seventeenth or twentieth century because classical names, of which Horace is one, were far more popular in the eighteenth and nineteenth centuries than those earlier and later. David W. Dumas shows in a study how traditional English, Biblical, and classical names varied in popularity in New England between 1780 and 1850.[5]

Surnames as First Names

Let us look at some examples of a surname being used as a first or middle name. James Madison Luce died at Athol, Massachusetts, on 28 November 1896, at age eighty-eight and thus was born ca. 1808. *Madison?* Should we look for Madison as a surname in his ancestry? Probably not. Probably we would do better by looking up James Madison in the encyclopedia and noting that the fourth president of the United States was elected to that office in 1808. As name evidence all we have here is a good indication that the parents of James Madison Luce were enthusiastic supporters of President James Madison (it should not be too surprising that James Madison Luce named a daughter, my great-grandmother, Marie Antoinette Luce).

Would we be on more solid ground with the case of Richard Baxter Mann, who was born at Petersham, Massachusetts, on 25 February 1825? I was really interested in the maternal ancestry of his sister, but after spending much time on the problem with no positive result, I decided – as part of a whole-family approach – to see if I could discover the ancestry of her siblings. The name Richard Baxter Mann seemed to offer a clue, and I began an extensive research effort that lasted years, off and on, trying to see if Baxter might have been a family name. There were certainly a number of Baxter families in Massachusetts in the generations before his birth, but all my efforts were to no avail. And then one day while looking up an unrelated matter in the *Encyclopedia Britannica,* I came across the name Richard Baxter, who lived from 1615 to 1691, "one of the greatest English Puritan ministers...[whose] influence on English Protestantism was more profound than that of any other 17th-century Puritan minister." His books were considered classics of Protestant devotional literature, and other books were still being written about him in 1830, 1925, and 1954. Here then was a likely, albeit not proven, explanation for the naming of Richard Baxter Mann. I also spent a considerable amount of research time in trying to see if Tyle (sometimes found as Tyler) Wilcox (see chapter 5) might have any Tyler ancestry, but without success.

On the other hand, I showed in a journal article[6] that the mother of an Ensign Mann, a Sarah whose maiden name was unknown, was most likely a Sarah Ensign. It is worth repeating what I collated in that article on some opinions of some leading American genealogists on the subject of onomastic evidence:

> George E. McCracken writes in *The American Genealogist* 54:108: "Let me emphasize also that endowing a newborn child with a first name that is a surname is also a very helpful clue to family connections and is called onomastic evidence in the trade." Earlier, in *TAG* 37:73, G. Andrews Moriarty gives a highly significant contemporary reference to show how the custom was regarded by people of the time: he notes that Judge Samuel Sewell in his diary recorded that his son Samuel had married Rebecca, daughter of Governor Joseph Dudley, and that when Rebecca wished to name a child Dudley, her mother objected because "her son might still have a son." Moriarty

explains that a child usually received a family name as a given one when "the mother's family was of some importance, particularly when it had died out in the male line." In commenting in the same issue upon Moriarty's remarks, Donald Lines Jacobus, the editor of *TAG*, agrees that there was a special inducement for so naming a child when the mother's family had died out, but he also notes that the custom seems to have been fairly common even when that was not the case; he adds, however, that "the use of a surname for a given name nearly always indicates descent of that individual from the family whose name was bestowed on him," although exceptions could be found (*TAG* 37:75). Jacobus's observations are of the customs of the early and middle colonial periods in New England; he notes that eventually some surnames became accepted as given names without any special significance, as is usually the case today.

In the case of Ensign Mann, I noted that there was a Sarah Ensign in his town of Scituate who disappeared from the records, and that the male line of the family of this Sarah Ensign had died out with the death of her brother in King Philip's War in 1676, a good number of years before Ensign Mann was born. This was a case where the onomastic evidence could not be ignored.

Naming a Child After a Deceased Spouse

I have observed also another tendency on naming patterns, one that we are liable to miss in the twentieth century, when the act of dying is considered something nasty, and people want no reminders of it. But in colonial times death was remembered, and sometimes the name of a deceased spouse was given to the child of a person by a later spouse. Note that although most of the following examples occur in the colony and county of Plymouth, I believe the custom was widespread throughout colonial New England and also was observed elsewhere in the English colonies in America. A few examples follow:

The first wife of Samuel Baker of Plymouth Colony, Eleanor (Adams) Winslow, died 27 August 1676, and he married secondly on 2 February 1677 Patience Simmons. His first child by Patience was born on 10 April 1679 and was named Eleanor.[7]

John Nelson of Plymouth, Massachusetts, married first (1667) Sarah Wood, second Lydia (Bartlett) Barnaby, and third (1693) Patience Morton. By his third marriage he and his wife named a daughter (born 1693/4) Lydia, most likely after his second wife, and another daughter (born 1695) Sarah, possibly after his first wife.[8]

Samuel Nelson of Plymouth, Massachusetts, married first (1704) Hannah Ford, second Bathsheba Nichols, and third (1718) Sarah Holmes. He named his first child by his second marriage (born 1707), Hannah, presumably after his first wife, and his first daughter by his third marriage (born 1719), Bathsheba, obviously after his second wife.[9]

James Fuller of Plymouth County, Massachusetts, married first (19 May 1725) Judith Rickard, and she died 23 February 1725/6. He married second (22 May 1729) Mercy (Jackson) Perkins, and he named his first daughter by his second marriage (born ca. 1730), Judith.[10]

Jabez Holmes of Plymouth, Massachusetts, married first (30 September 1730) Rebecca Harlow, who died 24 December 1730. He married second (12 November 1734) Sarah Clarke, and he named the first child by his second marriage (born 25 October 1736), Rebecca.[11]

Ruth Silvester married first (1719/20) Francis Cooke, second (1724/5) Samuel Ring, and third (1770) John Phinney, and she named a son by her second marriage (born 1737/8), Francis, probably after her first husband.[12]

Elisha Holmes of Plymouth County, Massachusetts, married first (7 March 1720/1) Sarah Bartlett, who died 4 July 1738. He married second (intentions 7 July 1739), Mary (Fish) Ellis, and he named his first son by his second marriage (born 2 April 1744), Bartlett Holmes.[13]

Richard Grinnell of Little Compton, then Massachusetts, now Rhode Island, married Comfort (Billings) Bailey, the widow of William Bailey, and he named a son (born 7 July 1759), Bailey Grinnell.[14]

Jeremiah Burlingame married at Little Compton (1 March 1778) Ruth (Grinnell) Palmer, the widow of Walter Palmer, and he named his first son (born 3 March 1780), Walter Palmer Burlingame.[15]

An awareness of the custom of naming a child after a deceased former spouse can be helpful as a research clue. For example, if a John Doe marries a Helen Roe, and for various reasons it is suspected that Helen Roe was a widow, it would be good practice to look in the same general area for the marriage of any _____ Roe to a Helen _____, and then to look for the death of whatever Roe is found to have married a Helen. However, if John and Helen (_____) (Roe) Doe named sons Moses, Jeremiah, and James, the search would have more to go on if one of those three names was found to be the name of a man with the surname of Roe marrying a Helen and then dying prior to the marriage of Helen with John Doe; that is, if the search shows a Moses Roe marrying a Helen Smith, and later a Moses Roe dies before Helen Roe marries John Doe, the fact that John and Helen Doe named a son Moses increases the possibility that the search has come up with the right man for Helen's first husband – not proof, just another bit of indirect evidence to add to the total.

Another important aspect of a child being named after a parent's deceased, prior spouse occurs when we know that a man had, say, two wives and ten children, but we do not know which children were by which wife. If the first wife was named Jerusha and the second Hepzibah, and the fifth child is named Jerusha and the sixth Hepzibah, a genealogist unaware of this custom could believe that the dividing line between the children of the first and second wives was between the fifth and sixth child, but it would not necessarily be so. Knowing this helps restrain us from jumping to unwarranted conclusions.

Keeping Names in the Family

The perpetuation of a number of first names from one generation to another can be a significant piece of indirect evidence, especially if it adds to other facts all pointing in the same direction. In an article on one of my Stratton ancestors,[16] I showed that an Elias Stratton had a wife Millicent, whose surname was not known. A Millicent Frost married in Sherborn, Massachusetts, in 1751 Abijah Sawin, and Sawin died in 1754. Elias and Millicent Stratton had ten children born at Sherborn between 1755 and 1773: Millicent, Sarah, Ebenezer, Elias, Jonathan, Hannah, Joseph, Jabez, Abijah, and Molly. Elias had a father Jabez, a brother Ebenezer, and a sister Sarah. Millicent (Frost) Sawin's parents were Joseph and Hannah Frost, and she had siblings Jonathan, Sarah, Joseph, and Hannah. The name Abijah could have been in honor of Millicent's deceased husband, though it was also the name of a brother of Elias Stratton; in either case, it contributes to showing that Elias and Millicent believed in perpetuating family names. There was additional indirect evidence such as Elias's wife, Millicent, being the same age as Millicent Frost. In this case the weight of the total evidence was very convincing, and onomastic evidence was a significant part of the total.

Not often, but every now and then we come across a man with two living children having the same first name. Humphrey Turner of Scituate in Plymouth Colony is a case in point, and in his will he named, among others, "my eldest son John Turner" and also "my son young John Turner."[17] Robert C. Anderson, F.A.S.G., in an unpublished study of cases where a man had two living children with the same first name, points out that almost invariably one such child was by one wife and the other by another wife. This suggestion has an important consequence for genealogists, as in the case of Humphrey Turner. His wife at Scituate, Lydia, has been called Lydia Gamer, though I have not seen convincing evidence of this surname. If she were Humphrey's only wife at Scituate, he probably had an earlier wife who may have died in England, in which case she, the unknown wife, would have been the mother of the older John, who married a granddaughter of Elder William Brewster. Descendants of the older John, many of whom have claimed Lydia Gamer as an ancestress (or put her down as I have with a question mark, for I descend from the older John) should look further for their real ancestress.

The emphasis on two "living" siblings above has the implication that it was much more frequent for a couple to have two children of the same first name when one had died before the second was born, and such is the case. It is very frequent in colonial times, and sometimes it seems pathetic to see a husband and wife naming child after child so as to perpetuate the father's first name, the mother's first name, or a grandparent's first name, as each child so named dies early, and the attempt must start all over again. In chapter 7, I mention a case where there was a need because of other facts to postulate the existence of a second Elizabeth Southworth, who is otherwise unknown in the records, but I felt safe in doing so because of the frequent occurrence of the phenomenon of a second child being given the name of a deceased child.

The implications in such a practice show again the need for careful research. Choosing the wrong date of birth for an ancestor in a family where there were two children with the same first name can seriously hamper further research, especially when there is a difference of many years between the two children. For example, suppose you find a death record for your John Doe in 1796 at age fifty, and you find a birth record for a John Doe in the right geographic area showing that he was born in 1728. Obviously you will dismiss the latter as a possibility, for he was born eighteen years too soon. But it is possible that the older John Doe died young, and it would not be out of the question that his parents named another son John who was born in 1746.

Some Significance in Names

Sometimes a name can imply some other significance. The name Francis was not often used by early colonial New England puritans because it was considered a "cavalier" or royalist name. The name Benoni (meaning "child of sorrow") was sometimes given in New England to a child whose mother had died in childbirth, and may thus be a clue in some cases to the possibility that the father had married more than once.[18]

Variations in Names

A common problem, especially for beginning genealogists, is the fact that a given person might be found in the records under more than one name. Not many people seem to know that Sukey was once a common nickname for Susanna. Ann can also be found as Nancy, Nan or Hannah, and Sarah as Sally. My wife put in considerable research to find her ancestor Miar Posey, and when she finally found him, she learned that his full name was Nehemiah. Judah was usually a male name but is sometimes found in colonial records as being interchangeable with Judith. Several names were used often for both sexes, "Experience" being sometimes a unisex name. When Latin was sometimes used in official documents, we may likely find Jacobus instead of James, Guilielmus instead of William, and Egidius instead of Giles.

The medieval genealogist should also be aware, as shown in appendix B, that names were not always as stable as in later centuries, and a twice-married widow might well choose to be known by the surname of her first husband. A knowledge of Latin is extremely helpful in genealogy. One of my correspondents – a good genealogist, but without much knowledge of Latin – wrote me that he had found information contradicting my assertions that the daughters of William and Eve (Marshal) de Braose had these marriages: Isabel to David, son of Prince Llywelyn of Wales; Maud to Roger Mortimer; Eve to William de Cantelou; and Eleanor to Humphrey de Bohun. His source gave the marriages as Agnes (instead of Isabel) to a Mr. _____ Wallie; Matilda to Reginald de Mortuo Mari; Eva to a man named de Cantilupo; and Eleanor to Uffrid de Boney, though he wondered if Boney should have been Bovey. I replied that "Wallie" was a form of medieval Latin meaning "of Wales"; Matilda was the same as Maud; Mortuo Mari was the Latin for Mortimer; Cantilupo was the Latin for Cantelou; and Uffrid de Boney was Humphrey de Bohun (pronounced Boon).

In medieval English genealogy, besides finding that Maude and Matilda are interchangeable, we also see that Isabel and Elizabeth, on the one hand, and Margery and Margaret, on the other, seem to be in many cases. However, *Complete Peerage* observes that the latter two sets were not always treated the same, and it notes that Michael atte Pole, Earl of Suffolk, who died in 1415, had one daughter named Elizabeth and another named Isabel.[19]

There is, of course, much more to the study of names in genealogy – indeed the subject merits a whole book by itself. In Greece there is a widespread custom of naming a first born son after the father's father. Both in Greece and in Russia, children are given a patronymic, in this case the father's first name becomes the child's middle name. As an example, the prime minister of Greece, Andreas Papandreou, has Georgiou (son of George) for his middle name, and Andreas's first born son is George Andrew (in Greek, Georgios Andrea) Papandreou. Welsh genealogy is impossible to understand without the knowledge that surnames did not generally come into use until the sixteenth century, and the patronymic was important to identify a child such as David ap Rhys

(David, son of Rhys, which, when surnames were adopted, could become David Price). In Spanish-speaking countries a child takes both parents' surnames, such as Juan, son of Jorge Gonzalez y Garza and Ana Martinez y Villarreal becoming known as Juan Gonzales y Martinez, and if Juan marries Dolores de las Casas y Fernandez and has a son Pedro, that son would be Pedro Gonzalez y de las Casas. It well behooves anyone interested in the genealogy of a given country to devote at least a little time to learning the onomastic practices of that country, past and present.

Like a sharp knife, onomastic evidence can be a powerful tool, but a dangerous one, especially in untrained hands.[20]

Notes

1. *Plymouth County Probate Records* 31:481-82.
2. *Mayflower Quarterly* 47 (1981):68-69.
3. *National Genealogical Society Quarterly* 74 (1986):83-110, 203-23; in particular, see footnotes 87 and 127.
4. I go back to Samuel Stratton, who appears in Watertown, Massachusetts, records in the 1640s. According to Harriett Russell Stratton, *A Book of Strattons,* 2 vols. (New York, 1908, 1918), 2:482, Gene Stratton Porter's grandfather, Daniel Stratton of Sussex County, New Jersey, is thought (but not proven) to be a descendant of Mark Stratton, an eighteenth-century resident of New Jersey. I cannot resist telling the story of how when I lived in Mexico, I was introduced to an American tourist as "Gene Stratton." When we parted company, she said, "It was nice to meet you, Mr. Porter."
5. "The Naming of Children in New England 1780-1850," *The New England Historical and Genealogical Register* 132 (1978):196-210.
6. "Mann-Ensign Notes," *The American Genealogist* 61 (1985):46-49.
7. Lysander S. Richards, *History of Marshfield, Mass., with Genealogy* (Plymouth, 1901, 1905), 2:142.
8. William T. Davis, *Ancient Landmarks of Plymouth,* 2d ed. (Boston, 1899), 2:193-94. I have not tried to verify the examples supported by Davis, or other undocumented secondary sources, since even if one or two examples might not be entirely correct, there are enough other examples to demonstrate that the custom was a frequent one.
9. Ibid., 2:194.
10. *Mayflower Families through Five Generations,* vol. 1, ed. Lucy Mary Kellogg (Plymouth, 1975), 68.
11. Eugene A. Stratton, "The Descendants of Mr. John Holmes, Messenger of the Plymouth Court," *National Genealogical Society Quarterly* 74 (1986):211.
12. Albert Henry Silvester, "Richard Silvester of Weymouth, Mass., and Some of His Descendants," *The New England Historical and Genealogical Register* 85

(1931):365; *Mayflower Families through Five Generations*, vol. 2, ed. Robert M. Sherman (Plymouth, 1978), 81-82.

13. *National Genealogical Society Quarterly* 74 (1986):211.

14. Benjamin F. Wilbour, *Little Compton Families* (Providence, R.I., 1967), 310-11. This source is known to contain a significant number of errors, but it is sufficient for the present purpose.

15. *Burlingame Manuscript* (located in the Rhode Island Historical Society and other places), 72-73. Additional information on this family, including more analysis of onomastic evidence, is given in chapter 8.

16. "Circumstantial Evidence: A Stratton-Frost Example," *The American Genealogist* 59 (1983):109-12.

17. A short biographic sketch on Humphrey Turner is given in my book *Plymouth Colony: Its History & People, 1620-1691* (Salt Lake City, 1986), 364-65.

18. In at least one case, that of Benoni Delano in Plymouth Colony, the name was used after it became known that he had been conceived out of wedlock, though his parents subsequently married.

19. *Complete Peerage*, vol. 3, appendix C, 618. This appendix should be required reading for anyone doing medieval English research. Another most useful onomastic guide for the genealogist is E. G. Withycombe, *The Oxford Dictionary of English Christian Names* (New York-London, 1947). An interesting article on the perpetuation of the feminine first name Violet can be seen in Haskell Venard, "When Violets Bloomed in Old Connecticut," *The American Genealogist* 46 (1970):206-8.

20. An interesting misinterpretation of a name was made in a recent book analyzing names. Along with such other puritan "message" names as Hopestill, Yetmercy, Thankful, Freelove, Mindwell, and Submit, the book pointed to the not uncommon feminine colonial name Tamesin as an ever-present reminder to "tame sin." The author was obviously unaware that this particular name was not puritanical at all but was an oft-found phonetic rendering of Thomasine, a then common feminine equivalent to Thomas.

Chapter 7

Analyzing Evidence

*Can anyone tell us who were the parents of Habakuk Lindsey
of Danvers, Mass., who married Mary Green of North Danvers 6 October 1741? A correct history of this branch is much
desired.*
—From the Lindsay Family Association 1906 Report

*Things are seldom what they seem,
Skim milk masquerades as cream.*
—Gilbert and Sullivan

Analysis, it is worth repeating, comes down to using common sense in
the light of specialized knowledge. The emphasis here has to be on
the words *specialized knowledge*. It does not take much analysis to understand when John Doe mentions in his will his "natural daughter," Joan,
the wife of Joseph Jones, that we have identified at least the father of Joan
Jones, assuming that there are not two contemporary Joseph Jones in the
area each with a wife named Joan. It might take a little more analysis to
identify Joan's mother, and it is helpful to have the specialized knowledge
that the word "natural" was not used in colonial times to mean illegitimate,
although Joan could still be John Doe's daughter by an earlier wife. As
we chain back in various genealogical lines, generation after generation,
we almost invariably come to a person whose identity requires more
analysis, and that means we require more specialized knowledge of what
the few available facts are likely to mean.

Obscured Facts

Sometimes family facts are obscured through either inadvertency or deliberate misstatements. My grandmother is a case in point. My parents and grandparents had all died before I took an interest in genealogy. In an old letter from my father I came across his statement that my mother's mother had run away from a strict family which had come to Boston from England. In my very gradual discovery of records on her, I learned that my grandmother, whom I had loved dearly, was a little liar. The records proved that, but because of all the lies, I had to go on a merry chase before I could find enough records to piece together a most likely biography. In the 1900 census, my grandmother showed herself to have been born in Canada in November 1869, and she had lived in the United States since 1883. However, by the 1930 census she had converted herself into a native U.S. citizen, born in Massachusetts, and age fifty-six, thus born ca. 1874.[1] When I found her marriage record, it showed that she was married on 3 July 1886 at age twenty-three, thus having been born ca. 1863, in a place called Brachburg, Canada. The Canadian government kindly answered my queries but assured me that there was no such place as Brachburg.

I had to make an analysis of what from the records was most likely to be true and eliminate the parts likely to be false. By doing this, I was able to reason that my grandmother had moved to Boston with her family as a young girl and had run away to marry a much older man. Her father, Nathaniel Chamberlain, had probably come to Canada from some unknown place in England and thus would be hard to trace. Her mother, however, was Myra Ann Sherman, who had been born in Saratoga, New York. This led me to a secondary source, a Sherman family history,[2] showing that Myra Ann Sherman had married a Nathaniel Chamberlain. Documentation for this part of the book gave the source as the Frank Dempster Sherman collection at the New York Public Library. On checking that collection I found that the ultimate source was the will of Edmund Jay Sherman, in which he mentioned Myra Ann Sherman, the wife of Nathaniel Chamberlain. I then went on to locate the complete will and related probate papers. One of the probate receipts was signed by the children of Edmund Jay Sherman, including "Myra Ann Chamberlain wife of Nathaniel Chamberlain residing in South West-Meath," Canada. A look at a map quickly showed that Westmeath, Ontario, Canada, was just a few miles from Beachburg (not Brachburg), Canada. A check of Canadian censuses for 1861, 1871, and 1881 showed that my grandmother had been born in 1860. Though I was able to trace her mother's side back to colonial New England of the seventeenth century and thence back to Dedham, Essex, England, her father's origin was still a mystery except that I had the additional information that he was born ca. 1814. These examples involving my grandmother well illustrate the fact that even primary records can at times be misleading or out and out wrong, especially if the source had a desire to exaggerate, suppress, or falsify evidence.

Misspellings of geographic names can be a problem in genealogy. When I was new in genealogy I searched a long time for Teacham, Vermont, until one day I noticed that the clerk's handwriting on the certificate I had was rather unusual, and that his *P*s looked like *T*s. Then I was able to make inquiries at Peacham, Vermont, which in turn took me much further back. A valuable aid to the specialized knowledge that helps in genealogy is a good gazetteer for the areas of interest.

Familiarity with handwriting of the times helps, too, and sometimes when two or more handwriting specimens are available, comparisons can help solve problems. The Mayflower Society had been bothered for years over the matter of two cousins named John Rickard, each with a wife named Mary. One John Rickard had married Mary Cooke, granddaughter of *Mayflower* passenger Francis Cooke, while the wife of the other John Rickard was of unknown parentage. The descendants of one John and Mary Rickard were eligible for Mayflower Society membership, while the descendants of the other couple were not. Analysis showed that the John Rickard who became guardian for a Josiah Doty was most likely the one married to Mary Cooke (Josiah Doty's mother was the sister of Mary Cooke). The original guardianship paper was available at the office of the Plymouth County Register of Probate, and it contained the signature of John Rickard. That signature was compared with specimens of the known signatures on other probate documents of each of the two John Rickards in question. The signature comparison showed clearly which John Rickard had married Mary Cooke.[3]

Know the History of the Times

Knowledge of the history of the times of our ancestors is indispensable in pursuing genealogy. Such historical knowledge is fascinating for its own

sake, but aside from the fact that nothing is dryer than a list of unembel-
lished begats, sometimes only a knowledge of history can help us solve
genealogical problems. I once deduced from indirect evidence that Sarah,
who married ca. 1678 Thomas Mann, had to be Sarah Ensign, but later I
found this Sarah Ensign mentioned in her brother John's will as Sarah
Wade. Were all my deductions in vain? However, I knew there were many
family ties between the Ensign and Wade families in Scituate, and that
both John Ensign and Joseph Wade were killed in 1676 in King Philip's
War. I now believe that Sarah Ensign married Joseph Wade, who died in
1676, and then a few years later the young widow married Thomas Mann.[4]
Knowledge of wars, famines, epidemics, dangerous occupations, and
other such facts can explain why there may be exceptions to normal
chronology.

Learn Something about Your Sources

It helps, too, to have more knowledge about the sources we use than
just the bibliographic information. It is well known among experienced
New England genealogists, for example, that the frequently used source
book, *Topographical Dictionary of 2885 English Immigrants to New
England 1620-1650,* attributed to Colonel Charles E. Banks, was actually
put together from his notes after his death by someone else who was not
as careful as Banks was. Many people tracing their ancestry back to early
New Jersey unfortunately rely on Ora E. Monnette's work. Jacobus points
out that "Mr. Monette seemed to delight in fanciful identifications, entirely without evidence and often contrary to the evidence....The genuine
records found here and there throughout the books, sometimes buried
beneath the weight of irrelevant and speculative matter, are often useful
and valuable. Many items are also included, copied uncritically from many
sources, good, bad, or indifferent, and often overlaid with the author's
opinions expressed with great positiveness and greater verbosity."[5]
In my capacity as the verifying genealogist for various hereditary
societies, I was asked to accept books such as these all the time in lieu of
any other evidence. For *Mayflower* genealogy, the Dunham family history
is frequently cited. Few books are so thoroughly condemned. Jacobus
called it "a genealogy of the Dunham family, published in 1907, poorly arranged, poorly indexed, and containing many errors and impossible statements." Barclay wrote that it "contains a vast amount of material poorly

arranged and much that is confusing and misleading. If fact, there are several serious errors and some statements that are absolutely impossible."[6] It seems to be far more common for people to find books such as Dunham's and Monnette's than to find the critical evaluations of them written in journals such as *The American Genealogist*, (*TAG*) not that *TAG* is difficult to find if one really wants to.

For one Royal Bastard application, I was asked to accept statements in the book *History of Woodstock* as sufficient support for several generations in a lineage. This multivolume work gives a good number of generations of the Bowen family. It was written by Clarence Winthrop Bowen, and it was not sufficiently documented, but, on the other hand, some of its volumes were edited by Donald Lines Jacobus. This type of thing could raise the question: Do we accept an undocumented (or insufficiently documented) work in which Jacobus had a hand? In this particular case the question was a moot one.[7] In the introduction to Volume 7, Jacobus himself wrote this disclaimer:

> Despite the large amount of manuscript material in Mr. Bowen's files which had to be studied, selected, and compiled, it was found that not much research had been done on these families in the probate and other primary sources....It was not possible, within the limits set to the work, to search also the land records in Woodstock. So far as the more recent generations are concerned, we have relied almost entirely on Mr. Bowen's manuscript, and must disclaim responsibility should any errors come to light....No systematic attempt has been made to check the earlier volumes of this series.

Sometimes good genealogical research may be reduced considerably in value by not being properly analyzed, documented, and compared to other sources. One of the most common mistakes in genealogical analysis is to find some information that seems to prove a genealogical connection, but then fail to check standard sources. It would be silly to accept a Bible record showing a fourth generation descendant of *Mayflower* passenger William White without checking first the *Mayflower Families* book on the first five generations of William White. There, for example, we might find that a previously unknown third wife and two children were claimed for third generation descendant Jonathan White, but that the evidence was all written in the same hand in a Bible which was not even printed until 1870.[8] Since the claim gave his third marriage as taking place in 1708, a Bible record of more than 150 years later (some five to six generations) was hardly contemporary. But someone coming across such a Bible among the papers of known ancestors might readily jump to the conclusion that it had to be true. Documentary proof is not proof without an analysis of the document. The fact that a secondary source is footnoted does not automatically give it the credibility of a primary source.

One of my pet peeves is the nineteenth-century English genealogist Dudley G. Cary Elwes, noted especially for his extensive writings on the medieval Braose family, which I have also been researching for years. Elwes is absolutely untrustworthy. The problem is that if he were merely bad, it would be easy to dismiss his writings entirely, but Elwes was a paradox. He was an amazingly good researcher, and he ferreted out numerous primary documents from British archives bearing on the Braose family through several centuries. It was in drawing conclusions from the good evidence he had discovered that Elwes failed so often. In one case he uses five pages to cite and often give excerpts from numerous original sources, and then he adds them up to the wrong conclusion. Ironically, among the excerpts that he gives appears the very clue that could lead to correct identification.[9] In another case, Elwes credits one of the Braose lords with possessing twenty-eight manors in Sussex, forty-seven in Hampshire, sixty-one in Berkshire, seventy-two in Wiltshire, and eighty-two in Dorset, figures which disagree completely with every other source of information on the subject. This so puzzled me that I made an effort to find out what Elwes based his figures on. I discovered by comparing Sir Harry Ellis's book explaining the *Domesday Book* with copies of the *Domesday Book,* itself that Elwes had actually recorded as the numbers of manors what Ellis had put down as *Domesday Book* chapter numbers.[10]

Chronology

I have mentioned chronology in other places in this book because the concept of chronology permeates all aspects of genealogy. Events occur not only in a place, but in a time. An understanding of chronological probabilities in genealogy is one of the most powerful tools available for genealogical analysis, both to support and to refute claimed lines. Here is a case that does both. Nahum Mitchell in his genealogies of Bridgewater, Massachusetts, families states that Eunice Leach, who married William Keith, was the daughter of Benjamin and Hepzibah (Washburn) Leach,[11] and this claim has been picked up as fact by at least three other secondary sources. Hepzibah Washburn's descent from *Mayflower* passenger James Chilton is given in some detail in chapter 8 of this book. *Mayflower Families Two* shows Hepzibah's marriage and fourteen children, though it mentions that "fourteen children appear a lot for one woman," and it comments that no contemporary records were found to support some, including Eunice Leach (whose husband is not given).

On receiving several applications on this line for *Mayflower* membership, I was bothered by the chronology. Not all the vital records were available to tie up the chronology neatly, but some dates could be approximated. Hepzibah Washburn married Benjamin Leach in 1702, and thus Hepzibah was born probably no later than 1685, and her claimed daughter Eunice Leach married twenty-three-year-old William Keith in 1767. Eunice could be expected (according to the averages) to be younger than her husband, or at the very least not too much older. Yet if she were as much as five years older, her mother would have been at least fifty-four years old (or much more) when Eunice was born, and we look very skeptically at that. A little research on my part, which should have been done by the applicants before submitting their applications, showed that William Keith died in 1824 at age seventy-seven, and an unnamed widow of William Keith (presumably Eunice) died in 1827 at age seventy-seven. Thus there was a presumption that Eunice was born in 1750, when mother Hepzibah would have been at least sixty-five. Clearly something was wrong.

A check of probate records showed several wills for Leaches of Bridgewater which might have been able to shed some light on the matter. The will for Joseph Leach, known to be a son of Benjamin and Hepzibah (Washburn) Leach, proved to be the answer. He died in 1755, and among his heirs were six daughters, including Eunice Leach (though Mitchell's genealogies showed only sons, no daughters, for him, but Mitchell contains many errors). Now we had the full story. Benjamin and Hepzibah married in 1702, had Joseph in 1705 (second child), and Joseph married in 1736 and had a number of children, including Eunice in 1750. Eunice married in 1767, when seventeen years of age, a man of twenty-three – all well within the normal, sound chronological ranges. Eunice

95

and her progeny were *Mayflower* descendants after all, but the secondary sources had skipped one generation.

Chronology only has to be approximated to be useful. Of course, it helps to know something about standard chronological ranges for the time and place. In medieval England among the nobility we expect very early marriages, perhaps as early as four years of age; consummation of marriage was deferred, but it was not too unusual (though perhaps somewhat more unusual than I had earlier thought – see chapter 13) for a woman to start having children shortly after the age of puberty. In colonial New England women might most commonly marry at age seventeen to twenty-three, while for men it would be more like twenty-one to twenty-seven. We do not expect children after a woman has reached her late forties. There will be exceptions, but then more careful study is required to determine if a given case really is an exception or if something is wrong.

Sometimes we are forced by the evidence to formulate theories that otherwise might seem unreasonable. Explain this if you can: Vital records show that Elizabeth Southworth was born in November 1672 to Edward and Mary Southworth of Duxbury, Massachusetts. She married Samuel Weston on 14 March 1716/7, when he was about twenty-seven years old. Thus she would have been forty-four years old, some seventeen years older than her husband. Her last child was born 30 April 1730, when Elizabeth would have been over fifty-seven years old. Some might say mistaken identity. How do we know that the Elizabeth Southworth who married Samuel Weston was the daughter of Edward and Mary Southworth? How do we know that the Elizabeth Weston who had Samuel's child in 1730 was his first wife? Could she not have died and he have married a second wife, also named Elizabeth? In the instant case those questions do not signify, for we also have the will of Elizabeth (Southworth) Weston's father, Edward Southworth, in 1719, and the will of her unmarried sister of 1761, which make it clear that Samuel Weston's wife Elizabeth was Edward Southworth's daughter. But this is virtually impossible, unless we invent an explanation. The Elizabeth Southworth born 1672 was one of the older children in the family of Edward and Mary. This Elizabeth must have died unmarried, though there is no death record, perhaps in her teens when her mother was still having children. As is frequently the case, the bereaved parents named a subsequently born daughter after the deceased daughter, even though there is no birth record (the second Elizabeth could easily have been seventeen or more years younger than the first Elizabeth). Can there possibly be any other believable explanation?[12]

The use of chronology as a tool in genealogy must also take into account changes or differences in calendars. For example, the Julian calendar continued to be used in England until 1752, long after other western European countries had adopted the Gregorian calendar (the Russians did not change from Julian to Gregorian until after the Soviet Revolution). English colonies in America followed the lead of the mother country. Quakers used a Julian calendar with numbered months, such as "2, 5th, 1710," meaning the second day of the fifth month of 1710, but the fifth month under the Julian calendar was July, for the year began with 25 March, with March called the first month and February called the twelfth month. It is very common in published genealogies to see dates erroneously transcribed, such as 10, 2nd being called February 10 instead of April 10. As an incidental matter, experienced genealogists usually put the day before the month, such as 10 April. As with any convention, once adopted it should be exclusively practiced, as I learned the hard way – when I see a date in file cards I made years ago, such as "5/8/1799," I have to analyze whether I meant 5 August or May 8.

The Habakkuk Lindsey Puzzle

Genealogical analysis often requires, as the above example shows, imagination. Let's conclude this chapter with a case study that ends with a question mark. I do not think anyone knows the answer. I certainly do not. Our case involves many of the methods and approaches discussed in this book. However, more than just a knowledge of methods is needed; knowing when to apply a given technique is equally important. Note that this is a real case, and that anyone may continue looking for the solution. Someone may find it. If so, and if that solution is not just guesswork or injudicious reasoning, but it is well-documented and convincing, the discoverer should write it up as an article for one of the genealogical journals, and I am virtually certain that it will be published.

Our case centers on Habakkuk Lindsey (the name is also found as Lindsay, among other variations), who married at Salem, Massachusetts, 6 October 1741, Mary Green. One writer, Margaret Isabella Lindsay, of the last century gave a brief undocumented account of him.[13] Her book reported that the Lindsays of Salem had a tradition that around 1680 an

97

English war vessel commanded by a Scotsman named Lindsay put into Salem for repairs. While there, his eldest son married a Salem woman and promised to return but was lost with his ship at sea. His widow had a son, who married and had a son, "and for two or three succeeding generations only one son likewise came into the family." The book then identifies the marriage of Habakkuk Lindsey to Mary Green as "the earliest existing record of this family." It further states that Habakkuk resided in North Danvers, and died young, leaving three children, Samuel, Hannah, and Habakkuk. Samuel is said to have died on a voyage to Jamaica. There was no record of Hannah. And the younger Habakkuk, born in North Danvers 10 April 1753, married Joanna, daughter of Captain Gidion Gowing of Lynnfield, Massachusetts. This younger Habakkuk served in the Revolution. He and his wife moved to New Salem, in central Massachusetts, where he died 12 January 1835, and she died 31 March 1831. They left two daughters, Mary and Anna, and five sons, Samuel, Stacy, Isaac, Daniel, and Ebenezer, all of whom had been born between 1777 and 1799.

Now this is a strange story. The author of the Lindsay book well knew of the existence of a much better recorded family which originated with Christopher Lindsey at Lynn, Massachusetts, in the first half of the seventeenth century, for she also covers this family in her book, though as a completely separate one. Though there is frequently something to family tradition (I find that it is usually not all true, but not all false), there is also found with great frequency what I call the genealogical myth, usually groundless, or with but a grain of truth. The story of an English sea captain who put into Salem for repairs long enough for his son to marry a local girl and then conveniently die at sea, leaving her pregnant, has all the aura of myth. Here we have a young man arriving at Salem around 1680, having a second generation, and then "two or three succeeding generations" leading to a Habakkuk Lindsey marrying in 1741. If Habakkuk were of normal marrying age, he might have been born around 1720, and there is not room for more than two generations at most between 1680 and 1720. Further, some of the children of the younger Habakkuk did not die until 1887, just two years before the Lindsay book was published. Surely we could expect either some written records prior to the 1741 marriage or some better family tradition than this story which would seem more appropriate to explain whole centuries rather than decades.

Also characteristic of mythical origins is the sudden change from vagueness to very specific information, names, dates, places, as we see here concerning Habakkuk Lindsey's marriage and children. Independent information allows us to know that some of the specifics are true. The younger Habakkuk did move to New Salem, then Hampshire County, now Franklin County, Massachusetts, and he died in nearby Prescott on 12 January 1835, age 81.[14] Though the Lindsay book states there is no record of Hannah, we find her also in central Massachusetts, dying at Prescott on 9 June 1828, age 81, as Hannah Moulton.[15] We know that Hannah Moulton was Hannah Lindsey because a deed dated 30 June 1786 shows that Daniel Moulton, cordwainer of New Salem, and Hannah, his wife, sold to Hab Lindsey of Danvers for £50 land in Danvers they had received from their "honored father Hab Lindsey, late of Danvers."[16] The death record of the younger Hab at age 81 in 1835 would have him born ca. 1754, very close to the date of birth of 10 April 1753 given him by the Lindsey book. The death record of Hannah (Lindsey) Moulton at age 81 in 1828 would have her born ca. 1747.

We know a little more about the senior Hab Lindsey of Danvers. He was a land grantee in 1745 from Sarah Moulton, administrator; in 1748 from Robert Moulton; and in 1753 from Joseph McIntyre and Benjamin Moulton. In the last deed Joseph McIntyre of Oxford, Worcester County, Massachusetts, on 22 January 1753, sold to Habakkuk Lindsey for £16 his interest in the estate of Robert Moulton, late of Salem, and also of Samuel Moulton, being the whole of that conveyed to Joseph by widow Mary McIntyre of Oxford by deed.

Once we discard the myth aspect to Hab's origins as given in the Lindsay book, we are left with a natural choice of the Christopher Lindsey family as the one for which we are searching. We are quite fortunate that just recently Marion A. MacDonald gave us the material with which to do a whole-family search for Habakkuk Lindsey in this other Lindsey family;[17] although the facts as recorded leave us with questions. The main problem is that there seems to be nowhere in the Christopher Lindsey family in which to place our Habakkuk.

The MacDonald article shows that Christopher Lindsey was survived by two sons, John and Eleazer. The article follows two sons of John, a younger John and a Christopher, both of whom moved early to Rhode Island and had families there. This might be called *lead one,* for though it is quite remote, it is possible that John or Christopher might have had a son or grandson in Rhode Island, who later returned to Essex County, Massachusetts. The senior John also had sons Samuel, Eleazer, and Nathaniel, on whom no further record was found, the presumption being that they died young. However, in spite of the presumption, this must be labeled *lead two*, for one of these could have had Habakkuk as a grandson. I am assuming here that the MacDonald article was based on diligent research of Essex County records, and thus the fact that no record was found is not very encouraging for us to try to connect Habakkuk to the senior John's branch of the family.

The other son, Eleazer, remained in Lynn, and in 1715/6 he deeded his real estate to his sons, Eleazer, Jr., and Ralph, for them to distribute among themselves, their sisters, their niece, and their nephew after the death of his wife. He named his daughters and two grandchildren, and he mentioned that he had already given his deceased daughter, Sarah James, her portion while she was living and that her children received their shares from this portion. The seeming completeness of the deed tends to eliminate the possibility of Eleazer having been survived by any of his other sons, who had probably died without issue.

Of Eleazer's two surviving sons, though Eleazer, Jr., was the older, we will take Ralph Lindsey first. Ralph stayed in Lynn and died there intestate. In 1747 his widow and five sons divided his estates. Habakkuk was not one of the five sons, and even the oldest of them, Ralph, Jr., born in 1712, was probably too young to be the father of a man marrying in 1741. Thus we can probably eliminate Ralph's family.

That leaves us with the family of Eleazer, Jr., who moved to Salem. Of his children, four were sons, Nathan (possibly this should be Nathaniel), born at Lynn, 7 November 1695; Habakkuk, born at Lynn, 1700; John, born ca. 1704; and Eleazer, born ca. 1714. Eleazer, Jr., a prosperous sea captain, died at Salem in 1717, and he left his land and houses at Lynn to his two oldest sons, Habakkuk and John. However, in 1727 his widow, Elizabeth, petitioned the court to divide the estate equally between her five children, Sarah Smith, Content Boyce, Elizabeth Trask, Lydia, and Eleazer Lindsey, and she specifically stated that her sons Habakkuk and John were "deceased without issue," the petition being granted 16 February 1727.

Obviously, Habakkuk[4] Lindsey (Eleazer,[3-2] Christopher[1]) was not identical with our Habakkuk Lindsey. In fact, our Habakkuk could seem a bit young to be of the same generation as the Habakkuk who was born in 1700[18] and died by 1727, for our Habakkuk, marrying in 1741, was presumably born between 1710 and 1725. Interestingly, Nathan, born in 1695, disappears without trace from the records, but not being mentioned in his mother's petition is a discouraging, though not completely eliminating, clue, and we should call this *lead three*. Admittedly, though, all three leads so far seem slight. On the other hand, the very existence of someone else with the name Habakkuk Lindsey is an onomastic clue. Our Habakkuk was presumably born later than this Habakkuk – could he have been named after him? Or did our Habakkuk come to Essex County as an adult from some other native area and of some other Lindsey family? If so, what a coincidence it would have to be for two Lindseys in the same area to have the very uncommon first name Habakkuk.

Cutting Through the Myth

I am beginning to smell some smoke. Go back to the Lindsay book: "The Lindseys of Salem have a tradition in their family to this effect: About the year 1680, or thereabouts, an English war vessel came," etc. And, "for two or three succeeding generations only one son likewise came into the family." This last statement could explain why our Habakkuk had no Lindsey relatives in the Salem-Lynn area, though it does not give any hint why there is no record of his parents and grandparents. At this point a digression into the subject of colonial New England bastardy might be helpful.

Anyone doubting the high incidence of premarital sex in colonial New England can find the subject fully documented in several publications.[19] Court records show that many sexual cases were discovered through resulting pregnancy, and though many cases came to light when the man and woman were married following pregnancy, there are a significant number where no marriage took place at all. A most interesting question for genealogists is what happened to the children of unmarried mothers? Did a mother marry someone other than the father and raise the child as a member of her new family, perhaps with the surname of her husband? Did the child go through life with the surname of the mother? Did the mother give the child the surname of the father even though no marriage took place? The answer is probably yes to all of these questions, though no full study has ever been made to show the distribution of cases into the various categories, and the records are rather silent on the matter.

The evidence to show that some, at least, illegitimate children existed is overwhelming, but records to show that this or that one of our ancestors was born a bastard are scant, though a few are available. I suspect, however, that the number of bastards among our colonial New England ancestors is small. Childhood death through illness was common, and the mothers of bastard children would in many cases have been forced to live on a bare subsistence level. Most premarital pregnancies resulted in subsequent marriage with the father. Children born where the father did not marry the mother seem to be a rather small percentage of all children born. Of that small percentage, a significant part could have been expected to die young. Still there did remain some known cases, and undoubtedly more unknown cases, where a bastard child survived the rigors of childhood, grew up, married, and had children.

An article by Gloria M. Christensen presents a plausible case to show that the Mary Howland who was married to George Conant at Plymouth, Massachusetts, on 3 November 1718, was the daughter of Sarah Howland, an unmarried daughter of Joseph Howland.[20] Sarah Howland confessed in church to fornication on 13 December 1691. In a codicil dated 23 December 1703, Joseph Howland bequeathed to "Mary the daughter of my daughter Sarah Howland deceased." This Mary thereafter disappears from the records, but some twenty-seven years later a Mary Howland, whose antecedents cannot otherwise be accounted for, married George Conant. A grandson of Mary (Howland) Conant wrote a letter in 1811 in which he mentioned that his grandmother Mary Conant died on 23 October 1756 in her sixty-third year of age. Allowing for the fact that stated ages at death were frequently off by a year or two, this would have Mary (Howland) Conant born very close to the time Mary, the illegitimate daughter of Sarah Howland, was born. Further, in the 1811 letter, the grandson mistakenly said that his grandfather Conant married Mary Southworth, when we know that he in fact married Mary Howland; however, Sarah Howland's mother was an Elizabeth Southworth, and thus the surname was in the illegitimate Mary Howland's family, This is not conclusive proof, but it is an indication that in one case a bastard child was given her mother's maiden surname, raised with her mother's family, and later made a respectable marriage and had many descendants.

As another example, *Mayflower Families in Progress* shows that Benjamin Foster, who died unmarried, was the probable father of a girl, Maria, born at Plymouth ca. 1685. The mother was a Mercy, who married Samuel Lawrence, and Lawrence in his will mentioned his wife, "her daughter Maria," and "our daughter Deliverance."[21] Nowhere in the records do we find anything stating that Mary Howland or Maria, the daughter of Mercy Lawrence, were illegitimate, and even today we cannot state it with certainty in either case. In another case, Elizabeth Hughes charged at the March 1690/1 session of the Plymouth county court that James Barneby had gotten her with child. Though Barneby denied it, in September 1691 he was ordered to pay child support. In 1693 Barneby asked the court for permission to "dispose of the Bastard child lately borne of the body of Elizzbeth [sic] Hughes unto his father in law [actually, his stepfather] John Nelson untill the said child shall attaine to the age of eighteene years," and his request was approved.[22] Thereafter the child seems to disappear from the records.

Just as with our Habakkuk Lindsey we seem to have hit a stone wall. All right, suppose our Habakkuk was of illegitimate birth, where would we look to get further information? There are several possibilities. We could conjecture that his father was the known Habakkuk, born 1700. Perhaps there was even a betrothal between the father and some local girl. She found out she was pregnant when the father was out to sea, and perhaps he did die in a storm. Under the circumstances, people were a bit more tolerant than usual. Perhaps she was able to give her son the name Habakkuk Lindsey. Perhaps the Lindsey family gave her some money for child support and a parcel of land for the young boy when he grew up. Having done that, with the passing years, the Lindseys would not want to be reminded of the rather embarrassing circumstances. When Elizabeth Lindsey told the court in 1727 that her sons Habakkuk and John were deceased without issue, this could be interpreted to mean without legitimate issue, since an illegitimate heir had no inheritance rights at law.

But it could also be that our Habakkuk got his Lindsey surname from his mother, who was perhaps a sister of the other Habakkuk. Perhaps the onomastic clue is the naming of a son by the mother after her brother. Our Habakkuk could even have been brought up by his mother after she married someone else, but in this case he would have kept the name Lindsey. He had to be brought up somewhere. There must be some trace of him in Essex County prior to his 1741 marriage, perhaps mention in a court record, a church record, a deed, or mention as a lesser heir in some related person's will. Most likely one parent was a Lindsey, and most likely he had relatives living in the area.

Among other clues we have the name Moulton. The Moultons were in Salem from very early times. In the three land transactions where our Habakkuk is a grantee, one is from Sarah Moulton as administrator, one from Robert Moulton, and one from Joseph McIntyre and Benjamin Moulton. The McIntyres were also numerous in the area, and had marital alliances with the Moultons. Indeed, Habakkuk's daughter would marry Daniel Moulton, son of John and Mehitabel (McIntyre) Moulton, though the marriage did not take place until 1770. We also have it from the Lindsay book that one of the sons of our Habakkuk's son, Habakkuk, was Stacy Lindsey. Stacy was not a common name then, but there were many Stacys in the Salem area. It was shown in chapter 6 that "the use of a surname for a given name nearly always indicates descent of that individual from the family whose name was bestowed on him."

This brings up the question of what do we know about our Habakkuk Lindsey's wife, Mary Green? If her mother, for example, were a Stacy, we probably should not pay as much attention to the Stacy clue as would otherwise be the case. Certainly more information can and should be found on Mary Green. There are other possibilities for analysis in this case, but of course it cannot be solved by confining oneself to the house, as Nero Wolfe used to do in solving murder mysteries. More research into original records is required, much along the lines of scientific method – that is, form a hypothesis, determine what information would be required to make that hypothesis true, check to see if such information can be found, and, if not, form a new hypothesis. The Habakkuk Lindsey puzzle can probably be solved from research into primary records of Essex County, Massachusetts, and many of these records can be made available all over the country via microfilms at one of the LDS Family History Centers.[23]

Notes

1. Someone suggested that we do not know for a fact that it was my grandmother who assumed for herself native-born American citizenship in the 1930 census, but remembering from childhood my very strong-minded grandmother and her very quiet, passive second husband, whom we called Wilbur, and knowing now how she changed records to suit her convenience, I feel sure that it was dear old grandmother who did it.

2. Roy V. Sherman, *The New England Shermans* (1974), 187.

3. Eugene A. Stratton, "Which John Rickard Married Mary Cooke?," *Mayflower Quarterly* 49 (1983):122-29.

4. For more details and references see my book *Plymouth Colony: Its History & People, 1620-1691* (Salt Lake City, 1986), 290, 366-67.

5. Ora E. Monnette, *First Settlers of ye Plantations of Piscataway and Woodbridge, Olde East New Jersey, 1664-1714* (1930-1935); Donald L. Jacobus, "Evaluation of Genealogical Writers," *The American Genealogist* 34 (1958):213-5. It should again be emphasized that this type of most helpful evaluation is just one of the many reasons why all genealogists should subscribe to the genealogical journals.

6. Isaac Watson Dunham, *Deacon John Dunham of Plymouth, Mass., 1589-1669, and His Descendants* (1907); Donald L. Jacobus, "Notes on Nathaniel Dunham of Wrentham and Hebron," *The American Genealogist* 29 (1953):22; Mrs. John E. Barclay, "Notes on the Dunham Family of Plymouth, Mass.," *The American Genealogist* 30 (1954):143.

7. See chapter 4, note 13. The answer is that in many cases we will accept an undocumented conclusion from Jacobus (and some of the other great genealogists of the past), particularly if 1) the conclusion seems reasonable and there are no counter-indications, and 2) it appears that Jacobus had made a first-hand study of the matter (keeping in mind that on matters peripheral to the main inquiry, Jacobus and others sometimes took some shortcuts, and in such cases their conclusions might not be as authoritative as when they made full investigations).

8. Lucy Mary Kellogg, ed., *Mayflower Families through Five Generations,* (Plymouth, 1975) 1:107.

9. Dudley G. Cary Elwes, "De Braose Family," *The Genealogist* 5 (1881): 318-22. See appendix B for more details regarding this matter.

10. Ibid., 4 (1880):133; Sir Harry Ellis, *A General Introduction to Domesday Book,* 2 vols. (1833; reprinted Baltimore, 1973), 1:386.

11. Nahum Mitchell, *History of the Early Settlement of Bridgewater* (Boston, 1840), 238-39.

12. References for the facts used in the Elizabeth (Southworth) Weston example are given in Eugene A. Stratton, "The Descendants of Edmund Weston Revisited," *National Genealogical Society Quarterly* 71 (1983):45-46, 58.

13. Margaret Isabella Lindsay, *The Lindsays of America* (Albany, 1889), 124-25.

14. *Prescott Vital Records,* from a typescript at The New England Historical and Genealogical Society, 42; he is there called Habakkuk Linzie.

15. Ibid., 32.

16. *Essex County Probate Record,* 156:50.

17. Marion A. MacDonald, "The Lindsey Family. Descendants of Christopher Lindsey of Lynn, Massachusetts," *The Essex Genealogist* 7 (1987):17-26, 71-76, 194-8.

18. The year 1700 for Habakkuk's birth is not guesswork but is taken from Lynn vital records, where only the year of birth is available.

19. See, for example, Roger Thompson, *Sex in Middlesex: Popular Mores in a Massachusetts County, 1649-1699* (Amherst, Mass., 1986), or chapter 12 "Morality

and Sex," Eugene A. Stratton, *Plymouth Colony: Its History & People, 1620-1691* (Salt Lake City, 1986).

20. Gloria M. Christensen, "Who Was Mary Howland, Wife of George Conant?," *Mayflower Quarterly* 45 (1979):138-43.

21. *Mayflower Families in Progress: Richard Warren* (Plymouth, 1987), 37; *The American Genealogist* 53 (1977):154-56.

22. *Plymouth Court Records,* vol. 1, ed. David Thomas Konig (Wilmington, Del., 1978), 208-9, 217.

23. I should mention that Marion MacDonald, compiler of the above-mentioned Lindsey article, does not subscribe to the "illegitimate" theory but feels that there is a possibility Habakkuk was a cousin or other relation to the Lindsey family of Lynn. Interestingly. MacDonald has a *Scholars' Ready Reference Handbook* to the King James version of the bible which includes in a synopsis in the back the quotation, "Of Habakkuk personally we know nothing."

Chapter 8

Indirect Evidence

Some circumstantial evidence is very strong, as when you find a trout in the milk.

—Henry David Thoreau

The Case Is Altered.
—Sometimes found in England as the name of a pub;
of unknown origin.

Nowadays genealogical authorities prefer the term "indirect" to "circumstantial" evidence, but they mean about the same thing. Let us define some terms as used in this book: evidence, direct evidence, and indirect evidence.

Evidence: Anything supporting a genealogical relationship. The most common type of evidence is something in writing, but it can be verbal as well. A tombstone inscription is evidence. Inclusion of a parent-child relationship in a family history is evidence. A grandfather's verbal account of who his parents were is evidence. Evidence is not necessarily true, and the weighing or evaluation of the evidence is an attempt to reach the truth, whatever it may be. A woman's age may be shown in a census record as thirty-nine, and that is evidence, but it is not necessarily true. Frequently in genealogy we find conflicting evidence. A birth record, a census record, and a tombstone record for the same person may differ from each other by several years on a person's age.

Direct Evidence: A positive assertion of a genealogical relationship, and again it need not necessarily be true. When John Doe in his will names "my daughter Anna, the wife of James Jones," we have direct evidence. In most such cases, it will be true, though we must allow for the possibility that, other than being his natural (that is, biological) daughter, Anna Jones could be John Doe's stepdaughter, adopted daughter, or the remarried wife of a deceased son. A published family history is full of direct evidence, though some of it may be in error.

Indirect Evidence: Support for a genealogical relationship deduced from the analysis of two or more statements that do not make positive assertions. One of the most common types of indirect evidence is where, say, a daughter Anna is born to John and Mary Doe in a small town, and twenty years later an Anna Doe marries James Jones in the same town. If no other appropriate Anna Doe is known, it is ordinarily assumed that the wife of James Jones is the daughter of John and Mary Doe, though there are cases where such an identification has been wrong. Indirect evidence almost always involves an assumption, whereas direct evidence almost never does. If there is no direct evidence of a woman's parentage, but in her will she refers to Richard Roe as her brother, and if Richard Roe's parentage is known (from some other document), it is assumed that the woman has the same blood parentage. Again, this does not have to be true, for brother could also mean half brother, stepbrother, adopted brother, brother-in-law, non-related close friend, or fellow church member.[1]

Sometimes indirect evidence can be quite strong, stronger even than direct evidence. For example, in an article I quoted from several contemporary sources to deduce that John[2] Holmes was the son of John[1] Holmes.[2] One document showed that Thomas[3] Holmes was the son of John[2] Holmes. Another document showed that Thomas[3] Holmes was the grandson of John[1] Holmes. Ergo, John[2] Holmes had to be the son of John[1] Holmes. Strictly speaking, if no other evidence was available, John[2] Holmes could conceivably have married a cousin named, as a hypothetical example, Mary Holmes, daughter of John[1] Holmes, and thus John[2] Holmes could have had some other father; however, in the present case we knew the identity of the wife of John[2] Holmes and mother of John[3] Holmes, and she was not a Holmes by birth. Thus we have a positive identification, albeit by indirect evidence.

Indirect Evidence Can Be Explosive

Ordinarily, though, indirect evidence is looked upon with caution by experienced genealogists, and with good reason. One new fact may explode what at first looked like an open and shut case. As a mythical case, say that there is a marriage record for Charles Jones and Martha Doe. A deed shows Charles and Martha Jones selling land that once belonged to John and Mary Doe. John Doe in his will mentioned his daughters, but did not name or number them. James Jones, the brother of Charles Jones, married Anna Doe, a known daughter of John and Mary Doe. Anna (Doe) Jones in her will mentioned "my sister Martha Jones." There appears to be good reason to believe that Martha (Doe) Jones was also the daughter of John and Mary Doe. However, since Anna and Martha married two brothers, they were certainly sisters-in-law, if not sisters, and that could explain the sister reference in Anna's will. Even the land transaction could be explained if John Doe gave the land to his son-in-law James Jones, and James sold it by an unrecorded deed to his brother Charles Jones. And Martha (Doe) Jones could be, as well as a sister, a first, second, or other cousin to Anna (Doe) Jones or not blood related at all.

In the example above, the main question is whether the indirect evidence is sufficient to identify Martha (Doe) Jones as the daughter of John and Mary Doe. However, in the example as given, not enough facts are presented to determine one way or the other. How numerous were the Doe families in the area? Is there any deed or will showing how and when Charles Jones obtained the land once owned by John and Mary Doe? How many daughters did John and Mary Doe have, and are they all accounted for? Were they known to have had a daughter Martha. Is Martha a family name (not strong support by itself, but it could add a bit to an otherwise good indirect case)? What other information is known about the Doe and Jones families?

As another example, a real case this time, in footnote 1 mentioning Barnabas Lothrop's sister, we have the additional information that the second wife of the Reverend John Lothrop was an Ann, whose surname and parentage is unknown. This Ann was the mother of Barnabas Lothrop. Suppose future research identifies Ann and shows that she had had a previous husband. Elizabeth, the wife of John Williams, then might have been her daughter by a previous husband and thus a half sister to Barnabas. This would certainly explain why the Reverend John Lothrop left us no baptismal record of a daughter Elizabeth Lothrop. Thus Elizabeth could be a blood sister to Barnabas, without being a blood daughter to John (who in his will mentioned "my Children both mine and my wife's". This is what I mean about other facts being able to change the appearance of what once looked like a solid circumstantial case.

Two Similar Case Studies

Let us go into a little more detail with two other real cases:

1. On 2 August 1687 at Plymouth, Francis Cooke married Elizabeth Latham. There is no direct evidence of Elizabeth's parentage. George Ernest Bowman accepted her as the daughter of Robert Latham and Susanna Winslow, and Susanna was a daughter of *Mayflower* passenger Mary (Chilton) Winslow. However, there is no birth record for Elizabeth in this family, nor is she mentioned in any probate or land record (neither Robert Latham nor his wife Susanna left a will). The compilers of *Mayflower Families Two* followed Bowman in accepting Elizabeth as the daughter of Robert and Susanna, pointing out that the children of Elizabeth and her husband, Francis Cooke, were named Susanna and Robert.

2. On 8 September 1702 at Bridgewater, Massachusetts (Plymouth County), Benjamin Leach married Hepzibah Washburn, whose parentage is not given by any known direct evidence. The compilers of *Mayflower Families Two* called Hepzibah "probably" the daughter of Joseph and Hannah (Latham) Washburn, Hannah being a *Mayflower* descendant via both her father (a great-grandson of *Mayflower* passenger Francis Cooke) and her mother (a granddaughter of *Mayflower* passenger Mary Chilton).

When I was *Mayflower* historian general, I accepted both Elizabeth Latham and Hepzibah Washburn as *Mayflower* descendants. My successor as historian general accepted the former but rejected the latter, stating that the evidence was not sufficiently strong. What does this tell us about indirect evidence? It would seem to confirm my view that standards of evidence cannot in the final analysis help but be subjective, and nowhere is this more true than when the evidence is indirect. No one can tell you what decision to make in a case like this, but it is possible to learn the analytical methods which may help you in making a decision.

Let's use a whole-family, total-history approach. This is not difficult, especially with colonial Plymouth, for probably no area has ever been studied as much from the genealogist's point of view. We know that in 1690 the population of Plymouth town was approximately 775 and that of Bridgewater about 440.[3] The Plymouth of Elizabeth Latham of 1687 and the Bridgewater of Hepzibah Washburn of 1702 would have had populations close to the 1690 estimates. Young girls of that time and place usually did not move to new towns by themselves. They usually stayed with family. Both the Latham and the Washburn families have been studied a good bit, though not all studies have yielded complete accuracy. We also have rather good and easily available records (vital, probate, land, etc.) of Plymouth and Bridgewater, and *The Mayflower Descendant* has published many of these. Though there is no really reliable family history of either the Latham or the Washburn families, use of *The Mayflower Descendant* can help us begin a reconstruction of appropriate family groups.

Latham is quite easy. The Robert Latham who married Susanna Winslow was the progenitor of the Plymouth Colony Latham family. Thus, in this case, we need not be concerned about first cousins, second cousins, and such. Though there was a William Latham on the 1620 *Mayflower,* there is no record of his having any children. The closest contemporary Latham family was that of Cary Latham of New London, Connecticut, and his two sons, Joseph and Thomas. Although chronologically any of these three could have been the father of Elizabeth, there is absolutely no reason to believe that any of them had anything to do with Plymouth. James Latham, the oldest son of Robert and Susanna Latham, was born ca. 1659 and thus was too young to be the father of a girl marrying in 1687.[4] Elizabeth Latham was married at Plymouth in 1687 and thus would have been born probably roughly around 1665. Robert and Susanna (Winslow) Latham were both living for many years after 1685; they had a known son Joseph born ca. 1663, and their next known child was a son, Chilton Latham, born ca. 1672. Susanna (Winslow) Latham was most likely in her late thirties in 1665 and was certainly capable of having children at this time when there is a gap of some nine years between the births of other children. Elizabeth (Latham) Cooke named her first two children Susanna and Robert.

Now let us change to the Washburn example. The Washburn family had several generations in the general Plymouth area by 1702 when Benjamin Leach and Hepzibah Washburn were married. The closest other family with the same surname, that of William Washburn, lived in Long Island, and contemporary records show no connection between the William Washburn family and Plymouth Colony/County.[5] Hepzibah's claimed father was Joseph Washburn, son of John and Elizabeth (Mitchell) Washburn. John and Philip Washburn were two brothers who had arrived in Plymouth from England as young boys in 1635. John married the daughter of Experience and Jane (Cooke) Mitchell, and thus, via his wife, his descendants were also descendants of *Mayflower* passenger Francis Cooke. Their children and grandchildren are well known from contemporary documents. John and Elizabeth moved to Bridgewater, and thereafter his family is especially associated with this town (although John married a second wife after the death of Elizabeth, he did not have any surviving children by her). His brother Philip married late in life and had but one son, John, born ca. 1671 (he died 17 June 1750 in his 79th year), who married ca. 1698 Lydia Billington, a granddaughter of *Mayflower* passenger Francis Billington, and they had many children – thus this John could not have been the father of the Hepzibah Washburn who married in 1702. Of the sons of John and Elizabeth (Mitchell) Washburn, most of their surviving children are known through wills and other contemporary documents. Son John married in 1679, and his first five children were recorded in vital records between 1680 and 1688 (he could have had an unrecorded daughter born in the 1680s, but it is unlikely (though not impossible) that he would have recorded those children born before and after her, but not her). Son Thomas, who left a will, had a daughter Hepzibah who married John Hutchinson. Son Samuel left a will. Son Jonathan's children are recorded in vital records as being born between 1684 and 1702 (it is possible, but again not so likely, that he could have had Hepzibah as an unrecorded daughter born prior to 1684). Son James married in 1693 and named his surviving children in a will.[6]

By the process of elimination, we are left with son Joseph, who married Hannah Latham ca. 1677. Joseph and Hannah lived and died in Bridgewater, where Hepzibah Washburn was married. Neither Joseph nor Hannah left a will, but land records and other contemporary documents prove they had sons Miles, Edward, Jonathan, Joseph, Ebenezer, Benjamin, and Ephraim. There is considerable room in this family for another child to have been born in the late 1670s or early 1680s, the most likely time for the birth of the Hepzibah who married in 1702. Two of the children of Hepzibah (Washburn) Leach were named Joseph and Hannah, the names of her claimed parents. The name Hepzibah also appears elsewhere in the Washburn family, for Joseph's brother Thomas named a daughter Hepzibah. Benjamin Leach witnessed a 1707 land record in which Joseph Washburn gave land to his son Jonathan Washburn.

These are the facts, then, that are available for interpretation. I see very little difference between the essential elements of the two cases. If you were historian general of the Mayflower Society, how would you interpret them? Would you accept descendants of either Elizabeth Latham or Hepzibah Washburn as *Mayflower* descendants? Would you accept descendants of both as *Mayflower* descendants?

The Identity of Lydia (Washburn) Ingals

I am going to use a later generation of the Washburn family – this time from Philip Washburn – for a somewhat more involved example of indirect evidence. First, let us note that the available evidence indicates that all people in Plymouth County with the surname Washburn, starting with the children of John and Elizabeth (Mitchell) Washburn and the children of Philip's son John Washburn (who married Lydia Billington) are *Mayflower* descendants. No other Washburn family was known to have lived in Plymouth County in the 1700s nor even in the 1800s. Of course, some unrelated Washburn might have come to live in the county, but we have no record of it. We would certainly have the odds greatly on our side if we identified any given Washburn found in Plymouth in the eighteenth or nineteenth century as a *Mayflower* descendant. Still, it would be wrong to accept *Mayflower* ancestry for such a Washburn without being able to 1) give the generation-by-generation ascent back to the *Mayflower,* and 2) provide satisfactory evidence to support each generation in the line.

Consider this case: A Boston marriage record shows that on 1 January 1807 Benjamin Ingals (Ingalls, Ingols) married Lydia Washburn. A contemporary newspaper, the *Columbian Centinel,* published on 3 January 1807, reported that Lydia Washburn "of Plymouth" married Benjamin Ingalls of Boston "Thursday last." A Boston death record showed that Lydia Ingalls, the wife of Benjamin, died on 5 April 1831 at age forty-four (and thus she would have been born ca. 1787). Another Boston death record shows that on 30 September 1890 a James Prince Ingols died, the son of Benjamin Ingols, who was born in Lynn, Massachusetts, and Lydia Washburn, who was born in Plymouth, Massachusetts. Aside from giving confirming information that Lydia Washburn was born in Plymouth, the death record of James Prince Ingols is of particular interest because of it showing his middle name to be "Prince."

William T. Davis, in *Ancient Landmarks of Plymouth,* asserts that Prince Washburn, the son of John and Lydia (Prince) Washburn, married Ruth Stetson in 1786, and their children were Ruth, Lydia, Benjamin, and George Washburn. As pointed out earlier, though Davis is very helpful for clues on Plymouth genealogy (indeed his book is one of the first places to look) it is undocumented and is known to contain many errors. It is not adequate evidence by itself. However, in defense of Davis, his error rate is not as high as some of his critics claim, and, based on my experience in using Davis many times, I would say the error rate might be 10 or 15 percent; certainly it is not as high as 20 percent, but let's use 20 percent for the sake of argument. If it were as high as 20 per cent, it would still mean that the identification of any given individual had an 80 percent chance of being correct, considerably more than a simple preponderance of evidence.[7] Also, note that we are getting more contemporary to the events, and Plymouth was a small town. Davis would have known and talked to people who would have known members of this Washburn family. That does not mean that he did talk to them, but he must have had some reason for crediting Prince and Ruth Washburn with four named children.

We can easily confirm some of Davis's information in this case from primary records, and thus we know that Prince Washburn married Ruth Stetson on 9 November 1786 at Plymouth, and that this Prince Washburn was the son of John and Lydia (Prince) Washburn, the grandson of John and Abigail (Johnson) Washburn, the great-grandson of John and Lydia (Billington) Washburn, and a descendant of Francis Billington of the *Mayflower.* However, Prince Washburn who married Ruth Stetson was most inconsiderate of his own descendants, for he did not record the births of any of his children. Plymouth church records show that Prince and Ruth did in fact have children because the records note that a child of Prince Washburn died on 30 November 1795, and another child of Prince Washburn died on 25 October 1798. Further research shows the existence in Plymouth of a George Washburn, of unknown parentage, who could have been the son George given by Davis to Prince and Ruth; this George Washburn was a mariner, as was Prince Washburn.

Is there enough indirect evidence to show that the Lydia Washburn who married Benjamin Ingalls was the daughter of Prince and Ruth? Let's get a few more facts. The 1790 census shows a Prince Washburn living in Plymouth with a family consisting of one male over sixteen years of age and two females. The 1800 census shows Prince Washburn in Plymouth with a family consisting of one male under ten, one male ten to sixteen, one male twenty-six to forty-five, one female under ten, and one female twenty-six to forty-five. Lydia Washburn should have been about thirteen years old in 1800. She could have been one of the two females in the 1790 census but apparently was not in Prince's family in the 1800 census.[8] Aside from the fact that census records can be wrong, such as calling a girl a boy, or getting someone in the wrong age category, it is a statistically more significant fact that it was a common custom at the time and place concerned to put young teenage children out to work in other houses. So the lack of just the right place for Lydia in the Prince Washburn household in the 1800 census does not necessarily indicate that Prince and Ruth Washburn did not have a thirteen-year-old daughter.

There is not much more evidence available on this case. There are two independent records showing that Lydia (Washburn) Ingalls was from Plymouth, a contemporary newspaper report showing her to be "of Plymouth," and the death record of her son showing that someone connected with the son believed that Lydia had been born in Plymouth. If she had been born in Plymouth, she most likely would have been of a Plymouth Washburn family, for no outside Washburn family was known to be living in Plymouth at the time. Whole-family research indicates that Lydia was not likely to be from a Plymouth Washburn family other than that of Prince and Ruth (Stetson) Washburn, who were having children at the right time to be the parents of Lydia. Prince is not found as a common name in the Plymouth Washburn family, and Prince Washburn undoubtedly received this name because his mother was of the Prince family. There is no known association of the Prince family with the family of Benjamin and Lydia (Washburn) Ingalls other than the claim that Lydia was the daughter of Prince Washburn. Prince Washburn had both a mother and a sister named Lydia. Davis specifically gives Prince Washburn a daughter Lydia, and again we should keep in mind that Davis, although his work contains a good number of errors, is still right much more often than he is wrong. These are the facts. In this example, we have used such genealogical techniques as onomastic evidence, whole-family genealogy, and a weighing together of primary (i.e., vital and church records) and secondary (i.e., Davis) sources. Are they enough? You be the jury and decide again, if you were historian general of the Mayflower Society, and dedicated to a principle not necessarily of truth beyond any conceivable doubt, but of preponderance of evidence, how would you decide?[9]

The Lydia Washburn case illustrates a very common problem in genealogy, that of an undocumented source giving us direct evidence that we cannot confirm by contemporary documents, and so must look for confirming indirect evidence. The following example is another good case in point because it depends on analysis of many facts, not just a few, that bear indirectly on an identification. This case will also show a growing conviction of mine of how – under some circumstances – we should treat undocumented assertions made in family histories. Some family histories are so poorly done, so sparse of detail, or so full of wildly extravagant claims that they are not even worth looking at, much less mentioning. But there are also a number of well-presented family histories that are rich in detail and display obvious proof of serious, judicious, and thorough research – are these to be consigned to oblivion because they lack what we now consider sufficient documentation?

The Identity of John Valentine Burlingame

Keeping in mind that standards of evidence are ultimately subjective, I suggest a way to handle the problem of good, but undocumented family histories. The example concerns the descendants of John Valentine Burlingame, who died at Kirkland, Oneida County, New York, on 26 September 1853 (see chart 3). Some of those who can document their descent from him made the assertion that he was the son of Jeremiah and Ruth (Grinnell) (Palmer) Burlingame. Jeremiah was a sergeant in the American Revolution, and he married at Little Compton, Rhode Island, on 1 March 1778 Ruth Grinnell, the widow of Walter Palmer. Ruth in turn was the daughter of Richard and Comfort (Billings) (Bailey) Grinnell; Comfort was the daughter of Richard and Sarah (Little) Billings; and Sarah was the daughter of Samuel and Sarah (Gray) Little and the great-granddaughter of *Mayflower* passengers James Chilton and Richard Warren.[10] There is no contemporary direct evidence to confirm the

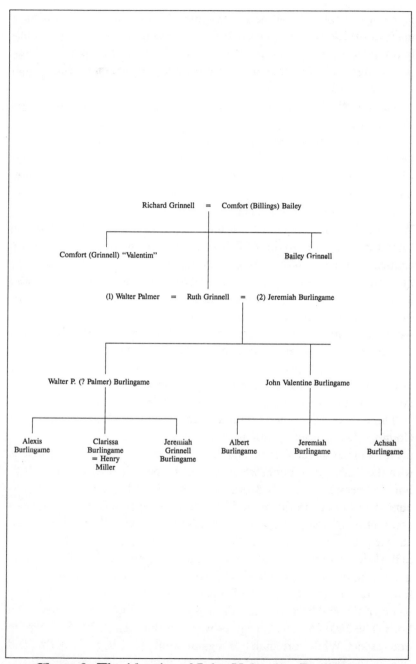

Chart 3. *The identity of John Valentine Burlingame.*

parentage of John Valentine Burlingame. However, a direct assertion is made in a thick typescript on the Burlingame family which was apparently compiled over a period of time by several people and based in some part on unspecified documents and in greater part on family records and remembrances.

The question is whether we can accept the Burlingame Manuscript. The manuscript gives a paragraph each on various family members, and for Jeremiah Burlingame it shows his marriage and movements and lists his children. The male children are later shown in their own paragraphs with information on their vital statistics, marriages, and children. John Valentine Burlingame is shown as the second child of Jeremiah and Ruth, born at Cranston, Rhode Island, on 20 June 1781, the first child being Walter Palmer Burlingame, born at Cranston, Rhode Island, on 3 March 1780. Jeremiah's service in the Revolution and the identity of his wife are confirmed by pension records at the National Archives.[11] Depositions on file with the pension records by people who knew both Jeremiah and Ruth, including Ruth's sister and niece, prove beyond any doubt that Ruth was the daughter of Richard and Comfort (Billings) (Bailey) Grinnell. Another document shows that a New York court appointed Walter P. Burlingame as the guardian of Ruth Burlingame, who was described as a lunatic, age eighty-five on 26 December 1838. The relationship of Walter P. Burlingame to Ruth Burlingame is not given, and there is no mention in the pension papers of John Valentine Burlingame.

The 1790 census shows a Jeremiah Burlingame in Windsor, Berkshire County, Massachusetts, with a family consisting of one male sixteen and over, six males under sixteen, and three females. This information agrees with the Burlingame book, which names six sons for Jeremiah and Ruth born between 1780 and 1788, one daughter born in 1787, plus another unnamed child born in this period who died young (the last is possibly an assumption on the part of the compilers to agree with the census record showing three females). The 1800 census shows a Jeremiah Burlingame in Berkshire County, Massachusetts, with a family consisting of four males under ten, one male twenty-six to forty-five, two females under ten, one female ten to sixteen, and one female twenty-six to forty-five. Obviously some of the children have left the family, and younger ones have been born. The 1800 census also agrees with the Burlingame book, except in one respect. While Jeremiah Burlingame would have been forty-five, and thus in the right age bracket, Ruth Burlingame would have been forty-eight; however, it would not seem far-fetched to suggest that she might have dropped a few years so as not to appear older than her husband (or that either the person giving the information or the census taker might have made a mistake). It should also be noted that the census shows other Burlingame families in the area who might have been related to Jeremiah. Aside from the agreement of Jeremiah's family in the Burlingame Manuscript with census records, land records of Berkshire County show transactions there for Jeremiah Burlingame between 1797 and 1806, including one where he sold land to Walter P. Burlingame in 1806. Walter P. Burlingame sold land in Berkshire in 1807.

The Burlingame Manuscript states that Jeremiah moved to Petersburg, Rensselaer County, New York. His death in 1811 is confirmed by pension records, and his move to New York state is supported by depositions, though the depositions neglect to mention his stay in Massachusetts. Land records show that Walter P. Burlingame and his wife Bethany sold land in Petersburg, New York, between 1823 and 1834. Records of the Oldenbarneveld Reformed Christian Church of Trenton, Oneida County, New York,[12] show that on 31 December 1834 Henry Miller married Clarissa Burlingame at the house of Alexis Burlingame (identified in the Burlingame book as Walter's son), and that Clarissa was the daughter of Walter Burlingame, "late of Rensselaer County, now of Trenton." Both Henry Miller and Alexis Burlingame were associated with Walter P. Burlingame in court papers when the latter was named guardian of his mother.

The same church records show that on 13 February 1829, a funeral was held for the unnamed wife, age about fifty, of Mr. J. V. Burlingame. On 3 September 1835 Albert Burlingame (identified in the Burlingame book as a son of John Valentine Burlingame), age twenty-three, married Mary Anne Baird. On 13 February 1837 Achsah W. Burlingame, daughter of "Mr. Valentine Burlingame of this town," married Daniel Thompson. The Burlingame book states that Walter P. Burlingame and his wife Bethany Crandall were buried in the Olden Barnveld Cemetery, "located on the dirt road" between Barnveld and Utica, New York, and also that John Valentine Burlingame and his first wife Betsey Whitney were buried in the same cemetery.

The 1850 census shows Walter P. Burlingame, age seventy, born in Rhode Island, living with the family of Alexis Burlingame in Trenton, Oneida County, New York, and Bethany Burlingame, age sixty-seven, is with the same family. The census also shows John Burlingame, age sixty-nine, born in Massachusetts, living with the family of Albert Burlingame in Kirkland, Oneida County, New York.

There is some good onomastic evidence in this case, too. The will of Richard Grinnell, of Little Compton, Rhode Island, dated 27 September 1787, proved 7 April 1789, mentioned his daughter Ruth Burlingham and also another daughter Comfort Valintim.[13] The surname Valentine (with spelling variations) is not very common in colonial New England (according to the International Genealogical Index it gets more common in the nineteenth century). Savage shows a John Valentine in Boston in 1675 as the only person with such a surname. The 1782 Rhode Island census has but one person with this name, a John Volentine living in Little Compton, Rhode Island. It appears that John Valentine Burlingame's claimed mother, Ruth (Grinnell) (Palmer) Burlingame, had a brother-in-law with the surname Valentine, and I suggest that this is one of those times when onomastic evidence takes on a considerable significance. It might also be noted that John Valentine Burlingame gave the name of his claimed father, Jeremiah, to one of his children. It is further of interest that Jeremiah and Ruth Burlingame named their first child Walter P. (presumably for Palmer), following, as noted earlier, a custom of the times to name a child after the deceased spouse of one of the parents.

That is the evidence. There is documentation that Jeremiah and Ruth Burlingame, not long after their marriage in Rhode Island, moved to Massachusetts, where they had most of their children (Walter P. Burlingame, the first child, was born in Rhode Island). The 1850 census shows that John Valentine Burlingame was born in Massachusetts ca. 1779. Son Walter is found in the same part of Massachusetts as his claimed father, Jeremiah, and he later moved to Rensselaer County, New York, the same place where Jeremiah died. Whether John Valentine Burlingame lived in Rensselaer County cannot be shown by contemporary records, but it is a fact that he later lived in Oneida County, New York, and when Walter moved there, both men and their families went to the same church. Walter P. Burlingame was named custodian of Ruth Burlingame, and though nothing in the contemporary records states that he was her son, the inference is quite powerful. He was born in Rhode Island shortly after Jeremiah and Ruth were married there; he was given the name of her late spouse; he was found in Berkshire County, Massachusetts, with them; and he was appointed her custodian – could there be any reasonable doubt as to whose son he was? (According to the Burlingame Manuscript, Walter also named a son Jeremiah Grinnell Burlingame, compounding his father's first name with his mother's surname.) It would also appear that John Valentine Burlingame received his middle name from the surname of the husband of Ruth (Grinnell) (Palmer) Burlingame's sister. We get a clear picture from the indirect contemporary evidence that John Valentine Burlingame and Walter P. Burlingame were brothers, both sons of Ruth. But is that evidence sufficient, and can we use the Burlingame Manuscript to supplement the indirect primary evidence?

Weighing an Undocumented Source

My view is that when an undocumented secondary source gives comprehensive information on a good number of members of a family (such as dates and places of birth, marriage, and death, together with occupations, migrations, church membership, and intimate details of family life), it merits some recognition. Further, when a substantial percentage of the assertions made in that source can be independently verified by contemporary sources, we are making a greater mistake in rejecting the smaller percentage of assertions where primary records are just not available for confirmation than we would be in giving some credit to the source, especially when there are no indications of contradictory information, and the assertions made do not violate common sense or otherwise seem suspicious. We should not discard that source entirely, but on a scale of zero to 100 we should be able to give that source a few points. How many points is a subjective matter, but not a lot, just a few. We certainly do not want to accept that source by itself as adequate sole evidence, but can it not in conjunction with other, primary, evidence be of some worth?

There may be some excellent genealogists whom I respect highly that will disagree with me on this point. However, I think Jacobus would agree. Like most of us, he learned through experience over the years. In a 1938 article he wrote:

> There are some excellent and generally reliable family histories in print, some of which are documented and others not. But, unless they are documented to the extent of showing the sources of their data, it is difficult to see how they can be considered evidence.[14]

But by 1958 Jacobus was writing:

> Each such family account [in undocumented county his-
> tories] should be carefully studied and considered by the
> genealogist, as the experienced eye can almost always judge
> how carefully or carelessly the account was prepared. True
> the people who had their families included in such books
> furnished the facts and dates themselves, but need they
> therefore be treated with suspicion? . . . I cannot see why
> records which were recent when the county histories and
> other such books were published and which were supplied
> by the families concerned should be considered unaccep-
> table. Both the society genealogist and the family historian
> should employ a rule of reason and use good judgment and
> discretion in handling all types of source material.
> Documentation should not become a fetish, nor should
> rules be set up more stringent than those followed in a court
> of law. Every case presented is different and should be
> judged on its own merits.[15]

Jacobus was obviously becoming more tolerant with the years. I do not
say that we should open up the flood gates and tolerate anything in print,
as has been done by many people in many times. But I am concerned
about throwing out the baby with the bath water. In the Burlingame example, we have a set of circumstances from primary sources showing that
John Valentine Burlingame was born in Massachusetts, about a year or
so after Walter P. Burlingame was born in Rhode Island. Their claimed
parents, Jeremiah and Ruth (Grinnell) (Palmer) Burlingame, were married in Rhode Island two years before Walter was born. Later both
Jeremiah and Walter are found in Massachusetts, and the 1790 census
shows Jeremiah had a family with him of a type that would ordinarily be
found for a man, wife, and children. Still later both Jeremiah and Walter
are found in Petersburg, New York, where Jeremiah died. John Valentine
Burlingame is found in Trenton, New York, simultaneously with Walter
P. Burlingame, and both are found in Trenton church records. Walter P.
Burlingame was appointed guardian for Ruth Burlingame when she became mentally ill. Valentine is not a common name of the times, but it
became the name (almost certainly through marriage) of Ruth
Burlingame's sister. Ruth's family (the Grinnells) show a more than

average use of family-connected surnames as first names, and Ruth's claimed son Walter P. (said to stand for Palmer) appears to have been named following a practice of the times after her first husband, Walter Palmer. Additional onomastic evidence shows that John Valentine Burlingame named a son Jeremiah Burlingame, and Walter P. Burlingame named a son Jeremiah Grinnell Burlingame. How do we explain away these facts if John Valentine Burlingame was not the son of Jeremiah and Ruth (Grinnell) (Palmer) Burlingame?

Other than a fantastic amount of coincidence, there could only be one alternative explanation. Walter seems with little doubt to be the son of Jeremiah and Ruth, but there were other Burlingames in both Rhode Island and in the area of Massachusetts where Jeremiah settled. Could a brother or cousin of Jeremiah have migrated with him from Rhode Island to Massachusetts? Could John Valentine Burlingame be the son of Jeremiah's brother or cousin, and thus not a son of Ruth at all? If Walter P. and John Valentine were cousins, it could be another possible explanation for their being members of the same church in Trenton, New York. As for John's middle name, Valentine, could it be coincidence, or could his hypothetical father have become entranced with the surname of Ruth's sister without being related himself to anyone with that name? These are legitimate possibilities, though still the middle name Valentine would seem to give just a little edge to John being Ruth's son.

Now we have two theories, both plausible. And if we put them in the two cups of the scale we might find that the name Valentine gives just a bit of extra weight to one of them, just a smidgen of preponderance. But we also have the Burlingame Manuscript which makes the positive assertion that John Valentine Burlingame was the son of Ruth. This document is full of detail of the type that would come from written family records and oral history, and it has proved to be accurate in every one of the many substantive details which have been checkable. We are not asked to accept the document as sole evidence. But can we not use it to obtain just a bit of extra weight to throw into one of the balance cups? The manuscript is too detailed for it to be innocently mistaken in identifying John. Either the manuscript is true, or it is a deliberate lie. Given all these facts, I have no difficulty in identifying John as the son of Jeremiah and Ruth Burlingame.[16]

At the beginning of the previous chapter I said that genealogical analysis comes down to using common sense in the light of specialized knowledge, and I emphasized specialized knowledge. As the chapter above shows, we should also emphasize the words "common sense."

Notes

1. In my book, *Plymouth Colony: Its History & People, 1620-1691* (Salt Lake City, 1986), 321, I quoted from a contemporary document to show that John Williams's wife, whose parentage was otherwise unknown, was the sister of Barnabas Lothrop, the known son of the Reverend John Lothrop. It did not appear that Elizabeth was Barnabas's sister through his wife, but, on the other hand, Elizabeth did not appear in the baptisms of children which the Reverend John Lothrop recorded during the period of years in which she should have been born. It might be assumed that Elizabeth was John Lothrop's daughter, but it is not proven. My conclusion from the evidence could not be that Elizabeth was his daughter, but that "probably" she was the blood sister of Barnabas.

2. "Descendants of Mr. John Holmes, Messenger of the Plymouth Court," *National Genealogical Society Quarterly* 74 (1986):86-87.

3. Stratton, *Plymouth Colony,* 128.

4. *Mayflower Families Two,* 13, 34.

5. John G. Hunt in an article, "Clues to the Origin of Washburne...," *The American Genealogist* 36 (1960):62-64, speculates that the Plymouth and the Long Island Washburn families were founded by brothers, but I have not seen any convincing evidence of this.

6. Robert S. Wakefield, Ralph Van Wood, Jr., et al., *Mayflower Families in Progress: Francis Cooke of the Mayflower and His Descendants for Four Generations* (Plymouth, 1987), 9, 39-44.

7. Although inclusion of a parent-child relationship in Davis would seem to have a greater than 80 percent chance for reliability, and thus seems to have a considerable preponderance of evidence, the concept of preponderance also presupposes that we are not relying on a single source.

8. A possible interpretation of the 1800 census record would be that it shows Prince himself and his wife Ruth, their sons George and Benjamin, and their daughter Ruth. Lydia would be out of town living in Boston with her uncle (as indicated in the following note). The two children who died young would not have been included by Davis in his mention of the family nor, of course, in the 1800 census.

9. After the above was written I received some additional evidence. My participation in this matter was in doing some of the research for a past client, Mary Lou Boegehold of California, who was gathering evidence to support the line of her husband, Richard A. Boegehold, for *Mayflower* membership, and I am grateful to her for supplying some of the additional details which appear in this chapter. Mrs. Boegehold is a most thorough and indefatigable researcher. I had stopped doing genealogical research for clients, but Mrs. Boegehold and I continue to maintain a correspondence. In a letter dated 11 October 1987, she shared with me the results of her continuing investigation: Plymouth Church records

show the baptism of James Washburn, son of John and Lydia Washburn, and a death certificate shows that James Washburn of Boston, who was born in Plymouth, was the son of John and Lydia Washburn; this James would thus have been the brother of Prince Washburn. Another contemporary Boston document shows that James Washburn married Mary Douglas on 29 July 1798, and the minister was the Rev. John Lothrop of the Second Boston Church, the same minister who married Benjamin Ingols and Lydia Washburn in the same church. James, of course, was Lydia's uncle, and quite possibly she met Benjamin Ingols while living with or visiting her uncle. Lydia's son, James Prince Ingols, was probably named James after her uncle and Prince after her father. James Prince Ingols was born in Plymouth, indicating that Lydia probably returned to her mother's home to have her first child. The documentary evidence regarding Lydia's uncle should be quite adequate to confirm Lydia's parentage beyond any question now.

But Mrs. Boegehold did not stop here. She continued her research with the whole-family approach, and she investigated the family of the mariner George Washburn, mentioned above, who might have been the son of Prince and Ruth Washburn and the brother of Lydia (Washburn) Ingols. She sent me copies of the documents from this research enclosed with a letter dated 1 November 1987. After the death of George Washburn, members of his family wanted to change the guardian of two of his children. Eleven relatives signed a petition to the court, and we can identify enough of them to be certain that George Washburn was the son of Prince and Ruth (Stetson) Washburn. Also among the signers were Lydia Ingols and Benjamin Ingols.

10. *Mayflower Families Two,* 91; Burlingame Manuscript at the Rhode Island Historical Society in Providence. A copy is also located at the library of the New England Historic Genealogical Society in Boston, and it may be seen on microfilm at the LDS Family History Library in Salt Lake City or its Family History Centers.

11. U.S. Pension File No. W16879.

12. Transcribed January 1940 by Louise Hasbrouck Zimm and available at the LDS Family History Library indexed as 974.762/71 V2Z.

13. Little Compton Probate Book 3:177.

14. "On the Nature of Genealogical Evidence," *The New England Historical and Genealogical Register* 92 (1938):213.

15. "Confessions of a Genealogical Heretic: Society Regulations and Hearsay Evidence," *The New England Historical and Genealogical Register* 112 (1958):87.

16. The John Valentine Burlingame case is based on work I performed for a client, Sally DeMars of California, who has kindly agreed to having it published in this book. I believe I am being objective when I say that the preponderance of evidence supports the identification and that it should be acceptable to any hereditary society other than the Royal Bastards, which by its nature requires stronger evidence.

Chapter 9

Forgivable Sins

The genealogist who brags that he never makes mistakes may or may not be a first-class genealogist, but he is surely a first-class liar.

—Donald Lines Jacobus

ELIZABETH TILLEY, d. 21 Aug. 1684. Her ancestry has not been found but she was definitely not the woman of this name who crossed on the Mayflower and married John Alden.[1]

—George E. McCracken

L et's start out with 1) a confession, and 2) an apology. First, I have made mistakes, and you do not have to go too far to find them. I recently published a correction of one error: "In 1980 I wrote that the original immigrant John Dingley died in 1658, perpetuating an error made by Savage, Arthur Adams, and others....We were only off by some thirty-one years."[2] In the first printing of the book *Plymouth Colony*, I made some typographical errors which at least let me know that people read the book, judging from the number of letters I received informing me politely that George Soule's name was left off the list of signers of the Mayflower Compact, and John Chipman married Hope, not Lydia, Howland.[3]

Second, I apologize to anyone who might misconstrue my motivation in writing this chapter. I do not write to heap scorn on anyone. My sole purpose is to establish the fact that any genealogist, the great as well as the beginners, can make mistakes. Once readers can understand this fact, then they have progressed a long way from that horrible, crippling malady of believing anything in print. In fact, they will now be less inclined to toss around even authoritative names such as Jacobus and Moriarty, and will tend more to go to the heart of the matter: What evidence has been presented to justify the conclusion? That Moriarty or Jacobus believed in a conclusion might help (and in some cases might help considerably) as one piece of support in a case built up on many pieces of indirect evidence, but by itself the statement that this or that authority said it was so, and so it must be true, is not fully sufficient as genealogical evidence.[4]

Different Types of Errors

At this point I should distinguish between different types of error makers. Good genealogists are good companions. They take you with them. They show you the way. They document their facts, and they put you in a position to analyze their facts and reach your own conclusions. They frequently teach you good, helpful techniques, and some even entertain you with their writing styles while giving you information. If along the way, they may commit an occasional error, you may forgive them, for they are human. You do not have to read their writings again, but you may wish to, especially if they write on families, times, or places that are of interest to you, or if they teach or entertain you. But if you cite their work to support genealogical conclusions you have made, you should do so mainly for their documentation, and, if you are yourself writing for either personal or public purposes, you should give some idea of the nature of their documentation and how their documentation supports your conclusion.

Beware today's writer who does not document, and be wary of the writer who generalizes documentation.[5] This is not to advocate excessive quotations from documents. But the key facts showing birth, marriage, death, parentage, and progeny should be given in enough detail so as to support fully the conclusions of the writer. If you keep your eye on the documentation, you are in a good position to walk through the genealogical mine field with some assurance that you are taking the right steps. Eventually you will get to know the writers whose works are used over and over, and you will be able to evaluate for yourself just how much you should check their documentation. The more important the matter is to you, of course, the more you should be willing to make the extra efforts required to do the checking. Good genealogists, when dealing with their own areas of interest, almost invariably do some checking. Ultimately an experienced genealogist is his or her own genealogical authority.

Examples from Genealogists

It might also serve a useful purpose to know how some mistakes are made. In looking at some errors made by the best genealogical authorities we might get some lessons. Such errors frequently concern identifications that are peripheral to a main line of inquiry. For example, Donald Lines Jacobus wrote in an article that the wife of Scotto Clark was Mary, the daughter of John and Patience (Soule) Haskell. Much was made of this fact a few years ago when the same identification was made in a *Mayflower* families book but was refuted in an article in *The American Genealogist*.[6] Proponents of the identification argued "but Jacobus approved it." But even Jacobus could be wrong – notice that in the quotation above about genealogists making mistakes, he does not say "except for yours truly."

G. Andrews Moriarty really botched up the family of Stephen and Mary (Ricketson) Wilcox, when he gave them two sons (Stephen and William) who did not belong to them and assigned the wrong wife to another son (Jireh).[7] He was corrected on the marriage of the latter by Mary W. Peckham, and he explained "this error arose from following the copy of Dartmouth vital records at New Bedford. I may say that as my chief interest was in his brother Culbut or Cuthbert, I did not make the same minute study of his brother Jireh." Again we see the error is made in a matter of peripheral interest. Another point here, though, is that when Moriarty speaks of following the copy of Dartmouth vital records at New Bedford, he most likely means that he checked only the secondary Leonard Papers at the New Bedford Library (he repeats errors found in these papers) and did not check, or at least not closely enough, either Dartmouth vital records or Bristol County probate records, for Moriarty names the children in Stephen Wilcox's will but omits Samuel and Jireh, (as Leonard had done).[8]

There are few genealogists whom I admire more than George Ernest Bowman, who was editor of the *Mayflower Descendant* for many years. His lessons on documentation and analysis as seen in the *Mayflower Descendant* were far ahead of his time. Even today his work may be read for great instruction and profit (even by genealogists who have little interest in *Mayflower* lines), for his methods are universal. So anyone trained in

Bowman's ways would ordinarily be only too ready to believe him when he makes an identification repeatedly and emphatically, as follows, on the children of Lieutenant John Tomson and his wife, Mary Cooke, daughter of *Mayflower* passenger Francis Cooke:

> The oldest printed reference to the son Adam, which I have found, is in "A Genealogy of John Thomson," by Rev. Ignatius Thomson (born 1774), published at Taunton, Mass., in 1841....Ignatius Thomson apparently paid no attention to probate and land records, and as a result his book contains many errors....The daughter Elizabeth Tomson, born 28 January 1654, married William Swift. She did not marry Thomas Swift, as stated by Ignatius Thomson.[9]

This has become a quite famous genealogical case. As Mrs. John E. Barclay pointed out in an article, Bowman was "known to have been exceedingly careful and cautious."[10] Barclay did not mention that Bowman also had the reputation of being quite stubborn and sometimes overbearing, which is probably why he dug in so tenaciously when his error was pointed out to him. In her article Barclay gives a brilliant analysis to show that William Swift and Thomas Swift each had a wife named Elizabeth, and each had a son named Thomas. William Swift had many children, and he was living when Lieutenant John Tomson made his will. Thomas Swift, who had died before Tomson made his will, left his wife and their only son Thomas. Tomson in his will, left £25 to Elizabeth Swift, and "to my grandson Thomas Swift £10 when he cometh to ye age of one and twenty and if he should dye before then it shall be forthwith paid unto his mother." An agreement of John Tomson's heirs was signed by his children including Elizabeth Swift and the husbands of three of his daughters but not by their wives. The inference was obvious. John Tomson's daughter Elizabeth married Thomas Swift and had a son Thomas by him before he died. Only her son Thomas was mentioned as a grandchild in John Tomson's will because she only had one son, while William and Elizabeth Swift had many children. Elizabeth Swift signed the agreement on her father's estate because her husband was dead, while William Swift was very much alive. Acting on this inference, Barclay, always one to be thorough, did more research and found a marriage record showing that Thomas Swift had married Elizabeth Tomson 22 September 1687 at Weymouth, Massachusetts. No one earlier had thought of looking in Weymouth for her marriage record because she did not live there, but she had a married sister living in Weymouth and was probably living with her at the time she became betrothed to Thomas Swift.

Thus we see another time when a very good genealogist made a mistake, and, from what I know of Bowman, he might have made it just because a clergyman who "apparently paid no attention to probate and land records" had made the claim that Elizabeth Tomson married Thomas Swift. Bowman did not suffer gladly those he considered to be fools. It is perhaps a concomitant trait of a number of people practicing genealogy, unfortunately some good ones along with the mediocre, to have a tendency toward either stubbornness or autocratic arrogance or both.

Above all in genealogy, let us beware of wishful thinking. I am behind no one in my admiration for the genealogical skill of Barclay, who so astutely showed Bowman to be wrong, and so I can perhaps be pardoned for noting that she joined the Royal Bastards under a line that was invalid.[11] There is nothing wrong in this, and, in fact, I did the same thing myself when I joined the Royal Bastards under the William Leete line (discussed in chapter 11). But I suspect there is a bit of unintentional wishful thinking involved when an experienced genealogist joins an hereditary society under an invalid line. A surprising number of good genealogists who have joined the Royal Bastards are in the same position of subsequently having their lines found wrong. This can be embarrassing when the line in question is one that was established by something written by the same genealogist wishing to join the society. It behooves all genealogists to be especially careful in 1) writing up their own lines that go back to an illustrious ancestor, and 2) accepting such lines when they are written up by friends. I know that at times I have been a bit lax in not wanting to tell a friend that the evidence in an article he or she has written is not as compelling as the friend seemed to believe.[12]

Examples from Historians

It is not only good genealogists who can make mistakes, good historians can, too. May McKisack, a distinguished English professor of history, writes that when William de Braose "died in 1320 his son-in-law, John Mowbray, seized both the barony of Gower and the lordship of Swansea."[13] In the bibliography of her book, McKisack mentions the *Complete Peerage,* showing that she presumably consulted it while doing her research. But in the *Complete Peerage* we find that William de Braose's son-in-law, John Mowbray, was hanged by King Edward II on 23 March 1321/2 following defeat of the adherents of the Earl of Lancaster at Boroughbridge, some four years before William de Braose died in 1326 (not 1320). Thus McKisack made a double mistake. Mowbray did not seize Gower and Swansea after Braose's death but was granted these vast estates by Braose while he was still living. There was a seizure made of them in 1320, but it was the king's favorite, Hugh le Despenser, the younger, who seized them then from Mowbray.[14]

Sir Maurice Powicke, a well-known University of Oxford historian, showed that he, too, could join the rest of us in making an occasional mistake. In one book, he had William de Braose (son of Reginald de Braose) hanged by Welsh Prince Llywelyn in 1232, when the actual year of this much publicized event was 1230. That perhaps could be a typographical error, but what are we to think of his statement elsewhere in the book that the contemporary cleric and writer Gerald of Wales "had much admiration for the lord and lady of Brecon, especially for its lady, Maud de St. Valery" (the parents of Reginald de Braose)?[15] Lewis Thorpe observes that Gerald of Wales had been highly critical of William de Braose, but since he "lived almost in the shadow" of William and Maude, he "toned down what he had written and added an admiring passage." After the agonizing deaths of William and Maude (William died in 1211, disgraced and as a pauper, following much persecution by King John, while Maud had been starved to death along with her son by King John in 1210), Gerald of Wales saw fit to "return to his earlier criticism." And then Gerald concluded in what, when we recall the last horrible years of William and Maud, must be considered a master craftsman's use of irony, "I can only hope that as a reward for their devout lives, they have both been granted eternal glory, just as they enjoyed grace and felicity here below."[16]

The *Complete Peerage* should not escape unscathed. But any discussion of errors in it should be explained first in the context of its total coverage: Any work that can produce so many solid facts laboriously squeezed out of meticulous research into thousands of volumes and manuscripts of varying degrees of obscurity and hiding places is above criticism. This observation applies also in general to all the people mentioned above, whose little peccadillos are illustrated in this chapter only because they were committed by the ones who are at the top of their profession. They should be judged by their total work, not their occasional lapse into the humanness of making an error. In an early volume of the

Complete Peerage we see that the father of William de Braose's wife, Mary de Ros, is William de Ros, but in a later volume the error is corrected by the same writer and her father is shown correctly to be Robert de Ros.[17] In the *Complete Peerage* coverage of the Haudlo family, it states that Sir Richard de Haudlo married Isabel, the daughter of Aumarie de St. Amand.[18] But *The Boarstall Cartulary* shows conclusively that Isabel's father was John de St. Amand, and it was her brother who was Aumarie St. Amand.[19]

Lessons Learned

This is a short chapter because it does not need any more space. The point has been made that even the best of genealogists and historians can make errors. It does not necessarily follow that anyone who makes errors is a great genealogist. Rather the number and seriousness of errors must be judged in comparison with a genealogical writer's total work. But the purpose of this exercise is to demonstrate the fallacy of concentrating on the name of the writer and ignoring the nature of the evidence.

It is true that even some of the best genealogical writers in the past left some work undocumented or only partially documented. In such a case we cannot take it on their authority that their conclusions have to be correct. Their assertions are part of the evidence and should be considered in the analysis of the total evidence. Though it may be difficult, we must attempt to find the material on which they based their conclusions. We may give them some allowance for their batting averages, but we do not just concede the whole game to them. And here we are talking about the writers of the past. Any genealogical writer today who presents conclusions without giving evidence or adequate references is not worthy of being quoted. The only acceptable procedure today is for the genealogist to give us the facts, and then let us see for ourselves how well the facts support the implicit or explicit conclusions.

Notes

1. Definitely not! The *Mayflower* Elizabeth Tilley married John Howland. John Alden married Priscilla Mullins.
2. Eugene A. Stratton, "John Dingley of Marshfield [Mass.] and What the Navy Driver Saw," *The American Genealogist* 61 (1986):234.

3. *Plymouth Colony: Its History & People, 1620-1691* (Salt Lake City, 1986). It is virtually impossible in books containing large amounts of genealogical data to keep out all sorts of what Neil Thompson calls "gremlins." In the case of *Plymouth Colony,* corrections have been made in the second printing, and an addenda sheet will also be made available to purchasers of the first printing who request it and send a stamped, self-addressed, legal-size envelope to Ancestry, Inc., P.O. Box 476, Salt Lake City, UT 84110.

4. See chapter 4, endnote 13, and chapter 7, endnote 7.

5. Generalizing documentation may take several forms. One is to write a long chapter full of genealogical assertions and follow it with an impressive bibliography, hinting, but not demonstrating, that every assertion in the chapter is fully backed up by one or more of the impressive grouped references. Another is to toss around phrases of vague meaning such as "several wills and deeds in Soandso County prove that John was the son of Joe." We want the wills and deeds identified, and we want pertinent parts given verbatim so that we may judge for ourselves if they really prove the relationship. Some writers (not all) generalize deliberately to obscure the fact that their works are not as well documented as they are trying to make them appear.

6. In *The American Genealogist* 47 (1971):6, Jacobus identified Mary Haskell, daughter of John and Patience (Soule) Haskell, as the wife of Scotto Clark, though this was a peripheral issue not central to the main idea of his article. Robert S. Wakefield and Ruth Wilder Sherman, "The Children of John and Patience (Soule) Haskell, *The American Genealogist* 57 (1981):80, show that John and Patience had a daughter Mary Haskell in Middleborough, but there was another contemporary Mary Haskell living in Rochester. One Mary Haskell disappears from the records, and there is no direct evidence to show which. However, Scotto Clark married his Mary Haskell in Rochester, and for lack of other evidence the presumption that she was the Mary Haskell known to be living in Rochester is stronger than the alternative.

7. "One Branch of the Rhode Island Wilcox Family," *The American Genealogist* 19 (1942):23-31.

8. For additional information on this family, see chapter 5. Another error made by Moriarty, in an earlier article on the William Bowditch family, was noted by George Ely Russell in the *National Genealogical Society Quarterly* 69 (1981):279.

9. "Lieutenant John Tomson's Children," *Mayflower Descendant* 30 (1928):49-53. See also Bowman's comments in *Mayflower Descendant* 19:135 and 30:110.

10. "Elizabeth[2] (Tomson) Swift of Middleboro, Mass.," *The American Genealogist* 36 (1960):164-70.

11. The John Washburn line noted in chapter 11.

12. The more genealogical books and articles I see, the more I have come to believe that wishful thinking is one of the most deadly enemies of genealogists, even those who normally know and practice all the rules. Accordingly, when a genealogist is writing on his or her own line and that line leads to some kind of illustrious ancestry, it should be examined with double care.

13. May McKisack, *The Fourteenth Century, 1307-1399* (Oxford, 1959; reprinted, 1976), vol. in *Oxford History of England.*

14. *Complete Peerage,* 9:379, 2:303.

15. Sir Maurice Powicke, "Loretta, Countess of Leicester," *The Christian Life in the Middle Ages and Other Essays* (Oxford, 1935), chart facing 147; 150.

16. Gerald of Wales, *The Journey Through Wales,* translated by Lewis Thorpe (Harmondsworth, Middlesex, 1978), 42, 82-83.

17. *Complete Peerage,* 2:302, 11:94.

18. *Complete Peerage,* 6:400.

19. H. E. Salter, *The Boarstall Cartulary* (Oxford, 1930), 74, 191. *Complete Peerage,* 11:298, 299, shows that John de St. Amand had both a brother Aumarie and a son Aumarie, but the brother died without issue, while the son was too young to be the father of Isabel.

Chapter 10

Pride of Ancestry –
Hereditary Societies

I am in point of fact a particularly haughty and exclusive person of pre-Adamite ancestral descent. Consequently, my family pride is something inconceivable. I can't help it. I was born sneering.

—Gilbert and Sullivan

When the ancestors of the right honorable gentleman were brutal savages in an unknown island, mine were priests in the temple of Solomon.

—Benjamin Disraeli

Often in my Plymouth office a visitor would ask me, "If I find I have *Mayflower* ancestry and join your society, what are the advantages of membership?" If you think about it, that is a tough question to answer. According to its constitution, the General Society of Mayflower Descendants is first an educational society, with a mission "to perpetuate to a remote posterity the memory of our Pilgrim Fathers." This is done by both the general and the state societies by widely distributing the Mayflower Compact in schools, by encouraging publicity about the Pilgrims, by publishing genealogical books which facilitate people finding they have *Mayflower* ancestry, by marking historical places associated with the Pilgrims, and by other appropriate means. The society has other patriotic and social purposes, but I think the educational one is the one most served.

Such reasons seem to satisfy many people, but to some they sound a bit abstract, and a number of people further inquire, "Yes, but specifically what do I get out of membership?" Sometimes one is tempted to say, a la Basil Fawlty, "Oh, perhaps a little snob appeal, too," but one usually holds one's tongue. I have frequently mentioned that membership often brings out a greater awareness of history, and a love of history can be its own reward. Also noting the social occasions, I have pointed out that most of the state Mayflower societies have at least two or three meetings, luncheons, banquets, picnics, or other types of entertainment yearly, sometimes (not always) with a very good guest speaker, and it is pleasant to get together with people with common interests. Sometimes I have pointed out, especially to people with a strong interest in genealogy, that one of the benefits of submitting an application is to get a thorough check by an impartial authority on how well the applicant's line is proven. Many of these reasons apply to other hereditary societies as well. Obviously membership in a hereditary society can mean different things to different people.

Probably the various reasons given above and below cover the motivation of most people joining most hereditary societies. Some societies may have, in addition to a patriotic motive, a political motive, but when hereditary societies play national or local politics, they endanger their existence, and they would be well advised to draw a strict and impassable line between patriotism in general and partisan politics in particular. I hasten to add here though that I am not talking about internal society politics, and there are undoubtedly some people who, having joined a society, find that the internal political intrigues prevalent in some societies make membership more interesting. Some societies stress a strong religious or ethnic reason for their being, just as some others are family associations, eligibility for membership being based on descent from a common ancestor, such as the Howland Society, the Stetson Society, the Eddy Society, the Rice Society, and many, many others. Another reason for joining some societies, and I am thinking of the Royal Bastards in particular, is the very fact that they are so difficult to join, and thus the application process becomes a challenge. And I suppose I should add to these reasons just the fact that a society is there; there are certainly some people who will join anything they find themselves eligible for, just for the fun of joining. Just as genealogists collect ancestors, some people collect societies.[1]

Regardless of the reasons, it is a fact that many people want to join one or more hereditary societies, and that to them one of the most important purposes of genealogy is as a means to a very specific end. I have had people write to me from all over telling me how much it meant to them to get to join this or that society. A lawyer in Alexandria, Virginia, wrote to see if I could expand his Stratton line so he would be eligible to join the Baronial Order of Magna Charta, which he said had always been one of his goals in life. It is sometimes sad to see the meaning that membership in the Mayflower Society has to some people who cannot find an adequately supported line for that purpose, such as when a woman wrote telling me that her ninety-year-old mother had not long to live, and the one thing she wanted before she died was to be accepted by the Mayflower Society.

Joining a Society

How then does one go about joining a hereditary society? For some societies, given the fact that you have a valid line, it is relatively easy, and for some it is easy even if you do not have a valid line. For some others it is difficult to join even with the best documented line in the world. First, one needs to decide which society to apply to. There are many, many societies, and most of them are described to greater or lesser extent (depending in part on how much they themselves want to be described) in the annual *Hereditary Register of the United States of America,*[2] which is available in many large libraries. Grahame Thomas Smallwood, Jr., who has belonged to and been an officer in more hereditary societies than anyone else I know, and is probably the country's leading authority on hereditary societies, has a chapter in *The Source*[3] entitled "Hereditary and Lineage Society Records," in which he gives information on many societies. The *Hereditary Register* does not name the many family surname associations, but Smallwood's chapter in *The Source* shows where information may be obtained on many of these.

My chapter here differs from other published information on hereditary societies in that I am not attempting to describe all existing societies in detail. On the other hand I will emphasize, with more than the normal candor perhaps, some of the inside aspects of several societies, particularly from the point of view of the genealogist. If I concentrate my examples on the General Society of Mayflower Descendants, it is because I know it (along with Royal Bastards) best, and thus it lends itself to giving more detailed illustrations. However, though the details may differ, most hereditary societies share in common a very difficult problem: How to base eligibility on genealogy and yet not embarrass present members or inconvenience applicants whose lines may be inadequately proven.[4]

Democratization

Before going into specifics on some societies, let me mention one important misconception which seems to be held by the general public regarding hereditary societies. In an age when democracy has become almost synonymous with egalitarianism, are hereditary societies democratic? To that question, I give a qualified *yes*. Some certainly are. The ones I have in mind are as democratic as bar and medical associations, unions, appointed political offices, veterans' organizations, and credit card companies, among others; that is, they have eligibility requirements which, if met, open them up to people of all races, ages, and creeds.[5] The trend, although it may be a slow one, increasingly shows that *the make-up of hereditary society membership tends to reflect the make-up of the nation as a whole.*[6]

There is a very scientific reason for this "democratization" of hereditary societies, and that reason is in some of the ramifications of procreation. For example, when I was in charge of the Mayflower Society office in Plymouth, one of the employees there was of a long-time Plymouth family. Her father had been born in Plymouth County, and virtually all his ancestors were born there. Under such circumstances, the number of lines he had back to the 1620 *Mayflower* passengers is astounding. This man married a first-generation Italian woman, and they had an only child, who was the woman who worked for me.

This woman married a man of Irish descent, and so her two daughters are one-quarter English, one-quarter Italian, and one-half Irish (assuming that her mother and her husband were respectively entirely of Italian and Irish stock). But these daughters have in their ancestry every single one of the mother's many *Mayflower* forebears. When the daughters marry, it is doubtful that they will be searching for pure WASP mates, and they could very easily marry someone of whole or part Portuguese, Polish, or Armenian descent. I give this as merely one out of many, many similar cases. I have a son who is of half English descent from me, and half Ukrainian descent from my first wife, and he married a girl who has

Italian and German ancestry; his two young sons might someday marry girls with completely different ancestry, and the national origin of their children will become even more diffused. Thus it is that with time *Mayflower* descendants reflect more and more the national ethnic composition.

Brief Descriptions of a Few Societies

The hereditary societies described below are some of those in which I have had membership or have otherwise had familiarity:

General Society of Mayflower Descendants. This is an umbrella society made up of individual state societies. There is a state society for every state in the union, plus the District of Columbia and Canada, and applicants join a state society not the general society. It is a bottom-up society in that all authority not specifically delegated to the general society is reserved to the individual state societies, which may therefore have different rules (and widely varying dues).[7] The main authority delegated to the general society is the sole right to determine valid *Mayflower* lines, and each application to a state society is forwarded from the state to the general society for approval of the lineage. It is a strictly bloodline society, and blood descent from a *Mayflower* passenger is the main membership criterion regardless of whether or not there may be illegitimacy in the line. Some state societies are perhaps more difficult to join than others, for some adhere strictly to the rule that an applicant must be endorsed by two existing members, while some tend to bypass the rule by routinely obtaining two endorsers for any applicant. One state society is notorious for being overly conscious about the social status of applicants, but most state societies are more concerned with the bloodline (however, more on this below). Although the general society constitution provides that no one shall be eligible who advocates the overthrow of the government, is guilty of treason, or is not of good moral character, I have known of only one case where an applicant with a valid line was refused membership on these grounds, and that was many years ago in the case of a man who had been described in a *Readers' Digest* article as having Nazi connections.

National Society Daughters of the American Revolution (DAR). The largest of all American hereditary societies with a membership of well over 200,000, the DAR has been much criticized as being perceived as an ultra-conservative organization of "little old ladies in tennis shoes." Although its stand on many issues, which it calls patriotic, may be characterized as considerably right of center, the DAR has been somewhat misunderstood and has within its ranks a significant divergence in opinions. It is a top-down organization in that ultimate authority rests in the national organization rather than in the state organizations and local chapters. Dedicated to older values, it still has shown itself ready to change in the present, just as the country itself goes through continuous change.

The criticisms against the DAR are well known, but the public in general does not know of this society's many good works. It has been active in generously supporting schools (including one for Indians and another for disadvantaged children), in conservation, in assistance to veterans, in welcoming new citizens at naturalization ceremonies, and, more recently, in promoting research into the contributions made during the American Revolution by black Americans (under the leadership of noted black genealogist James Walker). The DAR founded the Army Nurse Corps during the Spanish-American War, and when the United States government ruled that many of these nurses did not have enough service to be eligible for a federal pension, the DAR paid their pensions as long as they lived. The National Society of the Daughters of the American Revolution Library in Washington, D.C., ranks among the major genealogical libraries in the country.

The Society of the Cincinnati. One of the most difficult societies to join from the viewpoint of genealogical eligibility, it is also one of the most prestigious, as well as hands down the oldest. The Cincinnati was organized after the American Revolution by officers in George Washington's army to protect their mutual interests. Eligibility is limited to one male descendant at any given time from each of the original members, and the original members were officers of the Continental Army only, not the various local militia officers. Eligibility is thus passed down from father to oldest son or other main heir only, much like an honest coat of arms. Though there may be some hint of snob appeal in the General Society of Mayflower Descendants, it is not really an elitist organization, but the Society of the Cincinnati *is* elitist (though I am using "elitist" more in its original than its now pejorative sense).

Descendants of the Illegitimate Sons and Daughters of the Kings of Britain (Royal Bastards). Created as a reaction to the lax standards of evidence in many hereditary societies, the society was founded by a number of the country's best genealogists for the specific purpose of promoting genealogical scholarship.[8] The society has no meetings or other get-togethers, and it exists solely for promoting scholarship in genealogy. There is no criterion for membership other than having a valid line. I became the Herald/Genealogist in 1983 and kept this position until 1987. Eligibility is based on well-documented descent from one of the illegitimate children or grandchildren of British kings. The Royal Bastards has the reputation of being one of the most difficult societies to join and therefore one of the most desirable. However, there is a flaw in this organization's purpose in that after a number of early lines were determined, documented, approved, and published (the great majority of which went back to England via just a handful of American colonial immigrants), thereafter the British medieval ancestry requirement became satisfied for many applicants by citing references from previously approved lines. Sometimes the qualifying gateway ancestors (most of whom were prominent as governors, clergymen, or otherwise of the American colonial gentry) had a good number of their descendants documented in published family histories, such as Jacobus's *Bulkeley Genealogy,* making it relatively easy for later descendants to prove their lines. There are of course exceptions, for some new gateway ancestors are still being discovered (and this is the challenging part of Royal Bastards membership), and some people, such as Royal Bastards member Sir Anthony Wagner, have joined directly from England, where there is no need for a gateway ancestor.

The Royal Bastards is the only hereditary society I know of that annually publishes the generation-by-generation lines of all newly accepted members, together with an abbreviated form of the supporting evidence. Obviously this could be a dangerous practice for some hereditary societies, for it could expose to public ridicule how hypocritical their standards of evidence are. I think all hereditary societies having any pretense of being based on sound genealogical practices should be required to publish their lines regularly, but I think many would not care to do so, for the genealogical standards of some (certainly not all) of them are in varying degrees questionable.

Society of Descendants of the Colonial Clergy, and Hereditary Order of the Descendants of Colonial Governors. These are two separate societies which are discussed together only because the same remarks apply to each. The titles are descriptive of membership requirements.

These societies are especially interesting because the qualifying ancestors are among the men most likely to have had British royal ancestry. Colonial Clergy has from time to time published its complete membership lines, and these can be quite helpful as clues (but only as clues, for documentation is not given, and some lines are erroneous) as to where a non-member might find an ancestor to hitch onto. Given a line back to a colonial governor or a colonial clergyman, you have a good starting point for research that can take you, on the average, further back in your genealogy than most of your other American ancestors, and perhaps may lead to discovering a royal line (see also chapter 11). Standards of evidence are average.

Flagon and Trencher. The eligibility requirement is to go back to a colonial innkeeper. Anyone with a valid line can join. The purpose is to have an annual meeting with good food and drink at one of the surviving colonial inns or taverns. This society is good clean fun, and, via the speakers, a member may learn more about colonial inns, food, and beverages. Standards of evidence have been above average, as one might expect with the distinguished Kenn Stryker-Rodda as its genealogist for many years.

Order of the Founders and Patriots of America, and **Hereditary Order of Descendants of the Loyalists and Patriots of the American Revolution.** Again, these are two separate societies, but they have in common a twofold membership requirement. Founders and Patriots used to limit membership to finding qualifying ancestors with the surname of either your father or mother. My father was a Stratton and my mother a Holmes. On my Stratton side I would have to find a Stratton ancestor who settled in the colonies prior to 13 May 1657 (my founder), and I would also need a Stratton ancestor in the same line to me who served in the Revolution (my patriot). If I used my mother's line, I would have to find a Holmes in the colonies by the required date and a Holmes in the same line to me who served in the Revolution. I would not have been allowed to use any of the many other surnames in my ancestry. However, this society has recently relaxed its requirements to allow for four qualifying ancestral surnames instead of two, that is the surname of anyone of a person's four grandparents. In my case that would mean the double ancestor requirement could be satisfied by the surname Stratton, Holmes, Mann, or Chamberlain. Loyalists and Patriots requires two ancestors, one who served on the American side of the Revolution, and one who was a loyalist during the Revolution. The loyalist ancestor need not be in a direct line but can be as remote as a second cousin of a direct ancestor.[9]

Royal Societies. There are many of these: National Society of Americans of Royal Descent, Order of the Crown of Charlemagne in the United States of America, Baronial Order of Magna Charta, National Society of Magna Charta Dames, Order of the Three Crusades, National Society of Daughters of the Barons of Runnymede, and others. Though some societies might more properly be called baronial than royal, usually finding a baronial line can result in the same line or a related line going back to royalty. Though there has been some improvement in some royal societies, and some require much better standards of evidence than others, in very broad terms royal-line societies are a problem because they too often involve an injudicious mixture of lines, some few going back to a handful of well-proven colonial gateway ancestors and others established by something less than sound standards of evidence. Well-proven royal lines are not that easy to come by.

The standards of evidence used by some hereditary societies are deplorable. There are a number of reasons for this. First, the abilities and motivations of the approving genealogists vary considerably, even between two successive genealogists in the same society. Second, though many societies have acknowledged the weakness of their standards and tried to improve them, there is much opposition from members who balk at having to produce more and better evidence for their children than that which they used when they joined. Third, there is a matter of numbers (in terms of declining membership and declining financial balances when high standards prevent societies from bringing in more new members than they lose through attrition by death or drop out). When I applied what I considered a reasonable "preponderance of evidence" standard to one society, the head of that society wrote to me to say in effect, "While I sympathize with you on the need for high standards, I must be even more concerned with the fact that during your term of office we are suffering from negative growth." Not wishing to be a bottleneck, I resigned.

Levels of Exclusiveness

Not only is the standard of evidence a factor in joining a society, but whether they want you even if you have a valid line is another important factor. Some societies are gender conscious, as we have seen above with the DAR. But after allowing for these obvious factors, there are generally, aside from valid lines, three levels of exclusiveness in societies; call these levels first, second, and third. The first level is virtually unrestrictive admittance of anyone with valid ancestry, although they would draw the line, for example, at notorious criminals. Most of the Mayflower state societies practice this level (with one very notable exception),[10] as does Flagon and Trencher, Royal Bastards (even though the Royal Bastards application blank has a place for two endorsing signatures, I found that applications frequently came in with these places blank, and I paid no attention to it), and DAR to some extent, plus some others.

The second level is observed in those societies which feel more comfortable seeing modest references on their applicants. These societies prefer an applicant known to one or more of their members or, if unknown, at least to be someone with an educational, occupational, or family position that seems to admit of respectability. It is not difficult, if you can find a present member, to get an endorsement for this type of society. A variation of the second level of exclusiveness is practiced by those societies which like to have an applicant attend a meeting before inviting the applicant to join. DAR is partly like this, for though the national society practices no exclusiveness, the local chapters frequently like to see a prospective member before accepting the woman for membership, the view being that the chapter is a small social club as well as an hereditary society; however, DAR also allows a woman to join the national society directly as a "member at large," belonging to no chapter.

The third level is exclusiveness for the sake of exclusiveness, and there are some societies that accept no applicant other than someone whom they have decided to invite to join them. There are some societies that pay ten times as much attention to the social desirability of the applicant as they do to the validity of the line, including some that have committees to pass upon the social desirability of applicants. Some hereditary societies deliberately keep the names and addresses of officers secret from the general public because they do not want the public to find them – they take the view "if you don't already know one or more of our members, then we wouldn't want you in the first place."[11] In this sense they are more like exclusive social clubs.

My experience in general has been that the more attention a given society pays to social desirability, the less it pays to genealogical correctness. If an extremely exclusive society considers an applicant desirable, it may be more than willing to wink at weaknesses in the applicant's genealogical documentation (in fact, society genealogists sometimes have to face tremendous pressures from officers in given cases). I know of cases in the past at least where a society has allowed an applicant to give a personal affidavit of the immediate past five generations as the sole evidence of these generations. Under these circumstances applicants could (I have no knowledge that any did) deliberately tie onto a known line that was not theirs for the rest of the way back. Some so-called hereditary societies care not two figs for genealogy, especially when it involves the children of existing members who may have been accepted without any really valid evidence.

A Bit of Unpleasantness

I am going to give one unpleasant example of malfeasance by an hereditary society because I think it may encourage some future approving genealogist to hold the line and resist unfair pressure. Though the example involves Mayflower, I do not think this type of thing is more apt to occur in Mayflower than in other societies, and I know for a fact that it has not been practiced in recent years (but see below regarding the Mayflower Applications Appeals Committee). A number of years ago, one or more of the officers of one of the Mayflower state societies thought it would be nice to invite former British Prime Minister Winston Churchill to become a member. The state society would honor Churchill, whose membership would, of course, honor the state society, as well as the officers who brought it all about. I imagine the state officers knew little about genealogy, but they did believe at the time that Churchill had a valid *Mayflower* line.

Churchill was more fortunate than most applicants, for the state society spared him the trouble of having to research a line. They did all the work for him, prepared the typed application, and even signed it by proxy. A general society officer wrote to Mrs. John K. Allen, then historian general of the general society:

> I have a great problem with regard to the membership certificates for Sir Winston Churchill and Lady Eden [Churchill's niece]. [We] sent the lineage of Sir Winston and suggested he be made a member of the Society. From

147

then on [one of the officers] decided it would be splendid if he could present Sir Winston and Lady Eden with membership certificates in London....Both [Sir Winston and Lady Eden] have replied they would be most happy to have them....We sent word to have the papers made up as quickly as possible so that the unframed certificates could be ordered....[A state officer] said they would have to wait for a Board Meeting [for the state] office was closed during August. I suggested he assign numbers for these two applicants and ask you if you would be willing to assign the General Nos., all of which, of course, is unethical but [a certain officer] thought we might make an exception in this case. Mr. [another state officer] refused and that was that....Of course, the papers will not have the signatures of the applicants. I am writing to ask if you will approve these papers and assign the general numbers so that we can order the certificates....Sarah Churchill [Sir Winston's daughter], who is in Chicago at the present time, wishes to become a member and we will prepare her papers as soon as I secure some dates and places, etc....P.S. Would you approve the order for the certificates if they bear both *Mayflower* passengers' names, Richard Warren and Francis Cooke, even though the lineage papers are not ready for the Cooke line?

Mrs. Allen (to her everlasting credit) wrote back:

The lineage papers of Sir Winston Spencer-Churchill and of Lady Eden have been examined. Unfortunately, they are based on a line which has been ruled as questionable by the General Society, and therefore cannot be approved.

It had been well known for years by genealogists and published in genealogical journals that the line in question was most likely false, and certainly that it could not be proven true.[12] (See the discussion of the Wilcox family in chapter 5.) The pressure put on Mrs. Allen from various quarters was to say the least not gentle. Although she was renominated and re-elected historian general for another term, the following term she was passed over, and she then became state historian of the Massachusetts Mayflower Society. The application papers of Sir Winston Churchill and Lady Clarissa Eden were put away in the files to gather dust. Four years later an ambitious man of controversial (to say the least) character occupied the office of historian general. No new facts had come to light about the validity of Churchill's line, and it was still considered invalid then as it is now. Nonetheless, the new historian general dusted off the Churchill and Lady Eden papers, and he signed his name, thereby making Sir Winston Churchill and Lady Clarissa Eden Mayflower Descendants (though not *Mayflower* descendants). Though the Constitution of the Mayflower Society required the historian general's approval before the state society could elect the applicant to membership, the papers still bore the date of approval by the state historian, followed by a date four years later of approval by the historian general, followed by a date four years earlier for the election to the state society.

The Road to Advancement

Like some other societies, hereditary or otherwise, Mayflower likes a good fight every now and then. Most societies have self-perpetuating rules – the current head (or all the officers) selecting the nominating committee, which in turn chooses the next leaders – for in many societies elections are often a routine endorsement of the nominees. However, every now and then a good rousing floor fight takes place, as with the Mayflower General Society in 1972 (and in a quieter way 1987). Also, try though they might to perpetuate their own likenesses, no group of officers fully controls the nominees, and sometimes a person selected for the new head becomes a rather different person on election. There are well-established ladders for advancement. For example, in Mayflower one may first volunteer for state committee assignment, then be elected as a board member of a state society, and then advance to minor state society office and finally to state governor. State governors may be appointed to general society committees and gradually advance to minor and then major offices in the general society. All along the way there are dangers such as being identified with the wrong faction or advocating an unpopular policy, and an up-and-coming officer might find that suddenly the next step to advancement becomes closed. Thus sometimes advancement favors those who take a cautious course. The way for initial advancement, though, is voluntarism: today's volunteers are tomorrow's officers.

Controversies

The above is true to greater or lesser extent in most societies, not hereditary only. From the point of view of genealogy, though, I want to go into a bit more detail about the position of historian general, which I occupied from 1981 to 1983. Back in the old days, around the turn of the century and the following decades, as far as genealogy was concerned, the Massachusetts state society ruled the General Society of Mayflower Descendants, and George Ernest Bowman ruled the Massachusetts society. He was, as stated earlier, a superb genealogist, and, even though he was historian general for but a short time, he kept the accepted lines honest. As he aged, gradually newer historians general became less under his influence and more lax in approving applications. One of the biggest mistakes Mayflower made involves the publishing of indices to its lines.[13] The mistake, though, was not so much in publishing the index, as it was in accepting it as a bible. The practice grew of accepting in lieu of evidence a reference to Mayflower Index Numbers for one or more generations. As more and more erroneous lines were accepted by the society, the more serious the problem became. Also, in the 1970s, the general society started publishing the *Mayflower Families* series, giving five generations (plus the children of the fifth generation) in documented form. The Five Generations Project was conducted under the leadership of well-known genealogists, and thus within a short period of time many of the invalid lines, or lines inadequately proven valid, began to emerge, creating a paradox for the society.

A number of important actions, some quite controversial, took place within the Mayflower Society from the late 1970s through the 1980s. The most important from a genealogical point of view was that on the one hand the society tightened up its standards of evidence, going back to the George Ernest Bowman way, and this was a step forward for genealogy. On the other hand, the society took a number of ill-advised and arbitrary steps based on personalities and accordingly hamstrung its Five Generations publishing effort. The first book in the *Mayflower Families* series came out in 1975, the second in 1978, and the third in 1980. The third volume was prematurely published, and resulted in a black eye for the society (though a subsequent addendum has improved the correctness of the given lines). Thereafter the project could not seem to get back on track. In-fighting, personality conflicts, quarrels over format, concern about being the next act to follow the heavily criticized third volume, and other such distractions resulted in no new volumes being published as of the time this book is written. (However, the recent policy of publishing new, tentative *Mayflower Families in Progress* has been a step in the right direction.)

Other in-house quarrels resulted in attempts to change the Mayflower Society constitution so as to handcuff the historian general and reduce genealogical standards. Mayflower is still suffering from its middle period of abysmally low standards. Many members who came in during that period rose to officer positions and then saw their lines under potential attack as standards were improved. The threat of higher standards particularly was felt by those officers and other members who wanted to get their children accepted as members, which meant that the family line would have to be reviewed and possibly redocumented (or in many cases documented for the first time). This resulted in proposed amendments to the Mayflower Society constitution at the 1987 Triennial Congress at Plymouth to make the acceptance of existing members almost automatic (the burden of requiring the applicant to prove the line would have been removed, and the historian general would have been required to prove the negative) and to give vastly increased weight to undocumented secondary publications. I contributed to defeating those amendments, but the new historian general is in very unenviable position of walking a tightrope between the requirements of good genealogical principle and the knowledge that she can be easily overruled in the present and virtually fired in the future by not being renominated.[14]

It was obvious at the Mayflower Triennial Congress that most of the delegates did not understand what the issues really were. Many of them honestly felt that all previously approved applications had been based on adequately proven lines. Many of them simply were unaware of how little documentation had been required during the society's middle period. While they wisely voted down the anti-genealogy amendments, they approved the actions of an Applications Appeals Committee which had overruled the outgoing historian general (my successor) on three cases. All three of these decisions were bad, but one in particular was a travesty on any kind of reasonable standard of genealogical evidence. The historian general at the time sent an "Information Bulletin" to many of the officers and members of the Mayflower Society, with a request that they in turn pass it on to others. I considered transcribing that bulletin as an appendix in this book, for it is a solid indictment of completely unacceptable genealogical practices, but I decided not to because I want to avoid dealing in personalities insofar as possible. The more important thing is to alert in general terms the officers and members of hereditary societies as well as non-member genealogists who have interest in these matters, to the prevalence of serious problems existing in some societies, which in the past have been swept under the carpet.

It is my belief that the role of hereditary societies in this country will be sharply limited in the future if more of them do not pay attention to sound genealogical practices. Like it or not, their primary reason for being is genealogical, and those that ignore genealogy may face eventual trouble. I dislike using the Mayflower Society as the main example in this chapter, but it is the one I am most qualified to speak on. However, there are a number of other hereditary societies whose stance on good standards of genealogical evidence is much more equivocal than Mayflower's, and any lesson that may be derived from the above applies equally to them. I should also make it clear that many of the officers and members of Mayflower favor good standards of evidence, and that the new historian general has stated emphatically that she intends to enforce such good standards, continuing the reform that began some years back. Further, I have also been given to understand that there will be no more arbitrary acceptance of appeals from a historian general's rejection by a committee ignoring the genealogical facts in the case. Many societies today are paying for laxness in genealogical standards in the past, and the longer they delay reform, the more severe that reform will ultimately be.

I still think that hereditary societies can be interesting and fun to join and would certainly advise people with valid lines to apply for membership in any society they like. The more that people with valid, provable lines and an interest in genealogy join, the easier it will be to keep the societies on a sensible course. I belong to a good number of hereditary societies, and if anyone asks me what my favorite society is, I do not hesitate to say Mayflower.

Notes

1. *The Wall Street Journal* of 25 November 1987, in an article "It Isn't Easy to Join Mayflower Society – Even if You Want To," states that there is not much tangible benefit to membership, though it quotes social historian Stephen Birmingham as saying that *Mayflower* connections "might help people get into

fancy New York co-ops or certain boarding schools." Incidentally, the so-called Mayflower Madam was never a member of the Mayflower Society.

2. This book can be purchased from Hereditary Register, 444 W. Camelback Road, Suite 105, Phoenix, AZ 85013.

3. Arlene Eakle and Johni Cerny, eds., *The Source A Guidebook of American Genealogy* (Salt Lake City, 1984).

4. Some aspects of this problem were also discussed in my lecture "Between Scylla and Charybdis – The Plight of Hereditary Societies," given on 12 December 1987 at the New England Historic Genealogical Society in Boston.

5. Some societies are restricted to male only or female only membership, but usually in this type of society where the males have one, the females have their counterpart society. I would not be surprised if some of these societies eventually combined, though the results might not be satisfying to all people. It is interesting to note that the Daughters of the American Revolution (DAR) was founded specifically because females were not allowed to join the already established Sons of the American Revolution (SAR). Now the Daughters outnumber the Sons by about ten to one, and the Daughters might not now want to share what they have created with the Sons.

6. *The Wall Street Journal* article cited above quotes Philadelphia historian E. Digby Baltzell as saying that many hereditary societies nowadays include "a broad range of ethnic and racial groups in their membership," but "if you go to meetings, they're mostly sort of smug WASPs." I think he is using "smug WASPs" as a single word. I assume Mr. Baltzell is one himself, for he must attend such meetings in order to know. However, looking at the surnames of recent Mayflower society officers, who would of course attend meetings, I note Petro, O'Reilly, Pekowsky, Oedekoven, Matarazzo, Thivierge, Ruecki, Jizba, Rosencrantz, DeSa, Pedigo, Bilyeu, Orndorff, Aiwohi, Poblocki, Chiei, and Luzzi, among others, which are unfamiliar to me as WASP surnames. I think remarks such as made by Philadelphia historian E. Digby Baltzell are rather smug in themselves.

7. Each state Mayflower society requires an initiation fee plus either an annual fee or a one-time life membership fee. In general, with some significant exceptions, the size of the state society has an influence on how active it is in social, educational (including publishing), and other affairs. The figures given here are as of 1985 and are taken from the August 1986 issue of *The Mayflower Quarterly*. Total 1985 membership for all state societies was 21,165. The largest state society was Massachusetts, with 2,545 members. However, Massachusetts, being the home state of Plymouth, is an exception, for often people from other states join the Massachusetts society for sentimental or historical reasons (a person is free to apply to any state society), and possibly 50 percent of the Massachusetts membership resides out of state. Massachusetts had a $35.00 initiation fee, and dues of either $20.00 annually or $300.00 for lifetime membership. The state society with the largest in-state membership, 1,807, was California, where the initiation fee was $28.00 and the dues either $17.00 annually or $238.00 for lifetime membership. Some of the least expensive states were West Virginia (thirty-eight members) with an initiation fee of $2.00 and dues of $8.00 annually or $200.00 for lifetime membership; Maryland (196 members) with an initiation fee of $5.00 and

dues of $10.00 annually or $100.00 for lifetime membership; and North Dakota (forty members) with an initiation fee of $10.00 and dues of $8.00 annually or $90.00 for lifetime membership. Some of the most expensive state societies were New York (797 members) with an initiation fee of $50.00 and dues of $50.00 annually or $500.00 for lifetime membership; Massachusetts, given above; and Pennsylvania (690 members) with an initiation fee of $15.00 and dues of $17.50 annually or $300.00 for lifetime membership.

8. For additional details on the Royal Bastards, see my article "Royal, er, ahem...Bounders?" in the September-October, 1987, issue of the *Ancestry Newsletter*.

9. See note 1 in chapter 5 for comment on "direct ancestor." As of possible interest, I have an ancestor, Ensign Mann of Petersham, Massachusetts, who could be classified as both a patriot and a loyalist. As the young Harvard-graduate schoolmaster of Petersham, Ensign was a firebrand revolutionary and the local leader of the Sons of Liberty just before the Revolution. However, he fell in love with, and married, the daughter of the Reverend Aaron Whitney, one of the town's leading Tories, and his revolutionary fervor diminished. Though he was not what might be called an active Tory, Ensign thereafter was considered a Tory by some (he continued teaching school in Petersham during the Revolution). I once asked a DAR registrar how this type of thing would be handled by DAR, and was told that eligibility for DAR could be based on an ancestor who was a Tory first and a patriot after, but not vice versa.

10. I will not mention the name of this notable exception, but I will mention the other side of the coin, that the Massachusetts state society has been in the vanguard to remove any need to have endorsers for membership. At Mayflower Triennial Congresses, Massachusetts has proposed a constitutional amendment to eliminate the requirement of two endorsers for each applicant. It got some backing, as I recall from state societies such as Pennsylvania and Maryland, but was voted down by the majority of state societies. For itself, Massachusetts (as well as a few others) just ignores the rules about endorsers.

11. For the person with an overwhelming ambition to crash into some of the more exclusive societies, there is a "long and hard way" that might yield results. Join the easier societies, volunteer for the less desirable jobs, work up to the more prestigious positions, get to know fellow members who belong to other societies, through them join some of the middle difficulty societies, repeat the process and get to know members of the exclusive societies (often members of the most exclusive societies are also members of lesser exclusive societies), and, if you have gone about it the right way, you may be invited to join the societies you are really after.

12. See, for example, G. Andrews Moriarty, "The Mayflower Ancestry of the Descendants of Daniel Wilcox of Portsmouth, R.I.," *The New England Historical and Genealogical Register* 87 (1933):73. Sir Winston Churchill's line, via his American mother, Jennie Jerome, went through Daniel Wilcox, believed by genealogists to have been a son of the senior Daniel Wilcox by his first, unidentified wife and not by his second *Mayflower* descendant wife, Elizabeth (Cooke) Wilcox (see chart 2, page 63).

13. The Mayflower Index was not the same thing as publishing annually all accepted lines with references, for the index form made it difficult to follow, and the index contained no dates or references. Since the index was not published regularly, when an error was found in a line, it might be years after the event, and many more people might have come in on the same erroneous line in the meantime.

14. There was more than usual newspaper coverage at the 1987 Triennial Congress because it was known in advance that there would be a battle. *The New York Times* of 20 September 1987 quoted me as telling the delegates, "I don't like to reject people from this society, and it is with pain that I [have done so]. But we are running the risk of throwing genealogy out the window and becoming truly a society of possible *Mayflower* descendants." I could wish they had quoted other things I said, such as telling the delegates about the really sad lack of documentation on so many middle-period applications. I also made it very clear that I did not approve of arbitrary strictness in documentation requirements, and that there was a need for a happy medium between the reasonable and the unnecessarily strict. Some newspapers seemed to think that there was a battle between conservatives who wanted to have tight rules to keep more people out, and liberals who wanted to loosen the rules to democratize the society. The truth would seem to be more the opposite. The lower standards required by the amendments would have benefitted mainly the relatives of vested interest groups. Even giving more weight to undocumented secondary sources would have had more effect on relatives of members than on newcomers, for most of the sources in question were written decades ago when genealogy was more exclusively the interest of old-line families than of newer immigrant families. These newer families may be qualified because of intermarriage, but their descendants would be less likely than others to be helped by secondary sources (the mid-nineteenth-century immigrant who married a *Mayflower* descendant was not so apt to find himself in published family histories as was the English-surnamed banker or lawyer). The defeat of the amendments meant that the same standards (basically those used by law courts or advocated by Jacobus's "rule of reason") would have to be applied to both newcomers and the relatives of those already in.

Chapter 11

Royal Genealogy – Case Studies

The chances of getting your pedigree back further than the seventeenth century are remote.
—Gerald Hamilton-Edwards

Why do I rob banks? Because that's where the money is.
—Willie Sutton

One of these days I am going to start a new hereditary society called the Society of Descendants of Eleventh-Century Peasants. It will have absolutely no snob appeal, for any descendant of an eleventh-century peasant may join, and we all go back to at least one such peasant (perhaps even a few more somewhere back among our roughly one billion ancestors – including duplicates – of that time). For people of cultures that did not have peasants, we will also allow membership on the basis of descending from any other nonentity of the time. The only trouble is that if we use decent standards of evidence, we will not get any members. None at all! It will be the most exclusive society in the world. Why? Because it is absolutely impossible for anyone to trace himself or herself back generation by generation to an eleventh-century peasant. The records just do not exist.

Parish and Manor Records

Thomas Cromwell issued his edict on 5 September 1538 ordering every church in England to keep a book and "write the day and year of every wedding, christening, and burial" held in that church.[1] It is sometimes said that the beginning of parish registers in 1538 is thus the furthest-back, practical year for tracing Anglo-American genealogy. Gerald Hamilton-Edwards points out that you can get back somewhat further if the wills of your ancestors survive, perhaps as far as around 1400. He also mentions manor court rolls, which are becoming better known as sources in English genealogy, as possible means to go back two centuries earlier than 1538.[2] These rolls are private property, belonging to the present owners of the manors concerned, and they are rather spotty in their existence because all manor court rolls did not survive. They record much about the land holdings and heirs of tenants of the manor. Hamilton-Edwards concludes, "Apart from these possibilities, one is only able to trace further back than the mid-sixteenth-century people of distinction and rank, or those who owned land."[3] Of course those who owned land were for the most part people of distinction and rank.

Thus if a person wants to get back much further than the sixteenth century in Britain, it is necessary to do research in the area called "royal genealogy," or "medieval English genealogy." The practice of primogeniture in England was responsible for at least two aspects of the country's rather fluid class system. With the bulk of an estate going to the older son, the younger son of a younger son of a younger son might go down on the social ladder. On the other hand, with estates being divided equally among the daughters when there was no son, heiresses might marry a wealthy merchant emerging from family obscurity and give rise to new noble families. Probably the most significant barrier between classes was that between the broad upper and the broad lower, or between nobility/gentry and those of non-gentle birth, though even here there was some social mobility.[4] Thus when one traces ancestry back to the gentry (such as the lord of a small manor, a merchant who may have bought a landed estate, a minister of the Church of England, or a lawyer), there is a good possibility of going back even further by connecting into the lower nobility and thence into the higher nobility. The nobility frequently lead back to royal lines. We study noble and royal lines because they are there, and, with but a few exceptions, they are all that there is.

Tracing American Lines to England

My experience with royal genealogy has been tracing American lines back to the kings of England, usually in medieval times, with some of those lines also going back to various other European kings. Aside from researching those lines of personal or professional interest, from 1983 to 1987 I was the herald/genealogist for the Descendants of the Illegitimate Sons and Daughters of the Kings of Britain (also called Royal Bastards, or RBs). From my experience I can formulate several general observations.

Most such lines can be divided into two distinct parts, each with its own particular set of problems. The first part is tracing a line from a twentieth-century American back to a colonial gateway ancestor, "gateway" meaning the first of the line to arrive in colonial America. This type of genealogy is similar to tracing one's line back to a *Mayflower* passenger or a colonial clergyman. It requires all of the techniques necessary to do research in colonial American genealogy and none of the techniques peculiar to medieval English genealogy. The former techniques have already been discussed in many of the chapters in this book, and the latter techniques will be discussed in the next chapter.

The second part is to trace the gateway ancestor back to a time, place, and family in Great Britain, usually England, and thence back, usually through the gentry, to one of the noble families. Many noble families are well recorded in such books as the *Complete Peerage*[5] or in journal articles, and so in many, not all cases, once the gateway ancestor's family connects to a noble family, the bulk of the work is done. For some twentieth-century Americans, finding royal genealogy is as easy as falling off a log. Let's take a case in point. Many descendants of the Bulkeley family in both male and female lines find it easy to trace their ancestry back to the gateway Bulkeley family, thanks in good part to the work done by Jacobus in *The Bulkeley Genealogy*.[6] Among other Bulkeley connections, once the family is traced back to England, it almost immediately goes into the Charlton family and then into the la Zouche family and other lower and higher noble families. The colonial-American Richard Palgrave family goes back in just a few generations to the noble English FitzAlan family. And virtually every noble family of later medieval times can be traced back to kings of England or Scotland.

Like the Bulkeley and Palgrave families, some other gateway families have had their royal lines so well documented, that for many twentieth-century Americans the problem in joining an hereditary society has been more one of proving the American side to the gateway ancestor than to have to worry about the English side at all. This is true in connection even with the Royal Bastards, most of whose members trace their royal lines through just a handful of gateway ancestors, such as Bulkeley, Palgrave, Thomas Dudley, Jeremy Clarke, the Deighton sisters, Anne Marbury, Samuel Appleton, John Drake, George Reade, Henry Batte, and a few others. More will be said later in this chapter on some of the better proved gateway ancestors, as well as on some of those still accepted, but on weaker evidence.

It follows then that most work on royal-British genealogy really involves much more research on the American side. Very few new royal-British lines are being discovered, and usually those who discover them are highly experienced and knowledgeable genealogists who are known, among other things, for being specialists in this type of work. There is always room for newcomers, though, provided those newcomers recognize the need to study what has been done in the past, to understand what makes a valid royal line and why some so-called royal lines are invalid, and to educate oneself in both the techniques and the available materials of twelfth- to seventeenth-century British genealogy.

The easiest way for a beginner to find a new royal line is to concentrate on the immediate generations just before a gateway ancestor came to America. A good number of gateway ancestors have already had their parental and geographical origins in England discovered and published, and they represent a good starting point for research using British sources.[7] Perhaps even more promising are those cases where the English origin of the gateway ancestor has not yet been traced back to a time, place, and family in Britain, and that includes the great majority of gateway ancestors.[8] As newer versions of the International Genealogical Index for England are made available by the LDS Family History Library, even genealogists with relatively little experience have the opportunity of making new English origin discoveries.

Royal lines once considered valid are being demolished just about as fast as new ones are being discovered. It is most helpful for the student of royal lines to be aware of these invalid lines, why they were once considered valid, and how they have been shown not to be valid. Examples of some such lines will be given below.

Lines No Longer Considered Valid

John Dingley. I hope I put to rest once and for all the widely dispersed story that John Dingley, the seventeenth-century blacksmith immigrant who lived in Marshfield, Plymouth Colony, was a descendant of King Edward III, going back to that king in but surprisingly few generations.[9] The claim for the royal line was made by a descendant in the male line of the American John Dingley in a published family history, and once published, of course, it assumed a life of its own. The claim was based on the observation that the noble Dingley family in England had a son John (baptized in 1594), who disappeared from the records without marriage or burial. Ah, ha, the name's the same, and so the conclusion was drawn and written for the usual perpetuation. A man of a noble family disappears from the records in England, and somewhat later a man of the same name appears in New England as a blacksmith of unknown origin. Royal genealogy is not that easy. It is sufficient to say that no evidence was given, and that should end the claim; it should not be necessary to give the evidence against the claim, but in my article I did for the benefit of anyone interested. This example is typical of many claims of royal ancestry based on complete lack of evidence beyond a name.

John Washburn. The John Washburn claim would seem to stand on slightly firmer ground, but only because the difficult part of crossing the Atlantic is well proven. It is a fact that we can identify the immigrant John Washburn who came to Plymouth Colony no later than 1633, and we can see that he is identical with the John Washburn baptized in Bengeworth, Worcestershire, England, in 1596. The American immigrant John Washburn can be traced back to his great-grandfather John Washburn, also of Bengeworth. Then we find the same fatal jump as in the John Dingley claim. A John Washburn of a family with known noble ancestry in Wichenford, Worcestershire, some twenty miles away from Bengeworth, had a son, John, who later disappears from Wichenford records. The claim is then made that "it is not difficult to imagine the reasons why and the circumstances under which John struck out from Wichenford and migrated to the neighborhood of Evesham."[10] James Davenport, author of the quoted line, then goes on to explain away the fact that no John Washburn was mentioned in the will of the claimed father, John Washburn, because the father had remarried. He argues that the estate would have gone to the older son by the first wife, while the younger sons by the second wife would have become the father's favorites to the exclusion of the in-between son, whom Davenport calls the John Washburn of Bengeworth. The key word of this delightful tale is found in the phrase "It is not difficult to imagine," clearly showing that his identification is based on imagination. Another author, E. A. B. Barnard, however, completely demolishes the claim by showing that there were Washburn families in the neighborhood of Bengeworth for centuries prior to this time, and therefore it is superfluous and unreasonable to have to look outside Bengeworth for the origins of the John Washburn in question unless there are other compelling reasons for it.[11] More of the name's the same. Evidence, none.

William Dungan. In 1972 a claim was published that William Dungan (whose wife Frances (Latham) Dungan and daughter Barbara Dungan migrated to Newport, Rhode Island, in the seventeenth century) was the son of Judge Thomas Dungan, through whom the line went back to King John of England.[12] Some of the argument for the claim was based on a man said to have been born ca. 1607 getting baptized in 1628 because the church in which his marriage of more than fourteen months later took place was claimed to have insisted that one of the two partners to the marriage be baptized there, all of which was more conjecture than proof. Again, though it should never be mandatory to produce negative proof of a claimed line which rests on no or insufficient evidence, it is always neater when such negative proof is available. In the Dungan case, such negative proof was given in an article by Thomas P. Dungan.[13] The author shows convincingly that Judge Thomas Dungan married Grace Palmer, and among his children was a William, born 1622, who was killed at the Battle of Leicester in 1645 without any known surviving issue. William Dungan the Perfumer, through whom the American line descends, died in London in 1636, and he was the son of another Thomas Dungan, not the judge.

William Wentworth. Elder William Wentworth, a seventeenth-century immigrant to New Hampshire, has been thought to have a valid royal line via the Marburys, Blounts, Gresleys, and Gernons to the Colvilles and Braoses, eventually going back to King Henry I. The evidence cited for the claim would seem impeccable, three very well documented secondary sources by extremely good genealogists.[14] This case demonstrates once again, however, the need to get behind secondary sources, no matter how impressive, and trace the evidence back to the ultimate source. In one of the three secondary sources, Meredith Colket, Jr., makes no claim for Gernon ancestry but merely shows Sir Thomas Blount married Margaret, daughter of Sir Thomas de Gresley. In another source, Madan writes that the wife of Sir Geoffrey de Gresley (great-grandfather of Thomas) married Margaret, daughter of Sir John Gernon, of Lanington, near Oxford, but he adds cautiously "it is very difficult to discover the parentage of this Margaret Gernon." In order for the claim to be valid, the Sir John Gernon of Lanington would have to be identical with the Sir John Gernon who married Alice Colville. This Sir John Gernon had three wives, of which Alice de Colville was the second; no evidence is given anywhere to show that Margaret Gernon was the daughter of the second wife, Alice de Colville. In the third source, Waters names one child of John and Alice (de Colville) Gernon as a son, John, and states that they had other children, but he does not name them, and he does not claim that John and Alice had a Margaret. Nowhere, then, do we have even an assertion in these three sources, much less evidence, that Sir John Gernon of Lanington (father of Margaret who married Sir Geoffrey de Gresley) was 1) identical with the Sir John Gernon (not recorded anywhere as of Lanington) who had three wives, and 2) that Margaret was by the second wife, Alice de Colville. However, in a current article I go beyond that to show the existence of a fourteenth-century legal document (transcribed in full as appendix C of this book) which proves conclusively that John and Alice (de Colville) Gernon had but three children, John, Isabel, and Katherine – no Margaret. Thus the William Wentworth royal line breaks at Sir John Gernon of Lanington, who remains unidentified as to wife or parentage.[15]

John Alsop. Though John Alsop of Alsop-in-the-Dale, Derbyshire, England, did not come to America, in his will (dated 1643) he mentioned two unnamed brothers and a sister living in New England. Clarence C. Baldwin showed in 1892 the probability that these siblings were Timothy and George Alsop and Elizabeth Alsop, who married Richard Baldwin, all of Connecticut.[16] Among other things, Elizabeth named a daughter Temperance, and the mother of John, Timothy, George, and Elizabeth was Temperance. A royal line has been accepted by some knowledgeable genealogists for the Alsop siblings, going back to King Henry II via his natural son William Longespee and the Audley, Meinill, and Basset families, but I find that I cannot accept the line as adequately proven. Too much of the line depends on undocumented charts, one first published in

1829 by a Mr. Glover covering some twenty-three generations of the Alsop family (with many of the generations being nothing more than a name), and the other a pedigree given in Nichol's County Leicester,[17] cited as sole source for some seven generations. Experience has well shown how unreliable such charts can be. As far as I am concerned, the line is unacceptable unless and until better evidence can be produced.

Alice Freeman and William Sargent. Both lines are found in the current (fifth) edition of *Ancestral Roots,* going through Giffords, Throckmortons, and Besfords to Alexander de Besford, who had been believed to be the grandson of Robert and Joan (Corbet) Harley. A good number of Americans descend from one or the other of these two gateway ancestors. (Joan Corbet was believed to be a descendant of King John, this would depend on Margaret Verch Llywelyn being a daughter of Princess Joan, and this identification has been seriously questioned – see below.) An article by John G. Hunt and Henry J. Young showed the existence of two Robert Harleys, each having estates named Harley and Besford in both Shropshire and Worcestershire. It appeared from the evidence given in the article that Alexander Besford received estates of these names, and one other, from a Joan de Harley, whose maiden name was not known, the widow of a Robert Harley. Thus there seemed to be some coincidence both in surnames and the names of estates.[18] Because the chronology of the line was very tight (an average of about sixteen years each for five successive generations), the line had earlier been viewed with some suspicion, and the new finding made it appear more likely that the Joan, widow of Robert Harley, who was probably an ancestress of Alice Freeman and William Sargent, was not the royal-line-carrying Joan (Corbet) de Harley.[19] The line was no longer approved for Royal Bastard membership, and I continued the refusal to accept it based on this article.

Claimed Descendants of Princess Joan. Many Americans with royal lines find that, like *Mayflower* ancestors, they tend to come in clusters. Finding one such line frequently leads to finding others, and among royal lines held by a substantial number of Americans are those coming through the daughters of Prince Llywelyn the Great of Wales. But again, a recent article has put such descents in question.[20] The basic argument is that Welsh genealogy is different from English genealogy, which is certainly true, and one difference is that no distinction was made in the legitimacy of a man's children by his wife or by his concubines. Prince Llywelyn had married Princess Joan, an acknowledged illegitimate daughter of King

John, but Llywelyn was known to have had children by concubines. Since there was nothing in contemporary records stating that certain daughters of Llywelyn, who had married into the English nobility and were known to have American descendants, were specifically the daughters also of Llywelyn's only wife, Princess Joan, the matter of their maternity was inconclusive and indeterminate. Another factor was that again the chronology was rather tight.

Accordingly, William Addams Reitwiesner, the author of the article and my predecessor as Royal Bastard herald/genealogist, would no longer accept lines coming through these daughters as qualifying for membership, and I, after consulting with several expert genealogists, upheld this refusal. However, along with Walter Lee Sheppard, Jr., I believe that reasoning which might apply to the average Welshman of that time would not have necessarily applied to Llywelyn, who was struggling for acceptance by a Christian world in which illegitimacy was anathema in matters of inheritance. As mentioned in the article itself, "Llywelyn tried to bring Wales into line with contemporary principalities, in part by making his son Dafydd by Joan his sole heir instead of dividing his possessions among all his sons....As usual, changes at the top altered little underneath, and the Welsh continued in the system of partible inheritance until at least the 16th century." Here we have acknowledgment that in matters of inheritance Llywelyn went the English way, not the Welsh way. At this time the maternity of the questioned daughters (Gwladys's and Margred's maternity being the most important for American genealogists) must be considered indeterminate, but certainly the matter merits more study.

William Leete. Governor William Leete of Connecticut has been thought to have a very valid royal line. In fact, it has never been questioned before, but the facts given in chapter 5 force me to conclude that this particular line is wrong, and that Robert Freville's wife, Rose, was not the daughter of Sir Thomas and Margaret (Franceys) Peyton, as claimed by Weis and others. However, one modern source states that Rose, the mother of Judge George Freville, was the daughter of Anthony Haselden,[21] and this gives rise to a possibility – nothing more than a possibility at this time – of a replacement royal line. Certainly when we are dealing with a family of the higher English gentry (such as the Leetes) we may expect that some of the yet unexplored family connections might eventually branch into a royal line.

The above examples illustrate both the danger of accepting even documented royal lines without checking the documentation, and the difficulty of proving royal lines back through all of the many generations they inevitably involve. Now let me make a confession that is not often heard. Even though we genealogists who possess some authority or credentials in researching royal lines insist on seeing primary and direct evidence to support adequately every generation in a line, the truth is that we in fact accept many royal lines as valid without having every generation so proved. If we stuck to our guns and insisted on primary and direct evidence at every step in proving a pedigree, there would be far fewer accepted royal lines than appear today. In fact it is a rare royal line that can be proven solely by primary and direct evidence in all generations. Let's take a look at some royal lines that are generally accepted by knowledgeable genealogists but which rely on something less than the ideal.

Accepted Royal Lines with Some Weakness

John Alston of South Carolina. There is a royal line going through gateway ancestor John Alston, who died in South Carolina in 1719, as the son of William and Thomasine (Brooke) Alston of Bedfordshire, England. I have accepted this line as valid, as have other knowledgeable genealogists. The crucial generation, the parentage of immigrant John Alston, depends on three facts. First, an apprenticeship record shows that a John Alston, who became an apprentice in South Carolina in 1682, was the son of William Alston, gentleman, of Hammersmith, Middlesex (a suburb of London). Second, William and Thomasine (Brooke) Alston had a son named John baptized at Pavenham, Bedfordshire, on 25 February 1668. There is no direct evidence to connect these two facts. Are we just dealing with the name's the same again? The identification looks plausible, for John was the right age to become an apprentice in 1682. We have eliminated some possibilities of just dealing with a coincidence of names when we see that John's father in the apprenticeship document is a "gentleman," as was the William Alston of Bedfordshire. Though we have no evidence that the William of Bedfordshire resided at any time in the vicinity of London, he was a barrister and thus it was quite possible that at some point in his career he might have lived in a London suburb. With the third fact, we become a little more certain. The John Alston of South Carolina named children John, William, and Thomasine. John and

William were apparently named after himself and his father, and thus we know he favored family names. Thomasine is not a name found in the Alston family in general, but it was the name of the wife of William Alston of Bedfordshire. This is onomastic evidence (see chapter 6), and by itself it is not sufficient to prove a genealogical relationship. But in some cases it adds just enough to the other evidence to become important, and I think this is one such case. The evidence is not direct, though, and we must rely on making an assumption.

John Drake of Windsor, Connecticut. John Drake, who was born at Wiscombe, Devonshire, England, in 1601, definitely came to New England. A visitation specifically mentioned that he had emigrated to New England, and Kiepura presented primary evidence in an article to show quite clearly that in the 1633 will of a cousin of John Drake's father, John was mentioned as being in New England.[22] A competent genealogist with whom I correspond believes, however, that the royal line from John Drake of Windsor, Connecticut, is not valid. He bases his belief on various chronological problems which he intends to analyze in a future article, and he feels that there could have been two John Drakes in New England during early colonial decades, one with a royal line and the other John Drake of Windsor. Aside from the parentage of the gateway ancestor, there is also in this line some lack of primary evidence for some of the earlier generations. I have accepted this royal line for Royal Bastards, but I look forward also to seeing my correspondent's article when it is published.

Articles Need to Be Fully Documented

It is unfortunate that space is frequently limited in genealogical journals. Articles are often written by expert genealogists for other expert genealogists. Such articles may be well and sufficiently documented but still not give adequate verbatim excerpts from the documentation to put lesser experienced genealogists in a position to follow the reasoning behind the proof. They must take the word of the expert that the cited documents are in fact sufficient to make sound connections between each and every generation. I suspect, though, that we will see more and more articles in the future that are self-contained; that is, they can be fully understood on the basis of the text and not require having to look up the references to see what how the words prove the connection.

Accordingly, it is difficult to find textbook examples of fine and complete medieval genealogical work to help students see an entire line from an American gateway ancestor back to a king of England. More often, the student will have to settle for some of the excellent articles showing some self-contained parts pertinent to proving or disproving a royal line (but not the entire royal line) such as Mr. Dungan's article cited in endnote 13. For the intermediate student, some of G. Andrews Moriarty's articles, though a bit complex at times, are superb for study.[23] In appendix D, I present a new unpublished royal line which is self-contained and supported almost entirely by primary evidence (or by the *Complete Peerage*, which is the next best thing), but unfortunately it is somewhat flawed in the most recent generations. I understand that Colonel Charles M. Hansen, "The Barons of Wodhull with Observations on the Ancestry of George Elkinton, Emmigrant to New Jersey," *The Genealogist* 7-8 (1986-87):4-127, serves as a true self-contained textbook example of how to go about proving a royal line via primary direct evidence.

More such complete articles are needed. A mighty step forward was taken when it became the practice of authoritative genealogists to present articles with documentation. But for many intelligent, capable genealogists with less experience than the experts, documentation by itself, especially in an area like medieval genealogy which relies on so many relatively obscure and not easily available documents, is not enough. The reader should be led by the hand through verbatim excerpts of documents and shown specifically how each document supports the conclusion to which the writer is leading. Note that even the experts seldom check out all the references in an article such as Weis's on the ancestry of Governor William Leete (see above), and as a result the line has been accepted, though it is incorrect. In the courts lawyers are expected not only to present evidence, but to connect it as well. I think nothing less should be expected of genealogical writers.[24]

Notes

1. Cromwell's edict reminds me of what a high-ranking government official I used to work for once told me: "Gene, anytime I issue an order and get 25 percent compliance, I think I'm lucky." In some cases, Cromwell's edict did not get compliance until a hundred years later. The edict is transcribed in *The American Genealogist* 42 (1966):152-3. The *Phillimore Atlas and Index of Parish Registers,* edited by Cecil Humphery-Smith (Chichester, England, 1984), available from Genealogical Publishing Company, Baltimore, is an excellent source for English

county maps and tables showing parish boundaries, probate districts, and dates that each parish began keeping vital registers.

2. Professor David L. Greene points to Sir Anthony Wagner's *Drake in England* (New Hampshire Historical Society, 1970) as a superb study that traces American immigrant Robert Drake through the male line to the thirteenth century via the Great Malvern, Essex, manor court rolls, which began in 1248. Greene asks, "Is there any other thirteenth-century American immigrant of relatively humble origin whose male line has been traced fully to pre-1300?"

3. Gerald Hamilton-Edwards, *In Search of Ancestry* (London, 1974; reprinted 1976), 191-92.

4. Much social mobility occurred in steps – for example the child of a yeoman marrying a merchant's child; their child (or grandchild) marrying a minister's or army officer's child; their child marrying the child of a knight, and so on.

5. *Complete Peerage,* 13 vols. (London, 1910-59).

6. Donald Lines Jacobus, *The Bulkeley Genealogy: Reverend Peter Bulkeley. Being an Account of His Career, His Ancestry, the Ancestry of His Two Wives, and His Relatives in England and New England, Together with a Genealogy of His Descendants through the Seventh American Generation* (New Haven, 1933).

7. Gary Boyd Roberts, ed., *English Origins of New England Families,* first and second series, 3 vols. each (Baltimore, 1984, 1985), reprints many of the articles from *The New England Historical and Genealogical Register* showing one or several of the English generations immediately prior to the American immigrant. Henry F. Waters, *Genealogical Gleanings in England,* 2 vols. (Boston, 1901; reprinted Baltimore, 1981) should also be checked by anyone seeking English origins who is not particularly fond of reinventing wheels. Though efforts have since been made in many cases to trace some of these families even further back, there are still many good research opportunities available.

8. Robert Charles Anderson, "Seventeenth Century New England Research: A Review Essay and Status Report," *The Genealogist* 6 (1985):251-58, takes issue with Gary Boyd Robert's claim in the latter's Introduction to *English Origins of New England Families,* first series, 1:5, that "of the 25,000 or so immigrants to New England between 1620 and 1650, the English origins of approximately one-fifth – 5,000 or more – are known or have been reasonably hypothesized." Anderson believes that the English origins of only some 1,500 or so are known, and these would comprise some 30 percent of the total heads of families in New England between 1620 and 1650. Regardless of the absolute numbers, both writers would agree that the majority of gateway New England ancestors, at least in this period (which is the period of main immigration in the seventeenth century), are still of unknown British origins.

9. Eugene A. Stratton, "John Dingley of Marshfield [Mass.] and What the Navy Driver Saw," *The American Genealogist* 61 (1986):234-40.

10. James Davenport, *The Washbourne Family of Little Washbourne & Wichenford in the County of Worcester* (London, 1907), 36.

11. E. A. B. Barnard, *Some Notes on the Evesham Branch of the Washbourne Family* (Evesham, 1914), 7ff.

12. Robert J. Curfman, "Findings Regarding the Ancestry of William Dungan...," *Forebears,* 15 (1972):103-06.

13. Thomas P. Dungan, "Correcting the Ancestry of William Dungan, Perfumer of St. Martin-in-the-Fields, London," *The Genealogist* 4 (1983):187-202.

14. Falconer Madan, *The Gresleys of Drakelow* (Oxford, 1899); Meredith Colket, Jr., *The English Ancestry of Anne Marbury Hutchinson and Katherine Marbury Scott* (Philadelphia, 1936); and Robert Edmond Chester Waters, *Genealogical Memoirs of the Extinct Family of Chester of Chicheley, their Ancestors and Descendants*, 2 vols. (London, 1878).

15. Eugene A. Stratton, "The Cutting of a Royal Line – William Wentworth of N.H.," *The Genealogist* 7-8 (1986-87):127-31. Please note, however, that when an American line gets back to lesser nobility of the fourteenth century, as in this case, there are good possibilities of finding a replacement royal line, though none has been found yet for William Wentworth.

16. Clarence C. Baldwin, "Alsop and Harlakenden," *The New England Historical Genealogical Register* 46 (1892):366-69.

17. *The New England Historical and Genealogical Register* 46:366-367; J. Nichols, *History and Antiquities of the County of Leicester...*, 4 vols. (1792-1811; reprinted, 1971), 2:531-32. Jacobus, in editing the Ackley-Bosworth genealogy, observes that "one of [Meinill-DeThick-Basset-Alsop] pedigrees gives eighteen generations behind Elizabeth, but the first twelve generations are little more than names without verification by contemporary documents to establish the precise descent."

18. "Ravens or Pelicans: Who Was Joan de Harley?" *The Genealogist* 1 (1980):27-39.

19. William Sargent, however, still has a valid royal line going back to King Alfred the Great, as shown by Moriarty in *The New England Historical and Genealogical Register* 74 (1920):231-37, 267-83; 75 (1921):57-63; 79 (1925):358-78. Since the text was written, a new 6th edition of *Ancestral Roots* has been published, which drops royal claims for the Freeman and Sargent lines via the Harleys (but retains the correct Sargent line to Alfred the Great).

20. William Addams Reitwiesner, "The Children of Joan, Princess of North Wales," *The Genealogist* 1:80-95.

21. S. T. Bindoff, *The House of Commons* (London, 1982), 2:173. Bindoff in turn cites references, not all of which have been checked.

22. Genevieve Tylee Kiepura, "John Drake's English Connections," *The American Genealogist* 41:239; see also W. Lee Sheppard's articles in the *National Genealogical Society Quarterly* 59 (1971):255-61; and 60 (1972):32-34. Since writing the text on John Drake, I have heard that an article will be published by another genealogist disproving this line, and still another article will disprove John Botetourt as a qualifying ancestor for the Royal Bastards.

23. See especially Moriarty's series of articles on the royal line of the Reverend William Sargent, mentioned in endnote 19 above.

24. Another article not sufficiently documented is Charles Fitch-Northen, "From Charlemagne to President Rutherford B. Hayes," *The American Genealogist* 57 (1981):31-33. I understand that the author of this article has additional evidence which will be given in a forthcoming issue of *The Genealogist*. The article that appeared in *The American Genealogist* was a draft that was published inadvertently.

Chapter 12

Royal Genealogy –
Ways and Means

English research is a field in itself, and because of the great difference in conditions, a vast amount of special knowledge is needed before the genealogist is equipped to be an expert or specialist in English research.
—Donald Lines Jacobus

The outstanding feature of feudal genealogy is that, while the records upon which it is based are most voluminous, they are largely of a different sort from those employed for the construction of pedigrees from the sixteenth century onwards.
—George Andrews Moriarty

I cannot repeat it enough: The best way to get started in royal genealogy is to dissect published documented lines and see how the compilers reached their conclusions. And if the cited sources are not the ultimate sources, then to go further back yet to find and study the ultimate sources. This implies having a large and perhaps specialized genealogical library available, and perhaps that is the first step in deciding if one wants to get involved first-hand in royal genealogy. It cannot be done without the proper tools. There are a number of people well versed in a second-hand way in royal genealogy. This, too, can be a satisfactory pursuit. People who feel they cannot for one reason or another engage directly in primary source medieval genealogy can read the published writings of J. Horace Round, G. Andrews Moriarty, Donald L. Jacobus, John I. Coddington, Milton Rubincam, Walter Lee Sheppard, David H. Kelley,

Neil D. Thompson, Charles M. Hansen, John G. Hunt, Sir Anthony Wagner, and others, and they themselves can become experts on published royal lines. They can start by buying *Ancestral Roots* and *Magna Charta Sureties,* and then, if they wish to spend the money, they can purchase the newly reprinted, four-pages-on-one edition of the *Complete Peerage.*[1] Those becoming familiar with these various writings will simultaneously pick up some knowledge also of the techniques and materials used in medieval English research. They will be limited only in the amount of original research they can do and in their ability to "keep the experts honest."

Basic Materials

The three sources just mentioned are starting points for both those who want to acquire limited, secondary-source research capability and those who seek to work with primary materials. Accordingly, a brief description of these sources is in order. *Ancestral Roots* and *Magna Charta Sureties* were first compiled by the Reverend Frederick Lewis Weis and in later editions revised and corrected by Walter Lee Sheppard, Jr. The former book is currently in its sixth edition, and the latter is in its third edition; new editions will probably be available in the future – a completely revised, combined edition, would be most helpful. Both books use the same format, that of starting a line with a medieval king (usually of England but also of a number of other European countries) or with one of the men who acted as sureties for the Magna Charta. The beginning person is ordinarily number one in the line, and the line is continued with a child of number one, followed by a child of that person, and so on down to an American gateway immigrant. Each numbered generation in the line is identified by name; spouse; dates and places of birth, death, and marriage; cross references to other lines, as these items are available; and is concluded with abbreviated documentation.

Each line is therefore a single line of descent, but by the cross references a researcher can obtain, when available, a number of lines upward for the American gateway ancestor. Though a number of starting points (king or Magna Charta surety) are given with more then one line (so that a number of children, grandchildren, great-grandchildren, and so on of the starting person can be identified), the books are not intended to be complete in identifying all the children, grandchildren, and other descendants of any given starting person; thus they cannot be used to compile comprehensive royal- and noble-family histories. The documentation shown for each generation in a line is what makes the books so usable. Weis used the best documentation available to him regardless of whether it was primary or secondary, and, after the first edition was published, he was able to make additions, deletions, and other changes as readers notified him of the need. Sheppard has continued adding to and correcting the newer editions. The very number of editions over a relatively short period of time shows how fluid is our knowledge of medieval genealogy and how fast newer discoveries are being made and published. Sheppard gives a caveat in the third edition of *Magna Charta Sureties* that all users should constantly have in mind:

> The reader should note that not all lines have been verified, nor do the notations of corrections in a line indicate that all other generations have been checked and found to be correct. All compiled pedigrees in any book, including this one, are subject to copying or typographical errors no matter how careful the author, editor, or printer may be, and should be used with caution. Even though we believe this to be one of the most carefully compiled and most accurate books in this field, the user should verify all statements and dates with source material before transferring them to a lineage blank for application for membership in an hereditary society, or before incorporating them into a published genealogy.

Thus these books are not "proof," but are excellent guides, very desirable to have at hand when trying to keep up with the intricacies of intermarriage and the progeny of the medieval nobility.

Complete Peerage, originally published in eight volumes between 1887 and 1898, was compiled by George Edward Cockayne, or GEC as he called himself in the first edition. A second much revised and enlarged edition was published between 1910 and 1959 with various compilers (starting with Vicary Gibbs) continuing the work through successive volumes. This second edition, sometimes referred to as the *New Complete Peerage*, was completed in twelve volumes, with volume 12 issued in two books. Volume 13 came out in 1940 to cover peers created between 1907 and 1938 (and thus is not of much use to American genealogists), and a volume 14, containing additions and corrections to the earlier volumes, was to be published.

Peerages are given alphabetically by title, which is sometimes identical with surname, as is usually the case with barons, but is generally different with the higher peers, for example, the earldom of Oxford being held during the period of interest to us by the de Vere family or the earldom of Arundel being held by the FitzAlan family. There is no index (its biggest drawback), and thus only the title holder, together with whatever members of his or her family are given, can be looked up. It should be kept in mind that knights and baronets (the latter title not even created until 1611) are not peers. From the lowest to the highest, the titles of the peers of England are baron (baroness), viscount (viscountess), earl (countess), marquis (marchioness), and duke (duchess). *Complete Peerage* essentially gives the succession of each title from father to son, grandson, or nephew (or less often to female survivors) as the case may be; or from one family to another; or into abeyance, dormancy, or extinction as such changes occurred. Thus there is usually an abundance of information on heirs to the title, but lesser amounts on younger sons and daughters, some of whom are mentioned while some are not named at all.

Complete Peerage gives a considerable amount of authentic and valuable biographical and genealogical information on the title holder in narrative form including parentage, marriages, vital information when available, and career, with dates when known. Date of birth is seldom known directly, but dates are frequently found for succession to the peerage, marriage, and death, and thus often the date of birth can be approximated. What makes *Complete Peerage* such an authority that most knowledgeable genealogists are willing to accept it as tantamount to a primary source is the painstaking research by the compilers leading to footnotes which in the aggregate might comprise half the material in the work. Anyone seeking a survey of what kind of documents are used in medieval British genealogy need go no further than the footnotes of *Complete Peerage*. Virtually every type of known pertinent source document is used, frequently with extensive verbatim excerpts, so that we have in *Complete Peerage* the next best thing to the original. It would certainly deserve being called one of the seven wonders of the genealogical world.

Errors in *Complete Peerage* are few and far between. They exist, but as an amazingly small fraction of the whole (see chapter 9, which mentions such errors). Because of the large span of time between volumes, sometimes an error in an earlier volume is corrected in a later volume. Anytime a genuine error of identification can be found and thoroughly documented, it merits an article in itself for one of the genealogical journals. If *Complete Peerage* could do the impossible and cover all the children of the nobility as it does the heir to the title, then medieval British genealogy would be reduced to little more than consulting this work (but much of the pleasure of research and discovery would be gone, too). As it is, peripheral information can be most helpful at times on the younger sons and daughters – essentially it is a matter of luck whether the information one needs on the non-titled children is there or not. Certainly *Complete Peerage* should always be one of the starting points when dealing with families which may be of the nobility. For lines involving Scottish nobility, Sir James Balfour Paul, *The Scots Peerage*, 9 vols. (Edinburgh, 1904-14), is invaluable.

Background Sources

There is little in the way of textbook material on royal genealogy. The chapters in *Genealogical Research: Methods and Sources,*[2] written by G. Andrews Moriarty, John Insley Coddington, Milton Rubincam, Sir Anthony Wagner, and others in part 4, are a helpful introduction: chapter 1, "English Feudal Genealogy"; and chapter 2, "Royal and Noble Genealogy"; together with subsequent chapters on England, Wales, Scotland, France, Germany, and other countries. The in-text bibliographies given in these chapters are highly recommended. Walter Lee Sheppard's *Feudal Genealogy,*[3] is a good overview of the materials used in researching this area. It is worth repeating one of Sheppard's cautions, if only because it is so vital to give it more than lip service: "Never, and we underline this, try to research a pedigree in a time period and geographic area the history of which you do not know." Note also Sheppard's bibliography, which lists some of the most pertinent books and published records available, both general and specialized. Sir Anthony Wagner's *English Genealogy* is another virtually indispensable guide to the subject.[4]

For general historical background, the *Oxford History of England* series, especially the volumes covering the twelfth to seventeenth centuries, can be very helpful. Any of the books by J. Horace Round will be highly pertinent and educational and will make fascinating reading. I particularly recommend (if one can find them, for these books are out of print) two works by American authorities on medieval England: *The Reign of King John,* and *A Baronial Family in Medieval England: The Clares.*[5] One of the most valuable small booklets for medieval British genealogists is the guide to publications from the British National Archives, *Government Publications Sectional List Number 24,* frequently revised and available from Her Majesty's Stationery Office in London; it is also sold by some dealers in the United States specializing in official British publications. This lists availability and cost of the published volumes of records, the various roll series, inquisitions post mortem, calendars of state papers, and other official state documents dating back to the early Norman kings. There are other books and published materials available and helpful on the subject, but this mention is not intended to be a comprehensive bibliography. Those named here are a starter list, and they in turn will lead to others. In fact, if the books specifically named here were all obtained, or otherwise readily available (this is not unreasonable, for they are few in number, and not expensive, except for *Complete Peerage*), the reader would have a good basic library. Add to this list the hundreds of pertinent articles from the leading journals such as the American ones (*The American Genealogist, The New England Historical and Genealogical Register, National Genealogical Society Quarterly,* and *The Genealogist*) and the British ones *The Genealogist, Miscelanea Heraldica et Genealogica,* and various "Notes and Queries books," among others), and the person who reads them all diligently will be on his or her way toward becoming a knowledgeable medieval genealogist.

Getting Started

Historians today usually place the dividing line between modern times and medieval times as the reign of Henry VIII, and 1538 is as good a year as any to put a fine point on the matter. British genealogical research in the 1500s and 1600s is considerably different from research in medieval times, and people wishing to trace further a seventeenth-century immigrant American ancestor who has already been taken back to Britain, need to familiarize themselves with still different techniques and materials. Thus getting across the Atlantic is a first step, and then going back another century or so must be accomplished before getting into the pure medieval aspect. A recommended textbook for English genealogical research in general, including some coverage of medieval sources, is David E. Gardner and Frank Smith, *Genealogical Research in England and Wales,* 3 volumes (Salt Lake City, 1956, 1959, 1964). Another is Gerald Hamilton-Edwards, *In Search of Ancestry,* revised (London and Chichester, 1974). There are other good books to guide one on both sixteenth- and seventeenth-century English research and medieval English research, but I know of no good how-to book concentrating exclusively and in the desired fine detail on medieval English genealogy. The LDS Family History Library in Salt Lake City has good collections of both medieval and sixteenth- and seventeenth-century (as well as later) material for British genealogical research, though it should be noted that the British collection is not as extensive in terms of percentages of the whole as are some other collections, especially the Scandinavian collection. Of course, much of the collection of the Family History Library can also be made available at their Family History Centers (branch libraries) located all over the United States as well as in many places abroad. Especially valuable are the microfilms of British probate records and the International Genealogical Index (see chapter 1).

Finding British origins of colonial American settlers is again a subject in itself. Much has been done in *The New England Historical and Genealogical Register* articles over the years, and some of the best articles have been collected in the first and second series of *English Origins of New England Families,* 3 volumes each, selected by Gary Boyd Roberts (Baltimore, 1984, 1985). Among the other journals, *The American Genealogist* is especially known for its articles identifying the English parentage and geographical homes of American colonists. I know of no textbook as such that specializes in finding such British origins, but again a study of the articles themselves is one of the best ways to learn the techniques.

An older book collecting previously published *The New England Historical and Genealogical Register* material on English origins of early American settlers, but still a most valuable one, is Henry F. Waters, *Genealogical Gleanings in England,* 2 volumes (Boston, 1901; reprinted Baltimore, 1981). More recently Peter Wilson Coldham, F.A.S.G., has compiled several books giving abstracts of English records which mentioned people of the times known to be living in America.[6]

Best Possibilities for Finding a Royal Line

If you can go back to a number of English colonial settlers, and you would like to see if you can do research that will succeed in tracing their British antecedents with a view of possibly finding a royal line, I suggest you concentrate your efforts on those gateway ancestors which have the most promise of success. Especially promising are the many ministers who came to the English colonies, for they usually were university graduates at a time when most people who went to universities came from the gentry. Let us view the general picture, starting with the fact of mobility among the British classes. Primogeniture concentrated the great fortunes in but a few hands. Younger sons frequently had to make their own way in the world, and daughters who were not heiresses (heiresses usually being those daughters who had no surviving brother) frequently had to marry down a step in the social classes. At the same time new wealth, especially in the merchant class, was pushing a number of families up-wards, where the merchant's son might sometimes marry the knight's daughter. The child of such a marriage would have a merchant's line and a knight's line, and the knight's line might be traced back in a few genera-tions to the younger son of a baron or an earl and so on upward. When Puritanism became widespread among the general population in England, including the gentry as well as some of the noble families, some of the sons of these families became ministers, and a number of these emigrated to the colonies. Thus, as a group, colonial ministers offer a promising opportunity for successful search for a royal line.

There was a relatively large number of colonial ministers, and their descendants are quite numerous in the United States today. It is easier to find a colonial minister line first than a royal line, and once a minister line is found, there is probably a greater chance for successful search for a royal line than with any other group of colonists except for the leaders (such as the governors) at the top in colonial America – a much smaller group (though of course if you have a valid line back to a colonial gover-nor, do not neglect this likewise promising opportunity to find a royal line). Among colonial ministers, the best leads are those whose ancestry has already been traced back several generations within England but for whom a royal line has not yet been found.

Of course, it is axiomatic that one of the first steps in conducting re-search to find the English origins of a colonial American is to see what wheels have already been invented, what material has already been published. If you already have traced an ancestor to a family in England, then among the first places to look are three books which list by surname the various British pedigrees which have been published over the years in periodicals and books. The first of these books attempts to include all pedigrees showing any descent of three generations in the male line. The criteria for inclusion was modified in the next two, and the third book given below included "references to any fairly long passage of a family's history." Of the three books, each successive one was intended to cover especially any publications occurring since the previous one. Peerages are not included, but of course these can be found in *Complete Peerage*. These three immensely helpful guides can be found in most libraries with large genealogical sections:

> George Marshall, *The Genealogist's Guide* (1903);
>
> J. B. Whitmore, *A Genealogical Guide – An Index to British Pedigrees in Continuation of Marshall's Genealogist's Guide* (London, 1953);
>
> Geoffrey B. Barrow, *The Genealogist's Guide: An Index to Printed British Pedigrees and Family Histories, 1950-1975* (London and Chicago, 1977).

Though the three above books include reference to some American publications containing British pedigree information, they are not as comprehensive with American sources as British. Therefore, you should check insofar as possible to see what has been published in the United States. Unfortunately no thorough guide, such as Marshall, Whitmore, or Barrow, exists for the United States. At this time, probably the most thorough way for one having the time, is to review the annual index of each of the major American genealogical journals both for articles and for book reviews. Glancing over these journals can be most interesting for its own sake, and I have done it more than two or three times, each time finding something new as my genealogical knowledge and interests have increased. An index for the first sixty volumes of *The American Genealogist* has been produced, but for some reason it leaves out the articles which deal exclusively with British medieval genealogy. A comprehensive index for *The New England Historical and Genealogical Register* is being planned but will not be available when this book first comes out. *The Genealogical Periodical Annual Index* (*GPAI*) can be helpful for medieval British research, but there is the danger of missing something if these annual indices are used exclusively without covering also the annual indices of the journals themselves. One should not stop after checking in a single index.

The International Genealogical Index (IGI) of the LDS Family History Library should also be one of the first places to check for antecedents of a gateway ancestor. If you are looking for a name such as Augustine Castlethwaite, the job is easier than trying to find a John Smith (of course, there is not the slightest difficulty in finding a John Smith, but that is the trouble). The IGI for England is divided by county, and those people born or getting married in that county for which records have been located and put on microfiche will appear by alphabetical order. Thus for your Augustine Castlethwaite, you will have to search each of some forty counties. When you find the name, keep in mind some of the techniques mentioned earlier in this book. Use a whole-family approach, and get all the data on all the Castlethwaites of that area and time. Remember that the IGI is for finding clues, and do not stop there; trace the IGI entry back to a parish register, and then find the parish register. The register might show that some of the names contained typographical errors. It can also give additional information, such as occupations, titles (Mr., Esq., Captain, etc.), and family connections (such as showing that an uncle was a godfather). The IGI will give baptism and marriage information but not burial records, while the original parish register will often have all three types of vital records.

If the parish register has been published, then it is almost certain that the information will be in the IGI. However, some parish priests have not allowed their registers to be published or used for IGI purposes, but they will respond to inquiries from individuals in the United States or allow visitors to England to see the registers. In such cases it is customary to give a donation to the priest of around £3 or the equivalent. Very recently the British government has required all parish priests to submit copies of their registers to the county record offices, but it is not known how complete compliance has been. See endnote 1 of chapter 11. *Boyd's Marriage Index* is quite helpful for locating parish registers. As two examples of what can be done with parish registers, see the series of articles by Robert Leigh Ward mentioned in chapter 3, see also my article "Some Stratton Notes."[7]

Check For Wills

The above articles by Ward and Stratton reconstruct families using parish registers and wills. In sixteenth- and seventeenth-century England, wills were much more common than earlier and should be checked, though knowing where to look for them involves some prior knowledge. There are a number of books giving detailed information on locating wills, and the LDS Family History Library has put together much guidance material to help one find the appropriate microfilms where the original wills have been photocopied. Since this book is intended more to help in analyzing information rather than in describing sources, it will not go into the detail found in books written for the latter purposes. In general, wills – which at the time were administered by the church not the state – were maintained by different ecclesiastical jurisdictions, and the larger the estate, the more likely the will would be handled by a higher jurisdiction. Though exceptions seem to be sometimes the rule in English probate matters, usually a person's will would be proved in an archdeacon's court if all the property involved was located within the boundaries of that archdeaconry. Property in two or more archdeaconries under a single bishop would be proved in that bishop's court. If a person left property in two or more dioceses, the will would be proved in the court of one of England's two archbishops, the Prerogative Court of Canterbury (PCC) or the Prerogative Court of York (PCY). To complicate matters, some areas had special peculiars, where the jurisdictions (and the fees that probates produced) belonged to special church officials who need not even be of that area. Thus looking for a will can be a matter of trial and error. Obviously the beginner needs guides here. Some of the publications mentioned elsewhere in this book have sections on where to find wills, but more detailed information can be found in books written specifically for the purpose.[8] A valuable auxiliary book for information on both parish registers and probate jurisdictions is *The Phillimore Atlas and Index of Parish Registers,* edited by Cecil Humphery-Smith (Chichester, 1984, later published in the United States by the Genealogical Book Company in Baltimore). This gives maps of all counties showing the parishes and probate jurisdictions, plus charts by county and parish giving the dates for which parish registers exist, the dates for parish registers included in the IGI at the time,[9] availability of marriage indexes, and other similar information. Mr. Humphery-Smith is also the author of *A Genealogist's*

Bibliography (Baltimore, 1985), which is helpful as a county-to-county guide to various published primary and other English records.

The abstracts by F. G. Emmison of wills in Essex are other helpful leads to bridging the Atlantic.[10] Essex wills are especially important, for Essex is one of the three East Anglian counties from where most colonial New England immigrants originated. Emmison has also published special purpose abstracts of Essex wills as well as some Bedfordshire parish registers, which are of help to genealogists. There are also two volumes of will abstracts from Suffolk, England, another of the East Anglian counties.[11] These books include years when American immigrants are most likely to be found mentioned in English wills.

Research Techniques for the Medieval Period

The central feature of medieval records was their emphasis on keeping track of land and who had the legal right to possess it, particularly as it passed from one person to another. Land was the source of riches, power, prestige, and family pride, and the one fact of overwhelming importance was the need of people of the time to keep records of who was entitled to possess this or that landed estate. We can spend all day tossing around terms like muniments, cartularies, feet of fines, inquisitions post mortem, fine rolls, and other rolls, but they will mostly be of value to the genealogist because they show land passing from one generation to another. The particular distinctions between these terms and others can be mastered with time and use, but it is enough to know at the start that they exist, and that in great part they have to do with land records or with payments of money to the king from the nobles and payments to the nobles from others further down the hierarchical order. Moriarty in his above-mentioned "English Feudal Genealogy" gives brief definitions of some of the rolls and other series of documents (well-worth reading), and this book will define a few further below. Sidney Painter in *The Reign of King John,* mentioned above, gives much practical information and usage on the various types of contemporary documents. William Farrer in his writings demonstrates most convincingly how land records can be used to reconstruct family histories.[12]

An overview of the English land tenure system with special reference to aspects that would be helpful to the genealogist is given as appendix B. The records of the various types of land transactions, plus a few non-land records, are used by genealogists to determine directly or indirectly many of the details helpful in reconstructing genealogical relationships. For example, one of the most important details is to know, if only approximately, when someone was born, for that fact can help us check the chronology to see if we have the right family. The date that a ward pays relief to the king to take livery of his lands is a good indication that he was about twenty-one years of age at that time, though there are known cases of a minor receiving his estate. Keep in mind that there were many fine details in feudal customs, that they changed from time to time, and that there were exceptions. Further, keep in mind that even the experts can differ (sometimes rather violently) on definitions or interpretations of feudal terms. But there are enough generally agreed upon interpretations and techniques to serve as guidelines in helping us extract from some of these records the kind of information most useful to form genealogical hypotheses, which are then subject to subsequent verification.

Types of Medieval Records

Let us look at some of the records frequently used by genealogists (appendix B will be helpful in understanding some of the terms):

Inquisitions Post Mortem (IPM). In my research I have found the *Calendars of Inquisitions Post Mortem* to be of the greatest use. Calendar in this case means a published abstract of the original document, translated into English, and the published volumes are complete with index. IPMs were made by an official of the king called the escheator. The escheator began an investigation (inquisition) on the death of a tenant in chief, and thus this type of document is of use only when we are dealing with someone who held land directly of the king (although the information contained in the IPM might give us very valuable information on younger sons and daughters also). IPM records usually identify the heir to a deceased tenant in capite's lands. Sometimes heirs had to prove that they were of legal age, for if they were still minors, they would become wards of the king, and consequently lose more of the profits of the estate to him than would result from just paying a fine for livery of the estate. Sometimes the inheritance might be disputed, in which case witnesses might give testimony that could reveal many family relationships (see especially appendix C).

As an example of what can be found in an IPM, one of 1499 showed that Maurice and Elizabeth de Bruyn had Sir Henry Bruyn (elsewhere proved to be their son) as their heir, and Henry's heirs were his daughters, Alice and Elizabeth. Alice married Robert Harleston, and Alice and Robert had their son John Harleston as their heir. John predeceased his mother, and his son Clement, age five at the time of the IPM, was Alice's heir. Five generations in one document! Not all IPMs are so revealing, but as a whole they are invaluable. The Harleston example discussed here is from a generation-by-generation genealogy given in appendix D; elsewhere in that appendix there will be found other examples, such as one showing how IPMs can provide indirect evidence to help identify genealogical relationships. One word of caution: In reciting their family's genealogy over long periods of time, medieval witnesses could be subject to errors of memory just as much as people today, and we often find that a recited line of five or six generations has left out one or more generations. Names, ages, and relationships in IPMs can sometimes be wildly wrong, though usually they are close enough to the truth so as not to detract from the overall value of the document. Note also that if a deceased person were a tenant in chief in more than one county, there could be an IPM in each of the pertinent counties, and sometimes information in one IPM will differ from information on the same person given in another IPM.

Rolls. Documents were made on parchment, often pieces of sheepskin measuring some forty-eight by fourteen inches and then sewn together in a roll. Some of the most important of these were Charter Rolls, Patent Rolls, and Close Rolls. Charter rolls recorded charters granted by the king and were maintained by the king's chancery for the king's information, not for public information. Patent Rolls recorded letters written in the name of the king as an open matter. Some such letters conveyed the king's orders as they related to various individuals, and some could be used as passports showing that the bearer was under the king's protection. Close rolls also recorded letters, but these were private letters, such as orders to a sheriff. Though historians can define the various rolls with greater detail than given here, any given document might appear on some roll other than the one expected. Sidney Painter observes that any document of interest to the king and government might be entered on whatever roll happened to have some blank space.[13] Fine Rolls are especially helpful for they record the fines called relief, which an heir of a tenant in chief paid to the king before being entitled to take control of his estate. There are many other rolls, such as Curia Regis Rolls recording the disposition of legal matters in the king's courts. The originals are maintained by the Public Record Office, which has been publishing them gradually over many years.

As an example of a Close Roll document, a letter from the king dated 30 November 1395 was addressed to the king's escheator in Gloucestershire, who was instructed to give livery of the manor of Tettebury to Margaret, the wife of Thomas de Brewose, knight. The king assigned her the lands of her deceased husband which had come into the king's hands by reason of the death of Thomas de Brewose and the minority of his son, Thomas, who had died while a ward of the king (see chart 4, page 274). The lands remained in the king's hands because of the minority of Joan, the sister and heir of the younger Thomas, but Joan also died while a ward of the king. The assignment of the land to the widow Margaret was made with the assent of William Heroun, knight, who was married to Elizabeth, the cousin and heir of Joan.[14]

Observe what we have here. This is not some undocumented secondary source written 500 years after the event by an inexperienced genealogist who draws unwarranted conclusions from the fact that a *Mayflower* passenger had a similar surname to that of the noble de Warenne family. This is not information given by some parvenu merchant family to a venal herald for inclusion in a visitation to be held by the College of Arms. This is not the conclusion of a modern researcher expanding guesswork based on vague clues to unwarranted absolute identifications. This is not an assertion that every noble family in England with a son disappearing from the records must be represented in America by any blacksmith bearing the same name. This is positive, direct, contemporary, primary evidence. It is an unequivocal statement of family relationships determined by a contemporary jury under the direction of the king's escheator as a by-product of an investigation held mainly so that the king's representative could discover how much money was owed to the king. It is true that some contemporary statements might have been deliberately or inadvertently false, but that may be true of any primary document of any time.

As an example from the Fine Rolls, Agnes, widow of Peter de Brewosa, had paid a fine of 250 marks, and on 22 May 1313 she was granted the wardship of two parts of her late husband's lands, which were in the hands of the king by reason of the minority of Thomas, Peter's son and heir.[15]

In a Patent Roll we find that on 17 March 1296 at the request of the king's brother Edmund, Eleanor, widow of John de Verdun, a tenant in chief, was granted permission to marry Richard de Breous.[16]

Feet of Fines. What we would today call a fine was known as an amercement in medieval times. A fine in medieval times was a mutually agreed upon payment (though certain types of fines sometimes had the amount fixed), frequently for some favor from the king. One type of fine was a payment to the king for his permission for land transfers. Such transfers were written in triplicate on parchment, and the three copies thus created were cut in a patterned line, with one part given to the grantor, one to the grantee, and one, the foot of the fine, kept by the king's government. Thus the copies served as deeds, and could be brought back for comparison with the original in case of dispute. Since land transfers are such good sources of genealogical information, the feet of fines serve as an enlightening contemporary source. Though there is no one collection of published feet of fines, many have been published piecemeal in a variety of publications. The LDS Family History Library in Salt Lake City has prepared a list of the various publications it has in its collections that contain abstracts of feet of fines, which makes them easy to locate for visitors to that library.

A word should also be said about the ubiquitous Herald's Visitation. Sir Anthony Wagner, F.A.S.G., observes that some "proto-visitations" occurred as early as or even earlier than the mid-fifteenth century, but the proper ones began with Henry VIII's order of 1550 to Thomas Benolt, Clarenceux King at Arms, to visit the king's subjects to "reform all false armory and arms, if it be necessary," meaning to verify the right of those bearing coats of arms and stop anyone found unlawfully bearing them, and "to take the note of your descents," which resulted in the preparation by the heralds of genealogical charts for armigerous families.[17] All state officers were ordered to assist the King of Arms as he might require. Thereafter the heralds visited such holders of arms in their homes and at other places, and they prepared charts of descent based on the armigerous person's own testimony and the testimony of others.

These charts are among the private collections of the College of Arms in London, but some of them have been made available over the years bearing an official signature of a herald of the College of Arms. Others have been used with non-College of Arms material and conflated into the more numerous published *Harleian Visitations*. Round had a number of typical remarks to make on the venality of some, certainly not all, heralds, which need not be repeated here, though a few are mentioned in appendix A. The word "notorious" can honestly be applied in front of the word "visitations," but the main caution is in knowing how to use them. Some are good genealogical evidence and have been accepted by knowledgeable genealogists as adequate sole proof for one or more generations. Certainly those made by William Dugdale in the middle of the seventeenth century are honest although some errors have been found. Dugdale also wrote books which were the first to actually show documentation, and which have been of great help to modern genealogists.[18]

It is a great temptation when researching genealogical lines and finding a beautiful chart setting forth many generations going back to the noble houses of England and signed by an official of the College of Arms to feel that it must be authentic. It is not only in black and white, and signed by an authority on lineages, but it also confirms what one always knew that his or her ancestry just had to be noble. Why must the genealogical authorities always be so iconoclastic? I suppose because they know it is human nature to embellish the talent of one's children, the importance of one's life's work, and the nobility of one's descent, among other little fairy tales that we all weave at times. Sir Anthony Wagner comments:

> It has been thought strange that there should be an appreciable number of errors in the particulars of living or recently deceased persons, entered on the strength of family information. But this will hardly seem surprising to anyone who has had experience of collecting information in this way or who reflects how little opportunity such as a time table as Dugdale's can have given for checking.

Sir Anthony, a recognized genealogical authority, would naturally want to be circumspect in criticizing any of his predecessors in office, but if he makes this remark in connection with the best of the ones who prepared the visitations, then what must he think of those prepared by the worse? Further, Sir Anthony writes of the more numerous unofficial copies or "purported copies":

> The trouble with them is that, until they have been collated with the originals, their character and authenticity are quite uncertain. And it is from such copies that the editions printed by the Harleian Society and others are for the most

part taken. The additional matter may often, of course, be valuable, but it is important to ascertain where it comes from.[19]

The rule for using visitations should be one of caution. It requires a body of knowledge in itself to be able to evaluate any given one properly. As a rough rule of thumb, we might expect those dealing with the generations most contemporary to the person giving the information to be more correct than the remote generations, but even here we must keep in mind the temptaion to latch unto a noble family – if I knew that my grandmother's name was Mary Neville, obviously in my mind she would have to come from the noble Neville family, and not from the family of the village baker of that name – and note Sir Anthony's observation above on "errors in the particulars of living or recently deceased persons." The usual rules of checking chronology would apply, but in the majority of visitations not many dates are given. In all cases it is preferable to have other evidence to support assertions found in visitations. No visitation should be acceptable as sole evidence for a line of descent without at a minimum having some expert understanding of the reasons why it can be relied upon.

The resources mentioned in this chapter do not by any means exhaust the field of material available to the genealogist, but, again, some of the specialized source guides (given in both text and endnotes of this book) can be of further help.[20] This chapter is intended to be an introduction, but the reader can use references given here to access other references in other works, as one has need. The goal is to jump across the Atlantic, most likely in the seventeenth century, then use parish registers, probate records, and published genealogical material to go back into families of the higher gentry, and finally to start using the many extant medieval records to trace the higher gentry back to the nobility. The results of one such search may be seen in appendix D. Though someone may yet write a comprehensive textbook on English or British medieval genealogy, complete with descriptions of all of the most commonly used materials and perhaps also some of the more obscure ones, the appropriate chapters and appendices in this book may in the meantime get one started. Thereafter, it is a matter of using the described materials and techniques to gain a toehold and gradually go on to build up one's experience and expertise in the area. In England those taking honors in history at Oxford and Cambridge might have had an edge up on an American student, but this was not the case with Moriarty, Jacobus, John Insley Coddington, Milton Rubincam, Walter Lee Sheppard, Jr., Neil Thompson, David H. Kelly, and many others who have successfully pursued medieval genealogy. One just has to dig in and start.

Notes

1. These three books are virtually indispensable for keeping up with royal genealogy. The first two, *Ancestral Roots* and *Magna Charta Sureties* are inexpensive and can be purchased from bookstores specializing in genealogy or ordered directly from the publisher, Genealogical Publishing Company, 1001 N. Calvert Street, Baltimore, MD 21202. The 1981 reprint of the *Complete Peerage,* is rather costly. Most people would be inclined to use *Complete Peerage* at some large genealogical library without buying it, but it has been available for purchase from Alan Sutton Publishing Limited, 17a Brunswick Road, Gloucester, G11 1HG, England – be sure to write first to learn of current availability and price.

2. *Genealogical Research: Methods and Sources,* vol. 1, rev., ed. Milton Rubincam (Washington D.C.: The American Society of Genealogists, 1980).

3. Walter Lee Sheppard, Jr., *Feudal Genealogy* (National Genealogical Society Special Publication No. 39, 1975).

4. Sir Anthony Wagner, *English Genealogy,* 2d ed. (Oxford, 1972).

5. Sidney Painter, *The Reign of King John* (Baltimore, 1949); Michael Altschul, *A Baronial Family in Medieval England: The Clares* (Baltimore, 1965).

6. *Lord Mayor's Court of London: Depositions Relating to Americans, 1641-1736* (Washington, 1980) is especially helpful. Coldham's *English Adventurers and Emigrants, 1609-1660* (Baltimore, 1984) and *English Adventurers and Emigrants, 1661-1733* (Baltimore, 1985) give abstracts from the High Court of Admiralty with reference to colonial America, and his *English Estates of American Colonists, 1610-1699* (Baltimore, 1983) gives abstracts of information concerning people living in America from the records of the Prerogative Court of Canterbury.

7. *The New England Historical and Genealogical Register* 135 (1981):287-97.

8. See, for example, Anthony J. Camp, *Wills and their Whereabouts* (London, 1974).

9. Of special interest to genealogists is the information that the LDS Family History Library has issued a new set of the IGI in 1988. This will be especially useful for researching English origins, since the library has vastly increased its coverage of English parish registers since the last, 1984, issuance of the IGI. A word of caution on names in the IGI is in order. Names that may seem uncommon in one location, such as *Mayflower* passenger Degory Priest in early Plymouth Colony, may be much more common in some other places, such as Devonshire and Cornwall, England. Accordingly, due care should be taken on finding the name of an American colonial immigrant in some English county.

10. *Essex Wills (England), 1558-1565,* 3 vols. thus far (Washington, 1982; Boston, 1983, 1984).

11. Marion E. Allen and Nesta R. Evans, *Wills from the Archdeaconry of Suffolk, 1629-1636* and its companion volume for 1637-1640 (Boston, 1986).

12. William Farrer, *Honours and Knights' Fees,* 3 vols. (Manchester, England, 1923-25); William Farrer and Sir Charles Clay, *Early Yorkshire Charters,* 12 vols.

13. Painter, *The Reign of King John,* 98.

14. *Calendar of the Close Rolls, Richard II,* vol. 5 (London, 1925), 451.

15. *Calendar of the Fine Rolls, Edward II,* vol. 2 (London, 1912), 133.

16. *Calendar of the Patent Rolls, Edward I,* vol. 3 (London, 1895), 185.

17. Sir Anthony Wagner, *The Records and Collections of the College of Arms* (London, 1952), 55-56.

18. Of Dugdale's works, particularly valuable to the genealogist are *Monasticon Anglicanum,* 3 vols. (1655, 1661, 1673) and *Baronage of England* (1675-76).

19. Wagner, *Records and Collections,* 63.

20. Some other helpful publications are P.D.A. Harvey, "Manorial Records," *Archives and the User,* No. 5 (British Records Association, 1984); and "Mullins," *Texts and Calendars,* 2 vols., (London, 1978-82).

Chapter 13

Academia and Genealogy

*In Stubbs we have an illustrious historian who was also a
devoted genealogist.*

—J. Horace Round

*Since personal relationships played such an important role
in the economic and political lives of the merchants [of
seventeenth-century New England], much use must be made
of genealogical and biographic writings.*

—Bernard Bailyn

Time was when history and genealogy went hand in hand. But
Elizabeth Shown Mills notes a "twentieth-century cold war between
'real historians' and 'ancestor worshippers,'" which, however, she sees as
"ebbing noticeably." She gives as explanation:

> The past schism between academia and family genealogists
> has been grounded almost solely upon the issue of scholar-
> ship[1]....The resulting distinction between professional and
> amateur has been justified. Academic historians are
> theoretically bound to a code of scholastic standards that
> has not existed in genealogy until recently....However, the
> professional historian has also suffered academically from
> his self-imposed barriers against family historians, and his
> tardy recognition of this fact has at last begun to create an

academic interest in genealogy as a legitimate field of study.[2]

Robert Charles Anderson expresses the problem in somewhat different words:

> Genealogy should be viewed as one of the auxiliary disciplines of history and of the social sciences. Many lists have been published that include genealogy in this category, along with numismatics, historical cartography, paleography, diplomatics, and the like. But genealogy over the years has not received the same treatment as have some of the other "auxiliary sciences." University courses are available in paleography and diplomatics; funded summer scholarships are available for the study of numismatics, and so on. Even though these fields are not recognized by the academicians to the point where they may establish independent departments of paleography or the like, and where degrees may be granted in these disciplines, there has at least been a willingness to incorporate these studies in the regular curriculum of the university....The question immediately arises as to why similar civilities have not been accorded to the study of genealogy.[3]

Anderson names some of the barriers: a confusion between genealogy and family history, a misunderstanding of the methodology and literature of genealogy, and a view of genealogy as "filiopietistic antiquarianism." He then states:

> When all of these barriers to including genealogy as a proper member of the auxiliary disciplines are down, then perhaps it will be possible to bring genealogy, as it has been practiced for the past half century by the professional wing of the genealogical community, into the university. There would then be room for a handful of genealogy courses in the curriculum of the department of history or of sociology.

Anderson believes that the most important field in which the skills and works of genealogists may be of assistance to social scientists is in the study of human migrations. As another area, he mentions biography. In the field of collective biography, he points to the work of Professor David

L. Greene in *The American Genealogist* on the genealogy of all those who were executed in the 1692 Salem witchcraft persecutions as making new discoveries via genealogy which will benefit both historians and sociologists in future studies.

Academic Use of Genealogy

Though not strange in Round's day, it is a somewhat unusual phenomenon today to see genealogists writing about the academic aspects of genealogy, Mills and Anderson obviously being among the few exceptions. Yet, going even further, it might not be too surprising in the future to see academicians writing about the genealogical aspects of academic subjects. Not only are the methodology and results of the genealogist of potential great value to the academic social scientist, but the materials used by the genealogist have great significance, too. For example, the caveat is sometimes made by historians that their published findings might be unintentionally skewed because of the nature of the sources they must rely on. Historian John Demos, as a case in point, in writing of a fellow historian, says, "his extensive use of literary materials may tend to weight his conclusions toward the most affluent and educated class of people (particularly given a society that was only partially literate)."[4] Demos, lacking this type of material for his own area of interest, "tried quite self-consciously to reach the life of the 'average man.'" Among other resources, Demos used some wills and deeds to help reconstruct a model of various aspects of life in Plymouth Colony. But historians like Demos have been the exceptions (though the trend is for this type of history to become more popular).

For the most part a vast, almost untapped, mother lode of new historical insights exists in the readily available but mostly unpublished wills and deeds of bygone eras. Though ancient wills almost always contain some kind of boilerplate frame on which the testator's wishes were hung ("Know all people that I, John Doe, being old and sick of body, but of sound mind, etc."), but the wishes themselves frequently express the hopes, fears, philosophies, generosities, meannesses, contingency planning, economic framework, and many other cultural tenets of the devisor in his or her own words, and they often reflect the overall collective sentiments of the times. Heretofore wills and deeds have been considered almost the exclusive province of the genealogist, but that cannot continue. Just the inventories alone found along with wills in the probate books give us the means to interpret archeological discoveries as well as to make new discoveries per se as to how people lived, worked, and used instruments in their times. Neither the historian nor the archeologist can afford to ignore these tools of discovery, nor can the sociologist or demographer.

Let us examine a straight-forward case in the field of law. In 1976 and 1977 there appeared in a learned journal of legal history published by one of the nation's prestigious law schools, a series of articles attempting to discover what seemed to be a peculiar meaning of the word "spinster" in legal documents of the sixteenth, seventeenth, and eighteenth centuries.[5] The main argument was that "33 women included half of all the married women indicted" at court under criminal charges, yet they "are described as spinsters although they are married." A suggested solution was that "the justices, in identifying these women as spinsters, were trying to make certain that the women who had committed the acts and not their innocent husbands would be punished," with the author thus taking note of the fact that men at this time were in many respects held responsible for their wives. The article continued that the justices must have had the "hope that the appellation 'spinster' would insure that the indictment of the wives would not be voided for technical reasons."

Not so, said the second article. Rather "contemporaries, however, did not see the distinction between housewives and spinsters as sharply as we see it. As an addition for all women who lacked other rank or occupation by which they could be suitably described, 'spinster' was the ideal solution for wives as well as single women." The third article differed also, stating "it may be that the judiciary was suspicious too of claims of coercion raised by married women and consequently required, in cases where marital status was not proved at the indictment stage of the proceedings, that the prisoner plead to a modified indictment which recorded the claim to the status of wife without admitting that the accused was in fact and law a married woman." The conclusion of the third article was that "the lesson for the historian is more severe. He can never assume as a matter of course that a 'spinster' is a single woman," – something that genealogists have known all along.

These hypotheses were based on study of criminal court records of the time by three qualified legal scholars who seemed, however, to think that the use of the word spinster for a married woman or widow was fairly new as a discovery. Genealogists, from familiarity with land records, had been aware for some time of this unusual usage and had puzzled over the reason. However, in 1986 an article in *The American Genealogist* put forth a reason that would seem to be compelling. The article drew a few examples from court proceedings, but most were from land records, and one deed in particular seemed to be most elucidating, an 1825 Massachusetts deed signed by, among others, Samuel Mann, yeoman, and "Sally Mann, Spinster, wife of the said Samuel, and in her own right," for the sale of land she had inherited from her father. The article concluded:

> This, I believe, gives us a definition of spinster which has
> previously gone unnoticed, that of a woman legally capable
> of transacting business or otherwise acting on her own be-
> half. In some cases she might be acting in a dual capacity,
> such as also signing as her husband's wife, but it is her legal
> capacity that is being described by the term "spinster." Only
> this definition satisfactorily explains what is otherwise a
> rather mysterious appearance of the word "spinster" in cer-
> tain documents of interest to the genealogist.[6]

Apprenticeship contracts tell us of the aspirations people had for their children and also, by expressed prohibitions, show us what type of behavior might be expected of the youth of the times. Other records show us not only the laws of the times, but how well they were enforced or ignored. As I demonstrated in my recent book on Plymouth Colony, the courts could make stern laws against Quakers, but these laws did not help the constable very much when he tried to get people to help him apprehend a Quaker.[7] The small court cases showing over and over again how much people were with or against the policies of their governments are a significant part of history, but a part we might not fully understand without going into the microcosmic affairs of individuals – again, something ordinarily thought of as the domain of the genealogist.

Vital Statistics from the Distant Past

There appeared in a recent "advice to the lovelorn" newspaper column an item quoting a physician as saying that young girls are able to become pregnant at a much earlier age today than in medieval times. One could wonder how much study that physician had made into medieval times. I assume none. I assume that he was extrapolating from the fact that girls today seem to be able to become pregnant at an earlier age in general than several generations back. He probably believed that there was a completely linear trend in such matters. He may have been right, but suppose the physiological condition of young women varied according to time and place. Suppose they reached puberty earlier in medieval times, then later in intermediate times, and then earlier again in recent times – could this not have implications of an environmental or cultural nature, implications well worth studying?[8]

There are but few studies made on such matters as childbearing ages, average and median age of marriage and death, average number of children, and similar demographic topics in medieval times. The records exist, however, to allow us to make such studies. Obviously the results would be of considerable value in various academic fields. And just as obviously the genealogist is in the best position to make such studies. We already have some vague starting points. We know, for example, that marriage among the medieval nobility took place at a very early age, sometimes four years old.[9] While we may think of such marriages as more a contract or engagement to become married at a later time, it was still referred to at the time as a marriage, as if no subsequent marriage need take place. Of course, under these circumstances marriage and consummation are two different things, and it is likely that consummation did not customarily take place until the bride had reached puberty.

We could expect then that many times in the middle ages a young wife might get pregnant right after puberty, for many such wives had been married years before puberty. The medieval document given in appendix C shows clearly that girls could become mothers at the age of twelve or thirteen, though it seemed somewhat unusual to one of the women quoted in the document. From the fact of early marriages I had the idea that early motherhood was more the rule than the exception. However, when I looked for facts to back up my preconceived idea, I found that, at least on the basis of a limited sampling, quite the contrary, married mothers seemed to have their firstborn at an age similar to women in the twentieth century. I am not trying to draw any conclusions, but only want to point the way to a field rich for future research. I say "mothers seemed to have" because in most cases our records are of surviving children, and we know that the process of birth was one of the most mortally dangerous times for both mother and child, so that a mother may have had several children before her first recorded surviving child.

Eve la Zouche was a fairly young mother, having been born ca. 1281, marrying in 1289, and having a child born ca. 1296.[10] Edmund Coleville was a father at age seventeen, but we do not know the age of his wife, though since he married at age four, she was probably of similar age.[11] Isabel de Verdon was born on 21 March 1316/7 and gave birth to her son, William Ferrers on 28 February 1332/3, shortly before she reached her sixteenth birthday.[12] But most examples I checked showed a mother having her earliest known child born at an older age, and, studying two generations together, the age difference between the mother and the known first child of a known first child seemed more to average in the high thirties or low forties. This is hardly a scientific study, but it indicates some of the potentials existing for this type of endeavor.

Genetics

Even while this chapter is being written, a current news item tells of a new study based in good part on family records to examine possible causes of the illness toxemia, or preeclampsia, which "is associated with pregnancy and is a major cause of death among expectant women and their unborn children." Dr. Kenneth Ward, professor of maternal-fetal medicine of the University of Utah, said that there is believed to be a "genetic link" in the illness and studying the heredity of Utah's Mormon population may help to discover it.[13]

Genealogy and many of the academic disciplines are symbiotic – each scratches the other's back, as some of the above examples show. Certainly that is true with the science of genetics. There is little doubt nowadays that the genealogist's painstakingly collected family records covering a number of generations can be of much aid to the geneticist (as well as to medical researchers) in determining undesirable inherited characteristics such as the familial incidence of heart disease, diabetes, various types of cancer, hemophilia, sickle-cell anemia, Alzheimer's disease, and many others. Nor is it just diseases, for any inherited human trait is of interest to the geneticist. But what can the geneticist do for the genealogist? The answer to that question, I think, opens up one of the most promising doors to the future of genealogy. In fact, genetics and genealogy are so intertwined that I wonder why more has not been written in the past on genetics for the genealogist.[14]

Let us first go over very briefly the basics of genetics, with the emphasis on human beings.[15] Our loose way of speaking of "blood lines" not only is erroneous, but also gives an impression that the large number of ancestors we have many generations back have all made uniform biological contributions to our individual make-up, though the blood would be watered down from any one distant ancestor (such as Charlemagne). However, the facts are that our heredity passes not through blood, but through genetic material called chromosomes and genes, and further, if Charlemagne were one (or several) of a given person's ancestors, that person might have inherited a disproportionate amount of genealogical material from him − or none at all. We inherit genetic material from the ancestors back of our parents in an uneven way.

The basic component of life is DNA, found as long double helixes in the nuclei of living cells. DNA can duplicate itself, rarely changes (though infrequent mutations do occur), transmits biological information to the new cells it helps create (e.g., sex; blood type; height potential; color of hair, skin, eyes, etc.; intelligence potential; shape of nose, chin, mouth, etc.; and all the inherited characteristics that distinguish one human being from another); and it is the basic material of which chromosomes are composed. In human cells there are forty-six chromosomes arranged in twenty-three homologous or matched pairs. These forty-six chromosomes contain between them some 100,000 genes, those parts of DNA that transmit hereditary traits to new cells. A given gene may be responsible singly for a given trait, or it may together with one or more other genes create that trait.

Of the twenty-three pairs of chromosomes in a given human cell, twenty-two are like pairs; that is, each member of the pair contains genes of the same general kind and position (though of course the types of genes on each chromosome pair are different). The twenty-third pair contains two sex chromosomes and behaves differently from the others. If the person is female, both chromosomes are known as X chromosomes, but if male then one is the X chromosome and one the Y chromosome, with the Y chromosome being much the larger of the two.[16] The cells of the body have specialized functions, and though the XX or XY chromosome pair is present in all cells (see exceptions in endnote 15 above) regardless of specialization, they do not at first cause any sex differences in the developing embryo. Gradually specialized sex cells (gametes) are created: that is, the egg in the female and the sperm in the male. Each cell divides into two new cells, which also divide, and thus there is growth in the organism (either for increase of size of the immature organism or as replacement of cells in all phases of the organism's development). Normal cell division is by mitosis, with each chromosome growing in size and then dividing so that the two new cells each contain the full complement of forty-six chromosomes.

However, the specialized sex cells further divide by a process called meiosis. During meiosis each chromosome of a pair combines in a physical touching called chiasma with the other member of the pair. During chiasma, genetic material is mutually exchanged between the paired chromosomes, and this occurrence is called crossing over. The implications for genealogists of this crossing over of genes is vast. The chromosomes are no longer the same!

Let us continue in the same direction a bit further. Meiosis is a process of division of the sex cells. Mitosis, the other division process, takes a single cell with forty-six chromosomes and creates two new cells from it, each containing forty-six chromosomes. However, meiosis also divides the sex cell into two cells, but it sends only twenty-three chromosomes, one from each matched pair, to each of the new sex cells. The reason for this is that the male sex cell, the sperm, will combine with the female sex cell, the egg, and the fertilized egg will then again contain the full complement of forty-six chromosomes, twenty-three from the father and twenty-three from the mother. If the resultant child is a male, its cells will contain among its chromosomes a pair known as the X chromosome and the Y chromosome. If the child is a female, its cells will have two X chromosomes. It is the presence of the Y chromosome that makes a male a male. Note also that it is the random reassorting of genes caused by both meiosis and fertilization that produces the variance between siblings; otherwise all children from given parents would be like identical twins.

As the male sex cell, that is, the sperm cell, divides, one chromosome from each of the twenty-three pairs goes into a new cell. Each paired chromosome in twenty-two pairs is quite similar in gene content; that is, corresponding genes on the paired chromosomes are responsible for the same function, such as color of eyes, though the gene(s) on one chromosome may call for one color of eyes while the corresponding member on the other chromosome may call for a different color. When the pair splits so that one chromosome goes into one new cell, and the other chromosome goes into a different new cell, one color of eyes may now be in one cell, and another color in the other, but at least each new cell has something to determine that the eyes will have a color. The twenty-third pair, though, consists of an X chromosome and a Y chromosome, and so when they split the X chromosome goes into one new sperm cell, while the Y chromosome goes into the other new sperm cell. The female sex cell, the egg, contains two X chromosomes, and so when it splits each of the new egg cells will contain an X chromosome. Thus it is that the father determines the sex of the child. If a sperm cell containing an X chromosome fertilizes an egg, the fertilized egg will have two X chromosomes, and the child will be female. If the sperm cell contains a Y chromosome, it will be paired in the fertilized egg with the X chromosome from the female, and the child will be male.

Now here is a most interesting aspect of genetics which affects genealogy. Let us have a child, a father, a mother, a paternal grandfather (PGF), a paternal grandmother (PGM), a maternal grandfather (MGF), and a maternal grandmother (MGM). The child inherits 50 percent of its genetic material from the father (that is, twenty-three chromosomes together with all their genes) and 50 percent from the mother. The father in turn had received 50 percent of his genetic material from PGF and 50 percent from PGM, just as the mother had inherited 50 percent from MGF and 50 percent from MGM. So it would be easy to think that the child received 25 percent of its genetic material each from PGF, PGM, MGF, and MGM. If we went back another generation, the number of ancestors would double, and the amount of genetic material from each would now seem to be 12.5 percent. And another generation back would seem to reduce the amount − evenly − to 6.25 percent from each of the sixteen great-great-grandparents. But this is not so!

The child does not receive precisely 25 percent each from the four grandparents because of the crossing over of genes and independent assortment of chromosomes during meiosis. Each child certainly must receive 50 percent from each parent (twenty-three chromosomes from each), but consider what happens when the child matures, marries, and produces offspring. In both the male and the female of the new couple, something happens to change their chromosomes. In meiosis leading up to production of the sex cells of the father (and the same happens for the mother, too), the twenty-three chromosomes he received from his father line up with the corresponding twenty-three chromosomes he received from his mother. Each member of a pair of chromosomes touches the other member of the pair in chiasma, and the two members exchange segments of genetic material containing a varying number of genes, sometimes more, sometimes less. When this crossing over is ended, the resultant forty-six chromosomes are no longer identical with the forty-six chromosomes which started the process.[17] Twenty-three of these chromosomes go into a newly created sperm cell. Each of the twenty-two, non-sex chromosomes in the child will contain varying amounts of genetic material which the father received from both his father and his mother. Keep in mind that originally the child's father's genetic material was lined up in one chromosome of a each pair, and his mother's genetic material was lined up in the other chromosome. The facts of crossing over and the independent assortment of chromosomes during meiosis interfere with the father's passing on to his offspring exactly half of what he received from each of his own parents. Even if the exchange during meiosis resulted by chance in a precisely fifty-fifty measure in some isolated case, it would be too much to expect such chance to continue through the generations.

From the above we can see that, except from our parents, we do not inherit equally from our ancestors. The DNA making up the chromosomes is eternal material passed on from generation to generation, but it is composed of unequal parts from various ancestors. Further, after some nine or ten generations, we start to lose ancestors; that is to say, I might not have any of the genes from a given eighth great-grandparent (conversely, I must have received at least some genes from each one of my ancestors up to that ninth or tenth generation back). On the other hand, purely by chance I might have a considerable number of genes from some other eighth great-grandparent. I would probably have a good number of genes from some ancestors forty or eighty generations back, though mutations could cut the number down from what it might otherwise be. Further, if I have some 100,000 genes, then I could not be a product of more than about 100,000 of my far-back ancestors from any given generation, and that assumes only one gene from each, which is probably not the case.

However, for a male there is the interesting fact that the sex chromosome, and all the genes it contains, which he received intact from his father, his father received intact from his father, and so on back. Genealogists tend to make much of the agnate line, the unbroken male line. Surprisingly enough, genetics favors the agnate line, too, for, assuming that the unbroken male line of ancestors can be relied on for a fair number of generations back (that is, that each imputed father was in fact the biological father), it is the one line in which we know certain genes have continued (this holds true only for males because each son would have received his Y chromosome only from his father and one generation back from his grandfather, while the mother would have received her mother's X chromosome from either her maternal grandmother or her maternal grandfather). Dr. Roderick states that:

> The Y chromosome contains sufficient DNA variety among men that our agnate connections may soon be more understood by an analysis of our Y chromosomes. The authenticity of purported male connections may be shattered in many cases. And even more ancient male agnate connections may be put forth despite our lack of [other] evidence. I see this as a most exciting, new avenue for genealogy.[18]

Since genes are positional on chromosomes (a given gene is found in a given location), those closest together have the best chance of remaining together during crossing over. As more becomes known about this kind of linkage, we will be in a position to learn more about possible inheritance from a given ancestor by tracing certain traits of our own and comparing them with their traits. Not all traits come from a specific gene, but some may come from a combination of genes, and some traits are discontinuous while others are graduations (e.g., sex is either male or female, while skin color is determined by additive genes and may range through many intermediate shades of white, yellow, red, brown, or black). Because enormous strides are being made in genetics, it behooves all genealogists to learn as much fine detail as possible about their ancestors.[19]

Inbreeding

William R. Shields, who has been called "a controversial population ecologist at the State University of New York at Syracuse," has proposed a theory to explain why migrating animals (e.g., birds, salmon) come back with pinpoint accuracy to the same place each year. Shields reasons that they do this so as to mate with their relatives. He is quoted as saying "From a genetics point of view, the best mate you can have is something like a first cousin," so as to link "genes that work well together and have had a chance to prove themselves." Biologist John L. Hoogland of the University of Maryland, who at first looked askance at Shields's theory, has become a believer, saying that "my work has forced me to reevaluate things, and I am not alone in that."[20]

Since we are all the product of much inbreeding (see chapter 2), it is helpful for the genealogist to understand the effects of inbreeding on new generations. E. B. Ford puts it this way:

> Outbreeding leads to genetic variation, without which [evolutionary] selection cannot operate so as to adapt organisms to changing conditions. Inbreeding, on the other hand, tends toward genetic uniformity, so preventing the breakdown of favorable adjustments to the environment.[21]

Essentially Ford is saying that inbreeding is good when generation after generation of organisms live their lives facing uniform environmental challenges, because these organisms have developed genetically to favor those combinations and mutations which help them prosper against those challenges. Under changing or adverse environmental conditions, outbreeding is better because it allows for more variety in the succeeding generations, some of whom will be better equipped to meet the new challenges. Ford's ideal organism would be one that "passes back and forwards between outbreeding and inbreeding as required in any situation."[22] If we extend Ford's reasoning to human genealogy, we might reasonably conclude then that inbreeding in New England during the seventeenth, eighteenth, and nineteenth centuries (to use a specific example, but many other times and places would apply as well, such as the Roman Empire under those reigns described by Gibbon as the best of times) has on the whole been beneficial, though in our "future-shock" twentieth century outbreeding might be better. It does seem at a cursory glance to be under settled conditions that we see the most inbreeding, while there tends to be more outbreeding during unsettled times.[23] Perhaps nature knows best.

Of course, inbreeding of people who manifest dangerous recessive traits is obviously bad for the offspring. The laws of genetics are such that harmful hereditary traits tend to be reinforced by inbreeding so that bad traits recur in such lines much more frequently than in the population as a whole.

Acquired Characteristics

One of the raging battles of the biological sciences over the years has been over the question of environment versus heredity as the shaper of human characteristics. It is doubtful that much use of genealogy as a means of studying the respective influences of hereditary and environment took place in the Soviet Union during the Stalin regime. Under Stalin, Trofim Lysenko became supreme dictator of genetics, being shown great favoritism for his theories (now well rejected even in the Soviet Union) that there were no such things as genes and that environmentally-acquired characteristics could be passed on from one generation to the next with immediately significant effects. Geneticists advocating anything to the contrary were subject to secret arrest, and some mysteriously died.[24] Woe be to the geneticist of the time who might suggest "let's look at the long-term history of various families to see how genealogy might throw more light on the subject."

Eugenics

Lysenkoism is as much out of fashion currently as is a theory from the opposite end of the spectrum, eugenics, or rather that aspect of eugenics which was popular around the turn of the present century. Various scholars advanced the idea of theoretically improving the human race through the study of genealogy and genetics to "increase, from one generation to another, the proportion of persons with better than average genetic endowment."[25] If we read now some of the genealogical literature of the time, we find it strange, with much talk of managing human breeding in terms of raising race horses or improving the beef yield of cattle. This was a time when intellectuals looked to a Brave New World, a world that was forever shattered with the advent of Adolph Hitler and concepts of a master race and the genocidal Holocaust. Today interest in eugenics exists in a different sense as that part of biology which combines genetics, psychology, physiology, demographics, and other studies to forecast, and, in some voluntary ways, influence human trends (including genetic engineering in the laboratory). Obviously, sound genealogical data covering a number of generations in given families can be of great value here, but the advocacy of genetic manipulation, such as maintaining a sperm bank from members of Mensa (the society with membership requirements that a successful applicant have an I.Q. in the top 2 percent of the overall population) as was suggested by a few people in recent years, meets with very little current support. The well-rounded genealogist, though, will want, as a matter of historical knowledge, to be aware that eugenics was a concept far more frequently encountered in the past among genealogists than it is today.

The Future Of Academic Genealogy

A bit more than a generation ago, there was no such thing as a data-processing course in the universities. Today, of course, the case is altered considerably. The rapid acceptance of data processing by academia can be explained in great part by the fact that most of its graduates are highly employable and worthy of remuneration. For genealogy to become fully accepted in the universities, it will be a much slower, more gradual path. I think it inevitable, though, that we will see credit courses (not just the present non-credit "continuing education" courses) given in a number of universities, as well as chairs of genealogy in the history departments. Individual human beings influence the timing and the acceleration of institutional decisions, but the decisions themselves come about because of widely diversified collective response to manifest need. We are living in an age when the teaching of history itself is threatened by what appears to be a complete lack of interest by the great majority of people in what has happened in the past, and there is not much current demand for historians in occupations that enable a person to make a living. The entire history of the human race, however, gives us assurance that this is but a momentary aberration, and that the study of history will come back stronger than ever. When it does, it will encompass a number of respectable sub-divisions, one of which will be the academic study of genealogy.

Notes

1. Not all writers of historical texts are in a position to throw stones at the admittedly large number of self-styled genealogists who write with total disregard to scholastic discipline. The *Boston Globe* of 21 October 1987 carried an article entitled "Study Finds Distortions in History Books" reporting on a project by Columbia University Professor Gilbert Sewall, commissioned by the U.S. Department of Education, which delivered a "stinging critique" that "many U.S. history and social studies textbooks are distorted, boring, oversized and lifeless because

of 'cowardice, commercialism, condescension and crassness in the writing and publishing....American history textbooks often forsake good storytelling, energetic writing and even honest history to comply with adoption procedures, group pressures, the social studies approach, readability formulas, and other market forces....Textbooks should face historical conflicts and tensions squarely...not shrinking from class, religious, racial or gender controversies for fear of giving offense to potential book buyers.'" One of many recommendations was "the use of more primary sources that demonstrate the role of key documents in history," a plea similar to that continuously being made by responsible, knowledgeable genealogists to the far greater number of genealogical practitioners.

2. "Academia vs. Genealogy: Prospects for Reconciliation and Progress," *National Genealogical Society Quarterly* 71 (1983):99. It might be noted that among past and present prominent practitioners of genealogy are a great many academicians including, among others, Cameron Allen, Claude W. Barlow, David L. Greene, William J. Hoffman, David H. Kelley, George E. McCracken, Gary B. Mills, and Robert M. Sherman. Other skilled genealogists include lawyers and judges, doctors, religious leaders, civilian and military government officials, elected officials and legislators, engineers and architects, news and other media specialists, bankers, industrialists, and business executives. Perhaps because the study of genealogy encompasses so many other areas of knowledge, the educational levels and skills of good genealogists, including those whose university-level education is self-tutored, are in general exceptionally higher than those of the population average.

3. Robert Charles Anderson, "The Place of Genealogy in the Curriculum of the Social Sciences," *Generations and Change, Genealogical Perspectives in Social History,* ed. Robert M. Taylor, Jr., and Ralph J. Crandall (Mercer University, Macon, Ga., 1986), 79-88.

4. John Demos, *A Little Commonwealth: Family Life in Plymouth Colony* (New York, 1970; reprinted 1977), x.

5. *American Journal for Legal History,* published by Temple University School of Law: Carol Z. Wiener, "Is a Spinster an Unmarried Woman?" 20:27-31; J. H. Baker, "Male and Married Spinsters," 21:255-59; Valerie C. Edwards, "The Case of the Married Spinster: An Alternate Explanation," 21:260-65.

6. Eugene A. Stratton, "Spinster: An Indicator of Legal Status," *The American Genealogist* 61 (1986):167-70. It is perhaps indicative of the problems still existing between academia and genealogy that when I offered, with permission of *The American Genealogist,* to let the *American Journal for Legal History* reprint my article which would seem have important bearing on the spinster anomaly, I received a reply from Editor Diane C. Maleson, Professor of Law, that "we are unable to publish it. Our decision is certainly in no way a reflection upon the merit of your work. We receive many articles and have difficult choices to make." I would have thought that a learned journal which devoted three articles aggregating some fifteen pages or so to conjectures from court records as to the meaning of a peculiar, but wide-spread use of the word "spinster," would have been pleased to publish some four pages more pointing out that a different kind of contemporary record (land records) showed much more clearly what the term must really have meant.

It leads me, as well as other genealogists, including some with law degrees, to wonder what the purpose of a university journal is if it is not, *inter alia,* dedicated both to getting answers on matters it itself has raised and to correcting information it has published which draws erroneous or incomplete conclusions.

7. *Plymouth Colony: Its History & People, 1620-1691* (Salt Lake City, 1986), 95. It got so bad that the courts had to make an alternative law providing that if a constable was unwilling or unable to inflict the prescribed punishment on Quakers, he should bring the Quakers to the under marshal for punishment.

8. See endnote 12 of chapter 4 for some information on age at marriage and childbearing ages in American colonial and modern times.

9. John Giffard was married ca. 1236 at the age of four to Aubrey de Camville, who was then about four or five. He later rejected the marriage, saying that no one like him "would adhere to any wife to whom he happened to be married in his boyhood" (*Calendar of Inquisitions Post Mortem,* vol. 1 (London, 1904), 298-99). Maurice Berkeley married Eve la Zouche when they were both about eight years old (*Complete Peerage,* 2:129). Edmond Coleville married Margaret d'-Ufford when he was four (ibid., 3:274). When Robert Ferrers married Mary of Angouleme he was about ten and she about seven (ibid., 4:198, 201). These are just a few out of many similar examples.

10. Ibid., 2:129.

11. Ibid., 3:274.

12. Ibid., 4:347-348.

13. *New Hampshire Sunday News,* 4 October 1987.

14. I do not recommend the article in *The American Genealogist* (1981):219-24, which is misleading in several ways, especially in neglecting to consider "crossing over" during meiosis. On the other hand, an article which should be published in one of the national genealogical journals in the reasonably close future by Thomas H. Roderick, Ph.D., a career geneticist and Certified Genealogist, should be required reading for anyone wishing to look further into this fascinating field. I would guess that genetic literature for the genealogist will be increasing substantially.

15. In this all-too-brief thumbnail review, I am speaking in broad general terms, emphasizing the normal or most usual situation and leaving out the extremes. For example, it is sufficient for these purposes to say that the human cell has forty-six chromosomes, even though there are some rare exceptions, such as in Down's Syndrome and trisomic conditions. And of course the sex cells have only twenty-three chromosomes, while red blood corpuscles have none. In writing this section on genetics, I have learned much from Dr. Roderick, mentioned in the previous note, and I have also found helpful E. B. Ford, *Understanding Genetics* (New York, 1979) and Martin J. Gutnik, *Genetics* (New York, 1985).

16. An article in the *Boston Globe* of 23 December 1987 reported new genetic discoveries by a group of researchers, some of whom were connected with the Whitehead Institute for Biomedical Research, in Cambridge, Massachusetts. These researchers were able to pinpoint on the Y chromosome a single gene responsible for determining an organism's male sex. They also "in a surprising sideline to the discovery" found a similar gene on the X chromosome, which "may

play some unknown role." Dr. David C. Page was quoted as saying, "I think it's going to shake up people's notions of sex determination." This illustrates once again that our scientific body of knowledge is continuously growing, and the well-accepted concepts of today may become the discredited and cast-off notions of tomorrow.

17. It has been held by geneticists that crossing over occurs only in the twenty-two pairs of the non-sex chromosomes, and that the X chromosome and the Y chromosome continue from generation to generation without change other than the possibility of rare mutations. This non-change (lack of crossing over) of the sex chromosomes is assumed to be true in the discussion in this book, but we should keep in mind the caution mentioned in endnote 16 above that notions of sex determination may in the future be shaken up.

18. Letter from Dr. Roderick to the author.

19. From George S. Mann, *Mann Memorial* (Boston, 1884), 83, 106, I learn that my third great-grandfather (from whom I have two lines of descent), Ensign Mann, "was of vigorous frame, a great reader, and possessed remarkable memory ...though he had a slight impediment of speech." His son, my great-great-grandfather, Samuel Mann, "had a slight impediment in his speech." I recall that my parents had a doctor cut the frenum at the bottom of my tongue when I was quite young because I was slightly tongue-tied. When my own first son was born, the pediatrician examined him and found a need to slit the bottom of his tongue the same way. Now I want to learn if a tendency to be tongue-tied is an inherited trait, and, if so, if it could come from a single ancestor, as distinguished from those characteristics which result from contribution from more than one ancestor. If such a trait comes from a single gene, I would like to learn also what other genes are positioned close to it on a chromosome.

20. From an article by Bruce Fellman in the *Boston Globe,* 9 November 1987.

21. E. B. Ford, op. cit., 169.

22. Ibid.

23. The article about Shields also notes opposition to his theory, in part based on observations made at the National Zoo, that the effects of inbreeding on animals there have not been beneficial. However, it might be suggested in line with Ford's dicta that animals in a zoo are more under unsettled, than settled, conditions.

24. *Encyclopedia Britannica,* 14:484.

25. Ibid., 8:815.

Chapter 14

Computers and Genealogy

I can still recall sitting before my typewriter one of the hottest evenings of that summer, in my "office" on the top floor under an over-heated roof, clad only in jockey shorts, and with an electric fan playing on me, pecking out a chapter in two-fingered style, with the thermometer registering ninety-five degrees.

—Donald Lines Jacobus

Give me a place to stand, and I will move the world.

—Archimedes

The ancient Greek scientist was illustrating the power of the lever. A more figurative modern translation of his boast would be, "Give me the right tools, and watch my speed." To genealogists, the computer might be such a tool (and I am sure Jacobus would agree that air conditioning in summer is another).

Early Home Computers

I did not always feel this way, in spite of the fact that I was a computer professional before I became a genealogist. I worked with large-scale computers for more than a dozen years in the capacity of operator, programmer, instructor, systems analyst, section chief, branch chief, and finally director of a 100-person computer center. When home computers first arrived on the market, I was inclined to look upon them as toys. I could balance my checkbook without computerized help, and I did not need a computer to make a grocery list, two of the specialties of early home computers.

In 1982 I conceded that, yes, the word-processing aspect of computers had finally reached a point where it could be a considerable labor-saver for a genealogical writer. But even when I gave a lecture at Denver in 1984, "What Can Computers Do For Genealogy?," I was very cautious.[1] Let me quote just a bit from that lecture:

> The computer is probably the most overrated fad of this century, and this in no way is intended to detract from the acknowledged value of the computer as probably the greatest time-saver and problem-solver of our times. If this seems like a paradox, it is. We are exposed everyday to the virtues of this or that product being "computerized," as if they somehow acquired some transcendental quality not otherwise available. I do not think that food tastes any better just because it was purchased at a store where the prices were totaled by a computer instead of an old-fashioned cash register. We are confusing the product with the process....I get the vague impression that computers are being touted as if they were a solution to everyone's genealogical problem. In this case, the reality is not as good as the promise.[2]

The Cost Comes Down

The point I was making was that, yes, computers were a boon to genealogists, but at a cost. Were they worth the cost? For some, yes, and for others, no. But even when I spoke, the picture had been gradually changing, and it has continued to change ever since. What is the big difference? Simply that the power and convenience of the hardware and software have been going drastically up, while the cost has been going drastically down. When I bought my first computer in 1982, an IBM PC, I paid approximately $6,500 for the total configuration, computer, printer, and software. The printer alone, a letter-quality NEC Spinwriter 3550, cost over $2,000. I still have this computer, though I have changed the NEC printer for an Epson dot matrix. In 1987 I added a second computer (why? because my wife and I competed too much for use of a single computer), a fully compatible Leading Edge Model D with hard disk and an Epson EX-800 printer, which gives me draft speed of 300 characters per second and near-letter-quality speed of sixty characters per second. The total cost, including an upgrade of my software, was $1,600.

Someone else might not need as much power; I wanted to write articles and books. Many people could get by with two floppy disk drives, instead of a hard disk and one floppy, at a savings of $400, and they might not need an upgrade of my relatively expensive software, (the word-processing system that came free with the Leading Edge computer might do). A powerful computer and suitable printer capable of doing anything that most genealogists might wish could be had for little more than $1,000.[3]

I spent almost the entire year of 1986 writing the book *Plymouth Colony,*[4] with the aid of my IBM PC, two floppy disk drives, and an Epson RX-80 printer. The software was a rather primitive word processor, which I will not name, more suitable for writing letters than long articles or books. It had, for example, no word wrap, no automatic footnoting, and no way of combining files. Every time I made a change in a paragraph, no matter how small, I had to rekey the entire paragraph. I suspect that I wrote that book six times over. My word processor was better than a typewriter, but still it left much to be desired. Incidentally, I had other word-processing software, but I had started with the one with which I had the greatest familiarity, and I was reluctant to change in the middle of the book. What a difference in writing the present book with Wordstar 2000-Plus, version 2.0![5]

Kinds of Uses for the Genealogist

Another part of my 1984 talk has changed in the number of uses I see available to the genealogist with a computer. I then saw four general uses, but I think now there are at least six, with a seventh as a catch-all. Let us make a quick survey of all these uses and then go into more detail on some later:

Word Processing. This is the kind of software that first made home computers of use to genealogists. How spoiled we have become as each revised version of the various word processors on the market incorporates new features that make the older versions seem primitive. The versions available today take all the effort except the actual composing out of writing and revising anything from a letter to genealogical notes to a book.

Specialized Genealogical Systems. Specifically designed for the genealogist, these systems provide a structured way of keeping track of collected data. They make it easy to find information when it is needed again, and they also present data in a way that helps provide for meaningful comparisons. They do not take the place of research but help tremendously in storing, retrieving, analyzing, and formatting the results of one's research.

Telecommunications. A hardware device called a modem can be used with most home computers (other than those intended mainly for games) to enable one computer to transmit data electronically, usually via telephone lines, to another computer some distance away. Modems can be purchased for a few hundred dollars. The present value to the genealogist is mainly speed, if that is needed, but in the future telecommunications hold a promise of help for genealogists to access data banks that might not otherwise be readily available.

Data Base Management Systems (DBMS). Most of the commercially available specialized genealogical systems mentioned above, are a form of a DBMS. The specialized ones are convenient and user-friendly, but they are strictly limited to producing only that which is programmed in them. A general DBMS requires more time to learn and a higher computer skill level but is much more versatile than the specialized systems. In effect, users can designed their own specialized systems, modify them, and make them fit the peculiarities of their own data and needs. For example, a commercial specialized system might restrict all surnames to be no more than twelve letters; a user dealing with names that are sometimes extra long (such as East Indian surnames) could use a DBMS to design a system that would accept surnames of any desired length. Additionally, a DBMS is not restricted to genealogical use only, but it can be used for any purpose where large amounts of data need to be stored in a patterned way.

Graphics. The computer has long been used to create all kinds of fascinating graphics patterns, and many of the games we see using computers are a specialized form of graphics. Only recently, though, I have come to realize that graphics can offer the genealogist a wonderful tool in creating genealogical charts. I have not found the package best suited to my needs to do this yet, but I am looking.

Desktop Publishing. Fairly new, expensive, responsible for both some beautifully designed and some atrocious-looking publications, desktop publishing combines word processing and graphics, together with a matching hardware set (with emphasis on the printer), to allow the user to create professional-looking newsletters, journals, and even books. For genealogists and genealogical organizations, this promises to be a tremendous boon, though at present it is in its infant stage. I can recall years ago when I was editor of a four-page newsletter for the Massachusetts Society of Mayflower Descendants, and once every three months I could count on dedicating an entire weekend to getting a professional-looking (two justified columns per page) product out via my IBM Selectric typewriter. With appropriate desktop publishing hardware and software, I could probably do it after initial design in a matter of a few hours.

Programming Languages and Special Systems. This is the catch-all category. Some genealogists might want to write their own programs, using languages such as BASIC, COBOL, FORTRAN, C Programming Language, and others. This gets somewhat away from genealogy, though, and is just noted here. In the same way, there are many non-genealogical systems available that could be of some use to a given genealogist; for example, a professional managing a large genealogical business might find some of the accounting packages or the mail-order business packages of help, while someone in the genealogical publishing business could be interested in everything from electronic spreadsheets to full accounting systems plus of course the desktop publishing systems as mentioned above. Again the use of such aids is just noted here, and need not be covered further.

Be Informed Before You Buy

Any genealogist seriously considering an investment in computer hardware and software would be well advised to spend some time on studying the matter first. Do not make expensive decisions just on the basis of getting what a friend recommends. Most people have different needs. Even when someone has needs similar to a friend who has already bought equipment, the computer field is so fast moving that something bought a few months ago can already be superseded by new hardware or software available with better features at a lesser price. There is specialized literature for genealogists, and one good way to get up-to-date information is by subscribing to a periodical such as *Genealogical Computing.*[6]

Word Processing

A few years back a consumer magazine made some comparisons between word-processing systems on the basis of user response to questionnaires, which I felt was not too meaningful. Very few people are acquainted with all the systems available, and so not many people have any basis for comparison. I am using Wordstar 2000-Plus, version 2.0, and find it most responsive to my needs. I think that WordPerfect, with which I have had some experience, is a superb system, too, with a great abundance of features. Microsoft Word, which I have not used, is also said to be very good. There are many more on the market. The Leading Edge computer quite often can be purchased with a free word processor called the Leading Edge Word Processor (LEWP), and, when not free, it is available at a much lower cost than the others I have mentioned. I have tried LEWP and think it would be sufficient for most genealogists' needs; however, I do not like the cumbersome way of getting superscripts, and any genealogist using superscripts frequently, as I do in articles, might want something else.

I use underscoring frequently, as anyone reading this book can see, for all italics in the book originated as underscoring on my computer. I also use footnoting frequently, and I like the versatility I have in Wordstar of making footnotes automatically and placing them either at the bottom of the page or at the end of a chapter. The ability of a word processor to move and relocate entire blocks of information, large or small, is a required feature for me, and I have grown too fond of "windows" to ever give them up. The advantage of windows to me is that I can look at any two, or even more, files simultaneously, and I can copy information from one file to another, or combine files. This gives tremendous flexibility.

One feature I would especially recommend to any genealogist is a macro generator or, as it is sometimes called, a key glossary, and it also goes by other names. It is the function that counts, though, and it is not as difficult a concept to understand as some of the names identifying it might imply. A macro generator allows the user to redefine functions of the computer keyboard. One simple use would be to make (and instructions are quite easy showing one how to do this) a macro for closing a letter with "Sincerely" and then, four spaces down, your name. Thereafter, whenever you close a letter instead of keying all the letters that make up "Sincerely" plus your name, you merely depress one or two keys, and the computer automatically closes the letter for you. Another use would be to have a stock paragraph that you might use in many letters. Instead of rewriting that paragraph all the time, depressing one or two keys to get the macro would do it automatically. What I especially like about a macro generator is the ability to make frequently used computer instructions easier. For example, in Wordstar in order to get a superscript, I ordinarily would have to depress the control key along with the key for the letter "P," and then depress the plus (+) key, followed by the desired superscript number, followed by a repeat of the instruction; that is, depress the control key and the letter "P," and then depress the plus key. For the person using superscripts infrequently, this is not an unreasonably amount of keying. But for one using superscripts as much as I do, it is most helpful through a macro generator (which is provided in Wordstar) to redefine the superscript function. Now whenever I want a superscript, I depress function key "6," then my superscript, then function key "6" again. Thus the inclusion of a macro generator in a word processor allows us all to make easier those functions we each use very frequently, which might be the superscript for me, boldface for you, moving blocks for someone else, and so on. Such a word processor has the flexibility to be many different things to different people.

Genealogical Systems

For one of the specialized genealogical systems, I like Personal Ancestral File (PAF), created and sold by the LDS Family History Department of the Church of Jesus Christ of Latter-day Saints. I was living in Salt Lake City when they started working on the system, and they asked me to help test both versions 1.0 and 2.0. Some of my suggestions are incorporated in version 2.0. Input for the system consists of formatted data on individuals and families entered via the computer keyboard.[7] For an individual, the data consist of name, date and place of birth or baptism, and date and place of death or burial, together with a provision for entering whatever non-formatted sources and narrative might be desired. Family information additionally includes a marriage record and a means of tieing children in with the family. Each member of the family could thus have an individual record, be part of a marriage record (if married), and be part of a family record. The system automatically ties people together in a parent-child relationship.

Since the child of one family may be a parent of another family, the software system can put together all generations in a family. In the PAF system, for example, one output report consists of a complete four-generation chart starting with any given person, showing that person's parents, grandparents, and great-grandparents in horizontal chart form with names and vital dates and places. Another report starts with any given individual and cascades downward, showing by various indentations the starting individual and spouse, with subsequent lines showing the couple's children, starting with an indented presentation of the first child, followed by a doubly indented list of that child's children (and so on as long as a given child has children), and then it continues with the next child, and all that child's descendants, and so on. Keep in mind, of course, that any such system can rearrange only that data which has been input by the user. Anyone buying such a system who expects it to create data would be in for a shock.

There are other specialized genealogical systems, and I have heard some very good things about them. A friend of mine swears by the Family Roots system,[8] which is similar to the PAF system. I am not acquainted with the details of these other systems and am not in a position to compare them with PAF. There is literature available on most of them that will explain the differences in how they accept input and present output. Obviously, these systems are a tremendous aid in keeping track of one's own family. They can also be most useful in helping to solve genealogical problems via a whole-family approach or even a whole-area approach (such as mentioned in chapter 5). Users with more than average interest in particular areas of genealogy, such as medieval English lines, could input data from such books as *Ancestral Roots* and *Magna Charta Sureties,* and then create family chains of the various individuals included in these books.

Telecommunications

My interest in telecommunications is limited at this time. I see three possible types of use. The first is to experiment for the sake of experimentation or to prepare for future use, and I do not have the inclination for this. The second is to have the facility for rapid transmission of genealogical data in cases where the person on the receiving end also has telecommunications capability. If, for example, I needed to get an article to an editor fast, what faster way could there be than by connecting my computer with the editor's computer via the telephone line? But I do not really have the need for such speed. I can put a data diskette in a protective mailer and send it by mail, which is fast enough for my purposes. I have both sent and received diskettes that way, and I find it a very practical way.

The third type of use is to access distant data bases and get information from them. This merits a bit more discussion. In 1984 the LDS Family History Department asked me to participate as an outside representative in a six-day seminar examining future possibilities for the direction of their genealogical services. Naturally, much of the discussion had to do with computers. The Family History Department planned at that time to computerize the information on their vast numbers of family group sheets and make them available to users with computers and telecommunications facilities. Thus, someone from Boston, for example, could dial a given long distance number, connect a computer directly with a computer of the Family History Department, and ask for and receive family group sheet data. As far as I know, this is not a reality yet, but it could be in the not too distant future.[9]

I suspect that this facility would be of more interest to beginning genealogists than experienced ones. Most experienced genealogists are not looking for the kind of data found in family group sheets, which more often than not represent the conclusions of untrained genealogists, and they usually deal with generations from the nineteenth and twentieth centuries. I specialize in colonial and medieval genealogy, and I usually seek primary source information. From my participation in the LDS seminar, I know – because I asked – that at that time there was no intention of transcribing original source information into computer-readable form and making it available to users via their computers. It will be a long, long, long time before probate and land records are generally available to computer users. And this is true also for vital records, military records, medieval records, and other primary source materials which are at the heart of the experienced genealogist's work. I know of no genealogical library at this time which has plans for the near future to computerize the text of any substantial number of volumes. To put a significant amount of primary source data in computer-readable form at this time would be a tremendously costly undertaking. Most of the information available via computer, I expect, will be canned, undocumented conclusions. I think it is certain that by the time this situation changes, telecommunications equipment and capabilities will have so changed that anything bought now will be obsolete. Thus, at least for the time being, having telecommunications facilities does not interest me.

However, do keep in mind that the computer field changes rapidly, and that powerful advances are being made in electronic scanners. The drawback to putting much primary and secondary genealogical data into computerized form has been the tremendous cost of human inputting. When inputting can be done automatically, quickly, and cheaply by scanners, then the genealogist might not be able to do without some kind of telecommunications access to major computerized record depositories. The day is probably coming, though I would not attempt to predict the timing, when much primary source material will be available to genealogists via telecommunications, and that day will be a tremendous milestone in the development of genealogy.

Data Base Management Systems

I think one of the most exciting new frontiers for genealogists using a computer is in data base management systems. Everything else we have discussed is essentially a means of rearranging data where the genealogical relationships have already been discovered. This type of computer processing is most valuable to the genealogist in terms of convenience, speed, and saving of labor. To input given information one time, but be able to have it appear in different ways in ten different output reports, and further to be able to take the same information without reinputting it and use it in writing an article, these are marvelous technological advances. As wonderful as they are, though, they do not usually make discoveries for the genealogist.[10] DBMS software offers a potential way to make discoveries.

Here are some examples of large-scale DBMS programs in action. A few years ago, the FBI caught a mass murderer/rapist, and, according to the newspaper account, it was done with the aid of DBMS software used by credit card companies. The criminal traveled across country using his credit card. Credit card companies have large DBMS programs, and with their cooperation the FBI was able to pin where the fugitive had been almost as soon as he had been there. Then it was not difficult to predict likely places where he might go, and thus the FBI caught him.

One of the best-known types of a DBMS is that used by airlines for keeping track of reservations, such as American Airlines's pioneer SABRE system. Terminals at every reservation-taking office are connected to a large scale computer. Say there are three seats left on a given flight. Almost simultaneously two businessmen in Boston and a man and wife in New York ask their respective ticket sellers to make them reservations on that flight. I say almost simultaneously, but not quite. If the New York ticket seller's terminal gets connected to the main computer just a split second before the Boston computer accesses it, the New York couple will get two reservations, and the Boston businessmen will, a few seconds later, be told that there is only one seat available.

In genealogy the best example of a large data base management system I know of is the LDS Family History Library International Genealogical Index (IGI). Volunteers input vital records, parish registers, and other sources including family group sheets, showing people by parentage with date and place of birth, and by spouse with date and place of marriage, as input to a large system. The information from all over is sorted together and grouped by geographic subdivision such as state for the United States and county for England. All names are presented alphabetically, and the computerized information is then transcribed to microfiche, where it is available in Salt Lake City and at LDS Family History Centers (branch libraries) throughout the world. There are many uses for such a system, including of course looking up an individual of interest. Beyond this, though, if you have the name of a man and wife and know where they lived, you can not only look for their marriage date, but you can also search through all people with the same surname to discover all the couple's recorded children. Or, suppose you trace a couple back to a given town but cannot find where they came from. The IGI might allow you to find their older children in the town you know, and then it might show you that earlier they were having children in some other town, perhaps on the other side of the state. Now you are enabled to trace them further back. The IGI, a massive DBMS, has helped you discover something new, although the discovery has been by non-computer (manual) analysis.

Exciting Future Possibilities

Going further with the above example, I can envision in the near future a computer making the analysis. Individuals may, for example, be able to purchase given parts of the IGI on diskette and transfer the information to their own hard-disk home computers.[11] Such individuals may be able to design their own user systems via general purpose DBMS software, or they may be able to buy a customized ready-made user system. In either case, the user system could be programmed to search for all the likely children of a given couple, or the likely parents of a child, or the likely spouse of a person, and present the various possibilities to the user. An inquiry might be like this: "Search data base for possible parents of Deborah, wife of Edward Fish of Charlestown, Massachusetts, who was having children between 1714 and 1736, and who died on 2 April 1753." The user system might find a Deborah Tilson born at Charlestown in 1695, but also discover that this Deborah married a John Allen in 1720, and thus eliminate her, and then go on to present a Deborah Foster, born at Boston in 1692, who otherwise disappears from the records, as a possibility. The IGI data could be just the start of a huge data base, and the user could add probate records, land records, vital records, and other data as it was acquired, giving the genealogical discovery system more possibilities to work with.[12] In the example of Deborah Foster, given above, the computer could search all appropriate probate, land, and other records for further information on her. The system could be programmed to take into account all peripheral facts; for example, one of the sons of Deborah Fish might have died without children and in his will have mentioned an Uncle Peleg. The system could check the data base first to see if the husband, Edward Fish, had a brother named Peleg, and then to see if there might be a Peleg in any of the families discovered as possibilities for the identity of the wife, Deborah Fish. Perhaps whole volumes of scanned primary record input from libraries might also be available for purchase, or via telecommunications, to add to the individual's overall data base. The possibilities for making new discoveries might seem endless.

There are many DBMS software packages available commercially for the home computer, such as dBase III, which is one of the most powerful ones. They are especially helpful to people who want to publish genealogical material. I know of several people who have used, and are using, data base management systems to prepare books containing indices of probate and land records for given counties. I used such a system to keep track of royal lines when I was herald/genealogist for the Royal Bastards. There is no limit as to what a data base management system and a lot of imagination might do for strongly motivated genealogists.

When I think of the advances in home computers and software made since I bought my first configuration, and when I project this type of continuing advance into the future, I gain renewed respect for the computer as a tool for the genealogist. And apparently I am not the only one, for very few of the many genealogists I know are now without a computer. Computers and genealogy were made for each other.

Notes

1. Some of the material in this chapter was presented in September 1984 at a conference sponsored by the Federation of Genealogical Societies and the Association of Professional Genealogists.

2. I was not the only one with a bit of skepticism about the value of some computers. Mike Royko wrote in a column that the manufacturers of home computers failed in only one thing: to create enough practical everyday uses for their products, and I believe it was *Time Magazine* that once suggested that many people were holding off buying a home computer until one came out that could do the dishes, mop the floor, and iron the clothes. Even in my business association with computers, I had to deal with people who were not quite getting the concept. One user wanted my highly paid data professionals to design for him a computer system to keep track of the foreign languages spoken by the twenty employees he supervised. I told him it would be much more efficient (not to mention much less expensive) to get a file box and some three-by-five cards.

3. The Leading Edge computer was obtained in July 1987 from ISCA in Burlington, Massachusetts with a 30 megabyte hard disk for $1,199. With two floppy disk drives and no hard disk, the cost would have been $799.00. The Epson EX-800 printer was obtained from Arlington Computer Company in Arlington, Illinois, for $365.00. A somewhat less powerful but still suitable printer could be obtained for $250.00 or less.

4. *Plymouth Colony: Its History & People, 1620-1691* (Salt Lake City, 1986).

5. I no sooner bought version 2.0 than the maker came out with version 3.0.

6. Published by Ancestry, Inc., P.O. Box 476, Salt Lake City, UT 84110.

7. Formatted or structured means that blanks are provided to be filled in with name, date, place, etc. A format must be followed; that is, a given blank may be for surname and thus cannot be used for first name, or date, or place. There are limitations on how many letters or numbers can be inserted in a blank, and sometimes only certain data can be accepted; for example, a month blank may accept only "1" through "12," and a day blank may accept only "1" though "31." Unfor-

matted means that data may be entered in free form without restriction other than possible total size. Usually only formatted data is processed (that is, manipulated so that it can be retrieved in different forms). A date of birth, for example, would be put in a formatted blank and need be keyed in only once, but it might show on several output forms such as an individual form, a marriage form, a family form or in an index. Because the software system knows exactly what it is by virtue of it being found invariably in a certain place when input, it also knows how to present it on a multitude of outputs. Unformatted information is less restricted but cannot be manipulated by the computer system. The system has no idea what may be found in a given unformatted input area and can only present it in the same format it is input. Formatted data may be sorted; that is, the individual persons are entered in no particular order, but the computer will later be able to arrange them in sequence for one report by surname, for another by date of birth, for a third by place of marriage or for a number of other possible arrangements.

8. Available from Ancestry, Inc., and elsewhere.

9. As computer hackers know, the facility providing such computer information would be in a vulnerable position, because unscrupulous users with adequate technical knowledge, once connected to the host computer, could use the connection to vandalize all the information in the host computer. Expensive redundancy would be required here, with a dedicated single-purpose computer as the one accessible by telephone and a main computer to store and update information; periodically removable hard disks of updated information created by the main computer would replace the old disks in the accessible computer, and only the accessible computer would be vulnerable.

10. There is an exception. The systematic rearrangement of massive amounts of data from whole-family or whole-area research might allow a genealogist to make some discoveries through non-computer analysis of computer printouts. For example, if complete records of a small colonial village showed the marriage, spinsterhood, or death of every female child except one girl named Hepzibah, and if the records also showed the parents of every wife in the village of a certain age range, except Hepzibah, the wife of Theophilus Montmorency, non-computer analysis would produce a clue that the two Hepzibahs might be but a single person.

11. The IGI is already available for purchase by individuals on microfiche for home use, the present cost being fifteen cents per microfiche. A home microfiche reader is of course also needed.

12. The purchase of commercially prepared large-scale specialized data bases is already a reality, some of them using computer accessory compact disks. At the time of this writing, for example, the twelve volumes of the *Oxford English Dictionary* are available on three compact disks to be accessed in any number of ways by a computer, but the present cost is $1,250. This cost should go down drastically as such data bases become more popular. To my mind, the coming availability of large-scale genealogical data bases on compact disks is the most exciting new development in using computers for genealogy.

Chapter 15

The Organization of Genealogy

*In order to accomplish anything you have got to have a plat-
form.*
                                —Neil Kinnock and Joseph Biden

*Individuals may form communities, but it is institutions
alone that can create a nation.*
                                —Benjamin Disraeli

All it takes to become a genealogist is one hour visiting a local library
with a genealogical section. There is no apprenticeship mandated by
law, no required university degree, no licensing by local authorities. In
fact, one can save the hour and just declare, in front of a mirror or an
audience, "I am a genealogist," and who can dispute it?

People can also declare that they are historians, sociologists, or nuclear
physicists, but unless they have the degrees, the licenses, or the recognition of peers, they are not in danger of being taken too seriously. The
cause of history has not suffered because of history buffs asserting that
their interest in the subject gives them a right to the title. But genealogy
suffered for many years because people did take too seriously all those
who claimed to be genealogists. Anyone could write mediocre, undocumented, half- or quarter-correct family histories and send them to
libraries, and respectable genealogical libraries gratefully accepted these
offerings and put them on their shelves side by side with the works of
Jacobus and Walter Goodwin Davis. Anyone who could pay a printer

could have impressive name cards made with the words "Consulting Genealogist" under the name, and perhaps in the corner "Limited clients accepted."

But, happily, this is coming to an end. Oh, they can still call themselves genealogists, still write their inaccurate family histories, and still order name cards, but the difference is that they are no longer being taken so seriously. Today's sophisticated client in search of genealogical services will likely want to know, "Are you a Certified Genealogist, are you an Accredited Genealogist, or are you a member of A.P.G.?" And, with reference back to the quotation starting chapter 1, where Mills notes that the new breed of academician has been freely using the books put on the shelves of genealogical libraries to support significant general conclusions, more and more that new breed is inquiring also into the credentials of the person writing the book (and the level of documentation found in the book), before using material from that source to go out and publish gigantic boo-boos in his or her own learned dissertations.[1]

As with labor, minorities, doctors, and TV stars, so genealogists have become more and more organized. As Mills noted,[2] much of the schism between genealogy and academia has been due to the "issue of scholarship." Those genealogists whose mettle has been tested, especially in the learned journals (where they are like the guest of honor at a turkey shoot if they make mistakes), are fed up with being lumped together with armchair genealogists writing undocumented family histories "just for family." The organization of genealogy has been a slow, uneven, and sometimes painful process, but it has also been a continuing and lasting one. It behooves anyone in the field, or contemplating entering it, to know a bit about how genealogy is organized. What are the special interest groups, and how do they operate?

Early Genealogical Societies in America

Rabbi Malcolm Stern, F.A.S.G., points out that the first American heredity or genealogical society was the Society of the Cincinnati, founded after the American Revolution by regular army officers who organized in an attempt to get special privileges for themselves and their descendants.[3] This prestigious hereditary society, however, has not had much impact on the pursuit of genealogy as such, and it is noted here for historical purposes.

The next significant step in organization was the founding in 1845 of the New England Historic Genealogical Society (NEGHS), whose quarterly *The New England Historical and Genealogical Register* (*NEGHR*) has since been in continuous publication since 1847. The New York Genealogical and Biographic Society (NYGBS) was founded in 1869, and the first issue of its *New York Genealogical and Biographical Record* (*NYGBR*) came out in 1870.[4] Many of the founders and benefactors of both societies were well-educated people whose looking over the shoulders of those who filled the pages of their journals tended to make genealogical writers a bit more careful with their facts and conclusions than might otherwise be the case (even though many of the early articles are now known to have errors). NEHGS remained one of the leaders in genealogical education and publishing, and it has a lecture series at its Boston headquarters, sends its staff to speak throughout the country, and sponsors an annual fall tour to the LDS Family History Library in Salt Lake City, in addition to other occasional tours elsewhere. The NEHGS Library has been acclaimed as holding the best collection of books of any institute existing solely for genealogical purposes. NYGBS today is the leader in genealogical activities for New York and some surrounding areas such as close-in New Jersey.

The Founding of *The American Genealogist*

The founding of new genealogical journals encouraged better work (see chapter 3), and probably none more than Donald Lines Jacobus's *The American Genealogist*[5] (originally called *The New Haven Genealogical Magazine*), in a 1935 issue of which he gave his manifesto: "We maintain that it is our right and our privilege to apply to genealogy the same standards of research, documentation, and logical argument that are accepted in every other branch of historical study." Thus the learned journals carried the torch, and they served and are still serving not only as a source of enlightenment, but of education, for many people in the field: beginner, journeyman, or master alike. However, as with other forms of education, such as genealogical conferences, many times those who pay attention to the message do not need it, while the far greater number of those who really need it, do not put themselves in a position to receive it.

More Genealogical Societies and Annual Conferences

The National Genealogical Society (NGS), was founded in Washington, D.C., in 1903, as one out of many of the nation's local-area societies.[6] Its journal, the *National Genealogical Society Quarterly,* has at times resembled a local journal, and at other times under vigorous and talented editors, has been truly a national quarterly. In recent years NGS has been encouraged to expand its influence and become truly national, as its journal had already become. NGS began sponsoring national genealogical conferences held annually in different cities throughout the nation, with the 1988 conference held in Biloxi, Mississippi, the 1989 one scheduled for St. Paul, Minnesota, and the 1990 one scheduled for Arlington, Virginia. Attempting to get wide-spread attendance, the organizers of these conferences have obtained excellent speakers, with a deliberate mix of some of the best known genealogists in the country (indeed, the world, for speakers have come from Canada, England, Australia, Germany, and other countries), some of the best informed local-area specialists, and some promising newcomers on the genealogical lecture circuit. NGS is also engaged in many other educational, publishing, and social activities. It has taken a leading position in recognizing accomplishments in the field of genealogy by giving awards for that purpose, and it sponsors contests for genealogical articles by previously unpublished writers. It has recently initiated a Hall of Fame for genealogists (there have been two genealogists so honored thus far, first Donald Lines Jacobus and second Walter Goodwin Davis).

The other local societies formed to study genealogy in general, and their immediate surrounding areas in particular, have appeared almost spontaneously all over the country.[7] Sometimes a local historical society may function as a genealogical society, and vice versa. In some cases their influence has waxed and waned as they obtained or lost the services of strong, dedicated leaders. (It is also true for hereditary and many other societies that so frequently the strength of the organization depends upon the sacrifices made by one or two highly motivated individuals. This is highly commendable, but unfortunately once such leaders can no longer serve, the organization weakens unless there happen to be trained and motivated secondary leaders able to take over. A truly national organization will usually not be dependent on one or two individuals but will have a regular progression of leaders on all levels within the society.) For the beginning genealogist there are few better places to start than to visit a local genealogical or historical society, where one may find kindred spirits as well as the experience which may keep novices from having to reinvent the wheel.

Many local societies combined to form the Federation of Genealogical Societies (FGS), which also sponsors a national genealogical conference each year in different cities, working in coordination with a local society of the particular area.[8] The FGS thus can provide nation-wide educational services and also render a coordinating service to its individual member societies so that they can be more aware of what is going on in the genealogical world at large. The FGS conference in 1988 was held in Boston and in 1989 will be held in Seattle.

I have been pleased to lecture at both NGS and FGS conferences and to serve as chairman of a program sub-committee for the NGS 1985 conference in Salt Lake City. It is of course a task to put together such a conference, with many people involved in making local arrangements, handling logistics, arranging appropriately large and small rooms for the lectures and other meetings, organizing luncheons and banquets, contacting the mix of speakers and coordinating their various topics, and performing countless other activities to ensure that the conference will be a success.[9] Sometimes personality or organizational rivalries can cause special problems, and the conference chairmen must be good firemen. Often the area chosen for the conference influences the number of people attending, which has varied from a few hundred to a few thousand. Many of the participants mark it as an annual "must" on their activity calendars, while others are attending for the first time. Such conferences are a wonderful means of education, for lectures are carefully planned to serve the needs of all levels of beginning and experienced genealogists. They also serve as cross-pollination within the field, where people meet others who have common interests, have a chance to talk to genealogical writers with whose works they are acquainted, and get introduced to organizations and groups who can be of help to them. And far from the least attraction of conferences is the area set aside for "dealer tables," where large and small commercial organizations display and sell genealogical books and supplies, and which also serves as a social promenade, similar to walking to and fro past sidewalk cafes in large cities.

Problems of Conferences

Of course, state and local genealogical societies also hold conferences, and I heartily endorse all types, for they get genealogists to know each other and learn more both in particular and in general. There is nothing that will perpetuate ignorance more than isolation. I would note though a comment by Mills that "academicians are prone to berate the prevailing tendency of genealogical speakers to recycle their lectures, using the same fundamental presentations over and again before differing audiences."[10] Conference planners now have enough experience so that they make sure the offered menu is broad enough to have something of interest to everyone at all times, and the genealogical lecturer who is prone to repeat one speech over and over does not get invited to as many conferences as might once have been true. However, the other part of Mills's observations is still a problem: "The serious academician, schooled in the idea that a conference appearance demands a fresh paper based on new and original research, does experience difficulty appreciating the value of an effective genealogical lecture presented at the nonprofessional level." Several of us at the 1985 NGS conference tried to provide for the reading of learned papers providing never-before-published material by highly skilled genealogists. However, we found that this type of national genealogical conference, with its need to provide for attendees of widely differing backgrounds, was apparently not the place for "this time-honored custom among academicians."

There is still no platform available for genealogists to present and read papers, and I suggest that genealogy cannot fully become of age until some such facility is provided on a recurring basis. Since the large-attendee conferences do not need such papers, it might fall to some other organization, such as the American Society of Genealogists (ASG; see below) to arrange to invite some university historians to the annual ASG meeting and schedule a session for the reading of a few papers by historians touching upon genealogy, and genealogists touching upon history.

LDS Genealogical Activity

The LDS church has long been a leader in the area of organized genealogy, and, as mentioned, its Family History Library knows no peer in the world as a repository of genealogical materials. Since it is motivated by religious reasons, it spends a vast amount of money collecting, usually on microfilm, original genealogical records from all over the world, and it makes them available on a non-profit basis to any genealogist.[11] As Rabbi Stern points out regarding the LDS Family History Library, the "church has issued orders that no researchers are to be proselytized."[12] The LDS church has also sponsored international conferences on world records, family history, and other topics of interest to genealogists, and it also provides many other types of educational opportunities open to all.

In the above sense, then, the LDS church is indeed a leader in genealogy. However, by its own desire it does not attempt to "regulate" genealogy, and it has not noticeably been in the vanguard of those who try to improve genealogical reliability or standards. It encourages its members to research and submit family group sheets, and it provides voluntary educational courses, but it leaves the burden for accuracy entirely on the individual's shoulders. It makes these family group sheets and many, many commercially published and self-published books on family history available to library users with the caveat that it is not responsible for accuracy in the material. It does not require that its members submitting charts and published material adhere to the best genealogical standards and methodology. The main reason for this hands-off policy on standards and related topics is the LDS church feels that were it to do otherwise, it would be putting an unwelcome burden on its members. This is a pity because so many LDS members are engaged in genealogy, and it gives rise to the paradox that while the LDS church is otherwise such a recognized leader in genealogy, much of the research and analytical work done by its general membership is looked down upon as "amateurish" by other recognized genealogical authorities.[13]

Accreditation and Certification of Genealogists

One area, however, where the LDS Family History Library has taken an initiative to improve standards has been in creating an accreditation program. I mentioned earlier that very few people indeed make a living through genealogy. Although there are many professional genealogists providing services to clients for a fee, few work at it full time or continuously. The exceptions are those professional researchers in Salt Lake City who have made a career in providing services to clients from all over the world by using the library as their research center (it is open to them free of charge as it is to all others; and it might be noted that some of the Salt Lake City researchers are members of the LDS church, and some are not). The library runs an accreditation program intended to minimize any adverse effects the library might suffer by being associated, although quite unofficially, with inexperienced or incapable professional genealogists. The library provides a list of Accredited Genealogists, who are entitled to use the initials "A.G." after their names, to anyone inquiring about how to get in touch with a genealogical researcher.[14] Accreditation is given in different areas of research such as American, German, Polynesian, etc., and a person may be accredited in more than one area. To be accredited, a person must take written and oral examinations, which demonstrate how well the person knows general aspects of genealogy and particular aspects of the given area, though it should be noted that the emphasis is considerably on nineteenth- and twentieth-century sources. The existence of this accreditation system has been of considerable help in improving genealogy and making it more respectable.

There also exists a national program for qualifying the skills of professional genealogists administered by the Board for Certification of Genealogists (BCG).[15] The board was founded by the American Society of Genealogists (with NGS cooperation), but from the beginning has been a separate organization. Initially, its officers were Fellows of the American Society of Genealogists (FASG), and thus the board was in the hands of well experienced people who provided for a system of preempting new leaders to maintain the board's integrity. It now continues its functions under well qualified leaders and examiners chosen from certified people.[16] Certification is done by mail, involves a fee, and is entirely written (except that applicants for Certified Genealogical Lecturer must submit a tape recording of a lecture). There are different levels and types of certification including the highest, Certified Genealogist (CG), followed by Certified American Lineage Specialist (CALS), and Certified Genealogical Records Searcher (CGRS). In a category by itself is Certified American Indian Lineage Specialist (CAILS), and there are also Certified Genealogical Lecturers (CGL) and Certified Genealogical Instructors (CGI). The requirements vary according to category; for example, a Certified Genealogist must demonstrate great familiarity with primary sources and have ability to construct complete family genealogies, while a Certified Genealogical Record Searcher must show knowledge and ability to use all kinds of sources, but "is not certified to construct a pedigree or prepare a family history."

Neither the BCG nor the LDS Family History Library can guarantee the work of a certified or accredited genealogical professional. These various initials following a person's name mean that the respective grantor of them has examined the person and found him or her to be of a certain competence. They indicate a preliminary screening, not a blanket endorsement, but they do result in more desirable standardization in the field, and they help potential clients avoid selecting a genealogist on a purely hit-or-miss basis. Keep in mind, however, that there can be good professional genealogists who do not necessarily have initials after their names.

Professional genealogists in Utah some years ago organized a Association of Professional Genealogists (APG) to advance the interests of members, including providing standards for the relationship between genealogist and client. This has since become a nationwide, even international, organization with members from all over.[17] Genealogist-client relationships have been an area of some concern in genealogical circles because an unhappy client can put the integrity of the profession in question. First, there are undoubtedly people calling themselves genealogists who have taken money from clients and then given them shoddy service. Selecting someone who is certified, accredited, or belongs to the APG can minimize a client's chances of being cheated. On the other hand, there is something built into the genealogist-client relationship that sometimes leaves a disappointed client in spite of the fact that the genealogist may have behaved quite competently and conscientiously. The name of the villain is: *misunderstanding.* The genealogist is offering skilled services for hire, usually at an hourly rate, the same as a doctor or lawyer might do. But some clients feel that they are purchasing results. A competent doctor cannot cure a terminally ill patient, nor can a competent lawyer win a hopeless case. Nor can a competent genealogist find records where none exist. This might be a difficult concept for an individual to get across to an irate client, but an organization can help standardize situations and ensure that relations be better defined. Of course, this is not the only function of the APG, which has co-sponsored genealogical conferences, publishes a newsletter for its members, provides educational and advertising opportunities for members, and generally attempts to further the interests of the conscientious purveyor of genealogical information.

Fellows of the American Society of Genealogists

A word almost certain to strike an emotional chord from a knowledgeable genealogist (and some not so knowledgeable) is "fellow." It not only means different things to different people, but it can mean different things to the same person. For example, one of my greatest honors was in being elected a fellow. However, this has nothing to do with the fact that some years ago after I had written a few journal articles, I received a letter from England offering to make me a fellow in some international society of published writers. I had all the qualifications in my bank account, but I did not want to spend them (I forget the cost, but it was not cheap, something like $1,500 perhaps). There are fellows, and then there are fellows.

The society which honored me with my election as a fellow in 1985 was the American Society of Genealogists. Accordingly, you can consider anything I write below about fellows as prejudiced (and my comments certainly do not have an official sanction by the ASG), but I hope some objectivity will show through. The American Society of Genealogists was formed in 1940 by Dr. Arthur Adams, John Insley Coddington, and Meredith B. Colket, Jr., and in 1941 they were joined by Donald Lines Jacobus, Louis Effingham de Forest, Dr. Harold Bowditch, Milton Rubincam, Rosalie Fellows Bailey, G. Andrews Moriarty, and Walter Goodwin Davis. Other early fellows were Mary Lovering Holman, Clarence Almon Torrey, William Prescott Greenlaw, Walter Lee Sheppard, Jr., Sir Anthony Wagner, Noel C. Stevenson, George E. McCracken, and Sir Charles Travis Clay. These were some of the most experienced and acknowledged leaders in the entire field of genealogy.[18] The constitution of the society expressed its object:

> The purposes of the Society shall be the association of genealogists for the advancement of genealogical research and encouragement of publication of the results; and in general the securing for genealogy recognition as a serious scientific subject of research in the historical and social fields of learning.

Members were to be designated fellows and were to be chosen "on the basis of the quality and amount of their published genealogical work." The number of active fellows at any one time was limited to fifty (an inactive fellow may be given emeritus status and not count as one of the fifty). The deserved prestige of the early members and the determination of them and all subsequent fellows to perpetuate the organization by selecting only the best genealogical scholars in the country gave the society the reputation it has enjoyed for almost fifty continuous years. Other than having been selected for the quality and quantity of their published works, the fellows are not a homogenous group. They have included Ph.D.s and those without any degree; lawyers, doctors, and housewives; people as young as in their twenties and as old as in their nineties; computer analysts, government employees, and millionaires; knights of England and a professor of Mayan archeology; a general, a baron, a rabbi, several members of the LDS church, and a judge; and a few people who have depended on genealogy to earn a living.

No group of people can have a dominant influence in a field just by giving themselves titles. If the Fellows of the American Society of Genealogists are preeminent in the field of genealogy, and there are many people who say that they are, it is because they have been most conscientious about keeping true to the original purpose of the society. There are those who say that there are many more than fifty good genealogists in the country, and the numeric limit on fellows should be raised. But the society was not founded as a club for all good genealogists, and not many truly outstanding persons have missed being elected to fellowship (there are almost always a few vacancies, and because many genealogists have worked full time at other careers, a good number are up in years when first elected, so that attrition by death is not infrequent). There are also critics who say that still, some, if not many, outstanding genealogists have been passed over, and that may be true, but no organization of human beings is perfect, just as the study of genealogy itself is not perfect. And criticism has been voiced that certain cliques have taken over the society, but such criticism is usually hit-and-run, and cannot stand up to the facts. The Fellows of the American Society of Genealogists contain within their ranks some of the most respected genealogical authorities and prolific writers in the country, and, regardless of whether or not they are the best, they are indeed one of the main pillars of genealogy in America today. They themselves recognize that they are not the only pillars, and they have never claimed to be.

Other Fellows

There are other legitimate uses of the word "fellow" in the genealogical field. There has been a trend for various organized genealogical societies to honor some of their members by electing them fellows of the society. Some such societies base election on quality and quantity of service to the society, and at least one highly respected organization bases election on the amount of financial contributions. Some combine service and genealogical accomplishments as a joint criterion for election, and some use only genealogical accomplishment. Fellows of the Society of Genealogists in England (F.S.G.; and they include some Americans) once elected cannot maintain their honored status unless they also maintain membership and continue to pay dues in the society (the American Society of Genealogists has no dues or other required financial obligations), but this does not detract from the fact that people elected Fellows of the English Society of Genealogists are among the most knowledgeable genealogists in their field.

There are also, unfortunately, some individuals and organizations that use the word "fellow" in a covetous and highly misleading way to pretend or imply that their skills are more recognized in the field than is the case. One person interested in genealogy, stung by criticism of a poorly prepared book, where some of the critics were Fellows of the American Society of Genealogists attempted to organize a counter Society of Genealogical Disciplines (SGD) with 500 newly created fellows, though there were some who said the SGD stood for Sour Grapes Department. Some people have claimed to have created genealogical societies with names and initials similar to the better recognized ones, and undoubtedly there will be some innocents among the genealogical public who will salute fellows of these societies as if they were generally recognized genealogical authorities. Since many people reading this book may have an interest in knowing just who are the legitimate Fellows of the American Society of Genealogists, I will include all the names of living ones.[19] Though members are of course honored by being elected to a prestigious society, in the long run a society can keep its prestige only by the honor bestowed upon it by the recognized worth of its members.

Genealogical Coordinating Committee

In 1980 a number of genealogical societies formed the Genealogical Coordinating Committee as an umbrella organization to maintain coordination among themselves. These societies were the American Society of Genealogists, the Association of Professional Genealogists, the Board for Certification of Genealogists, the Federation of Genealogical Societies, and the National Genealogical Society. Non-voting observers have included the Genealogical Society of Utah and the U.S. National Archives. Among the functions of this committee is a semi-political one of encouraging genealogists all over to be active in supporting policies by federal, state, and local government to advance genealogy and oppose attempts by government officials to curtail access to genealogical records. Among its efforts was participation in a successful national move to obtain independence for the U.S. National Archives from the General Services Administration (GSA). The Genealogical Coordinating Committee has also created and administers a National Archives and Records Administration (NARA) Gift Fund, accumulated by the Federation of Genealogical Societies, to reproduce copies for the regional branches of the National Archives of records useful for genealogical research.

Genealogical Institutes

A number of universities and other public institutions have been active in one or more ways in genealogical areas. Some of the direct activity promoting genealogy has been by Brigham Young University in Utah, which has courses and degrees in the field of genealogy, as well as summer programs in genealogy and family history. On an advanced level, the Genealogical Coordinating Committee each summer presents a one-week National Institute on Genealogical Research in Washington, D.C., aimed at the experienced genealogist and hosted by the National Archives. The Committee selects the director, who has the full responsibility of advertising, recruiting attendees and faculty, and administering it.[20] After the National Institute, the oldest regularly scheduled genealogical summer institute in the country is that of Samford University, which presents a variety of courses for genealogists on all levels.[21] George Mason University in Fairfax, Virginia, has begun a new Middle Atlantic Genealogy and History Institute presenting summer courses on various levels, beginner through advanced.[22] Among other academic institutions featuring special genealogical educational opportunities is Westfield State College in Westfield, Massachusetts, which has begun an annual conference on biography, family history, and genealogy.[23]

Libraries, Publishers, and Booksellers

There are of course other organizations that contribute toward giving genealogy the respect of a serious scientific endeavor, but space is lacking to name them all. However, special mention must be made of those main ones who make the indispensable books available. The LDS Family History Library and the NEHGS Library have already been mentioned. The Library of Congress in Washington, D.C., would naturally be a superb place to find needed genealogical books. Many of the larger public libraries have well-stocked genealogical sections, New York City possibly being the most complete. Chicago is fortunate in having the Newberry Library, possessing one of the largest genealogical collections in the country. The Fort Wayne & Allen County Library in Indiana is another of the nation's most significant genealogical libraries. Among other excellent genealogical libraries is the Peabody Institute in Baltimore, with its virtually unmatched collection of medieval English sources. There are tremendous collections of appropriate material in many university libraries, such as Harvard's Widener Library. Some libraries have a special purpose, such as the Mayflower Library in Plymouth, Massachusetts. Sometimes a smaller but closer library can serve most of a person's needs, 60 or even 75 percent of the time, and they should be used as much as possible and supplemented with infrequent trips of a greater distance to a more complete library.

There are only a handful of companies specializing in publishing a significant number of genealogical books. The first that comes to mind for me is Ancestry, Inc., which has published my own books.[24] Genealogical Publishing Company in Baltimore is also one of the larger genealogical publishers.[25] This company is especially noted for its reprints, although it publishes some originals, too. Other large genealogical publishers are Everton Publishers,[26] and Heritage Books, Inc.[27] There are of course many smaller or specialized genealogical publishers, and some genealogical societies (such as NEHGS and NGS) also publish books. Two of the largest retailers carrying large stocks of genealogical books are

Goodspeed's, serving the Boston area, and Hearthstone, serving the Washington area.[28] There are a surprising number of other good retail stores for genealogical books all over the country, and a check through the telephone yellow pages can usually find them. Almost all these book stores, large and small, can special order almost any desired book and obtain it quickly for a customer.

The Interlocking Whole

It should not be thought that the various organizations mentioned above are mutually exclusive. Many of the leaders in genealogy are active in more than one organization; therefore, there is an interlocking overall organization of genealogy. There are perhaps individual rivalries and at times feuds between individuals and within organizations (just as there are in the governmental, business, and academic worlds), but there is also a moderating influence of the emerging total organization that tends to minimize violence and keep long run attention on the major goal of advancing the cause of honest genealogy and conscientious genealogists. And there is always room for many more genealogists to participate in one or more parts of this growing organization.

Notes

1. Elizabeth Shown Mills, "Academia va. Genealogy," *National Genealogical Society Quarterly* 71 (1983):103, observed that "demographic histories are being produced [by Ph.D.s], based upon 'rich genealogical sources,' which the genealogical community has long since proven to be unreliable."
2. See the beginning of chapter 13.
3. Malcolm H. Stern, "The Genealogical Researcher Past and Present: Images and Realities," a talk given at Chicago, 30 August 1986, to the Society of American Archivists. I have also used other material from Rabbi Stern's talk as background information in the preparation of this chapter.
4. Information may be obtained on the New England Historic Genealogical Society by writing to it at 101 Newbury Street, Boston, MA 02116, and on the New York Genealogical and Biographical Society by writing to it at 122 East 58th Street, New York, NY 10022.
5. The address of *The American Genealogist* is 128 Massasoit Drive, Warwick, RI 02888. Information on *The Genealogist,* mentioned in chapter 3, can be obtained from 255 North Second West Street, Salt Lake City, UT 84103-4545.

6. Information on the National Genealogical Society may be obtained by writing to it at 4527 17th Street, North, Arlington, VA 22207.

7. For the best comprehensive list of such societies, see Mary K. Meyer, *Meyer's Directory of Genealogical Societies in the U.S.A. and Canada;* this book is updated frequently and information on it may be obtained from Mary K. Meyer, Box 29, Lintihicum Heights, MD 21090.

8. Additional information on the FGS may be obtained from the Federation of Genealogical Societies, P.O. Box 220, Davenport, IA 52805.

9. A newcomer invited to speak at such a conference would be well advised to provide for "hand-outs" to the audience, which expects them and becomes like roaring, starved tigers if they do not get them.

10. Mills, op. cit., 105.

11. There is no charge for using the facilities of the LDS Family History Library in Salt Lake City. Family History Centers (branch libraries) in other places do not charge for the use of materials they have on hand, but require a small fee for the use of material, such as microfilms, which must be ordered from Salt Lake City.

12. Stern, op. cit.

13. As validating genealogist for a number of hereditary societies, I would not accept LDS family group sheets as evidence for applications. Many of my counterparts in other societies would not accept them either. However, some validating genealogists have gone further and refused to accept, say, marriage certificates of couples in LDS temples, which showed a lack of understanding. A marriage certificate by a clergyman of any religion is primary evidence. All genealogists should make careful distinctions between LDS primary materials and secondary materials (see chapter 4 for definitions), and the universal rule holds here, too: Secondary evidence may be useful for clues, but it is not acceptable by itself except for any readily-checkable documentation it provides. There has been wonderful cooperation between the LDS Family History Library and the non-LDS genealogical world, and I would not want anything I write to be construed as anything other than constructive criticism. Glade I. Nelson, one of the Library managers and a highly skilled genealogist himself, in a talk to the Fellows of the American Society of Genealogists in 1986, put in excellent perspective the fact that there is some difference between the goals of the overall LDS genealogy program and the needs of outside genealogists. Honest recognition of this difference by both groups aids their mutually beneficial cooperation.

14. This list is available to anyone writing to the LDS Family History Library, 35 North West Temple, Salt Lake City, UT 84150. Have the now well-established courtesy of sending a stamped, self-addressed envelope, and this of course applies to making inquiries at any other address mentioned in this book.

15. P.O. Box 19165, Washington, DC 20036-0165. The BCG will mail a list of certified persons to anyone who asks for it and encloses a check for $2 plus a stamped, self-addressed, legal-size envelope. Certified persons are listed by the state(s) or foreign area(s) in which they specialize.

16. As of late 1987, the trustees of the board consisted of four fellows and eleven non-fellows.

17. Inquiries to the APG may be made at P.O. Box 11601, Salt Lake City, UT 84037.

18. The American Society of Genealogists has published two volumes, which are now being distributed by Ancestry, Inc. These are *Genealogical Research: Methods and Sources,* vol. 1, edited by Milton Rubincam (Washington, D.C., revised 1980), and vol. 2, edited by Kenn Stryker-Rodda (Washington, D.C., revised 1983).

19. The Fellows of the American Society of Genealogists as of September 1988 follow: Enid L. Adams; Cameron Allen; Robert C. Anderson; John D. Austin, Jr.; Rosalie F. Bailey; Rachel E. Barclay; Timothy F. Beard; Raymond M. Bell; John I. Coddington; Peter Wilson Coldham; F. James Dallett; David C. Dearborn; Winston DeVille; J. Frederick Dorman; Jane F. Fiske; David L. Greene; Charles M. Hansen; Mary M. Harter; Henry B. Hoff; Winifred L. Holman; Henry Z. Jones, Jr.; Roger D. Joslyn; C. Frederick Kaufholz; David H. Kelley; Virginia P. Livingston; MacLean W. McLean; W. Blake Metheny; Elizabeth Shown Mills; Nils William Olsson; Gerald J. Parsons; Paul W. Prindle; Christine Rose; Milton Rubincam; Jean Rumsey; Donna V. Russell; George Ely Russell; Kenneth Scott; W. Lee Sheppard, Jr.; Ruth Wilder Sherman; Kip Sperry; Malcolm H. Stern; Noel C. Stevenson; Eugene A. Stratton; Kenn Stryker-Rodda; Neil D. Thompson; Sir Anthony Wagner; Robert S. Wakefield; Elizabeth P. White; and George O. Zabriskie.

20. Information on the institute can be obtained by writing to it at P.O. Box 57280, Washington, D.C. 20037.

21. Information may be obtained from Samford University Library, Birmingham, AL 35209.

22. Information on the Middle Atlantic Genealogy and History Institute may be obtained from George Mason University, Office of Community Services, 4400 University Drive, Fairfax, VA., 22030.

23. Details may be obtained from Westfield State College, Westfield, MA 01086.

24. P.O. Box 476, Salt Lake City, UT 84110.

25. 1001 N. Calvert Street, Baltimore, MD 21202.

26. P.O. Box 368, Logan, UT 84321.

27. 1540 E. Pointer Ridge Road, Bowie, MD 20716.

28. Goodspeed's Book Shop, Inc., 7 Beacon Street, Boston, MA 02108; and Hearthstone Bookshop, Potomac Square, 8405-H Richmond Highway, Alexandria, VA 22309.

The Validity of
Genealogical Evidence

[*This article was first published in the* National Genealogical Society Quarterly *72 (1984):273-85, and was in turn based on a talk I gave on 14 September 1984 at a genealogical conference in Denver, Colorado, sponsored by the Federation of Genealogical Societies and the Association of Professional Genealogists. The copyright is owned by the National Genealogical Society, and I am grateful for their permission to reprint the article here. Though I would not be reprinting it if I did not feel it is as true today as when first conceived, still with continuing experience I might not express my thoughts and beliefs today in precisely identical words.*]

Perhaps a better title for this talk would be "An Introduction to the Validity of Genealogical Evidence," for the subject is a huge one. I will attempt in this introduction to give you an understanding – not by definition, but by example – of how to judge the validity of evidence. By validity I mean the relative strength of the evidence to support the conclusion one draws from it. If I dwell a bit on the negative, giving examples of what is not valid evidence, please forgive me, but this particular subject, I think, needs some shock treatment.

The Two Nations

That great British prime minister and intellect of the last century, Benjamin Disraeli, who was also a novelist, in his book *Sybil*[1] coined a phrase which by its aptness captured the imagination of British politicians and scholars for many years and is still used today. In one scene, Lord Egremont remarks to two strangers, "'Say what you will, our Queen reigns over the greatest nation that ever existed.' 'Which nation?' asked the younger stranger, 'for she reigns over two.' The stranger paused; Egremont was silent but looked inquiringly. 'Yes,' resumed the younger stranger after a moment's interval. 'Two nations between whom there is no intercourse and no sympathy; who are as ignorant of each other's habits, thoughts, and feelings, as if they were dwellers in different zones or inhabitants of different planets; who are formed by a different breeding, are fed by a different food, are ordered by different manners, and are not governed by the same laws.' 'You speak of – ' said Egremont hesitatingly. 'The rich and the poor.'"

I want to speak today about the "two nations" that exist in genealogy, two nations between which there is no intercourse and no sympathy; who are as ignorant of each other's habits, thoughts, and feelings, as if they were dwellers in different zones or inhabitants of different planets; who are formed by a different breeding, are fed by a different food, are ordered by different manners, and are not governed by the same laws. One nation is that small minority that respects documentation and evidence, and the other nation is that vast majority to whom the validity of genealogical evidence is a meaningless concept.[2]

I naturally assume that virtually all of you who are here today are in the former group. But should there be any of the latter group among you, I do not mean to speak insultingly but rather helpfully and sympathetically, for I was once there myself. I would attempt to open up to you new vistas in genealogy, new understanding, greater compassion, higher satisfaction. I would attempt to take you out of the quicksand and place you on solid ground.

Hereditary Society Standards

As historian general of the Mayflower Society for two years, I processed some 3,500 applications for membership and examined the evidence submitted to support each generation from the applicant back to a 1620 *Mayflower* passenger. Before my time this documentation was referred to as "proofs," but I soon changed that, for I found that what was called a "proof" very often proved nothing. I was frankly appalled not only by what people offered as evidence, but also by the general lack of understanding of what had been going on in the field of genealogy. People who would not believe the promises made by a presidential candidate would accept what a mountebank such as Sir Bernard Burke might write in *Burke's Peerage* as if it were the gospel truth. They would accept the words of charlatan pedigree peddlers as if engraved on stone and carried down from Mount Sinai. They might not trust their slightly dotty Great Aunt Minnie to make change for a dollar, but if she wrote a family history, that part of her image would be transported to become someone worthy of abiding in the Hall of Fame for Historians, side by side with Samuel Eliot Morison. That anything appearing in print might be based in any part on wishful thinking, mistaken identity, misinterpretation of facts, unthinking gullibility, or just plain intention to deceive was a concept alien to their powers of ratiocination. That there might be two or more people in a given state with the name of Lydia Jones or Ebenezer Jackson was a far-fetched notion. Dates and places were abstractions that validating genealogists wanted to see filled out on application forms just to justify their existence, and thus they would become perturbed, angry, and antagonistic if the approving official wrote back to point out that they had a child born thirty years before the parent. Likely ages for marrying or child-bearing were so much trivia, and they found nothing wrong in a man marrying at age ten or a woman giving birth at age sixty. And they would become indignant if the approving genealogist observed that the Anna Smith getting married in Louisiana in 1830 might not be the same Anna Smith born in Maine in 1795. If the name of an ancestor was not with the other children of a family in the desired father's will, nor in vital records, nor in land transactions, nor in census records, all that would not hold a candle against the more impressive fact that it was a family tradition. I have had people come into my office and tell me that their name was White or Brown or Cooke, and since there were passengers of these surnames on the *Mayflower*, obviously they were *Mayflower* descendants, and would I please fill in all the intervening generations?

Currently, I am the herald/genealogist for the Descendants of Illegitimate Sons and Daughters of the Kings of Britain, sometimes called the Royal Bastards. Now why would anyone want to join a society which broadcasts one's descent from illegitimacy? But there is a good reason, and in fact it is considered one of the most desirable of hereditary societies to join. And the reason is given in a letter which one of the founders wrote to me some years back. The purpose, he said, was "to ridicule the lousy scholarship used by some of the extant precolonial societies by requiring high scholarship for membership in a society that could not possibly have snob value – a VIP ancestor. How the tables have been turned, and it is now the society to join!" I hasten to add that many of the other societies – and Mayflower I know from personal experience – have necessarily been tightening their standards in recent years. Still, as far as I know, the Royal Bastards is the only hereditary society where the requirements specifically call for documenting a line according to scholarly standards. As one Fellow of the American Society of Genealogists, who is not a member himself, called it, it is a genealogist's hereditary society.[3] But therein lies a paradox. The main reason for joining is that membership is a guarantee that the line has been examined and found true under very strict standards, and most of our applicants appreciate this, though some seem to want to keep the standards high – but for the other fellow! I am still receiving some applications from well-meaning people who expect me to accept many generations based only on unsupported secondary sources. But mark you, these applicants are not trying to get away with anything. They believe in good faith that finding a line recorded somewhere, anywhere, in print, is proving a line according to scholarly standards.[4] It is a matter which needs much education, for again the "two nations" have different views of the validity of genealogical evidence.

Genealogical Research Not Easy

I would recommend to you for further reading an article by that superb American genealogist, G. Andrews Moriarty, in the 1925 issue of *The New England Historical and Genealogical Register* entitled "The Royal Descent of a New England Settler."[5] In one part of this article he wrote:

> Occasional perusals of the Genealogical Department of the *Boston Evening Transcript* and other publications have convinced the writer of this article that, in spite of the fact that "all men are created equal" and in spite of the good old American contempt for royalty and the "effete nobility of Europe," the American genealogical public have an exceedingly strong desire to deduce their descent by hook or by crook from the same "effete" royal and noble houses of Europe. Furthermore, an investigation of these claims

usually shows that not one in twenty of such pedigrees can stand up under the searching test of modern scientific investigation. These lines are usually based upon the works of Dugdale and their derivatives, upon printed county histories, and upon the notoriously inaccurate so-called visitation pedigrees of the sixteenth and seventeenth centuries edited by the Harleian Society; and, when these fail, the most wild and careless statements are relied upon.

And later in the article Moriarty wrote:

The present article is written as an indicator, to point out the path in which those who desire to deal with medieval genealogy in a serious manner must travel; and it is written solely to encourage such work. No statement will be made without citing the original document relied upon for it, so that the reader may judge for himself the value of the evidence and decide whether the conclusions reached are justified. To prepare such a pedigree is no easy matter; and I especially wish to show those persons who write glibly of "royal descents" how much labor is involved if a careful pedigree is to be presented.

Yes, it is no easy matter to prepare such a pedigree, and yet I am constantly being told by people that they have this or that royal line, often in a context of, "Oh, I have two of these, and three of the other, and five of those," as if they were picking out pastries in a patisserie.[6] When I say people, I mean educated people, people with responsible positions, people whose livelihoods depend of their everyday discernment of true or false statements, – lawyers; doctors; church officials; university professors; and people in real estate, insurance, and investments – and yet people who, when it comes to genealogy, seem to abandon every principle of common sense that they ever knew. They know that royal lines are hard to come by – for the other fellow! But they consider themselves an exception because some relative told them they had a royal line, or they came across it in a book, or they figured it out one rainy afternoon at the public library while perusing Burke's *Peerage* or Virkus's *Compendium of American Genealogy*. It reminds me of a remark by Justin Winsor in his *History of the Town of Duxbury*[7] to the effect that pedigrees by the well-known genealogist Horatio G. Somerby were always amazingly detailed. We know now that the detail in Somerby's pedigrees was so amazing because Somerby went as far as he could from the records and then filled in the rest from his fruitful imagination. Needless to say, Somerby was in much demand as a genealogist by people who were just begging to be taken in. P. T. Barnum missed his calling when he neglected to become a genealogist.

Probably the best known respectable books for Americans on royal and noble lines are *Ancestral Roots of Sixty American Colonists* and *Magna Charta Sureties*,[8] both by Weis and Sheppard. Yet note that the former is now available in the fifth edition, and the latter in the third edition, and there is no doubt that there will be still newer editions. The whole implication of continual revision is that when we are dealing with medieval genealogy we are dealing with a very fluid subject. The paucity of evidence alone gives rise to much conjecture. Gradually, as scholars examine and reexamine those best known medieval lines, they are becoming weeded out. Lines once held to be valid by the best of scholars are subject to being cut if the latest evidence requires it. Inclusion of a line in one of these books is no guarantee that it is accurate. Walter Lee Sheppard in his introduction to the latest edition of *Magna Charta Sureties* observes, "The reader should note that not all lines have been verified, nor do the notations of corrections in a line indicate that all other generations have been checked and found to be correct." And he adds, "Even though we believe this to be one of the most carefully compiled and most accurate books in the field, the user should verify all statements and dates with source material before transferring them to a lineage blank for application for membership in an hereditary society, or before incorporating them into a published genealogy."

No matter who the writer is, anyone can make errors in genealogy. I have found mistakes in Jacobus, Moriarty, and the *Complete Peerage*. I am certainly no exception and have found errors in my own published articles. As the great genealogists of the past, starting with J. Horace Round, have discovered, there is no substitute for putting the reader in possession of all the facts. If the genealogist has drawn a wrong conclusion, or if newer evidence invalidates a genealogist's earlier assessment, the citation of all the material that the genealogist relied on will allow subsequent readers to put everything in proper prospective. A writing can be no more reliable than the sources it cites.

Errors in Sources Usually Considered Accurate

Good genealogical research is not easy. It is amazing how people who would not dream of flying an airplane without lessons, removing an appendix without medical training, or remodeling a house without some form of apprenticeship will appoint themselves full-fledged genealogists after three visits to the genealogical section of the local library. Let me try to give you some idea of what a researcher may be up against. I wrote an article called "The Elusive Luces" for the February 1981 issue of the *Mayflower Quarterly*.[9] In researching the article, I came across errors in no less than four source materials generally considered accurate. First, the marriage of William Luce in Concord is reported in the book *Weston Births, Marriages and Deaths*,[10] thus giving an impression that he was of Weston. This was no doubt because another book, *Concord Births, Marriages and Deaths*,[11] in showing the marriage called him "of Western." The compiler of the Weston book probably knowing of no town called Western, reasoned that it meant Weston. A little more background in Massachusetts history would have told him that a town of Western did in fact once exist but had changed its name to Warren in honor of the Revolutionary War general. William Luce had lived in Warren when it was still known as Western.

The town name change was the cause of a second error when someone years ago obtained a true copy of the births of some of William Luce's children from the town clerk of Greenwich, Massachusetts. A true copy is a certification that it is an exact transcription of public records, but in this case it really was not true, for the town clerk left off three significant words "born in Werston." They were probably meaningless to him, but of course this was a typical misspelling for the town of Western, which by the time of the town clerk was known as Warren.

The town of Greenwich was flooded to make way for a reservoir, and its records were never published in book form. However, the DAR transcribed the records and sent copies to a few large genealogical libraries.[12] I have great respect for the DAR in preserving thusly so many valuable genealogical records which might otherwise be lost to us. It was by means of their transcription that I learned of the missing "born in werston" phrase from the true copy. But transcriptions are seldom 100 percent accurate, and in fact the average error rate is generally considered to be around 5 percent. It was only because I went to the reservoir headquarters where the original Greenwich records are kept that I was able to pick up an important marriage record, which had been skipped over by the person making the DAR transcription.

A fourth error involved a published transcription of the 1800 census, where I found William Luce, but not his son, William, Jr. All the other evidence indicated that William, Jr., had to be in that town at that time, and so I checked a microfilmed copy of the original census records, and found, sure enough, that both William and William, Jr. were there, one immediately after the other. Four errors in sources usually considered correct just in researching a seven-page article! If this is the general state of affairs, how can we ever expect to find anything reliable in genealogy? Well, the answer is that we just have to do everything possible to keep error rates as low as possible; to get as close as possible to the original source so as to eliminate transcription error; and to make it standard practice to learn about the areas we are dealing with before we write about them, so that we will know about town name changes or about jurisdictional changes which might mean that a town's records could be located in some county other than its present one. But my point here is not so much good research practices, as important as they are, but rather I am concerned with the recognition that so many people writing family histories cannot or will not put good research techniques to use. Who, for example, living in the midwest, can afford to go to the Quabbin Reservoir Headquarters in Massachusetts to double-check DAR transcriptions? The resources available to most compilers of family histories are scant, and the inclination to double-check information is not strong. Is it any wonder that family histories as a group are given so little credence by genealogical authorities or by the validating genealogists for hereditary societies? It is a fact that most published family histories contain significant error. In fact, Stevenson quotes one writer as stating that only 10 percent of them are worth the paper they are printed on, but that is an exaggeration in the other direction.[13] Perhaps only 10 percent of them have fair-to-high reliability, but the other 90 percent can be useful in varying degrees for clues – starting points prior to more detailed investigation.

Mayflower Society Examples

Let me now give some examples from Mayflower cases of how genealogical evidence plays an indispensable part in determining correct lineages. Let's start with a difficult one. Ruth Church was a great-granddaughter of *Mayflower* passenger Richard Warren, and consequently all her blood descendants would be *Mayflower* descendants. Ruth's second husband was Joseph Child of Watertown, and they had a daughter, Lydia Child. Watertown vital records show that James Fay of Westborough and Lydia Child of Watertown were married in 1727. No other Lydia Child was found in Watertown records. When many years ago applications for Mayflower membership used this line there was no reason to suspect it. This is a case which could have fooled any but the most painstaking researcher. It was only when other applications for Mayflower membership came in from descendants of a David Ingersoll and his wife Lydia Child that it was required for the Mayflower Society to look further.[14] And a further look showed that Lydia Child's father died in 1711; his widow Ruth, the *Mayflower* passenger's great-granddaughter, moved across Massachusetts to Springfield, and she married Thomas Ingersoll. Daughter Lydia must have moved with her, for she was under fourteen when her mother remarried. A year after the mother's remarriage, we find a Lydia Child marrying David Ingersoll, son of her mother's new husband. Thus we have two contemporary Lydia Childs, one in Watertown marrying James Fay, and one having moved from Watertown to Springfield with her mother and marrying David Ingersoll. It was obvious now which was the *Mayflower* descendant. As a clue for the descendants of the Lydia Child who married James Fay, it was found that there was another Child family in Waltham, near Watertown, and it seemed that another daughter of that family had married a brother of James Fay. The salient point of this example is that it is wrong to presume, when a man and wife are known to be in one town, and some years later a boy or girl of the same surname marries in that town, that they must necessarily be parents and child. Real life takes place in a flux. People move into town. People move out of town. Surnames usually occur in clusters spread out over areas, so that confining a search to a given town, instead of the entire area around that town, can lead to erroneous identifications. Or to put it another way, to be certain of a given parent-child relationship, we need more than just the same surname in the right time and place – we need positive identification from such documents as probate and land records.

Now let's take an easy one. Ann Dodge was a sixth generation descendant of *Mayflower* passenger Richard More. An application claimed that this Ann Dodge was identical to an Amee Dodge who married Ebenezer Maynard. I do not have any difficulty in accepting that Ann may later be called Amee; but I do have a problem with chronology in this case, for the documentation showed that Amee Dodge who married Ebenezer Maynard did so thirty-one years before the *Mayflower* Ann Dodge was born. Needless to say, this application was quietly withdrawn. The lesson would seem to be to watch your chronology, but notice once again that the mistake was the most common of all, assuming that two people with the same or similar names must be identical. Numerous similar examples could be given, such as the two Elizabeth Spragues, the two John Kingsleys, the two Sarah Cookes, the two Thomas Russells, the two Anna Moshers, the two Sarah Snows, the two John Sampsons, the two Mary Haskells, the two Jonathan Whites, etc.; in each of these pairs, one or more *Mayflower* applicants had confused the identities.

The test of a genealogical fact must be a series of questions: What is the ultimate source? How contemporary to the event is the ultimate source? How well does the event agree or disagree with other known information? Is the event sufficient to support a genealogical identification? Let me give you one more Mayflower Society example. The facts are these: First, Jonathan Morey married a widow, Mary Bartlett Foster, who was a granddaughter of *Mayflower* passenger Richard Warren. Second, a generation later an unidentified Mary married Nathaniel Atwood. The claim has been made by descendants of Nathaniel and Mary Atwood that she was a daughter of Jonathan Morey and Mary Bartlett Foster Morey. The obvious facts against it are that there was no vital record of Jonathan having a daughter Mary, nor was a daughter Mary mentioned with other children in Jonathan Morey's will nor in any land transaction. In other words, no contemporary evidence. On the other hand, the supposed daughter is shown in the *Shurtleff Genealogy* by Benjamin Shurtleff, a respected writer. Alfred Wood, a disinterested writer, also gave her the Morey surname in his book *Middleborough Deaths,* and further Nahum Mitchell, compiler of the *History of Bridgewater,* wrote a letter to a Mary Atwood descendant, saying, "Your proofs are sufficient to show [Nathaniel Atwood's] wife to have been Mary Morey." There is also a letter written by the above-mentioned Benjamin Shurtleff telling why he included her as a Morey in his Shurtleff book.[15] He said his grandfather's brother, Dr. Nathaniel B. Shurtleff, a highly respected historian, was quite interested in the family genealogy and left "all these scraps of paper with little memoranda on it. Nothing was in any shape or form except a few cases." Benjamin Shurtleff collated the scraps of paper and used many of them in his family history. In other words, we seem to have a good bit of secondary evidence for the assertion that Mary Atwood's maiden name was Morey. However, I showed in an article in the *Mayflower Quarterly*, August 1982,[16] that it was likely Wood and Mitchell were merely repeating information from Shurtleff. The fact was that there was no information on this Mary Atwood's parentage in the seventeenth or eighteenth centuries. George Ernest Bowman, the patriarch of *Mayflower* genealogy, did not accept her as a Morey. Florence Barclay, an acknowledged authority on Pilgrim genealogy, wrote an article against it in which she gave good circumstantial evidence to show that Mary Atwood's maiden name was Lucas, not Morey. So what it all comes down to is the mere assertion by Benjamin Shurtleff, who, as a descendant himself of Mary Atwood, could hardly be called impartial. We have then an assertion made 150 years after the fact by an interested party supported solely by unspecified words on an unseen scrap of paper found among his grandfather's brother's completely disorganized genealogical notes. See how that good bit of secondary authority, when analyzed, comes down to nothing more than a rather flimsy single piece of evidence which, by any reasonable standard, is totally insufficient. What I emphasize here is the absolute necessity of getting back to the ultimate source.

I am going to give an opinion as to why Shurtleff never disclosed the contents of his scraps of paper. My experience in examining thousands of applications for hereditary societies has shown me that people do not like to lie in matters concerning genealogy. When it comes to lying, most of the out and out falsehoods that I know of have come from the professional pedigree peddlers of the past, Sir Bernard Burke being one of the most notorious. But the furthest most people go is to suppress evidence. I have sometimes had people submit a page from a book supporting a claim, but they neglect to send the very next page which denies or contradicts the first page. And far more prevalent than lying is drawing a completely unwarranted conclusion from insufficient facts. If Shurtleff had lied and said that one of his scraps was a contemporary letter stating that

Mary Atwood was a daughter of Jonathan and Mary Morey, he most likely would have been taken at his word, and the line would have been accepted. However, I think he probably deduced the relationship by drawing from his scrap of paper a highly subjective, unwarranted conclusion based on some words which might have set up a very weak circumstantial case. I think he might have withheld the contents of his scraps because he would have been ashamed to let others know how weak was the evidence on which he was making such an unflinching claim. I could be wrong in this case, but if so it would still not invalidate my overall belief that many times people dealing with genealogy prefer to give us their conclusions rather than their facts because they instinctively know that their conclusions are not objectively and rationally justified.

Notice that I just mentioned for the second time that old purveyor of purloined pedigrees, Sir Bernard Burke of *Burke's Peerage.* Lest anyone think I am unjustly picking on him, I will mention a few references to him from Noel C. Stevenson's book *Genealogical Evidence.*[17] Stevenson gives Jacobus as the source for the comment that, "Only genealogical novices rely on Burke." A more indignant quotation comes from the noted English historian Edward Freeman, who wrote in words which seem to roar, "What for instance can be the state of mind of Sir Bernard Burke? Does he know, or does he not know, the manifest falsehood of the tales he reprints year after year?" So much for Sir Bernard, though I should also note that *Burke's Peerage* (since Sir Bernard) has gradually improved over the years. Noel Stevenson's book, incidentally, is very quotable, and I could easily pad this lecture with numerous remarks of his, but instead will just refer you to his book as one which belongs in every genealogist's library.

Errors in Typical Printed Sources

After confused identity, probably the most customary mistake involving the validity of genealogical evidence comes from the perpetuation of errors from undocumented secondary sources. In a recent issue of *The Genealogist,*[18] I have a correction noting how three of the most commonly used secondary sources on colonial New England genealogy, that is, Savage's *Dictionary,* Mitchell's *Bridgewater,* and Davis's *Ancient Landmarks,* are all wrong in concluding that immigrant Philip Washburn did not have children. These and similarly impartially written books giving genealogies by locality are excellent for clues, but totally unacceptable as proof. When it comes to family histories, in which the writer usually has a direct personal interest, the situation is often worse. Let me quote a few remarks from Mayflower Society cases involving some such books: "Mary who was the wife to Samuel Sturtevant of Halifax was not of this Prince family and probably did not even have the Prince surname, although Davis erroneously gives her the Prince surname in *Ancient Landmarks of Plymouth*"; and "this is another case where Mitchell's *History of Bridgewater* is wrong"; and "the various sources mentioning Ansel Burrows (such as *Ancient Landmarks of Plymouth; History of Paris, Maine; History of Cornish, N.H.;* and *Cutter*) give conflicting information"; and "the author of [this] genealogy, which had made the erroneous claim, wrote to say that as a result he checked further and found evidence to confirm our rejection"; and "Mary Delano did not marry William Spooner, as claimed by the *Spooner Genealogy*"; and "Monette is unreliable and the *Dunham Genealogy* is self-contradictory"; and "the author of the *Faxon Genealogy* had made an error"; and the "line in the *Church Genealogy* is now known to be incorrect"; and "this means that *Colonial Families in America* is incorrect"; and "the cause of error is in the *Hinds Family Genealogy*"; and "the identification of Jireh Wilcox as being identical with Tyle Wilcox, as given in the *Ricketson Genealogy,* is entirely wrong." I could go on and on, but I think the point is made. Keep in mind that these are typical of the printed secondary sources which are habitually used by people as the "proof" of their genealogical endeavors.

Medieval Pedigrees, Visitations, and County Histories

Let me move on now to use English medieval genealogy as a background for some other kinds of examples. But first, it might be useful to ask, how does one go about compiling a medieval pedigree in the first place? Again, I would refer you to the 1925 article by Moriarty. There you will find that he has painstakingly sought out contemporary documents of the eleventh and following centuries, many of them in Latin, to build up meticulously step-by-step, generation-by-generation, a firm foundation. Fortunately some of the documents he needed had been published, but many had not; we are a bit luckier today because more have been published, but far from all. While Moriarty gives you the fruits of his labors, he does not go into detail about the labors themselves. For this we must go to another, and I cite *The Trowbridge Genealogy,*[19] much of the English part of which was gathered by Lothrop Withington. Though a bit later than medieval, it shows similar research problems. In a letter to the person commissioning the genealogy, Withington writes of the efforts of himself and two assistants:

> We so organized our work as to give every possible chance of immediate result. At Wells we went through every existing transcript of the over five hundred parish registers of Somerset, largely repulsive, rotten and faded fragments, to find if possible the marriage of John and the baptism of Thomas. At Exeter we not only used the diocesan and probate registries for the available points, but also the old registries of St. Petrock and St. Kerian, to some purpose. Our main attack however was at Taunton where things seemed absolutely hopeless after the partial failure of the hopeless muddle in the Castle and the exhaustion of every likely name of the probate registry. We saw there was nothing for it but to go through the files for a hundred years and look at every Taunton will and also any oddments. Hence our triumph. We could only do this, however, with exceptional official friendly relations at Taunton, and doing at a moderate estimate three months' work or one or two months' work for three in less than a week....I enclose the John Trowbridge will.

Please observe here that we have another case dealing with disorganized scraps of paper, but here, unlike Shurtleff's case above, we are told the exact contents of those scraps of paper, which are published in *The Trowbridge Genealogy.* We are allowed to see for ourselves just how convincing they might be.

As far as medieval pedigrees in general are concerned, it is worth repeating a bit from Moriarty; "An investigation of these claims usually shows that not one in twenty of such pedigrees can stand up under the searching test of modern scientific investigation. These lines are usually based upon the works of Dugdale and their derivatives, upon printed county histories, and upon the notoriously inaccurate so-called visitation pedigrees of the sixteenth and seventeenth centuries edited by the Harleian Society; and, when these fail, the most wild and careless statements are relied upon." What does he mean "the notoriously inaccurate so-called visitation pedigrees?" The visitations occurred because there was royal concern about people bearing coats of arms to which they were not entitled. There were people then just as eager to claim false ancestors as there are some now. Heralds were sent all over England to examine those claiming armigerous rights, and they had authority to order those not entitled to arms to cease use of them, even to the extent of causing stone carvings of false arms in churches to be effaced if need be. They compiled records of their findings which are still held privately in the College of Arms in London, though some became publicly available.[20] Many have been published by the Harleian Society, frequently with augmentations not authorized by the heralds. These are usually in the form of pedigree charts showing lines of descent for a few or for many generations. The basic information was given to the heralds by a bearer of the arms in question, but the herald was empowered to make other inquiries for confirmation. The accuracy of these charts depends on a number of things: first, on the honesty and the knowledge of the bearer of arms; next upon the ability, and unfortunately in many cases upon the lack of venality of the herald; and finally upon the faithfulness of the transcription available to us. Dugdale was the best of the heralds, and he strove for accuracy, even though he made a considerable number of errors. Glover is good, though of course with errors, too. But listen to what J. Horace Round, who more than any other person made genealogy into an honest woman from having been a harlot, says about heralds Dethick and Cooke in exposing a forged pedigree, "Just about what we would expect to find from these two wretched heralds." And he further speaks of heralds Bysshe and Segar and Philipot as continuing the "evil work" of the Elizabethan heralds.[21] Queen Elizabeth herself knew how bad they were, as Moriarty showed in quoting her famous remark to the successor of herald Cooke, "If he were no better than his predecessor, it were no great matter than that he were hanged."[22] This then is some, but far from all, of the background to Moriarty's remark about the notoriously inaccurate visitation pedigrees, pedigrees which today are still heavily relied on as the proof for many a claimed royal line.

This is the type of material which is seized upon by those who do not have the time, talent, training, or tenacity to go track down each generation in a pedigree by searching for contemporary documentation. On the one hand, they want to be thought of as genealogists, but on the other, they want everything laid out for them in summary form, conveniently located on the local library shelf. Hence the popularity, too, of the English county histories, mostly published in the eighteenth and nineteenth centuries. Again, I emphasize that these county histories are excellent for clues, and they cannot be ignored. They are one of the starting points for any scholarly research into medieval English genealogy – the pity comes from many people using them also for the finishing point, for they are subject to many, many errors. Let me give you some detailed comments on a typical county history.

I recently had to consult Manning's *History of Surrey*[23] for an article I was writing on the medieval Braose family.[24] There were only a few pages concerning the Braoses, page 80 being one of them, and I decided to list the mistakes I found on that one page. I will quote a line from that page first, and then give my comment:

> Line 9: "Agatha, who married William de Ros." Wrong. We are dealing here with two families, de Ros and le Rus. Agatha did not marry William de Ros, but William le Rus.

> Lines 9-10: "The second husband of Maud [de Fay] was William de Braose." Wrong. The Maud who married William de Braose was not a de Fay, but a de Clare, an entirely different family.

> Lines 10-11: "It appears that he [William de Braose] held this manor of the moiety of Brumleigh." Wrong. Bromlegh first came into the Braose family when this William's grandson, Richard de Braose, married Alice le Rus.

> Lines 15-16: "She left Alice daughter of William de Ros and the aforesaid Agatha her heirs." Wrong. Alice was not the daughter of William de Ros, but of William le Rus.

> Lines 20-21: "On her [Alice's] decease without issue." Wrong. Alice is well documented as being survived by heirs who were issue of her body.

> Lines 23-24: "We find the said William de Braose in possession of this moiety." Doubtful. A reference is given which I have not been able to check, but this contradicts a good number of contemporary sources.

> Line 24: "He married three wives: 1. Isabel, daughter of Gilbert de Clare." Wrong. He did not marry either an

Isabel or a daughter of Gilbert de Clare. His first wife was Aline de Multon.

Lines 26-27: "Mary, the daughter of William Lord Ros." Wrong. At last he gives us a true daughter of the de Ros family, but Mary was not the daughter of William de Ros, but of Robert de Ros.

Lines 32-34: "Mary his wife [survived] who held the moiety in dower and afterwards successively married Ralph Lord Cobham and Thomas de Brotherton Earl of Norfolk." Wrong. It was the granddaughter of this Mary who successively married these two nobles.

I might note also that Manning's *History of Surrey* is generally considered one of the more accurate county histories. I have found similar, or more grievous, errors in every country history I have consulted. Yet time and again these county histories are cited as if they were the very epitome of veracity. And this is true of most other secondary sources or virtually anything in print. If people can find what they want in a book on a library shelf, it must be true; why look any further? If law or medicine or engineering or beating the stock market were as easy to master as genealogy seems to be to some people, we could all be successful lawyers and doctors and engineers and millionaires simultaneously and in our spare time. But genealogy takes training, too, and to be good at it, one needs to serve a long, drawn out apprenticeship. Above all, he or she who would be a genealogist must have a thorough understanding of the validity of genealogical evidence, what evidence is sufficiently valid, and what evidence is not sufficiently valid, to make a sound genealogical connection.

Despair or Hope?

The genealogist with not much more available than the local library might wonder in despair, "Should I quit genealogy altogether?," but I do not think it is as bad as that. I would suggest that such a genealogist learn how much can be accomplished by mail and then follow three easy rules:

1. Make an effort to learn how valid various commonly used sources are. For this, I would highly recommend subscribing to and reading the genealogical journals, which are most educational.[25]

2. Unless you are absolutely certain of your source (that is, you have firsthand knowledge), qualify your remarks a bit. Maintain a bit of healthy skepticism.

3. Cite sources for every genealogical statement.[26]

Human nature being what it is, I do not look for any quick, miraculous overall change. But progress is being made, and there is hope for the future of genealogy. Conferences such as the one we are attending now are becoming more frequent, and both directly and indirectly they aid in the formation of standards for genealogy and the quickening of desires to learn the right way. Hereditary societies in general are tightening standards and relying more on contemporary documentation rather than unsupported, secondary sources.[27] The periodicals in the field are monuments to the quest for truth in genealogy, good research practices, and above all education. Universities, particularly in the history departments, are finally paying more heed to both the conclusions of genealogy and the methodology of genealogy.[28] There is hope, then, that the "two nations" of which I speak might someday become one.

Notes

1. Benjamin Disraeli, Earl of Beaconsfield, *Sybil or the Two Nations* (Hughenden Edition, London, 1881), 76.

2. The barbarities committed in the name of genealogy by myriads of well-meaning individuals, as well as some organizations, are in great part responsible for the low standing of genealogy as a field of scholastic endeavor. That the standing of genealogy is indeed low in the academic world was vividly brought out by Elizabeth Shown Mills, "Academia vs. Genealogy – Prospects for Reconciliation and Progress," *National Genealogical Society Quarterly* 71 (1983):99-106, the first lines of which begin with, "A young Southern historian began his teaching career on the university level and simultaneously showed an interest in family history. Superiors promptly cautioned him not to get involved in genealogy or his career would be ruined."

3. Charter members were the Reverend Arthur Adams, Walter Goodwin Davis, Harold Minot Pitman, Walter Lee Sheppard, Jr., George Andrews Moriarty, Donald Lines Jacobus, The Rev. Harry Gilbert Doane, Richard LeBaron Bowen, Sir Anthony Wagner, and William Johan Hoffman, all then or subsequently Fellows of the American Society of Genealogists.

4. Standards vary considerably among hereditary societies. The Descendants of Illegitimate Sons and Daughters of the Kings of Britain was founded for the specific purpose of establishing certain difficult lines through a high level of scholarly research, not simple preponderance of evidence. Most other societies

were founded for other purposes – educational, patriotic, social, etc. – based on descent from a group of common ancestors, and accordingly preponderance of evidence would seem sufficient to establish the line. Donald Lines Jacobus frequently commented on the standards of hereditary societies, as in "Confessions of a Genealogical Heretic: Society Regulations and Hearsay Evidence," *The New England Historical and Genealogical Register* 112 (1958):81, where he stated that there was no reason why hereditary societies could not except books by capable family historians, that were written when documentation was not considered so necessary, to support the generations of "those who were living when the genealogy appeared and of their immediate progenitors...nor should rules be set up more stringent than those followed by a court of law." Elsewhere in the article Jacobus makes a plea for the "rule of reason," saying that documentation should not become a fetish, nor should approving genealogists become "angels with flaming swords" to keep applicants out. This has been misinterpreted by some applicants to mean that anything in print goes. But Jacobus does not say that undocumented family histories and other writings should be accepted for assertions of events occurring long before the lifetime of the writer. In "On the Nature of Genealogical Evidence," *The New England Historical and Genealogical Register* 92 (1938):213, he points out, "The only evidence, aside from personal knowledge, for a line of descent are records, private and public....The present writer has never yet inspected ancestral charts based on printed sources and found all the lines correct....There are some excellent and generally reliable family histories in print, some of which are documented and others not. But, unless they are documented to the extent of showing the sources of their data, it is difficult to see how they can be considered evidence."

5. G. Andrews Moriarty, "The Royal Descent of a New England Settler," *The New England Historical and Genealogical Register* 79 (1925):358. In the same vein, see also 74 (1920):231, 263; and 75 (1921):57, for other pertinent articles by Moriarty showing the level of documentation necessary to establish medieval English lines.

6. I have observed that with experience in genealogy, one's royal lines tend to decrease. At one time I had twelve royal lines. Now I am down to two, and one of these is a little shaky.

7. Justin Winsor, *History of the Town of Duxbury, Mass., with Genealogical Registers* (Boston, 1849; reprinted Boston, 1970), 316: "The following pedigree was procured by Horatio G. Somerby, Esq....In its details, as regards intermarriages, etc., it is uncommonly full, much more so than most of so early a date." Another uncommonly detailed pedigree by Somerby, of the Bright family, may be seen in Henry Bond, *Genealogies of the Families and Descendants of the Early Settlers of Watertown, Massachusetts,* (Boston, 1860), 708-09.

8. Frederick Lewis Weis and Walter Lee Sheppard, Jr., *Ancestral Roots of Sixty Colonists Who Came to New England between 1623 and 1650,* 5th ed. (Baltimore, 1976), and *The Magna Charta Sureties, 1215: The Barons Named in Magna Charta, 1215, and Some of Their Descendants Who Settled in America 1607-1650,* 3d ed. (Baltimore, 1979).

9. Eugene A. Stratton, "The Elusive Luces," *Mayflower Quarterly* 47 (1981):23.

10. *Town of Weston – Births, Deaths and Marriages, 1707-1850* (Boston, 1901), 276.

11. *Concord, Massachusetts. Births, Marriages and Deaths, 1653-1850* (Boston, 1895).

12. The DAR transcript of Greenwich, Massachusetts, vital records may be found, among other places, in the libraries of the DAR in Washington, and of the New England Historic Genealogical Society in Boston.

13. Noel C. Stevenson, *Genealogical Evidence: A Guide to the Standard of Proof Relating to Pedigrees, Ancestry, Heirship and Family History* (Laguna Hills, Calif., 1979), 147.

14. Letter dated 8 December 1982, from the historian general to a state historian, with enclosure dated 9 September 1954.

15. Letter written in 1950 by Benjamin Shurtleff to an inquirer.

16. Eugene A. Stratton, "Mary, Wife of Nathaniel Atwood," *Mayflower Quarterly* 48 (1982):127.

17. Stevenson, *Genealogical Evidence* 31, 34. J. Horace Round, *Family Origins and Other Studies* (London, 1930; reprinted Baltimore, 1970), 12, also quotes "'There is somewhere,' said Freeman of Sir Bernard Burke, 'a last straw that breaks the back even of a King-of-Arms.'"

18. Eugene A. Stratton, "Billington-Washburn-Cooke – A Correction," *The Genealogist* 4 (1983):202.

19. Francis Bacon Trowbridge, *The Trowbridge Genealogy* (New Haven, 1908), 34.

20. A good book for information on the visitations and their varying degrees of reliability is G. D. Squibb, *Visitation Pedigrees and the Genealogist* (London, 1978). See also Sir Anthony Wagner, *The Records and Collections of the College of Arms* (London, 1952); the appendix is especially helpful as background material on the visitations.

21. Round, *Family Origins* 12, 103.

22. G. Andrews Moriarty, "English Feudal Genealogy," *The American Genealogist* 19 (1942):7.

23. Owen Manning, continued by William Bray, *The History and Antiquities of the County of Surrey*, vol. 2 (London, 1809).

24. Eugene A. Stratton, "The Medieval Braose Family," to be published in a future issue of *The Genealogist*.

25. I suspect that there is a high degree of correlation between the one fact that the "two nations" in genealogy are so disproportionate in size, and the other fact that some of the best genealogical journals in the country have a relatively low number of subscribers.

26. A good guide for citing sources is Richard S. Lackey, *Cite Your Sources, A Manual for Documenting Family Histories and Genealogical Records* (New Orleans, 1980). One should know the rules before feeling free to break them. This is an excellent manual, though as George E. McCracken suggests in *The American Genealogist* 57 (1981):127, its use without modification could make one's writings bulky. Know the rules, consider your purpose and audience, and the decide how many of the rules apply in a given situation.

27. Some hereditary societies have made starts toward insisting on reasonable amounts of documentation to support applications, the Daughters of the American Revolution being a case in point. Their 1983 publication, *Application Papers – Information for their Preparation,* mentions that their 1965 booklet, *Is that Lineage Right?,* was "intended to increase interest in genealogical research and enhance the quality of documentation." Many other hereditary societies lag behind, most likely not because they refuse to recognize the need for improvement, but because they are afraid to confront the issue of requiring children of existing members to submit better documentation than the parents had to submit in the old days.

28. Note, for example, the words of historian Sumner Chilton Powell in his Pulitzer-Prize-winning, *Puritan Village – The Formation of a New England Town* (1963, Wesleyan Paperback, 1970), xiv: "Any young historian would do well to appreciate the precision and careful handling of documents, which are the sine qua non of any professional genealogist."

Essay on Medieval English Land Tenure

Think of medieval English land tenure as a series of ever-widening concentric circles, with the king as the center circle.[1] All land was owned by the king, and the other circles represent tenants (from the Latin word meaning one who holds or possesses). The last circle, or tenant, was the demesne lord, the one who actually made use of the land and enjoyed the benefits. All the intermediate tenants were mesne holders, except those who held directly of the king, the tenants-in-chief, although for all practical purposes the land tenure rules and customs of tenants-in-chief followed the same rules as mesne lords.[2] The number of circles could vary considerably. There would be just one circle if the king himself was also the one who directly exploited the land, in which case the land would be called the king's demesne land. There would be two circles if a tenant-in-chief, also called tenant in capite, was also the ultimate exploiter or user. Or there could be a number of other circles if there were a number of mesne tenants between king and tenant-in-chief on the one hand, and the exploiter (the demesne tenant) on the other.[3] Outside the last circle was the "villein," the non-free worker, who was tied to the land and who performed the labor necessary for his family to subsist and to yield a profit for the demesne lord.

Starting with the king, each circle at one time had given land to the next succeeding circle outward, and owed protection and justice to that tenant or circle. Conversely, starting with the demesne lord, each circle owed a fixed payment or service to the next inward circle, usually on an annual basis. This was feudalism, a system of mutual upward and

downward obligations, as they applied to the land. In the beginning, starting with the conquest in 1066, William the Conqueror rewarded his most
important followers with large grants of land. Many of his principal barons
were given manors from different parts of the country, so that many holdings were quite scattered, and subsequent infeudation, inheritance, marriage of heiresses, and other changes of tenancy resulted in an even
greater scattering of the manors held by a given tenant.[4]

The collective total of a lord's estates was known as his "honour,"
though, as Stenton mentions, the term in practice "came to be reserved
for the fiefs of the king's greater tenants."[5] Further, a tenant-in-chief was
required to have a "caput," which was the one manor designated to be in
effect his address, the one place where he could be reached if the king
should want him. Manors could be divided, and in fact the word "moiety,"
meaning one-half, is found quite often in contemporary documents in
reference to manors; but the manor known as a caput could not be divided,
just as titles, such as baron or earl, could not be divided.[6] The number of
manors held by higher lords was quite large. Painter notes that Roger de
Montgomery held 793 manors, Alan of Brittany held 442 manors, and
Baldwin of Exeter held four in Somerset and 162 in Devon, where he was
by far the largest landholder.[7]

Every higher lord was like a miniature king (indeed, some of the fron-
tier lords on the Welsh marches were at times autonomous and acted in
a quasi-regal way, even having their own chanceries), surrounded by lesser
barons and knights who needed to be rewarded. Thus an original tenant-
in-chief might keep so many manors for himself, but grant other manors
to his leading followers, who in turn had their own followers to reward.
This is why the circles expanded outward. The relationship of each higher
(or inner) circle, including the king, to the next subordinate was that of
lord to vassal, and the vassal owed homage, or loyalty, to his lord. When
a vassal had a number of manors, some held of different lords, the lord
to whom he owed his main loyalty was known as his liege lord. The king,
of course, was not a vassal in his own land, but as Duke of Normandy he
was, at least nominally, a vassal to the king of France.[8]

Land was usually held by knight service, spiritual tenure, or sergeanty. The last term, also seen as serjeanty and sometimes serjeantry, came
from Latin and meant service, in this case any service other than knight
service or spiritual service, but it was always service to the king.[9] Such
other service might be from the lower lord to provide the king with bows

and arrows, provisions for his table, two new falcons each year, or to wait on him at his meals, maintain his wine cellar, stable his horses, or assist him in many other forms of servitude. Doris M. Stenton points out that there was no original differentiation of such service into grand serjeanties and petty serjeanties, but ultimately those services which brought the provider into immediate contact with the king became known as grand serjeanties.[10] Grand serjeanties included being the king's marshal and other high officers of the crown. One distinction of land held by serjeanty was that it could not be sold or divided by heirs, because it would be impossible or inconvenient to divide the service owed the king. An interesting example of tenure by serjeanty can be seen following the death of Philip Marmion in 1291 without male heir. He had been the king's hereditary champion, and among his possessions were Tamworth Castle and the manor of Scrivelsby. His main heirs were a granddaughter, Joan, wife of Alexander de Freville, and a great-granddaughter, Margaret, wife of Sir John Dymoke. Joan, as daughter of Philip Marmion's older daughter, Mazera, inherited Tamworth Castle, while Margaret inherited Scrivelsby Manor. The Freville descendants through whom Tamworth Castle passed believed that they had also inherited by right of possessing Tamworth Castle the serjeanty of being the king's champion, but this was contested by the Dymoke heirs. In 1377 a court determined that it was Scrivelsby Manor which was held by the serjeanty of being the king's champion so that the Dymokes had the better claim and thus this family became the new champions.[11]

Spiritual service (frank almoign) would seem self-explanatory, for it meant that land was held in return for certain spiritual services, such as saying prayers for the soul of the deceased higher lord. However, the large ecclesiastical estates, such as held by bishoprics, abbeys, and priories, more often held the land by knight service, the same as most landholders in England. Knight service is thus the most important to understand. In essence the tenant held an estate of a higher lord in return for providing so many knights for given times each year (such as for guard duty) or given occasions (such as war).[12] An estate might be held by one knight's fee, or two, six, or ten knights' fees, a knight being understood to mean a fully equipped knight, accompanied by a fully equipped squire and their retinue. An estate could even be held by a fractional knight's fee, such as one-half, one-third, or one-eighth; this would occur, for example, when an estate held by one knight's fee was divided, for lack of a male heir, to two or more surviving daughters. In 1199 there were approximately 197 lay and thirty-nine ecclesiastical baronies in England owing a total of some 7,200 knights' fees.[13]

With the passage of time, it became inconvenient and inefficient to raise armies in this manner, and by the twelfth century tenants were already beginning to be allowed to substitute a money payment in lieu of providing knights, this payment being called a scutage.[14] Thus the term knight's fee became more a measure of an annual rent or tax from the vassal to the higher lord, though traditional knight service in some few cases lingered until mid-fourteenth century, much later than has usually been supposed. Where there were one or more mesne lords between the king and the demesne lord, each lower lord held of the higher lord by a given number or fraction of knights' fees, but the unsystematic way in which land was subinfeudated resulted in the number bearing little relation to either value or any other number in the chain of tenancy. Certainly in the process of subinfeudation each tenant-in-chief and mesne lord generally exacted a higher fee from the next tenant than he himself was paying up the line. Baldwin de Redvers, for example, owed only fifteen fees for his vast Plympton barony but had eighty-nine fees owed to him.[15]

To the genealogist a knowledge of these terms and customs is indispensable for any research in contemporary records. Sometimes, it is true, a document gives a sufficient understanding of a genealogical relationship that emerges anyway, but even then a fuller understanding may be desirable. A simple case of relationships is shown in the following document:

> Surrey. Brumleghe manor was hold of the king in chief by John de Fay by service of 3 knights' fees, after whose death it was parted between his two sisters Maud and Philippa, and from the said Maud issued a daughter Agatha, and from her Alice, who was the wife of the said Richard [Lungespeye] (and still survives); and the said Richard and Alice held a moiety of the manor in chief of the king by service of 1 1/2 knights' fee.[16]

This is the summary of an inquisition into the estates of Richard Lungespeye in response to a writ dated 27 December 1261. Of course, in analyzing data such as this, we would have other information (else how would we get this far in the first place?). Putting the above together with other discovered information, we get this genealogical story:

Surrey. Brumley manor was held of the king by a tenant-in-chief [not necessarily redundant, for a non-tenant-in-chief might temporarily hold of the king] John de Fay for three knights' fees. After his death the manor was divided between his two sisters Maud and Philippa [each getting a moiety]. Maud married Roger de Clere, and they had a daughter Agatha. Agatha married William le Rus, and they had a daughter Alice, who is still living, and who married Richard Lungespeye. Richard and Alice held one-half the manor of Brumley in chief by service of one and one-half knight's fee. [The other half would be held by the heirs of Philippa de Clere.]

I say this is a simple example, but there are some ramifications of it that become more difficult. Up to this time, the so-called definitive work on the medieval Braose family was done in the last century in England by Dudley G. Cary Elwes, F.S.A., especially in a series of articles in the English *The Genealogist*. I have commented elsewhere on Elwes, who was very good in researching data from contemporary medieval manuscripts but was unbelievably obtuse when it came to interpreting the raw data.[17] In these articles Elwes wrote that John de Braose's "mother was Matilda, daughter of Ralph, and sister and co-heir to John de Fay, and not as the pedigrees that I have consulted state, by birth, Matilda de Clare; she married after William de Braose's death in 1210, a Roger de Clere, which was probably the source of the error."[18] First we should distinguished between the Clare family (of the major nobility) and the Clere family (of the minor nobility) even though the spelling at times might be used interchangeably. Elwes assembled and quoted from a very impressive amassing of documents, inquisitions, Charter Rolls, the Testa de Nevill, and others to show the possession of various estates by members of the Clere and Braose families, including contemporary mention of "Matilda de Clere, who was the wife of Wm. de Breus."

Many Americans who can claim royal lines will go back to the Braose family, and for them Elwes's identification can make a significant difference in their genealogy. If the wife of William de Braose, mother of John de Braose, was Matilda (or Maud, which was another form of the same name) de Clare, there is a royal line, for Matilda de Clare was the daughter of Richard de Clare, a descendant of Charlemagne and a Magna

Charta Surety, and his wife, Amice, the Countess of Gloucester, and Amice was a granddaughter of Robert de Caen, a natural son of King Henry I. On the other hand, if Matilda was the daughter of Ralph de Fay, and wife of Roger de Clere, there would be no royal line, nor Royal Bastard, Charlemagne, or Magna Charta Surety line.

Elwes devoted some five pages to support his assertion identifying the wife of William de Braose and concluded "the above [impressive documents], I think, sufficiently prove the correctness" of his claim. However, none of the documents gives the parentage of Matilda, who married William de Braose. Elwes relies heavily on the fact that as a widow she called herself Matilda de "Clere," from which he assumes that she remarried and was identical with the Matilda who was the wife of Roger de Clere, who was proven to be the daughter of Ralph de Fay. Believing he had made his point, Elwes then went on to continue the Braose family history and mentioned that John de Braose had inherited the manor of Buckingham "from his mother."[19] This should have given him the real clue to the identity of William de Braose's wife, for the manor of Buckingham was held by the famous Clare family as tenant-in-chief of the king.

Elwes even cited Lipscomb as his source[20] but completely ignored the significance of what Lipscomb reported, especially his information that Richard, Earl of Clare, "did not long retain Buckingham as part of his demesnes. In the 16th year of King John (1215), he granted it in frank-marriage to William de Braose, with his daughter Matilda, to be held of himself, as the superior Lord." Lipscomb was obviously wrong on the year 1215, for William de Braose had been starved to death by King John in 1210. But the essential element remains: How can it be explained that the manor of Buckingham passed from Earl Richard de Clare to William de Braose? Why did William's widow call herself Matilda de Clare (Elwes had fudged the truth a bit in reporting her name on the document as de Clere, when it is actually found there as de Clare)? It is difficult to believe that Elwes, scholar that he was, was ignorant of the custom (and again I stress the importance of knowing customs) of a woman in a time when surnames were not hard and fast, often being known (especially as a widow) by whichever of her various surnames was the most important, prestigious, or recognizable. This Matilda, born a prestigious Clare and widowed from a disgraced Braose, chose to call herself by her maiden name.[21] Thus we are dealing with two Matildas (or Mauds), one a Fay, married to Roger de Clere, and the other a Clare, married to William de

Braose. The final proof of this is given partly by the *Complete Peerage,* where it is shown that Richard, Earl of Clare, had a daughter Maud, and partly by Moriarty, who cites Dugdale and a patent roll of the time of King John to show that the wife of William de Braose, first name not given, was a daughter of "R. Earl of Clare."[22]

Among terms often found in records of land tenure is "advowson," in the context of a tenant having the manor and the advowson. It means that the tenant had the right of appointing the vicar to the church going with the manor, a form of political, or often familial, patronage. A messuage was a building, and a parcel was a part or fraction of a stated unit of land, and the unit could be a manor, a moiety (half) of a manor, or an entire barony. Frequently, a tenant had various rights (sometimes expressed in land documents) such as a view of frank pledge, the right to hold courts baron or courts leet, or the right of infangentheof and outfangentheof (respectively the rights to hang thieves found on the property and to hang thieves who had left the property and were found elsewhere). However, these terms are not of much genealogical value in themselves, though the records of manor courts, when available, can be valuable.

An understanding of money units can be helpful. The standard coin was the penny, which had varying values at different times. Other units of money are found frequently in land documents, such as the shilling, mark, and pound. However, these were not actual coins in medieval England but were units of accounting or calculating, and when cash was paid it usually involved the equivalent amount in pence. The shilling was worth twelve pence, and the pound was worth twenty shillings. The mark, a very popular unit but one which never existed as a coin in England, was two-thirds of a pound and is also found frequently in documents in its equivalent form, thirteen shillings, four pence.

If a tenant died without heirs, the lands he died seized of would escheat (or go back) to the higher lord to dispose of then as he saw fit (sell, give away, or keep for himself). Of course, the king, from the mere number of estates which were held directly of him, would routinely be having estates escheat to him all the time, and for this purpose he maintained officers known as escheators. One of the main duties of an escheator was to hold an inquisition post mortem on the death of a tenant-in-chief. The purpose of the inquisition was to determine that a tenant-in-chief had died, whether he was survived by heirs, whether the heir was a minor (in which case the king would profit by the wardship), and what relief the heir must pay in order to obtain livery of seizin. The records of these inquisitions post mortem provide us with a wealth of genealogical information.[23]

Three of the most rewarding benefits attaching to mesne tenancy (and also owed by tenants-in-chief to the king) were reliefs, marriages, and wardships. When a vassal died, his heir did not automatically take possession of the estates due him. First he had to pay a relief to the higher lord, and then he could receive livery of seizin from his lord which would allow him officially to have his estate. Magna Charta set the relief of a barony at £100, regardless of the number of knights' fees it had owing to it, while other estates paid relief at the rate of £5 per knight's fee.[24] A. L. Poole also states that by the second half of the twelfth century, 100 shillings (£5) was considered a just relief for a knight's fee.[25]

The time of paying relief can gives us clues to ages, especially if the person receiving livery of seizin had been a minor when his parent (or perhaps grandparent) died. Normally a young heir had to be at least twenty-one, if male, and about fifteen, if female. Edmund de Coleville, son and heir of Roger de Coleville, proved his age at an inquisition of 14 February 1309 by having a number of witnesses testify that they knew his age for a fact. One witness said he was in the service of Edmund's grandfather the year he was born, and he stated that he was named Edmund by his father in dedication to St. Edmund; Edmund had reached twenty-one on the past St. Edmund's day. Other witnesses testified that they had a son or other relative born in the same year or on the same day, or a father had died the Christmas before Edmund was born, or a sister was married that year. Though this was not the most precise way of dating, the number of witnesses was impressive. Edmund was now ready to pay relief and enter on his estate.[26] Often we do not have any record of the proving of age but just the date on which a son took livery of seizin. If we have reason to believe he had earlier been a ward, we can assume that he was probably around twenty-one years old on taking over his estate, though there are records of a few heirs, usually quite rich and important, being granted livery of seizin at an earlier age.

The proof of age for Lucy, wife of Robert Mautravers and daughter and heir of Beatrice de Braose, was taken at an inquisition of 1312/3, and witnesses testified that she was born on Whitsunday, in 1297. She had completed the age of fifteen at the past feast of Holy Trinity. One witness testified that his mother had died around the feast of Holy Trinity fourteen years ago and Lucy was then more than one year old and in the wardship of Giles de Braose. Another witness testified that Lucy was over a year old when her mother, Beatrice, died in 1298. The Giles de Braose who purchased her wardship was probably her father's first cousin.[27] Another inquisition of 6 March 1305 on the estates of Lucy's father, Giles de Braose, obtained evidence that Lucy was age seven at the last feast of St. Michael (29 September), thus confirming that she was born in 1297. Note that she was already married by age fifteen. Lucy was the only surviving child of Giles and Beatrice (de St. Elen) de Braose. Though Giles had a surviving son by his second wife, Lucy was the heir of her mother, and the property was of the inheritance of her mother, Beatrice, the daughter and heir of John de St. Elen. This land was included in the estate of Giles de Braose, obviously because he had obtained a lifetime interest in it by the courtesy of England after the death of Beatrice. At this date the land was probably entailed and had to go to an heir of the body of Beatrice but was obviously not tail male.[28]

English kings always maintained their right of approval to the marriage of a daughter of a tenant-in-chief, and this right in turn became asserted by the tenants-in-chief as due them from their own tenants, and so on outward through the feudal rings. Sometimes this right was asserted and enforced in connection with sons, especially the sons of the king's immediate tenants, those in chief. Custom dictated that an arranged marriage had to be suitable and that an heir or heiress would not be disparaged, but otherwise the right to marry heirs and heiresses could be sold by the higher lord, thus bringing in considerable revenue. Sometimes a widow, especially if young, could be resold for marriage, while at other times the widow of a tenant-in-chief might pay the king a fine in order to remain single or choose her own subsequent husband.[29]

Wardships were an important, though not of course inevitable, right of the higher lord. A wardship occurred when a tenant died leaving an underage heir. By virtue of wardship, the higher lord assumed responsibility for the heir and direct control and use of the heir's estate. Use meant enjoying the annual, renewable profits. Of course, the higher lord could not sell the estate, and he was expected by custom to leave it in the same condition he found it. He could not (or at least should not) strip off timber, let buildings get in disrepair, or sell the cows along with the milk. Where part of an heir's estate consisted of mesne tenancy of other estates, the higher lord would receive the annual financial payment determined by the number of knights' fees owed by the lower estate.[30] It is worth noting that when a higher lord obtained the wardship of one or more young heiresses (and sometimes heirs, too), we often see the subsequent marriage of that heiress to a relative of the higher lord, who had a natural interest in wanting to provide new estates to a younger brother or son.[31] The right of wardship, including the right to farm a ward's estate, that is, to enjoy its profits, could be sold by the higher lord to someone else.

It is helpful to remember in genealogy that under feudalism a number of people might have different interests in any given piece of land. That interest could be a present one, but it could also be a future one; for example, the widower of a woman who had a son by a previous marriage might have possession and control of the land in the present (under the concept of what was called the "courtesy of England," roughly a widower's equivalent of a widow obtaining a life interest in dower land), but he would not be able to sell it or pass it on to his heirs, for his wife's son by her earlier marriage could have an interest (called a reversionary interest) in the land after the man's death. Given this fact of different interests held at the same time in the same piece of land, it is all the more indispensable that students know the terms, for else they could never make accurate deductions from land tenure evidence, which is by far the most important evidence we have for medieval genealogy.

The right of a tenant (mesne or demesne) to alienate his or her interests in the land was limited by law. Because of the historical development of this or that piece of land, some estates could be alienated more freely than others. Further, because of new laws and new practices to circumvent the law, a given piece of land might be more freely alienated at one point of time than another. Whatever a mesne or demesne tenant might legally do to change his interest in a holding, that change did not affect the interests of others in that land. If A held of B, and B sold the land to C, C obtained both the land and whatever obligation B owed to A in connection with that land. If A sold his interest to D, then C now owed that obligation to D.

The form of tenancy most similar to out and out ownership was fee simple, and a tenant having land in fee simple could sell it, give it away, or pass it on to his heirs. Of course, to sell the land might require the approval of a higher lord, but this could usually be arranged for a payment (one of several types of payments called fines). The process of subinfeudation, that is, of a tenant changing from a demesne to a mesne tenant by granting some or all of his land to a new demesne tenant to hold of him (creating a new estate) was prohibited in 1290 by the Statute of Quia Emptores.

A man could not directly bequeath his estate to anyone in a will. On the tenant's death, the estate had to pass to his oldest surviving son or, if there was none, equally to his daughters or, if none, then to his nephew and so on to other family members in a prescribed way. K. B. McFarlane makes the point that many a man might wish to provide for younger sons on the one hand but would not want to repeat King Lear's mistake and give away his lands during his lifetime.[32] However, some men did divest themselves of land to younger sons while still living, but in 1285 the Statute of De Donis Conditionalibus put restrictions on such grants.[33] This statute required that grants to younger sons (or to daughters as a gift of maritagium) had to be in fee tail, meaning that the land could not be sold, and thereafter had to pass to heirs of the body, not collateral heirs, for three more generations. If there were no direct heirs for three generations (for example, say a grantee younger son had a son and grandson, but the grandson failed to leave children), then the land passed back to the line of the original grantor's main heir. The fee tail could also be made fee tail male, which restricted the inheritance to males of the body only; that is, if the grantee had a daughter, but no son, after his death the estate would have to pass back to the grantor's main heir.[34] An entail had a peripheral advantage in that it protected the estate in case a tenant was convicted of treason (and in medieval England it was quite easy for lords and gentry to get caught between warring sides and, if on the losing side, be condemned for treason). The estate of a convicted traitor was confiscated by the crown, unless it was entailed, in which case it passed on the tenant's death to his son or, in the case of a deceased son, to his grandson.

We see what appears to be a contradiction in the fee tail in the manor of Tettebury, which was said by an inquisition of 16 May 1367 to have been held of the king in chief by the late John de Braose in fee tail male by knight service "to hold to the said John and Elizabeth his wife, and the heirs male of their bodies" (see chart 4). John had received the manor as a gift from his parents, Thomas and Beatrice Braose, with contingent reversion to them. John's heir was said to be his brother, Thomas, age fifteen.[35] However, an inquisition of 27 November 1395 showed that the manor of Tettebury came into the king's hands on the death of Thomas de Braose. This inquisition states that the king took over the manor be-

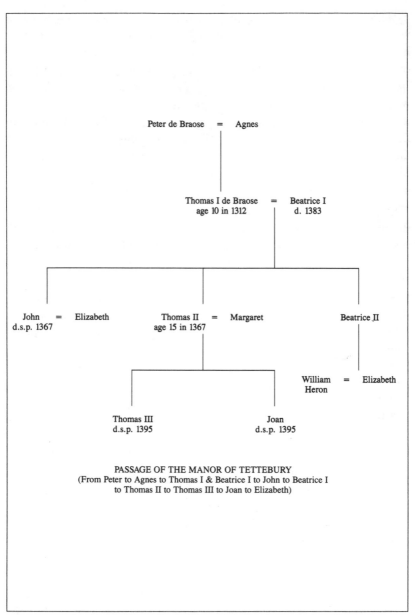

Chart 4. *Passage of the manor of Tettebury (from Peter to Agnes to Thomas I and Beatrice I to John to Beatrice I to Thomas II to Thomas III to Joan to Elizabeth).*

cause of the minority of Thomas de Braose and his sister, who both died while wards of the king. Joan died 10 February 1395, and "her next heir is Elizabeth, wife of Sir William Heron, knight, daughter of Beatrice, sister of their father Thomas."[36]

There are some important questions here. If John's brother Thomas was fifteen years old in 1367, then he was not the Thomas de Braose who died a minor as the king's ward around 1395. If Joan inherited, and then Elizabeth, what ever happened to the tail male? The first inquisition shows that the young Thomas de Braose, John's brother, was John's heir, but Thomas did not necessarily inherit the manor in that capacity. On John's death without issue, the manor should have reverted back to his father and mother, but John's father predeceased him. Thus the manor reverted back to John's mother Beatrice. The important thing for our discussion is that the tail male would have expired with the reversion. Once the estate had gone back to Beatrice, she now possessed it in fee simple, as she and her husband had before they gave it in tail male to John. On the death of Beatrice in 1383, Thomas, as oldest surviving son, did inherit the estate in fee simple, and when he died his heir was his young son, a third Thomas. Since the third Thomas was a minor, the king took over the manor in wardship, and when the third Thomas died, his sister Joan became heir. But Joan was also a minor, and she lived only three days more than Thomas. At that point, the inheritance passed to Elizabeth, daughter of a younger Beatrice, who was the daughter of the older Thomas and Beatrice, the sister of John and the junior Thomas and the aunt of the third Thomas. (Mention of another aspect of this case in chapter 12 shows that the widow of the second Thomas, Margaret, mother of the third Thomas and Joan, was given a life interest in the estate before possession was to pass to the last-named Elizabeth, with the consent of Elizabeth and her husband.)

Now I have supplemented the information coming from the inquisitions with information coming from other research, but conversely I have supplemented information coming from my other research with information coming from the two inquisitions. By analysis of both, we come up with knowledge of a considerable number of members of this family, but we could not have done a proper analysis without understand the meaning of such terms as tail male, reversion, wardship, lifetime interest, and such. It can also be helpful to keep in mind that the manor came into the king's hands only because of the minority of the heirs, not for lack of an heir. Had there been no heir at all of a reversionary tenant when John died, with the manor in tail male, the manor would have escheated to the king, who then could have granted it to someone else. The new grant would not have had to have the same fee conditions as the old grant; that is, the king could have received it with a tail male condition, but could have granted it anew in fee simple, or fee tail not male, had he desired. Manors were sometimes surrendered to the king or other higher lord, and regranted to the same tenant for the very purpose of changing the estate condition (usually with the higher lord paid a fine for his trouble).

The word maritagium, mentioned above, meant a gift of land in free marriage (also called frank marriage) to a daughter during the grantor's lifetime on the occasion of her marriage. It was in itself a conditional gift, and the husband had no right to it until an heir was born. The birth of an heir created an immediate right to a lifetime estate, which would pass to the husband on the death of his wife by the concept called "courtesy of England." Only on the widower's death would the estate go to his late wife's heir, who could be his child or grandchild, but the heir could also be his wife's child by a previous marriage. If there were no children of the marriage on the death of the wife, the estate would revert to the main heirs of the original grantor. Although maritagium was required also to be entailed by De Donis Conditionalibus, McFarlane points out that gifts of land in frank marriage had virtually died out before the end of the thirteenth century, and a daughter's marriage portion thereafter took the form of money.[37]

Sir Maurice Powicke tells us of Loretta, Countess of Leicester, who, when she married,

> became, as any other wife became, a woman of property. She received a maritagium, or marriage portion from her father, and at the church door her husband allotted her a dower, upon which she had the right to enter when he died....Loretta, after her husband's death, was allotted her dower, not a dowry which had already been defined, for Earl Robert does not seem to have made a precise allotment, but 100 librates of land....A widow's reasonable dower was normally one-third of her husband's lands. The husband may have endowed her with less, and at any rate until 1217, the third was regarded as a maximum, although before the Great Charter of 1217 a husband would some-

times say that if a specific dowry did not amount to a third, his widow should have enough in addition to bring the whole up to a third part of his total inheritance.[38]

We see an example of the above in an inquisition dated 7 March 1312 on the estates of Peter de Braose, again concerning the manor of Tettebury. Peter had been given the estate of Tettebury by William de Braose [his father], and he held it of the king as a tenant-in-chief by service of one knight's fee. Peter's heir was Thomas de Braose, age ten (this Thomas was the senior Thomas of the example given above). Peter's widow Agnes had a lifetime interest in the land and the inquisition noted that Peter had "assigned the said manor to Agnes his wife at the church door."[39]

In the story of Countess Loretta, we can see another of those seeming exceptions which so frustrate those who would neatly catalog rules on medieval land tenure, though in this case the answer is not determinable as it was above. Powicke, a noted British medieval historian,[40] points out that "if there were no children [the maritagium] would go back to the donor or his heirs...Loretta, so far as we know, had no children." But in the next paragraph Powicke shows that the maritagium land passed to Loretta's niece, "Maud, or Mariotte, to whom Loretta gave it later." How can childless Loretta be giving land in which she held only a lifetime interest to a niece? But Loretta came from an exceptional family, a most exceptionally unfortunate family, which had incurred the wrath of King John, and several members of her family had perished ignominiously. In her case, all kind of things might have been possible. Powicke, in the story of Loretta has given us a good illustration of both the maritagium and dower systems. The dower was a woman's lifetime interest in a part of the lands of her deceased husband. It would pass to his heir when she died (his heir could be a son by an earlier wife). In Loretta's case, her husband apparently provided for a specific amount of land at the church door, without saying which land. In such a case, it would first be up to the woman and the reversionary heir or heirs to see if they could work out a peaceful settlement of which lands she would get.[41] A married woman (or a widow from a jointure) might possess in fee simple lands coming to her from her family, and these she could give (or bequeath when it became possible to dispose of land by a will) to one or more of her younger children.

In spite of continuing legal attempts to keep estates together in the hands of heirs of the body, a number of ways were discovered to get around this hindrance. McFarlane shows that the use of the jointure was one such device. A jointure was land held jointly by man and wife, and after the death of one, the land would be held by the survivor in an unrestricted estate. This was no lifetime interest, for a surviving wife could sell or otherwise alienate her lands obtained by jointure. A husband might on marriage create a jointure with his wife for some of his lands instead of giving her a dower, and, if she were a wealthy heiress, he might have to give her a jointure in all he had in order to marry her in the first place. McFarlane points to the example of Lady Joan Mohun, who after being left a widow without male heirs and having married off her daughters, sold the reversionary interest in Dunster to the Luttrells and then kept them waiting for it thirty years before she died.[42] But in this manner, Dunster passed to the Luttrells instead of to the husbands of Lady Mohun's daughters.

Tenants were devising land indirectly by will as early as the fourteenth century, after a way was found for a tenant to give away land during lifetime and still enjoy the use and disposition of it. A man could grant land to a number of friends, called feoffees, to be held to his "use," as he instructed them and then have them pass it on to his heirs when he died. The concept of uses thus gave a person considerably more flexibility in controlling land during both life and death, and the instruction in the will to have it granted to one's heirs could be in fee tail as well as fee simple, as the original tenant might desire. Such a device had the advantage of protecting the land from forfeiture in case of treason and also excluding the higher lord from gaining the heir's payment of relief (or a wardship if the tenant died with an heir still a minor).[43] In 1535 the Statute of Uses destroyed the effect of the device by converting one's use interest into a legal estate, subject to all the obligations of possessing a legal estate.

As an example of uses and also of the intrafamilial rivalries caused by such devices as uses and entailments, an inquisition of 1 November 1498 showed that Thomas Brewse (evolving from the surname Braose) was seized in fee of the manor of Wakelynes in Fresingfeld, Suffolk, and he enfeoffed John Paston and others "to the use of himself for life, and for the performance of his last will." While he lived, Thomas enjoyed the profits of the manor "by permission of the said feoffees," and in his will he said that the manor should go to elder son, William, with remainder in default of heirs to Giles Brewse, William's brother, and "the heirs male of his body." This seems a bit ambiguous. Clearly it was Thomas's intent to put the manor in tail male as far as Giles was concerned, but tail male is not specified as a condition of William's inheritance, though the implication is there. On the death of Thomas, William received the profits from the manor "by permission" of the feoffees, and later William died without heir male of his body [though not without heir]. Again with permission of the feoffees, Giles Brewes took the profits of the manor, until Thomas Hansard, knight, and other "ill-doers and disturbers of the peace" took over the manor, disseising Giles, who now pleaded that he was in fear of his life if he came near the manor.[44] We see elsewhere that Sir Thomas Hansard was the husband of Thomasine Brewes, the elder daughter of William Brewes,[45] and thus niece of Giles Brewes. Did the family quarrel over the manor start because of looseness in the terms of Thomas Brewes's grant of the manor to his feoffees? Alas, these documents do not always tell us the conclusion of the issues they relate.

Though this is far from being a complete study of medieval English land tenure – many volumes written by people making a lifetime career of the subject would be required for that – it should enable the reader to make sense out of many of the commonly encountered documents dealing with landed estates.[46] The other appendices dealing with medieval genealogy should be read in the light of these explanations. Again, it must be emphasized that analysis of land tenure documents is the major tool we have for doing research in medieval genealogy, for the simple reason that little else exists.

Notes

1. It is impossible in a small space to give perfect definitions to English feudal terms. This was not a game with rules created for once and all time to guide all players under all circumstances. The rules varied according to different times, different conditions, and different degrees of arbitrariness. Sometimes it is even difficult to get the experts to agree on what different terms meant, and when agreement is found, there are sometimes exceptions. This article is intended more to convey a general background to help students understand the terminology and materials involved in English medieval land tenure than to cover all the possible exceptions. The reader should be warned that, when it comes to putting a fine point on something, historians, as much as genealogists, love a good interdisciplinary fight. The highly motivated student will find much helpful information on land law in Bracton's *Note Book,* Plunknett's *A Concise History of the Common*

Law, Milsom's *Historical Foundations of the Common Law,* and C. F. Kolbert and N. A. M. Mackey's *History of Scots and English Land Law.* Note also that inheritance practices were much more fluid before the time of King Henry II.

2. *Oxford English Dictionary* defines a mesne lord as "one who holds an estate of a superior lord"; it quotes Selden as writing of a person who "held of a mesne lord, and not immediately of the king," and Hume in talking about men "whose duty was immediately paid to the mesne lord that was interposed between them and the throne." Desmesne, on the other hand, is illustrated in the dictionary by a quotation from Professor F. W. Maitland, "In every case, the ultimate (free) holder, the person who stands at the bottom of the scale, who seems to be most like an owner of the land, and who has a general right of doing what he pleases with it, is said to hold the land in demesne."

3. J. Horace Round, *Family Origins and Other Studies* (London, 1930; reprinted Baltimore, 1970), 49, observes that contemporary documents did not necessarily mention all the mesne lords, but that they were there nevertheless: "When we find Baldwin de Rosey [holding certain estates] we may be sure that William de Blancmuster's name as mesne tenant is omitted, for these manors with North Barsham were held by him of the Earl," and "Conversely, when Henry de Walpole is found subsequently holding at 'Houghton' of the fee of 'Blanmuster,' we may be sure that the name of the Warennes as tenants-in-chief is omitted."

4. Sir Frank Stenton, *Anglo-Saxon England,* in the *Oxford History of England* series, 3d ed. (Oxford, 1971; reprinted 1975), 629, observes in a footnote that the popular conception of William deliberately splitting the holdings of his tenants-in-chief, so as to prevent them from having autonomously compact baronies, is wrong.

5. Ibid., 627. At least as early as mid-twelfth century, some tenants-in-chief are found with more than one fief and more than one honour.

6. It is beyond the scope of this essay to go into defining who was a baron or earl, and how the titles were created, for even today it can be a matter of much learned dispute. Suffice it to say that in looking backwards, the experts say that this or that person became a baron on this or that day by tenure (if he held such and such land, he must have been a baron), or writ (summoned by the king to parliament), or by charter or patent (created a baron specifically by royal command). Sidney Painter, *Studies in the English Feudal Baroney* (Baltimore, 1943), notes that Stenton had suggested that in the Norman period an estate held for five or more knights' fees was a barony, and he adds that certainly in the eleventh and early twelfth centuries, the more important tenants-in-chief called their leading vassals barons, but by the end of the twelfth century, official usage restricted the term barony to fiefs held in chief from the crown.

7. Painter, *Studies in the English Feudal Barony,* 17.

8. Though we say that a lesser lord held an estate from a higher lord, this is for convenience, and does not necessarily mean that the lord "held of" is always of higher rank. The vagaries of birth, marriage, death, and political fortune were such that manors, or parts of a manor, could be shuffled and reshuffled from one honour to another, and in such a shuffle an earl might find himself holding a manor of a knight. Such a situation is shown in an inquisition [*Calendar of In-*

quisitions Post Mortem, Edward III, vol. 11 (London, 1935), 430] of 1364 on the estates left by John de Nerford in Suffolk, where Thomas of Brotherton, Earl of Norfolk and brother of King Edward III, held the manor of Soham of John de Nerford, knight, who held it of Edmund de Bereford, but the earl "did not attorn to Edmund de Bereford for homage, fealty, or other services."

9. *Oxford English Dictionary* cites several documents from past centuries to show that serjeanty was tenure of land held always directly of the king and only of the king. Further, a glossary in the published *Pipe Rolls Series,* 3:94, states that "serjeanty signifies a service that cannot be due from a tenant to any lord but the King." However, serjeanty is described in the *Encyclopedia Britannica,* (1971), 20:253, as meaning "a form of land tenure granted in return for the performance of some specific service to the lord, whether the king or another." The author of this article, Doris M. Stenton, is an acknowledged authority on medieval English history, and she should know. I cannot think of any examples of land held by serjeanty of any lord other than the king, but I would not be surprised if there were a few isolated cases.

10. Ibid., 20:253-54.

11. *NCP* 8:505-14. See especially footnotes *b* and *c* on page 513 showing that both sides could make their claims with some justice for Tamworth was held "of the king in chief ... by service of coming to the King's coronation, armed cap-a-pie with royal arms ... offering himself to make proof for the King against all opposing his coronation," while Scrivelsby was "held of the King in chief by grand serjeanty, viz. of being armed on the day of the King's coronation for the defence of the King's estate." See also J. Horace Round, *The King's Serjeants and Officers of State, with their Coronation Services* (1911; reprint London, New York, 1970), in which Round shows some exceptions to the widely held theory that tenure by serjeanty was impartible.

12. Sir Frank Stenton, op. cit., 682, points out that although some form of feudalism (service for land tenure) existed in England before the conquest, the Normans introduced the practice of knight service for tenure: "It is now half a century since Round made what was then the daring claim that, in England, tenure by knight-service was a Norman innovation. After a generation of research Round's theory has been confirmed at every point."

13. Sidney Painter, *The Reign of King John* (Baltimore, 1949), 19.

14. Ibid.,125ff, regarding scutage.

15. Painter, *Studies in the English Feudal Barony,* 27.

16. *Calendar of Inquisitions Post Mortem, Henry III,* vol. 1 (London, 1904), 143.

17. See chapter 7.

18. *The Genealogist,* 5:318ff. See also 5:69 and the chart in 5:164.

19. Ibid., 5:322.

20. George Lipscomb, *The History and Antiquities of the County of Buckingham,* vol. 2 (London, 1847), 548.

21. Another example of this custom may be seen in the daughter of an earlier Braose family. Sybil de Braose married, first, William de Ferrers, Earl of Derby, and, second, Adam de Port. After the death of Adam de Port, Sybil was known as the Countess of Ferrers. See *NCP* 11:321. Elwes, op. cit. 4:139, again displayed

how little he could understand genealogical evidence when he had Sybil married but once, to Ferrers, and then created a fictitious unnamed sister of Sybil as the wife of Adam de Port.

22. *NCP* 6:503, fn d; Moriarty's Notebooks at The New England Historical and Genealogical Society, 15:147.

23. See chapter 12.

24. Painter, *Studies in the English Feudal Barony,* 11ff.

25. A. L. Poole, *From Domesday Book to Magna Carta, 1087-1216,* 2d ed., in the *Oxford History of England* series (Oxford, 1955; reprinted 1975), 20.

26. *Calendar of Inquisitions Post Mortem, Edward II,* vol. 5 (London, 1908).

27. Ibid., 239.

28. *Calender of Inquisitions Post Mortem,* vol. 4 (London, 1913), 214.

29. Painter, *Reign of King John,* 217.

30. Ibid., 216.

31. As an example of how analysis of the marriage of an heiress in wardship to a higher lord's relative was helpful in making a genealogical identification, see my article on Richard de Braose in *The Genealogist* 6:88-89.

32. K. B. McFarlane, *The Nobility of Later Medieval England* (Oxford, 1973), 63-64.

33. *Encyclopedia Britannica,* 8:549, states that De Donis Conditionalibus created the fee tail, or entail; however, McFarlane, op. cit., 64, shows in a footnote that fee tail was used at least as early as 1227.

34. Still later, De Donis Conditionalibus was interpreted as meaning a perpetual restriction, but gradually ways in the form of legal fictions were found to get around it. An interesting dramatic background is made of the fee tail male in Jane Austen's novel, *Pride and Prejudice,* taking place in the early nineteenth century, where Mr. Bennett has no son but five daughters, who if not married by the time of his death would have no foreseeable means of support when Mr. Bennett's distant cousin, Mr. Collins, would inherit the estate.

35. *Inquisitions Post Mortem for Gloucestershire,* vol. 47 of the *Index Library* (London, 1914; reprinted 1968), 43.

36. Ibid., 194.

37. McFarlane, *Nobility of Later Medieval England,* 64.

38. Sir Maurice Powicke, "Loretta, Countess of Leicester," *The Christian Life in the Middle Ages and Other Essays* (Oxford, 1935), 152-55. Note that a widow could have dowers in more than one estate, such as the Countess of Shrewsbury, "Bess of Hardwick," who outlived four husbands and possessed four dower estates.

39. *Calendar of Inquisitions Post Mortem,* vol. 5 (London, 1908), 182.

40. See his *The Thirteenth Century,* 2d ed. (Oxford, 1962; reprinted 1970 with corrections), in *The Oxford History of England* series.

41. See, for example, Public Record Office, Calendar of the Fine Rolls, Edward I, A.D. 1271-1307 (London, 1911), 290, showing that on 1 March 1291 the Justice of Wales was empowered to endow Mary, surviving wife of William Braose, with land from the estate of her late husband, unless she were willing to receive an assignment of dower from her stepson, the heir.

42. McFarlane, *Nobility of Later Medieval England,* 55, 65.

43. Ibid., 69.

44. *Inquisitions Post Mortem,* second series (London, 1908), 2:131.

45. *NCP* 2:307. Notice that the thoroughness and accuracy of the *Complete Peerage* is due to extensive research by its compilers through the vast number of extant state papers of the type shown in the few examples given in this essay.

46. An excellent up-to-date bibliography can be found in C. Warren Hollister, *The Making of England 55 B.C. to 1399,* 5th ed. (Lexington, Mass., 1988).

Appendix C

An Interesting Medieval Document

The document translated below is presented as valuable evidence of genealogical connections; as a most interesting description of medieval life and manners; and as a tribute to Professor Donald W. Sutherland, of the University of Iowa, who did the translation, and who died suddenly of a heart attack in October 1986. Professor Michael Altschul of Case Western Reserve University said of Professor Sutherland, "Everyone who knew him, however slightly, respected and valued him." On forwarding me the translation, Professor Sutherland wrote, "Working on the document, I found it unusually interesting. I have studied fourteenth-century legal writings for many years but had never seen anything like it nor did I know that there were such pieces as this." And he concluded his letter with the generous statement, "Especially since I feel as well rewarded as I do that you have given me the chance to make the acquaintance of such a document as this, I hope that you will not feel under any obligation to me for the transcript and translation, or for any use that you may make of them in publications."

Robert E. C. Waters, *Genealogical Memoirs of the Extinct Family of Chester of Chicheley; their Ancestors and Descendants*, 2 vols. (London, 1878), 1:198, referenced an unpublished fourteenth-century document, which he had obviously seen, as support for what he was writing on a Sir John Gernon. Waters was in turn one of three sources customarily referenced to show that Elder William Wentworth of colonial New Hampshire had a valid royal line.[1] However, the document also appeared to give some valuable information on the medieval Braose family, which has been of prime interest to me. I therefore determined to get a copy of the document, and did so with some help from Neil D. Thompson, F.A.S.G., and Peter Wilson Coldham, F.A.S.G. Though identified by Waters as "Esch. 4 Rich. II, No. 29," Dr. Thompson helped me learn that it had been recataloged as "C260/92/6 in the Chancery Miscellanea." Actually the material consisted of three documents:

1. IPM, 7 Edw. III, on tenements (including Abington, etc.) late of Guy Guband whose son was his next heir.

2. Depositions, 49 Edw. III, regarding the parentage of Sir John Gernon.

3. IPM, 4 Rich. II, on the manor of Bakewell, Derby, late of Sir John Gernon, whose next heir was his son John.

At the time I was only able to get document 2, which promised to be the most revealing. This document was in Law French, and the copy was in such bad condition that it could hardly be called legible. To translate it would require an expert in both fourteenth-century Law French and in the handwriting of the period. Through the help of Professor Altschul, I made contact with Professor Sutherland. Professor Sutherland very kindly agreed to translate this most difficult document, and not much later he forwarded me his transcription of the original and his translation of the transcription into English. In his accompanying letter, Professor Sutherland noted the rough condition of the copy I furnished him, and he cautioned that some parts of his translation might be wrong and need to be redone. However, I found his translation to be fully consistent with itself and with my other knowledge of the families involved. Although it much augmented Waters's summary, it did not change his conclusions; however, it did omit several items mentioned by Waters (because they were not in our copy of the document).

Waters had mentioned a Peter de Braose and a Monsieur de Argentine, whom Professor Sutherland did not find. He wondered if Waters might have taken the "le piere" (father) as "Peter" and "Anguileme" (Angouleme) as "Argentine"; however, he quickly pointed out that this would be to suggest that Waters was not competent, which did not seem likely. Certainly there was a Sir John de Argentine alive in England at this time, and his family had a distant connection with the Braose family. Thus Waters was probably correct, and as Professor Sutherland suggests, probably something is missing. Given the context of Waters's summary, it would not seem likely that Waters obtained the names Peter de Braose and Monsieur de Argentine from documents 1 and 3, above (though that is of course possible), for only document 2 was concerned in any way with the identity of John Gernon's mother (document 1 was dated prior to Alice's marriage to John Gernon, and document 3 seems to be the court's decision on the matter a few years after the testimony was taken).

Chronology

The document itself is undated. Both Waters and Professor Sutherland thought that from internal evidence the depositions must have taken place around 1370, and I agree. However, the time given to the depositions, 49 Edward III, would have been 1375. It is possible that the various depositions were given over a period of years, starting perhaps in 1370 and ending in 1375 (even so, most of them would seem to be 1370). Chart 5 on page 287 will be helpful for following the names.

Waters's Summary

> Sir John Gernon was not allowed to take possession of his moiety of the Coleville estates without a struggle, for his right of succession was disputed by the elder coheir of this mother's first marriage. She had issue by Guy Gobaud two sons John and Guy, who died without issue; and two daughters Elizabeth and Mabel. Mabel Gobaud married William Lampet, and had many children; but her elder sister Elizabeth left an only child, Alice, who was in 1370 the wife of John Wyke of Scredington, Lincolnshire. Wyke and his wife now asserted a claim to the inheritance of Coleville, on the ground that Sir John Gernon was not the son of Alice Gobaud, but of his father's first wife, Isabella Bygot. They alleged that Alice Gobaud was past the age of child-bearing when she married her second husband, the elder Sir John Gernon, and they appealed to the testimony of Monsieur Thomas Roos, who deposed that when he was about ten years old the elder Sir John Gernon and his son paid a visit to his mother at Donnesby, and that when they told his mother that Sir John Gernon the son (who was then between eight and ten years old) was born of Isabella Bygot

when she was only thirteen, she expressed great surprise that a woman of such tender age could bear a child so well grown and well formed; whereupon the elder Sir John Gernon replied that Monsieur John St. John, who was one of the tallest and properest knights in the country, was born when his mother was only twelve years old. This witness, however, was contradicted by the evidence of several relations of Lord Coleville, who agreed in asserting that Sir John Gernon had always been recognized in the family as the son of Alice Coleville, and their testimony was supported by Monsieur de Argentine, who deposed that Robert Lord Coleville at the siege of Calais acknowledged Gernon as his cousin, and as the son of his aunt Alice. The evidence of Sir Peter de Braose and of Sir John de Braose the elder and younger, who were Alice Coleville's cousins through her mother, was confirmed by Thomas Lampet the son of Alice's daughter Mabel Gobaud, who had been educated in his uncle Gernon's household, and was himself one of the coheirs of the Coleville family, if Sir John Gernon was not the son of Alice. Lampet's brother-in-law William Boyton of Suffolk (the husband of his sister Alice Lampet) bore testimony to the same effect, and judgment was pronounced in favour of Sir John Gernon by the Court of King's Bench in 1380.

The Full Text

[The full translation as furnished by Professor Sutherland (with perhaps a part of the original text missing), together with bracketed comments by both Professor Sutherland and me, is as follows (see chart 5)]:

First, Sir Thomas Roos of Dunsby [Lincolnshire], being examined upon his oath, says that the said Alice Gobaud [that is, Alice (Coleville) (Gobaud) Gernon] was fifty years of age or more at the time when she was married to John Gernon, the father of the present Sir John Gernon, and so that she was big and heavy of body and past the age of bearing children.[2] It being asked of him how he knew, he says that he was in the

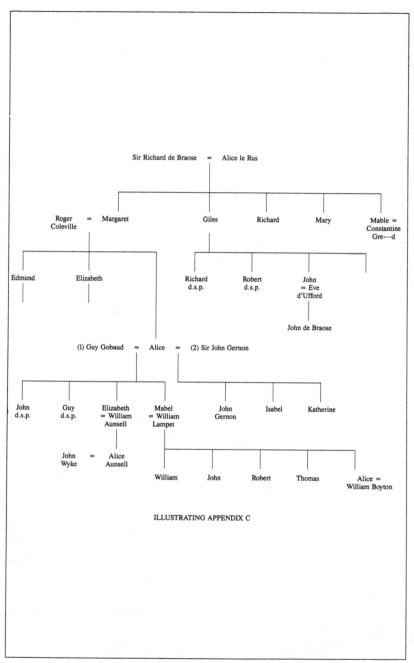

Chart 5. *Illustrating appendix C.*

company of his father at the time when the said John Gernon the father came to Dunsby in the company of Sir Thomas Newmarch the father and that the said present Sir John Gernon came with him, being at that time a child of eight or nine or ten years. At this time the said Sir Thomas de Roos was ten years old or more. It being asked of the said Sir Thomas of what age he is now, he says that he is more than sixty years old.[3]

It being asked of him when the marriage was celebrated between the said John Gernon the father and the said Alice, he says that he did just not know when it was, but he says that within a quarter of a year after the wedding the said John Gernon the father came to Dunsby as is above said.[4] It being asked of him, since he was of so tender age at the time when Sir John Gernon came to his father's house, how he remembered that this present John Gernon is that same person who was of such and so tender age then, or whether he ever had dealings with him after he was grown up, he says that he never afterwards had dealings with him, for he had been engaged [far?] from this land since he was a child and has not known the business of....But he says that the people of Rippingale [Lincolnshire] and others where Lady Gobaud had lands say that John Gernon the father never had any legitimate male issue except this present John.

And he well remembers that when John Gernon the father came to Dunsby he told my lady, the mother of the said Sir Thomas, that his son, who was then present there, was born of his mother when she was only thirteen years old. And my lady his mother said that it was amazing that a woman of such age could bear a child of such stature and so well made. To which the father of the said Sir Thomas said that it was not amazing, for Sir John St. John was born of his mother when she was only twelve years old, and yet the said Sir John St. John was one of the tallest and best made knights of this land.[5] It being asked of him how he remembers these things, and such words, he says that he well remembers many things that happened when he was of the most tender age. It being asked of him what was the name of the mother of Sir John Gernon, he says it was Isabel; for a knight, Sir John Bygot, and William Coleville, who are relatives of the said Isabel that John Gernon had first married, said openly at Lincoln that they considered that the said Isabel was the mother of the said Sir John Gernon. And thereupon he says that he heard Sir Robert Coleville, lord of Bytham [Lincolnshire], say that the wife of John Wyke, issue of Elizabeth the daughter of the said Alice, would be one of his heirs if he died without an heir of his body. And so he [Thomas de Roos] says upon his oath, for the reasons stated above, that the wife of the said John Wyke is one of the heirs of Robert, kinsman and heir of Robert Coleville, and that Sir John Gernon is not the son of Lady Alice Gobaud born of her body.

William Coleville, parson of the church of Harrington and brother of the said Sir Thomas [possibly brother-in-law][6] says upon his oath just as the said Sir Thomas...has said....It being asked of him of what age he was when he saw the said Sir John Gernon at Dunsby with John Gernon his father, and whether this John Gernon is the [same person as] the child who was there at that time, the said William says that whether this Sir John Gernon is the same person or not, he does not know in truth, for he never had any dealings with him afterwards. But he says that he himself was then about the age of three years, and immediately afterwards he rode in a horse-drawn car with his mother from Dunsby to Lincoln in the company of his father when his father was going to the battle of Stirling [Bannockburn, 1314].

Jordan, Abbot of Colchester, being examined upon his oath, says that upon the command of the Bishop of London he examined many honest people about the mother of Sir John Gernon and about his birth. And before him Sir John de Sutton the father, now deceased, in the presence of Sir John de Sutton the son, Sir Richard de Sutton, and Sir Guy Sinclair, said upon peril of his soul that he was at the manor of la Garonner when Lady Alice Gobaud, the mother of the said Sir John [Gernon] was churched [brought to church for a public thanksgiving following a successful delivery of her child] after the birth of the said Sir John. And he [the abbot] also saw the aforesaid knights [John de Sutton, Richard de Sutton, and Guy Sinclair] and many others of the parts where the said Sir John was born, both men and women, and they have testified before him that the said Sir John is the son of the said Lady Alice, born of her body, as appears by a certificate made to the said bishop and exemplified under the seal of the said bishop, which certificate the said abbot shows, sealed, and [says] will always be ready to be seen and....Lady Fitzsimmons acknowledged before the abbot that she saw the said Lady Alice when she was great and pregnant of the said Sir John Gernon, whereof a certificate was made and shown to us [the investigators] by the said abbot, which certificate and other evidences remain in the keeping of the party until they shall be called for.

John de Braose the father says upon his oath that Margaret Braose, the...[sister] of Giles de Braose...was married to Sir [Roger] Coleville, and that of them were born Edmund Coleville and two daughters, Elizabeth and Alice. Edmund had a son, Robert Coleville, lord of Bytham. And Elizabeth was married to Basset of Sapcote, the grandfather of the present Sir Ralph Basset of Sapcote.[7] And Alice was married to Sir G ...a... the son [this would be Alice's first husband, Guy Gobaud]. From Alice came [were born] John Gobaud, Guy Gobaud, Elizabeth, and Mabel [Mabille]. John Gobaud died without an heir [of his body]. After his death his brother Guy sold his heritage to Sir Robert Coleville. And Mabel was married to William Lampet, and she has many descendants still...namely....And...[Elizabeth's daughter, Alice Aunsell] is the wife of John Wyke. And after his decease Lady Alice Gobaud was married to John Gernon the father; to them was born the present Sir John Gernon. It being asked of him how he knows, he says that Sir Richard de Braose is his uncle,[8] and to him the said...and Constantine Gre...d, who had married ...bille, the sister of the said Margaret de Braose,[9] [they] said to him many things...that it was so. And so he says that the said Sir John Gernon was the son of the said Lady Alice, born and begotten of her body.

William Boyton, being examined upon his oath, says that two years before the first epidemic [which occurred in 1348] he was staying with Sir Richard de Braose, who had married the said William's aunt. This Sir Richard had said that he would be very glad if the said William [should become one of his?] family, and afterwards upon the provision of the said Richard he was married to Alice, the daughter of Mabel, the daughter of the said Lady Alice Gobaud...[who] bore the same baptismal name as the said Lady Alice. And after he married her he lived continuously with the said John Gernon and always thereafter considered him as his...because of that...Mabel...Lady Alice. And so he says upon his oath that the said John Gernon and Mabel...were issue, son and daughter, of the said Lady Alice Gobaud, born and begotten of her body.

Sir Hamo de Felton, being examined upon his oath, says that he had married Margaret, widow of Sir William Weston. This Margaret [belonged to the?] Gobaud family as is said, and she said that Sir John Gernon was her kinsman begotten of Lady Alice. Thereupon, when he [Sir Hamo] [was] at Angouleme and was informed by Sir John Ancel [Aunsell?] of the death of Sir Robert Coleville and was in doubt whether his own issue begotten of his own dear wife [Margaret] would be heir of the said Sir Robert or not, he went to Bordeaux to talk with Sir Thomas de Roos of Dunsby, the mayor of Bordeaux, to find out the truth from him, because he [Hamo] was in his [Thomas's] pay and at board with him. And when he was seated at supper among his company and with him, the said Sir Thomas said to him that he had nothing to say and nothing to...in this [heritage?]. And this happened when the said Sir Thomas was about to lay down the office of mayor. And if the said Sir Thomas will deny it, the said Sir Hamo is ready to prove it in whatever way the court of our lord the king shall prescribe.

Sir Richard de Swinnerton, cleric,[10] says upon his oath, that he saw him [John Gernon the son] in the company of the late earl of Hereford when the said earl went to the papal court in the time of our lord the present king. And at that time he was no more than fifteen years old. And since that time he [Sir Richard de Swinnerton] has always considered him [John Gernon] to be the son of Lady Alice, and to the best of his knowledge he [John Gernon] is the son of the said Lady Alice, born of her body. Sir Robert de Swinnerton says, upon his oath, that the said Sir John Gernon and he have worked together for ten years and more. And the said Sir John has often told him, and this long before the death of Sir Robert Coleville, that Lady Alice Gobaud his mother had a daughter named Mabel who was married to one William Lampet, and that of that marriage Thomas Lampet, John, Robert, and two other brothers were born, and he considers them to be his kinsmen on his [Gernon's] mother's side, and that many of his kin on his mother's side were in Lincolnshire. And so he [Robert de Swinnerton] says upon his oath that the said Sir John is the son of the said Lady Alice, born and begotten of her body.

Sir Robert Gedding, of the age of fifty years, says that he has heard that Sir John de Sutton the father, now deceased, often said while he was alive that he had been at la Garonner in Essex...the said Sir John was [born?] of the said Lady Alice and [was?] there when she was churched and that afterwards, to the time of his [John de Sutton's] death, he had known him and...he heard when my lady Fitzsimmons said that she...when the said Lady Alice was great and pregnant of the said Sir John. And so he says upon his oath that the said Sir John is the son of the said Lady Alice.

Sir John de Braose the son, of the age of thirty-six years, being examined upon his oath, says that the late earl of Suffolk,[11] in whose company he was...since he was eight years old, and the said earl questioned him often about his family, and [this when] he [was] of tender age...said right...family of my lady Alice Gobaud, who was the mother of Sir John Gernon, who was of the family of Coleville, and so he was of the same family.[12] And so the said Sir John de Braose says upon his oath that the said Sir John Gernon is the son of the said Lady Alice Gobaud, born of her body.

Sir John de Bur...says upon his oath...of the time that he...was acquainted with the said Sir John Gernon with the earls of Northampton and of Hereford, that he told...and...that he had no other mother than my lady Alice Gobaud, and also that he has heard many people of the parts where the said Sir John Gernon was born say that the said Sir John Gernon had no other mother than the said Lady Alice. And so he says that he [John Gernon] was the son of the Lady Alice.

Edmund Breton, of the age of forty years, says upon his oath that Sir Robert Coleville [son of Edmund Coleville and grandson of Sir Roger and Margaret (de Braose) Coleville] often, when he [Breton] came to Weston Coleville [Cambridgeshire] and there were present only he and Thomas Breton, his brother, and he [Robert Coleville] entertained them and they stayed there with him and he often asked them about their family, and they told him that they were kinsmen of the present Sir John Gernon, and the said Sir Robert said to them that he and Sir John Gernon were kinsmen, and further that the earl of Suffolk and the said Sir John were kinsmen too. And Sir John Gernon also said to him ten years ago that in case Sir Robert Coleville should die without an heir begotten of his body he [John Gernon] would have land in Lincolnshire. And further he says that William Lampet and Thomas, John, and Robert, his brothers, the sons of Mabel, daughter of the said Lady Alice, often said to him that the said Sir John was their uncle on their mother's side and they considered him and acknowledged him as such all their lives, and still consider him so. And so he [Edmund Breton] says that to the best of his knowledge the said Sir John is the son of the said Lady Alice, born and begotten of her body.

Thomas Tue, of Suffolk, also says upon his oath that he was in the parts where the said Sir John was born and the said Lady Alice buried, and that there many people, both men and women, of great age, said and acknowledged before him that the said Sir John was the son of the said Lady Alice, born of her body. And he showed there [before the investigators] a paper bill in which were contained all their statements and their [testimony?] and how [they came by their knowledge?], which bill he handed in when he was examined....

Thomas Lampet, being examined upon his oath, says that William Lampet, his father, had married Mabel, the daughter of Lady Alice Gobaud. And he says that the said William his father had many children, and nine years after the first epidemic [the epidemic of 1348], because the said Thomas was of tender age, he was...by his father to the present Sir John Gernon, the uncle of the said Thomas on his mother's side, to learn of him...and to stay with him, for it was reasonable that the said Sir John should treat him well and should be to him a good master [teacher?]...said Sir John and Mabel, the mother of the said Thomas...and were born of the same mother, namely...the said Lady Alice Gobaud [was the mother of the?] mother of the said Thomas that he and his four brothers all their lives have considered and still consider the said Sir John to be their uncle on the side of Mabel their mother...that Mabel his mother all her life considered the said Sir John Gernon to be her uterine brother...and [that] the said Sir John also [considered] the said Mabel his sister and...each to other as brother and sister. And so he says upon his oath that the said Sir John is the son of the said Lady Alice, born and begotten of her body. And if it were not so then he or one of his brothers would be co-heir of the Gobaud inheritance [it is really the Coleville inheritance] on account of his mother, who is the daughter of the said Lady Alice.

William, vicar of the church of Wythmondford, which is under the patronage of the prioress of Wykes and of the foundation of the earl of Hereford, says upon his oath that he has been vicar there for twenty-four years. In this church the said Lady Alice is buried. And many of his parishioners, both men and women, of whom many are of the age of eighty or more, have told him and shown him, both in confession and otherwise, that the said Lady Alice, when she was great and pregnant of the said Sir John, she was moved from one manor and came to the manor of la Garonner, and when she came there, in the said parish, they saw her in that condition great and pregnant, and there was delivered of the said Sir John. This John was baptized in the said church. The said Lady Alice also had afterwards two daughters begotten by John Gernon the father of the said Sir John, of whom one was named Isabel and the other Katherine. And he says that the said Lady Alice afterwards died and was buried...before...in the chancel of the said church....At the time when he first became vicar there he found in the chancel a large stone resting over the said Lady Alice, as appeared by the inscription...asked what lady and of what estate she was, and his parishioners told him that she was the mother of the present Sir John Gernon. And further the said vicar says upon his oath that the said Sir John in his time [that is, after his parents' deaths] has caused masses to be sung and other...for John Gernon his father and Lady Alice his mother, espressly, by name. And so he says surely and upon his oath that the said Sir John is the son born and begotten of the body of the said Lady Alice. And to the best of his knowledge he [John Gernon] is of the age of fifty-four years.

Alexander Deryng of Wythmondford says upon his oath that when he was of the age of thirteen years he was staying with Roger Gernon in the company of John Gernon the father of the said Sir John at the manor of la Garonner in the parish of Wythmondford, and he saw the said Lady Alice when she came there, great and pregnant of the said present Sir John. And immediately afterwards William Gernon, the grandfather of the present Sir John gave up the manor aforesaid to John his son, who had married the said Lady Alice, for his support, and in the same manor, in a room that is called the Brothers' Room she was delivered of the said present Sir John. And he says that the said Lady Alice afterwards had there two daughters, Isabel and Katherine, with [that is, fathered by] the said John Gernon late her husband, and one of them lived with the...lady de Wygton, the lady who was afterwards [after the death of Lady Alice] wife of the said John Gernon the father [his third wife]. And he says that the said Lady Alice lived with her husband for about ten years, and that he [Alexander Deryng] lived continuously with Sir John Gernon the father of the said present Sir John after the birth of the said child...the life of the said Alice and all her life she considered him to be her son. And he says further that he has known the said Sir John Gernon well ever since then. And so he says upon his oath that the said Sir John is the son begotten and born of the body of the said Alice.

John Foucher of Easthorpe [Essex] says upon his oath that his father died forty-three years ago. After his death he [John Foucher] was claimed by the father of the present Sir John Gernon to be in wardship, and he lived for three years in the house of his [the present John Gernon's] father, until his father (Gernon) learned that he had no right to the wardship. And at that time the said present Sir John was a fine child, and he [John Foucher] then often went with him to hunt the hare and the fox, since they were both children and about the same age. And he [Foucher] has known him [Gernon] since then. And he says that at that time the said Alice had there a son named Guy [by her first husband, Guy Gobaud]. Guy slept in his mother's room, and the present Sir John Gernon slept in another room with the squires. It was often asked there about this, why the said Sir John slept outside and the said Guy inside. And Roger Gobaud then said [that it was] because the said Lady Alice was [both] father and mother to the said Guy, and the said Sir John was the son of the said Lady Alice and had a father there present. And further he says that the said John Gernon the father and Lady Alice had together two daughters, Isabel and Katherine. It being asked of him whether the said John the father had any wife before the said Alice, he says that his mother told him often that the said John the father had first married one Isabel Bygot who died at the age of thirteen years at Messing [Essex] in the company of Lady Baviard [or Bainard, or similar] and was buried in the church of Great Birch because the church of Easthorpe was at that time suspended [under a bishop's ban?]. And his mother also told him that she went to the church of Great Birch with the body of the said Isabel and that two fine horses were led to the church before the body of the said Isabel and that when she was buried his mother rode home on one of the two horses because she was great with child and could not travel easily. And so he says upon his oath that the said Sir John Gernon is the son begotten and born of the body of the said Alice...to the best of his knowledge that the said Sir John is now about the age of fifty-four years, and that his father and the said Isabel once his wife never had any children between them.

Robert Beleigne of Great Birch says upon his oath that Isabel Bygot the first wife of John Gernon the father died in childbirth when she was of the age of thirteen years,[13] and that there was never any issue between the said John and the said Isabel. This Isabel is buried in Great Birch, as said above. And [he says] that about two years after the death of the said Isabel the said John married the said Lady Alice. Afterwards, when she was great with child, she was brought to the manor of la Garonner, near Great Birch, and there the said Robert saw the said Alice great and pregnant of the said Sir John Gernon often before she was delivered and immediately after. And he knew the said Sir John well from that time on, for the said Sir John was raised there and lived continuously in those parts. And he says that the said Lady Alice all her life considered the said present Sir John to be her son and loved him more than any other...living. And also he says that the said Lady Alice had with John Gernon the father two

297

daughters, Isabel and Katherine. After the [death of Alice?] John Gernon the father married...Margaret of Wygton, between whom...there was never any issue, neither son nor daughter. And he says that the said present Sir John Gernon is about the age of fifty-four, and without doubt the son of the said Lady Alice, upon his oath.

Austin...of Suffolk says upon his oath that William Lampet married Mabel the daughter of Lady Alice and that the present Sir John Gernon often came to Bucklesham [Suffolk] to the said Mabel to enjoy himself there with his sister. And for thirty years after the said Austin has been continuously...with the said William Lampet and the said Sir John considered...and called the said Mabel his sister...of...Sir Robert de Braose, Sir John de Verdon...that they were...considered the said Sir John Gernon to be the brother of the said Mabel...to William...Robert son of the aforesaid William Lampet and Mabel. [end of document]

Notes

1. See chapter 11, which disproves the Wentworth royal line.

2. It appears from the bulk of the other testimony that Sir Thomas was lying, and it can be shown that he was wrong on Alice's age. Her mother was most likely born in the late 1260s, and her father died in 1288; thus she was probably born about 1285, give or take a few years. Alice's second husband, Sir John Gernon, who was age thirty in 1327, died in 1334; she had predeceased him, and he had married a third wife. According to another witness she was married to Sir John for some ten years before she died. Since Sir John Gernon the father was born ca. 1297, Alice would have been about twelve years older than her husband, a not unusual difference in medieval times in the case of a wife bringing valuable property into the marriage. Still, Alice must have been well under forty when she gave birth to Sir John Gernon the son, who most likely was born ca. 1316 (see testimony), and certainly could not have been born much later than 1321, and she would have been well within childbearing ages when she gave birth to John's two sisters.

3. People of the time were not precise on ages, but we have to try to make use of them because we do not have much on which to base chronology. From the testimony of William, the vicar of Wythmondford, and of others given below, Sir John Gernon was fifty-four years old at the time of their depositions. If the depositions were made in 1370, then Sir John would have been born in 1316, but if made in 1375, he would have been born ca. 1321. If Sir Thomas is telling the truth on ages (and since he is apparently lying in the main respect, he cannot be considered especially reliable in other respects), he, Sir Thomas, would have been born no later than 1310 (if he testified in 1370) or 1315 (if he testified in 1375). In either case, Sir Thomas's testimony on ages seems to be a discrepancy with the testimony

of others. Waters believed that the older Sir John Gernon lost his first wife, Isabel, in 1311, and we have testimony in the present document that he married Alice about two years later, that is, ca. 1313, perhaps 1314, which would be reasonable if the younger John was born ca. 1316.

4. There is good testimony that Isabel died at age thirteen. If the younger John were her son, and he were eight to ten years old when Sir Thomas saw him, Isabel would have been a mother at age three to five.

5. These comments would show that although at that time and place it was somewhat unusual for a mother to give birth at twelve or thirteen years, it occurred. See also chapter 7. It is interesting to see that Waters translated the Law French "plus bien fourne" as "properest" and Professor Sutherland as "best made," both conveying the meaning, though "best made" seems closer to the original.

6. Sir Thomas de Roos seems to have a personal interest in the inheritance (as is also implied later in the testimony of Sir Hamo de Felton). If Sir Thomas were married to a sister of William Coleville (who, being a parson, would not have been married himself, and thus would not be a brother to Sir Thomas by having married a sister of the latter), and if William Coleville were related to Alice (Coleville) (Gobaud) Gernon, Sir Thomas might be harboring a possibility of sharing in the estates of Alice, thus accounting for his testimony, which is so contradictory to that of the great majority of witnesses.

7. At the time I wrote the article "The Evidence that Sir Richard de Braose Who Married Alice le Rus Was the Son of John and Margaret (verch Llywelyn) de Braose," *The Genealogist* 6 (1985):85-99, I did not yet have the translation of the present document. While the document does not invalidate the conclusion of that article in any way, nor does it change the main part of the article, pp. 85-90, the second part, pp. 90-93, headed "The Evidence from Association," was partly speculative, and now in the light of this new information, must be considerably revised.

8. This Richard de Braose would be the second son of Sir Richard and Alice (le Rus) de Braose. According to Moriarty's Notebooks (15:162) at The New England Historical and Genealogical Society, Richard obtained the manor of Stradbroke from his mother and died without issue before her, his heir being his older brother Giles. This is not correct. Richard is clearly identified by the testimony both of Sir John de Braose the father and later in this document of William Boyton, who said Richard was married to Boyton's aunt and was living in 1346. Further, a *Calendar of the Patent Rolls* (London, 1908), 3:132, shows that the king granted Richard de Braose the right to hold an annual fair at his manor of Stradbroke, Suffolk, on 12 December 1309; thus he could not have predeceased his mother, who died almost ten years earlier. W. A. Copinger, *The Manors of Suffolk* (Manchester, 1909) 4:84-85, states that Stradbroke was held by the le Rus family and was inherited by Alice le Rus, who had no brother. Copinger continues, "It is said that Sir Richard [de Braose, second husband of Alice le Rus] died in 1296, but this seems doubtful, as we find in 1309 a grant of free warren and of a fair in Stradbroke made to Richard de Brewse [variation of Braose] this year." Copinger was probably fooled by the fact that the heir of the older Sir Richard de Braose was Giles de Braose, but in this case Sir Richard's wife Alice le Rus

must have given Stradbroke to a younger son, Richard, while she was still living. Copinger mentions that in 1358/9 a fine was levied on this manor by Sir John de Wingfield and Alianora his wife, and thus it is possible that Alianora was a daughter (or granddaughter) of the younger Richard de Braose. Thus we see how this contemporary document can correct erroneous impressions held by secondary genealogical writers of later centuries.

9. This name was probably Mabille (Mabel), whose sister Margaret later named one of her daughters after her. This is apparently the only extant record showing that Richard and Alice (le Rus) de Braose had a daughter Mabel.

10. In this period priests were customarily given a courtesy title of "Sir," but it did not mean they were knights. Knights were frequently distinguished by having the word attached to their names, as in Sir John Doe, knight.

11. It is now possible, by adding new information from this document to information previously obtained for my article "The Medieval Braose Family" (to be published in *The Genealogist*), to identify Sir John Braose the father and Sir John de Braose the son. Robert d'Ufford, Earl of Suffolk, (1298-1369), was the maternal uncle of John de Braose the son. John de Braose the father, who gave earlier testimony, married Eve d'Ufford, sister of the earl. John the father was the son of Gile de Braose, the brother of Margaret de Braose who married Roger Coleville, and thus a first cousin to Alice (Coleville) (Gobaud) Gernon. I had previously had John the son as being born ca. 1332 (a document called him age fifty-four in 1386), but the present document, if correct in showing him to be age thirty-six in 1370, would have him born more around 1334. However, keep in mind that people did not keep good track of their age, and ages given in testimony such as this were frequently approximations or best guesses. For example, Alice (le Rus) (Longespey) de Braose, was called in a document of 1253 to be six years old and in a document of 1260 to be fourteen or fifteen years old.

12. The meaning of this episode cannot be determined because of illegibility. However, Lady Alice's brother Edmund Coleville had married Margaret, the daughter of Robert and Mary d'Ufford of Ufford, Suffolk, and thus there would have been a relationship between the Colevilles and the Uffords, as well as the Braoses and the Uffords, which is perhaps what is meant here.

13. Again we see an example of early pregnancy.

Appendix D

A New Royal Line: John Harleston of South Carolina

Royal lines are hard to find, hard to prove, and especially hard to document by primary evidence. The following new royal line relies almost entirely on primary evidence, or on the *Complete Peerage,* which is generally considered the next best thing and which can usually be translated into primary evidence. Admittedly, at the end of this line, the immediate generations leading to colonial South Carolina immigrant John Harleston, we have something less than primary evidence, and it is hoped that someday this deficiency can be overcome. In the meantime, though, the line has the "feel" of authenticity, and, perhaps more important, it would seem to be more strongly supported than many royal lines that are now accepted by virtually all genealogists.[1]

In presenting this line, I will give each succeeding generation, together with spouse, followed by the appropriate references, and then will discuss how the referenced information supports the current generation as the child of the next previous generation. This manner of presentation takes up more space than a simple list of generations followed by abbreviated references and little or no discussion. But it has the advantage of allowing readers to draw their own conclusions, so that all may readily see that the line is or is not adequately supported in all generations. If this method were used more often, we would not have the unfortunately common problem of having a new royal line claimed in one article, and then years later shown to be false or not adequately documented in another article.

It is convenient to start the line with Isabel de Clare, who married William Marshal, and who had Maud Marshal as her daughter. There is no need to support the line back to Charlemagne, for this part of the line is well known,[2] and is as follows:

Charlemagne (A.D. 747-814) married Hildegarde,
and had

Pepin, who by a daughter of Duke Barnard had a natural son Bernard, who married Cunigarde
and had

Pepin,
who had

Herbert I de Vermandois, who married Beatrice
and had

Herbert II de Vermandois, who married Leigarde
and had

Albert I de Vermandois, who married Gerberga
and had

Herbert III de Vermandois, who married Ermengarde
and had

Otho de Vermandois, who married Parvie
and had

Herbert IV de Vermandois, who married Adela
and had

Adelaide de Vermandois, who married Hugh Magnus
and had

Isabel de Vermandois, who married Robert de Beaumont
and had

Isabel de Beaumont, who married Gilbert de Clare
and had

Richard de Clare, who married Eva MacMurrough
and had

Isabel de Clare, who married William Marshal
and had

Maud Marshal, who married Hugh Bigod.

The documented line now continues:

1. MAUD MARSHAL (d. 1248) married (1) Hugh Bigod, Earl of Norfolk, son of Roger Bigod, both Magna Charta Sureties.

Reference: *Complete Peerage* (*CP*) 9:589-590.

Discussion: See next generation.

2. ISABEL BIGOD married (2) Sir John FitzGeoffrey (d. 1258).

Reference: As above.

Discussion: *CP* 9:590 (fn c) shows that Isabel Bigod who married Sir John FitzGeoffrey was the daughter of Hugh and Maud (Marshal) Bigod.

3. MAUD FITZ JOHN (d. 1301), married (2) William de Beauchamp, Earl of Warwick.

References: *CP* 4:265, 12 (2):309-10.

Discussion: The first reference shows that Hugh le Despencer married the widow of Patric Chaurces, Isabel, daughter of William de Beauchamp, Earl of Warwick, by his wife, Maud, daughter of Sir John FitzGeoffrey. The second reference shows that William de Beauchamp, Earl of Warwick, married Maud, widow of Sir Gerard de Furnivale, and daughter of Sir John FitzGeoffrey by Isabel, daughter of Hugh Bigod.

4. ISABEL DE BEAUCHAMP (d. 1306) married Hugh le Despencer, Earl of Winchester.

References: *CP* 4:265, 11:299.

Discussion: Both references show that Isabel, widow of Patric Chaurces, and wife of Hugh le Despencer, was the daughter of William de Beauchamp, by Maud, daughter of John FitzGeoffrey.

5. MARGARET LE DESPENCER married John de St. Amand (1278-ca. 1330).

Reference: *CP* 11:299.

Discussion: The reference shows that John de St. Amand married Margaret, daughter of Hugh le Despencer, Earl of Winchester, by his wife Isabel.

6. ISABELLA DE ST. AMAND (d. 1361) married Richard de Haudlo (d. between 1340 and 1347).

References: H. E. Salter, *The Boarstall Cartulary* (Oxford, 1930), 74, 191, and other references given in the discussion.

Discussion: This is one of the few times when the *Complete Peerage* can be proven wrong. *CP* 6:400 states that Richard de Haudlo married a daughter of Aumarie (Almeric) de St. Amand, though she was in fact a sister of this Aumarie de St. Amand. Salter (p. 191) shows that John de Haudlo in a 1229-30 agreement with John de St. Amand (Sancto Amando) gave several properties to Richard, son of John de Haudlo, and Isabella, his wife, and to their issue, or if no issue then the right to dispose of the land would go as John de Haudlo pleased. In this agreement John de St. Amand gave properties to his son Almaric de St. Amand and Almaric's wife Joan (thus a son and daughter of John de Haudlo married a daughter and son of John de St. Amand, as Salter points on p. 74).

John de St. Amand had a brother Almaric, but he died without issue (*CP* 11:298), and he had a son Almaric, but he was born ca. 1315 (*CP* 11:299), and was too young to be Isabella's father. The double marital agreement shown by Salter is a primary source and leaves no doubt that the *Complete Peerage* was wrong in this case, in fact, doubly wrong, for *CP* 11:300 has the younger Almaric married to an Eleanor (____) but makes no mention of his marriage (proven by the above agreement) to Joan de Haudlo.[3] Additional confirmation is found in *The Index Library*, vol. 47, *Inquisitions Post Mortem for Gloucester* (London, 1914; reprinted, 1968), 15, where Isabel de Haudlo was shown following her death to be jointly possessed with her husband Sir Richard de Haudlo of several properties, one of which was in Coln St. Aldwyn, and one of the properties John de Haudlo had given Richard and Isabella was in Coln St. Aldwyn.

7. ELIZABETH ST. HAUDLO (b. 1339; d. between 1362 and 1374) married Sir Edmund de la Pole.

References: *Calendar of Inquisitions Post Mortem, (IPM)* 12 vols. (London, 1904-38; reprinted, 1973) 8:489, 493; 10:243, 362, 367. Also *The Index Library*, vol. 47, *Inquisitions Post Mortem for Gloucester* (London, 1914; reprinted, 1968), 15, hereafter *Gloucester IPM.*

Discussion: *IPM* 10:367 shows a petition by Sir Edmund de la Pole and Elizabeth his wife, sister and one of the heirs of Edmund de Haudlo, dated 12 March 1358. On 13 April 1358 Elizabeth's proof of age showed that she was born on 5 June 1339. *IPM* 8:489, 493, show that Edmund, son of Richard de Haudlo, deceased, who was the son of John de Haudlo, was the heir of the said John de Haudlo, who died 5 August 1346. *IPM* 10:243, 362, show that Edmund de Haudlo died on 1 June 1356, and his heirs were his sisters Margaret and Elizabeth. Although one part of the inquisition confuses the ages of the sisters, it is clear that Elizabeth, who by 20 May 1358 was married to Edmund de la Pole, was the younger, and had been born on 5 June 1339 (see proof of age, above). *IPM* 8:489 shows that this Edmund de Haudlo was age seven years and more on 22 August 1346, and thus was born prior to 22 August 1339. Thus either Edmund and Elizabeth were twins, or he was the older of the two.

It is necessary in a case such as this to show that not only was Elizabeth the daughter of Richard de Haudlo but also the daughter of Isabella de St. Amand, who carried the royal line. *IPM* 10:243 shows that "the mother of the deceased," that is, Edmund's mother, had married Robert de Ildesley after the death of her husband Richard de

Haudlo. Since she survived Richard de Haudlo, and since it is shown that she was Edmund's mother, any children Richard de Haudlo had after Edmund would have been by the same mother. Thus it is shown that the Elizabeth de Haudlo who married Edmund de la Pole was the daughter of line carrier Isabel de St. Amand.

This is deductive reasoning, but sometime after I had done the above research for my client, I discovered another document that confirms the above with direct evidence. The *Gloucester IPM* gives the 1361 inquisition on lands held by Isabel de Haudlo at the time of her death and specifically states that "Margaret Chastelon and Elizabeth att Pole, daughters of the said Richard and Isabel, are her heirs and are of full age."

8. ELIZABETH DE LA POLE (b. 14 July 1362; d. 14 December 1403) married Sir Ingram Bruyn of South Ockendon, Essex (b. Titchfield, Hampshire 6 December 1353; d. 12 August 1400).

References: *CP* 2:356; Henry A. Napier, *Historical Notices of the Parishes of Swyncombe and Ewelme in the County of Oxford* (Oxford, 1858), 291-92.

Discussion: *CP* 2:356 shows that Sir Ingram Bruyn of South Ockendon married Elizabeth, elder daughter of Sir Edmund de la Pole by his first wife, Elizabeth de Haudlo, younger daughter of Richard de Haudlo and sister of Edmund de Haudlo. Napier quotes from a fly-leaf of a psalter which gives the birth of Elizabeth, daughter of Edmund de la Pole and Elizabeth his wife, daughter and heir of Richard de Haudlo, on 14 July 1362. Napier states that she married Sir Ingelram Bruyn, who died in 1406 [*sic*], and left a son Maurice Bruyn as heir.

9. SIR MAURICE DE BRUYN (1386-1466) married Elizabeth Retford.

Reference: *CP* 2:357.

Discussion: The reference shows that Sir Maurice Bruyn, who was born at South Ockendon 14 September 1386, and died 8 November 1466, was the son of Sir Ingram and Elizabeth (de la Pole) Bruyn. Maurice's third wife was Elizabeth Retford, who died 20 May 1471, the daughter of Sir Henry Retford of Lincoln.

10. SIR HENRY BRUYN (d. 1461) married Elizabeth Darcy.

Reference: *CP* 2:357.

Discussion: The reference shows that Sir Henry Bruyn, who died on 30 November 1461 during the lifetime of his father, was the son of Sir Maurice and Elizabeth (Retford) Bruyn, and that he married Elizabeth, daughter of Robert Darcy.

11. ALICE BRUYN (d. 15 Feb. 1472/3) married (2) Robert Harleston.

Reference: *CP* 2:357-58.

Discussion: The reference shows that Alice Bruyn, who died 15 February 1472/3, was the daughter of Sir Henry and Elizabeth (Darcy) Bruyn. Alice married (2) Robert Harleston of Shimpling, Suffolk, who was slain at Barnet Field 14 April 1496.

12. JOHN HARLESTON I (d. ca. 1496), wife unknown.

Reference: *IPM,* 2d series, 2:236-37.

Discussion: The reference shows that Maurice and Elizabeth Bruyn had Sir Henry Bruyn as their heir [*sic;* Henry predeceased his father], and Henry's heirs were his daughters Alice and Elizabeth. Alice married Robert Harleston, Esq., and they had John Harleston as their heir. Clement Harleston, son of the said John Harleston, who was five years old at the time of the inquisition, 31 October 1499, was the heir of Alice.

13. SIR CLEMENT HARLESTON (1494-1546), wife unknown.

Reference: As in 12, above.

Discussion: As in 12, above. It should also be noted that among the properties inherited by the young Clement Harleston was "Southwekyngdon" (that is, South Ockendon) in Essex.

14. JOHN HARLESTON II (d. 1569) married Mary (possibly Brinklies; but if so she would not have been the mother of 15.)

Reference: F. G. Emmison, *Elizabethan Life: Wills of Essex Gentry & Merchants* (Chelmsford, Essex, 1978), 7-9, 46.

Discussion: Emmison (p. 7) transcribes the will of John Harleston, Esq., of South Ockendon, dated 20 April 1567, proved 22 March 1570 (ER 11A/66), giving the names of his wife Mary; his sister Mary Harleston; his late father Sir Clement Harleston; his brothers Clement, Anthony, and Henry; his sons Robert, Thomas, and William; and his unmarried daughters Jane, Frances, Elizabeth, and Ann. His sons Thomas and William and the four daughters were to get £80 each at age twenty-one. Thus Thomas, No. 15 below, must have been born between 1547 (if under twenty-one in 1567) and 1557 (since he had a son born 1568-1573).

The will mentions others by name, including "Goddistocke my old servant." Pages 8 through 9 give the will of his son Robert Harleston, Esq., of South Ockendon, dated 21 January 1571, proved 9 February 1571 (who must have been his father's first main heir), who of the Harleston name mentions only his uncle Henry Harleston. Among others, Robert also names "Godstocke my father's old servant." Page 46 gives the will of Henry Harleston, gentleman, of South Ockendon, dated 21 April 1589, proved 4 February 1590, but no one is mentioned as a relative or with the Harleston surname.

From a typescript vol. 395 of Boyd's Marriages (LDS Family History Library 942.67/V25b/v.1), a John Harleston married Mary Brinklies in S. Ockenden in 1562, and she is possibly the Mary who was married to generation No. 14, but if so, she would have been a second wife.

15. THOMAS HARLESTON (b. ca. 1550, d. 1572) married Mary, the daughter of Rowland Lytton.

References: F. G. Emmison, *Elizabethan Life, Wills of Essex Gentry & Yeomen* (Chelmsford, Essex, 1980), 94-95, 121-23.

Discussion: Emmison (p. 94-95) gives the will of Thomas Harleston, dated 6 August 1572, proved 5 October 1572, naming his wifc Mary, who gets as part of her dower the reversion of his messuage or farm called Mollandes in South Ockendon; his beloved father-in-law Rowland Lytton, Esq.; his sisters, who are unmarried; and his son John, a minor. If John has no heirs, successive remainders go to Thomas's brother William Harleston and his male heirs, and then to his sisters.

Emmison (p. 121-23) gives the will of Robert Sampson, Esq., of South Ockendon, dated 1 October 1589. Sampson married Mary, the widow of John Harleston (No. 14), and Mary predeceased Sampson. Sampson refers to his term of years of land he had under the grant of Robert Wingefeild, Esq., deceased, during the "nonage of John Harlestone, her Majesty's ward," in the tenement called Rowles, South Ockendon, and to his term of years in South Ockendon Hall (that is, he still has possession of these lands at the time he made his will). He names Anne Dinglie his "daughter" and her mother "late my wife, when she was married to Mr. John Harleston esquire, her father." Also, "whereas the right honourable Lady Jane Wentworth in her widowhood did leave in my hands in trust to the use of Anne daughter of Clement Harlestone gentleman deceased £17 and there is £14, 10s., 3 3/4d., the just portion of Mistress Mary Harlestone deceased, remaining in my hands and due to her, and £10 of a legacy given by her to one Mary, another of the daughters of Clement, and due to Anne, I appoint my executor to pay the said sums to her; to Anne, whom my loving wife did bring up, 40 marks." (Note another Wentworth connection in No. 16, below).

16. JOHN HARLESTON III (b. 1568-1573, d. 1624) married (1) Elizabeth (source unknown) and (2) Jane (possibly Dauthen) (d. 1626).

References: Emmison, *Wills of Essex Gentry & Yeomen, 121; W. R. Powell, editor, The Victoria History of the Counties of England, A History of the County of Essex* vol. 7, (Oxford, 1978), 118-20.

Discussion: Sampson's will, under No. 15, above, would indicate that John was born no later than 1573 (if his father died in 1572), and being under 21 in 1589 would have been born no earlier than 1568.

Powell, a well-documented secondary source [though I have not checked all his references] (p. 118-20) shows that the manor of South Ockendon passed through various families to the Bruyns and the Harlestons, and that in 1499 the heirs were William Tyrell and John Harleston's five-year-old son, Clement. The manor was divided in 1531, and Clement Harleston took the hall and most of the lands in the south southeast of the parish, and thereafter this part of the old manor was called the manor of South Ockendon Hall. Sir Clement was succeeded by his oldest son John, who in turn was succeeded by his sons, first Robert, and then Thomas. Thomas was succeeded by his son John, who died in 1624. "In 1615 John Harleston and his second wife Jane sold the reversion of the manor after their deaths....In 1625 Jane surrendered her life interest to Lord Petre" and thus the manor passed from the hands of the Harleston family. The estate of Mollands was in the southeast of the parish, and by 1540 was a part of the demesne of the manor of South Ockendon Hall. "It descended along with the manor until John Harleston's death in 1624. He had previously settled Mollands on his wife Jane (d. 1626) with remainder to their sons John and Thomas." Powell adds that "the subsequent descent of Mollands has not been traced until 1692."

17. JOHN HARLESTON IV, wife unknown.

References: Powell, op. cit.; John Venn and J. A. Venn, *Alumni Cantabrigiensis,* part 1, vol. 2 (Cambridge, 1922), 308.

Discussion: Venn shows that John Harleston "doubtless the son of John of South Ockendon, Essex," matriculated in 1627 and was admitted to Gray's Inn 28 April 1629. He was the brother of Robert (1635/6) and Thomas (1629/30). Robert and Thomas are given also as separate items, and both are said to be sons of John of South Ockendon, Essex. John is not shown with a degree, while Thomas and Robert received M.A.s in 1637 and 1643 respectively. Thomas migrated to Pembroke.

Thus far each generation would seem to be unquestionably correct, having been well supported by primary evidence and the *Complete Peerage.* Powell has showed via primary source documentation [Prob 11/54 (P.C.C. Daper) and other references] that John Harleston III had sons John and Thomas; and Venn, from his study of the records of Cambridge University, shows John, Thomas, and another brother Robert (all incidentally family names), as students at Cambridge. At this point the line starts relying in part on indirect evidence.

18. JOHN HARLESTON V, of Malling, Co. Essex (d. bef. 28 December 1698), wife unknown. Brother of Affra (Harleston) Coming.

References: Theodore D. Jervey, "The Harlestons," *The South Carolina Historical and Genealogical Magazine* 3 (1902):151-55; Agnes Leland Baldwin, *First Settlers of South Carolina 1670-1680* (University of South Carolina,

Columbia); Caroline T. Moore and Agatha A. Simmons, compilers, *Abstracts of the Wills of the State of South Carolina, 1670-1740* (1960), 1:20.

Discussion: Jervey cites the Shaftsbury Papers, Collection of the South Carolina Historical Society, vol. 5, p. 134, as the source for Affra Harleston's name appearing on a list of those on board the *Carolina,* preparing to sail 10 August 1669. Her brother Charles was said to be in Carolina in 1678 but subsequently went to Barbados and disappeared. Affra's father was said to be John Harleston, the older brother "apparently" of Secretary Robert Harleston. Affra married John Coming, and she died in 1699, leaving all her estate jointly to Elias Ball of Devonshire, a half brother to her husband, and "to my nephew John Harleston of Dublin in the Kingdom of Ireland the son of John Harleston late of Malling in the county of Essex" (Will Book 1687-1710, p. 23, Probate Court, Charleston County, South Carolina). Jervey adds that Elias Ball was in South Carolina in 1701 and married a sister of John Harleston.

Affra (Harleston) Coming's will is abstracted by Moore and Simmons. She is of Berkeley County, South Carolina, the widow of John Coming, gentleman, and in her will dated 28 December 1698, proved 9 March 1699, she bequeaths all her estate "to nephew John Harleston of Dublin, Ireland, Gent., son of John Harleston late of Malling, County of Essex, England, Gent., deceased, and Elias Ball, son of William Ball, half-brother of said John Coming." Among the witnesses is James Child, probably the James Child who is shown below as having land next to John Harleston, No. 19.

19. JOHN HARLESTON VI (d. 1738) married Elizabeth Willis.

References: As above for No. 18. Also Walter B. Edgar and N. Louise Bailey, *Biographical Directory of the South Carolina House of Representatives, 1692-1775* (Columbia, S.C.), 2:308; A. S. Salley, Jr., editor, revised by R. Nicholas

Oldsberg, *Warrants for Land in South Carolina, 1672-1711*
(Columbia, S.C., 1973), 605, 611, 617.

Discussion: Jervey identifies him as the John Harleston
who married Elizabeth Willis in 1707, he apparently coming to South Carolina shortly after the death of his Aunt
Affra. Jervey also refers to him as a "particular friend" of
Chief Justice Mr. Nicolas Trott in Carolina whom, along
with the Governor, John Harleston invited to his wedding
(from a letter by John Harleston to John Page, subsequently Lord Mayor of Dublin, Ireland, as shown by Jervey, 2:47-48.

From Salley (p. 605) we see that James Child (one of the
witnesses to Affra's will) had a warrant dated 19 August
1702 for 800 acres of land on an inland plantation joining
southwesterly on lands belonging to Elias Ball and John
Harleston. John Harleston had a warrant dated 17 September 1703 for 500 acres of land he already owned at the eastern branch of the Cooper River (p. 611). Two consecutive
warrants, each dated 8 May 1704, for 200 and 150 acres of
land respectively to John Harleston and Elias Ball are
shown on page 617. These items prove that Affra's nephew
did come to South Carolina in the very early 1700s. Edgar
and Bailey (p. 308) state that the immigrant John Harleston died in 1738, and his son Nicholas inherited from him
Bossis, a plantation on the eastern branch of the Cooper
River in the parish of St. John Berkeley. There is no other
person of the name John Harleston in South Carolina at
this time.

Jervey (3:151) refers to a coat of arms with Harleston
quartering Wentworth. This is described in the achieve-
ment (possibly from the back of the coat of arms in a
descendant's house, or possibly from Berry's Encyclopedia) as belonging to Robert Harleston, Secretary in
1640 to William Louthal, Master of the Rolls and Speaker
of Parliament, "second son of John Harlstone of South ofin-
don [*sic*] in the County Essex and Jane Dauthen Coheirs
of Philip Wentworth a younger brother of the Lord
Wentworth." Jervey (3:154) has a footnote referring to

Affra as "a Lady of eminent piety and liberality; benefactress of the Church in Carolina....Her father's 'inventorie' shows the furniture of the early home at Mollyns from 'the seller, the parlour, the Inner parlour, the hall, the kitchen, the larder, great Chamber, the hall chamber, the painted chamber, the nursery, the buttrie chamber the back 1 chamber the gallie to 'the garrets.'" (Note by Langdon Cheves, Esq. to Shaftesbury Papers, Collections of the South Carolina Historical Society, vol. 5, p. 394. Here we have another variation of the estate Mollands. It would be helpful to have the father's inventory identified more. What we have here is something purporting to be a primary source, but possibly no longer available for checking.)

Nonetheless, we have the abstract of Affra's will clearly showing that her nephew John Harleston VI was the son of John Harleston V "of Malling, County of Essex." John Harleston IV was identified by Powell on the basis on primary evidence as the heir to Mollands in South Ockendon, Essex. A check of gazetteers showed no other place in Essex likely to be "Malling." Again, neither Essex nor colonial South Carolina were filled with members of the gentry. The Harleston family which owned Mollands was clearly of the gentry, as was John Harleston of South Carolina. The evidence is questionable in only one sense: Could there have been two John Harlestons at this time in Co. Essex, one with an estate called Mollands and one with an estate called Malling? The question is a legitimate one, but the answer is clear that there is no evidence for two John Harlestons owning similarly named estates.

I would call this line adequately proven under the legal concept of preponderance of evidence. I would have to stop short of calling it proven beyond any reasonable doubt, and thus I would not have been able to approve it for membership in the Royal Bastards – yet there are approved Royal Bastard lines that are not as well supported as this John Harleston line.

Notes

1. My acquaintance with this line is due to work I did for a client, Mrs. Gordon F. Jacobsen of Utah, and I am grateful to her for giving me this opportunity of demonstrating how a new royal line may be documented.

2. Anyone interested in lines from Charlemagne should consult as a starting point the monumental work of Erich Brandenburg, *Die Nachkommen Karls des Grossen* (1935). Unfortunately this work is not available in English translation.

3. Arthur Adams, *The Elkinton Family in England and America* (Hartford, 1945), 13, correctly shows that Isabella, the wife of Richard de Haudlo, was the daughter of John de St. Amand, but Adams was unaware of the error in the *Complete Peerage,* since volume 11 of the latter was not published until 1949.

Index

A

Academic studies, 10
Accredited genealogists, 224, 229
Ackley-Bosworth genealogy, 170
Acquired characteristics, 204
Adam and Eve, 12
Adams
    Arthur, 74, 127, 232, 315,
    Enid L, 239
    Henry, 29
Adoptions, 44
Advowson, 269
Affidavits, 44, 51
Age, 270
    at childbirth, 96
    limits, 54, 195, 207,
Alden, John, 15, 23, 76, 133
Alfred the Great (King), 170
Allen,
    Cameron, 206, 239
    David Grayson, 13
    John K. (Mrs.), 147
    Marion E., 190
Alsop,
    Elizabeth, 163
    George, 163
    John, 163
    Timothy, 163
Alston,
    John, 166
    Thomasine (Brooke), 166
    William, 166
Altschul, Michael, 3, 12, 189, 285
American Archivists, Society of, 237

American Genealogist, The, 12, 27, 30, 39, 176-77, 179, 225, 237
American Journal for Legal History, 206
American Society of Genealogists, 230, 232, 235, 239
    Fellows of the, 230, 232-33, 238, 244
Americans of Royal Descent, National Society of, 145
Amice, the Countess of Gloucester, 268
Ancel, Sir John, 292
Ancestral Roots, 170, 172
Ancestral Roots of Sixty American Colonists, 246
Ancestry, Inc., 236
Ancestry Newsletter, 34
Anderson, Robert Charles, 4, 37, 83, 169, 206, 239
Andrus, Hannah, 25
Appleton,
    Samuel, 160
    William Sumner, 6
Apprenticeships, 195
Archimedes, 209
Archives and the User, 190
Argentine,
    John (Sir), 286
    Monsieur, 286
Arms, College of, 5, 186, 255
Arms, The Records and Collections of the College of, 190
Army Nurse Corps, 142
Arnold, James N., 59
Athenae Cantabrigienses, 74
Atwood,
    Mary, 250
    Nathaniel, 250

    Sarah, 76
Audley, 163
Aunsell, Alice, 292
Austen,
    Jane, 282
    John D., Jr., 239

B

Background sources, 175-76
Bailey,
    Comfort (Billings), 81
    N. Louise, 312
    Rosalie Fellows, 232, 239
    William, 82
Bailyn, Bernard, 191
Baird, Mary Anne, 119
Baker,
    Eleanor, 81
    Hannah, 25
    J. H., 206
    Samuel, 80
Baldwin,
    Agnes Leland, 311
    Clarence C., 163, 170
    Richard, 163
    Temperance, 163
Baldwin of Exeter, 264
Ball, Elias, 312-13
Baltzell, E. Digby, 153
Banks, Charles Edward, 6, 73, 92
Bannockburn, battle of, 291
Barclay,
    Florence, 92, 251
    John E. (Mrs), 38, 105, 130
    Rachel E., 239
Barlow, Claude W., 206
Barnaby, Lydia (Bartlett), 81

Barnard,
    Duke, 302
    E. A. B., 161, 169
Barneby, James, 103
Barnum, P. T., 246
Baron
    by charter or patent, 280
    by tenure, 280
    by writ, 280
Baronage of England, 190
*Baronial Family in Medieval
    England: The Clares, A,*
    176
Barony, 270
Barr, Robb, 34
Barrow, Geoffrey B., 179
Barrows,
    Jemima (Drew), 76
    Joseph, 76
    Peleg, 76
Bartlett,
    Joseph Gardner, 6
    Sarah, 81
Basset, 163
    Sir Ralph, 292
Bastardy, 101
    factor, 25
Batte, Henry, 160
Battle Abbey Roll, 5
Baxter, Richard, 79
Beach, Tyle, 68
Beaman, Alden G., 74
Beard, Timothy F., 239
Beauchamp,
    Isabel, 303
    William, 303
Beaumont,
    Isabel, 302
    Robert, 302
Bedford, Henlow, 37
Beerman, Eric, 37
Beleigne, Robert, 297
Bell, Raymond M., 239
Benoît, Thomas, 186
Bereford, Edmund, 281
Berkeley, Maurice, 207
Bernard, son of Duke Bernard,
    302
Besford, 164
    Alexander, 164
Bible, 25
    records, 51, 93
Biden, Joseph, 223
Bigod,
    Hugh, 302-03

Isabel, 303
    Roger, 303
Billings,
    Richard, 116
    Sarah (Little), 116
Billington,
    Francis, 63, 112, 114
    Isaac, 63
    Lydia, 62, 112-13
    Seth, 63
Bindoff, S. T., 170
Birmingham, Stephen, 152
Black ancestry, 38
Blount, 162
    Sir Thomas, 163
Board for Certification of
    Genealogists, 230, 235,
    238
Boarstall Cartulary, The, 133,
    304
Boegehold,
    Mary Lou, 124
    Richard A., 124
Bohun, 77
    Humphrey, 85
Bond, Henry, 259
Bonney, Desire, 63
Book reviews, 31
Booksellers, 237
Boston Globe, 60
Botetourt, John, 170
Bowditch,
    William, 134
    Harold, 232
Bowen, Clarence Winthrop, 93
Bowman, George Ernest, 33,
    62, 110, 129, 150, 251
Boyce, Content, 100
Boyd's Marriage Index, 180
Boyton, William, 292, 299
Bractonn's Note Book, 279
Bradford, William, 37
Brandenburg, Erich, 315
Braose, 77, 94, 162, 256, 285
    Agnes, 185, 277
    Beatrice, 270, 273
    Eleanor, 85
    Elizabeth, 185, 273
    Eve, 85
    Giles, 271, 279, 292, 299-
        300
    Isabel, 85
    Joan, 185, 275
    John, 267, 273, 292-93,
        299-300

Lucy, 270
    Margaret, 185, 292, 300
    Mary, 282
    Maud, 85
    Peter, 185, 277, 286
    Reginald, 132
    Richard, 186, 282, 299
    Sybil, 281
    Thomas, 185, 273, 277-78
    Thomasine, 279
    William, 85, 131-33, 267,
        277-78, 282
Breton,
    Edmund, 294
    Thomas, 294
Brewster, William, 83
Brigham Young University,
    235
Brinklies, Mary, 308-09
British National Archives, 176
Brownson, Lydia B. (Phinney),
    38
Bruyn,
    Alice, 184, 307
    Elizabeth, 184
    Henry (Sir), 184, 307
    Ingram (Sir), 306
    Maurice, 184, 306
Bulkeley, 159
Bulkeley Genealogy, 143
Burke, Bernard (Sir), 243, 251-
    52
Burke's Peerage, 243, 245, 252
Burlingame,
    Achsah W., 119
    Albert, 119
    Alexis, 119
    Bethany, 119
    Clarissa, 119
    Jeremiah, 82, 116
    Jeremiah Grinnell, 121
    John Valentine, 116
    John Valentine, *chart*
        117
    Ruth (Grinnell) (Pal-
        mer), 116
    Walter Palmer, 82, 118
Burlingame Manuscript, 87,
    118, 125
Burrows, Ansel, 253
Bygot,
    Isabel, 297
    Sir John, 290
Bysshe, Herald, 255

C

Caen, Robert, 268
Camp, Anthony J., 189
Camville, Aubrey, 207
Cantelou, William, 85
Caput, 264
Carroll, Lewis, 41
Case studies, 110-13
Census records, 51
Cerny, Johni, 10, 38, 153
Certified genealogists, 224, 230
Chamberlain,
    Henrietta, 25
    Nathaniel, 20, 90
Chambers, Valarie N., 34
Charlemagne, 17, 26, 35, 39, 70, 170, 198, 267, 302
Charles, Bonnie Prince, 2
Charlton, 159
Charter Rolls, 184
Chastelon, Margaret, 306
Chastity, 25
Chaucer, 38
Chaurces, Patric, 303
Chester, Joseph Lemuel, 5
Chester of Chicheley, 70
Cheves, Langdon, 314
Chicago Manual of Style, 57
Child,
    James, 312-13
    Joseph, 249
    Lydia, 249
Chilton, James, 95, 116
Chipman, John, 127
Christensen, Gloria M., 102, 106
Chromosomes, 198
Chronology, 76, 94-97, 183, 287
Church of Jesus Christ of Latter-day Saints (LDS), genealogical resources of, 7-10
    Family History Centers, 104, 238
    Family History Department, 44, 215, 217
    Family History Library, 7, 9-10, 125, 160, 177, 180-81, 186, 189, 225, 228, 236, 238
Church records, 51
Church, Ruth, 249

Churchill,
    Sarah, 148
    Winston (Sir), 74, 78, 147-48, 154
Cincinnati, Society of the, 224
Clare, 3, 77, 176, 267
    Gilbert, 302
    Isabel, 302
    Matilda, 267
    Richard, 302
Clark, Scotto, 129, 134
Clarke,
    Jeremy, 160
    Sarah, 81
Clay, Charles Travis (Sir), 190, 232
Clere, 267
    Agatha, 266
    Roger, 267
Clerk's copy, 53
Cleveland, Dutchess of, 12
Close Rolls, 184
Clough, Arthur Hugh, 29
Cockayne, George Edward, 173
Coddington, John Insley, 171, 175, 189, 232, 239
Coldham, Peter Wilson, 177, 189, 239, 286
Coleville,
    Alice, 288, 290, 292
    Edmund, 197, 207, 292, 300
    Elizabeth, 292
    Robert, 290, 292, 294
    Roger, 292, 300
    William, 290
Colket, Meredith B., Jr., 13, 163, 170, 232
Collateral ancestor, 73
Colonial Clergy, Society of Descendants of the, 143
Colonial Governors, Hereditary Order of the Descendants of, 143
Colville, 162
    Alice, 163
    Edmund, 270
    Roger, 270
Coming,
    Affra, 311, 313-14
    John, 312
Compact disks, 222
Compendium of American Genealogy, 245

Compiled genealogies, 32
Complete Peerage, 85, 131, 132-33, 159, 168-69, 172-73, 246, 269, 283, 301, 304
Computers, 209-22
Conant,
    George, 102
    Mary, 102
Concise History of the Common Law, A, 279
Concord, Massachusetts, Births, Marriages and Deaths, 1653-1850, 247, 260
Contemporary evidence, 52-53
Cooke,
    Elizabeth, 66
    Francis, 81, 91, 110, 130, 148
    Herald, 255
    Mary, 130
    Robert, 110
    Sarah, 250
    Susanna, 110
Coolidge,
    Hepzibah, 20
    John, 36
    Tabitha 20
Cooper,
    Ann, 37
    Charles H., 74
    Humility, 37
    Thomson, 74
Copinger, W. A., 299
Corbet, Joan, 164
Cosby, Bill, 38
County histories, 253
Court records, 51
Courtesy of England, 271-72, 276
Courts
    baron, 269
    leet, 269
Cousins, marriage of, 18
Crandall, Bethany, 119
Cromwell, Thomas, 158
Crown of Charlemagne in the United States of America, Order of the, 145
Cunigarde, 302
Curfman, Robert J., 169
Curia Regis Rolls, 185

D

Dallett, F. James, 239
Daniels, Almon E., 38
Darcy, Elizabeth, 307
Darling, Hopestill, 76
Data Base Management Systems, 212, 218-219
Daughters of the American Revolution, 141, 146, 153-54, 247, 261
  Library, 142
Daughters of the Barons of Runnymede, National Society of, 145
Dauthen, Jane, 310, 313
Davenport, James, 161, 169
Davis,
  Walter Goodwin, 223, 226, 232
  William, 46, 114, 252
De Donis Conditionalibus, 276
Dearborn, David C., 239
Declaration of Independence, 35, 39
Dedham, Essex, 36
Deighton sisters, 160
Delano,
  Benoni, 87
  Ebenezer, 55
  Lydia (Delano) (Wormall), 54
  Mary, 253
DeMars, Sally, 125
Demesne lord, 263
Democratization 140-41, 155
Demos, John, 13, 193, 206
Deryng, Alexander, 296
Desktop Publishing, 212
Dethick, Herald, 255
DeVille, Winston, 239
Diaries, 51
Die Nachkommen Karls des Grossen, 315
Dingley, John 127, 161, 169
Dinglie, Anne, 309
Direct ancestor, 73
Direct statements, 51
Disraeli, Benjamin, 137, 223, 241
DNA, 198
Documentary proof, 94
Documentation, 41-60, 245
  formats, 55-58

Dodge,
  Amee, 250
  Ann, 250
Dorman, John Frederick, 33, 239
Doty,
  Edward, 30
  Ellis, 39
  Ethan A., 39
  Joseph, 30
  Josiah, 91
Double standard, 42-44
Dower, 276, 282
Dowry, 276
Drake, John, 160, 167
Dudley,
  Joseph, 79
  Rebecca, 79
  Thomas, 160
Dugdale, William, 5, 187, 190, 245, 254-55, 269
Dumas, David W., 78
Dungan,
  Barbara, 162
  Frances (Latham), 162
  Thomas, Judge, 162
  Thomas P., 162, 168, 170
  William, 162
Dunham, 92
  Isaac Watson, 105
  Jonathan, 68
  Tylee, 68
Dunham Genealogy, 253
Dunster, 278
Dymoke,
  John (sir), 265
  Margaret, 265

E

Eakle, Arlene, 153
Early Yorkshire Charters, 190
Eddy Society, 138
Eden, Lady Clarissa, 147-48
Edgar, Walter B., 312
Edward II (King), 132
Edward III (King), 161, 281
Edwards, Valerie C., 206
Elizabeth I (Queen), 255
Elizabeth II (Queen), 16
Elkinton, George, 168
Elliot, Wendy, 10

Ellis,
  Deborah, 30
  Elizabeth (Freeman), 39
  Harry (Sir), 94, 105
  John, 39
  Mary (Fish), 81
Elwes, Dudley G. Cary, 94, 105, 267
Emmison, F. G., 182, 308-10
Encyclopedia Britannica, 11, 79, 208, 281-82
Endogamy, 19
England, American lines, 159-60
English Genealogy, 175
English Origins of New England Families, 177
Ensign,
  John, 92
  Sarah, 79, 92
Ensign, The, 12
Entailed land, 271
Escheat, 269, 276
Escheator, 183, 269
Essex County, 33
Essex Genealogist, The, 33
Essex Institute Historical Collections, 33
Ethiopia, 3
Eugenics, 204-05
Evans, Nesta R., 190
Everton Publishers, 236
Evidence,
  analyzing, 89-106
  indirect, 107-25
  validity of, 241-61

F

False Pedigrees, 25-26
Family group sheets, 9, 229, 238
Family Roots (computer program), 216
Farrer, William, 182, 190
Fawlty, Basil, 138
Fay,
  James, 249
  John, 266-67
  Mary Smith, 38
  Maud, 266
  Philippa, 266
  Ralph, 268
Fee simple, 272

Fee tail, 273
Fee tail male, 273
Feet of fines, 186
Fellman, Bruce, 208
Felton, Hamo (Sir), 292
Ferrers,
Countess of, 281
Robert, 207
William, 197, 281
Feudalism, 263
Fine Rolls, 184
Fiske, Jane F., 33, 68, 74, 239
Fitch-Northen, Charles, 170
FitzAlan, 159, 174
FitzGeoffrey, John (Sir), 303
FitzJohn, Maud, 303
Fitzsimmons, Lady, 291, 293
Flagon and Trencher, 144, 146
Ford,
E. B., 203, 207
Hannah, 81
Forest, Louis Effingham, 232
Formatted data, 221
Forst-Battaglia, Otto, 12
Fort Wayne and Allen County
Library, 236
Foster,
Benjamin, 102
Maria, 102
Mary Bartlett, 250
Foucher, John, 296
Founders and Patriots of
America, Order of the,
144
Frank almoign, 265
Frank marriage, 276
Frank pledge, 269
Freeman,
Alice, 164
Edward, 6, 252
French, Elizabeth, 6
Freville,
Alexander, 265
George, 71, 165
Joan, 265
Robert, 71, 165
Frost,
Hannah, 83
Joseph, 83
Millicent, 83
Fuller,
James, 81
Judith, 81
Furnivale, Sir Gerard, 303

G

Gamer, Lydia, 83
Gardner, David E., 177
Gateway ancestors, 159
Gazetteer, 91
GEC, 173
Gedding, Robert (Sir), 293
Genealogical Computer Systems, 212, 215-16
Genealogical conferences, 226-29, 231, 258
Genealogical Coordinating Committee, 235
Genealogical Disciplines, Society of, 234
Genealogical Evidence: A Guide to the Standard of Proof Relating to Pedigrees, Ancestry, Heirship and Family History, 260
Genealogical Gleanings in England, 177
Genealogical Guide - An Index to British Pedigrees in Continuation of Marshall's Genealogist's Guide, A, 179
Genealogical guides, 179
Genealogical Helper, The, 34, 39
Genealogical institutes, 235-36
Genealogical journals, 29-38
Genealogical Periodical Annual Index, The, 179
Genealogical Publishing Company, 236
Genealogical Research in England and Wales, 177
Genealogical Research: Methods and Sources, 175, 239
Genealogical societies, 224
Genealogical Societies, Federation of, 221, 227, 235, 238, 241
Genealogical Society of Utah, 235
Genealogist, The, 30, 176, 237, 252
Genealogist's Bibliography, A, 181
Genealogist's Guide, The, 179

Genealogist's Guide: An Index to Printed British Pedigrees and Family Histories, The, 179
Genealogists, American, 6
Genealogists, American Society of, 230, 232, 235, 239
Genealogists, Board for Certification of, 230, 235, 238
Genealogists, Fellows of the American Society of, 230, 232-33, 238, 244
Genealogists in England, Society of, 234
Genealogists, professional, 7
Genealogy,
history of, 5
modern, 5
origin of, 2-3
purposes of, 3
royal, 157-90
General Services Administration, 235
Generations, 15-16
Genes, 198
Genetics, 197-202, 207
Genetics, 207
George I (King), 16
George Mason University, 235, 239
Georgia, 38
Gerald of Wales, 132
Gernon, 162
Alice (Coleville) (Grobaud), 300
Isabel, 163, 295-96
John, 163, 285, 288
Katherine, 163, 295-96
Margaret, 163
Roger, 296
William, 296
Gibbs, Vicary, 173
Giffard, John, 207
Gifford, 30, 164
Gilbert and Sullivan, 15, 89, 137
Giron y, Jeronimo, Moctezuma, 37
Glass,
Hannah, 63
James, 63
Mary (Pontus), 63
Glover, 164
Herald, 255
Robert, 72

Gobaud,
    Alice, 288
    Elizabeth, 290, 292
    Guy, 292, 297
    Isabel, 297
    John, 292
    Katherine, 297
    Mabel, 292-93, 295, 298
    Roger, 297
Goodspeed's Book Shop, 237, 239
Gowing,
    Gidion, 98
    Joanna, 98
Grand serjeanties, 265
Graphics, 212
Gravestone records, 51
Gray, Tyle, 68
Green,
    Christopher, 72
    Mary, 97
Greene, David L., 6, 32, 34, 39, 60, 169, 191, 206, 239
Greenlaw, William Prescott, 232
Gregorian calendar, 97
Gresley, 162
    Geoffrey (Sir), 163
    Margaret, 163
    Thomas (Sir), 163
Grinnell,
    Bailey, 82
    Comfort (Billings) (Bailey), 116
    Richard, 81, 116
Guinness Book of World Records, 60
Gunderson, Robert C., 12
Gutnik, Martin J., 207

H

Haley, Alex, 38
Hamilton-Edwards, Gerald, 157-58, 169, 177
Hansard, Thomas, 279
Hansen, Charles M., 37, 168, 172, 239
Harding, Anne Borden, 38
Harleian Society, 187, 245, 255
    Publications, 74
Harleian Visitations, 186

Harleston,
    Affra, 308, 311
    Ann, 308
    Anthony, 308
    Charles, 312
    Clement, 184, 307-09
    Elizabeth, 308
    Frances, 308
    Henry, 308
    Jane, 308
    John, 184, 307-13
    Mary, 308, 309
    Nicholas, 313
    Robert, 184, 307-08, 311-13
    Thomas, 308-09, 311
    William, 308-09
Harley,
    Joan (Corbet), 164
    Robert, 164
Harlow, Rebecca, 81
Harter, Mary M., 239
Harvard's Widener Library, 236
Harvey, P. D. A., 190
Haseslden, Anthony, 165
Haskell,
    John, 129, 134
    Mary 129, 134, 250
    Patience (Soule), 129, 134
Hatch, Deborah, 30, 39
Haudlo,
    John, 304
    Richard (Sir), 133, 304, 315
Hayes, Rutherford B., 170
Hayford, Mercy, 59
Hearthstone Bookshop, 237, 239
Heiresses, 266
Henry, Matthew, 38
Henry I (King), 70, 162, 268
Henry II (King), 163
Henry VIII (King), 176, 186
Heralds, College of, 5
Hereditary Register of the United States of America, 139
Hereditary societies, 10, 137-55
    standards for, 242
Hereford, Earl of, 293, 295
Heritage Books, Inc., 236
Heroun,
    Elizabeth, 275

    William, 185, 275
Hildegarde, 302
Historical Foundations of the Common Law, 280
History, 3, 91, 138, 191, 205-06
History and Antiquities of the County of Surrey, The, 260
History of Scots and English Land Law, 280
History of Surrey, 256
History of the Town of Duxbury, 245
Hoff, Henry B., 33, 239
Hoffman, William J., 206
Hollister, C. Warren, 283
Holman,
    Mary Lovering, 232
    Winifred L., 239
Holmes, 77
    Bartlett, 81
    Elisha, 81
    Jabez, 81
    John, 38, 46, 78, 108, 124
    Josiah, 76
    Jeremiah, Jr., 76
    Nathaniel, 78
    Rebecca, 81
    Ruth, 25
    Sarah, 81
    Thomas, 108
Honour, 264
Hoogland, John L., 202
Howland,
    Hope, 127
    John, 133
    Joseph, 102
    Mary, 102
    Sarah, 102
Howland Society, 138
Hughes,
    Elizabeth, 103
    Howard Robard, Jr., 38
Hume, David, 280
Humphrey-Smith, Cecil, 168, 181
Hunt, John G., 124, 164, 172
Husband, Richard L., Sr., 34
Hutchinson, John, 112
Hyde, Myrtle Stevens, 35

I

Identification, 12
Ildesley, Robert, 305
Illegitimate children, 102
Illegitimate Sons and Daughters of the Kings of Britain, Descendents of the, (Royal Bastards), 142
In Search of Ancestry, 177
Inbreeding, 202-03, 208
Indian Affairs, Bureau of, 10
Infangentheof, 269
Infidelity factor, 25
Ingals, Benjamin, 113
Ingersoll,
    David, 249
    Thomas, 249
Ingols, James Prince, 114
Inheritance, 2
Inquisitions Post Mortem, 183, 269
International Genealogical Index, 8, 120, 160, 177, 180, 189, 219
Is That Lineage Right?, 261
Islands, 24

J

Jacobsen, Gordon F. (Mrs.), 314-15
Jacobus, Donald Lines, 4, 6-7, 9, 12, 26, 32, 34, 47, 51, 53, 60-61, 73, 80, 92-93, 105, 121, 127-29, 134, 143, 155, 159, 169-71, 189, 209, 223, 225-26, 232, 246, 252, 259
Jacobus revolution, 60
James, Sarah, 100
James II (King), 1
Japan, 3
Jerome, Jennie, 154
Jervey, Theodore D., 311
Joan (Princess), 164
John (King), 132, 162, 164, 277
Jointure, 278
Jones, Henry Z., Jr., 239
Jordan, Abbot of Colchester, 291
Journals, 29-39
Joslyn, Roger D., 239

Julian calendar, 97
Junior and senior, 76

K

Kaufholz, C. Frederick, 239
Keith, William, 95
Kelley, David H., 171, 189, 206, 239
Kellogg, Lucy Mary, 86, 105
Kiepura, 167
    Genevieve Tylee, 170
King Philip's War, 80
King's champion, 265
Kingsley, John, 250
Kinnock, Neil, 15, 223
Knight service, 264-65
Knight's fees, 265
Kolbert, C. F., 280
Konig, David Thomas, 59, 106

L

la Pole,
    Edmund (Sir), 305
    Elizabeth, 306
la Zouche, 159
    Eve, 197, 207
Lackey, Richard S., 57, 260
Lambert, Isaac, 59
Lampet,
    Alice, 292
    John, 293
    Robert, 293
    Thomas, 293, 295
    William, 292-93, 295, 298
Land,
    changing an estate's condition, 276
    records, 51, 182, 186, 194
    tenure, 263-83
    various interests in, 272
Lapham Bathsheba, 66
Laslett, Peter, 18, 61
Latham,
    Cary, 111
    Chilton, 111
    Elizabeth, 110
    Hannah, 112
    James, 111
    Joseph, 111
    Robert, 110

    Thomas, 111
    William, 111
Lawrence,
    Deliverance, 103
    Mercy, 103
    Samuel, 103
LDS, *see* Church of Jesus Christ of Latter-day Saints
le Despencer,
    Hugh, 132, 303
    Margaret, 304
le Rus,
    Alice, 266, 299
    William, 267
Lea, J. Henry, 6
Leach,
    Benjamin, 95, 110
    Eunice, 95
    Hepzibah (Washburn), 95
    Joseph, 95
Lear (King), 273
Leete, William, 70, 131, 165
Leonard Papers, 129
Letters, 51
Libraries, 236
Library of Congress, 236
Library: A guide to the LDS Family History Library, The, 10
Lindberg, Marcia Wiswall, 33
Lindsay,
    Margaret Isabella, 97, 105
    Christopher, 98
    Eleazer, 99
    Elizabeth, 100
    Habakkuk, 73, 97
    Hannah, 98
    John, 99
    Lydia, 100
    Nathan, 100
    Nathaniel, 100
    Ralph, 100
    Samuel, 98, 100
    Stacy, 104
Lindsay Family Assoication, 89
Lipscomb, George, 281
Little Commonwealth: Family Life in Plymouth Colony, A, 206
Little,
    Samuel, 116
    Sarah (Gray), 116

Livery of seizin, 270
Livingston, Virginia P., 239
Llywelyn,
    Gwladys Verch, 165
    Margaret Verch, 164-65
    of Wales, 85
    Prince, 132
    the Great, 164
Lockridge, Kenneth, 13
Longespee, William, 163
Lord Mayor's Court of London:
    Depositons Relating to
    Americans, 1641-1736,
    189
Loretta, Countess of Leicester,
    276
Lothrop,
    Ann, 109
    Barnabas, 109
    John, 109
Louthal, William 313
Loyalists and Patriots of the
    American Revolution,
    Hereditary Order of
    Descendants of the, 144
Luce,
    Henry 63, 73
    James Madison, 20, 78
    Marie Antoinette, 20, 78
    Sarah, 20
    Thomas R., 74
    William, 64, 247
Lungespeye, Richard, 266
Luttrell, 278
Lysenko, Trofim, 204
Lytton,
    Mary, 309
    Rowland, 309

M

MacDonald, Marion A., 99,
    105-06
Mackey, N. A. M., 280
MacMurrough, Eva, 302
Macy, Harry, Jr., 33
Madan, 163
    Falconer, 170
Madison, James, 78
Magna Charta, 3, 270
Magna Charta, Baronial Order
    of, 139, 145

Magna Charta Dames, Nation-
    al Society of, 145
Magna Charta Sureties, 70, 172,
    246
Magna Charta Surety, 267
Magnus, Hugh, 302
Maitland, F. W., 280
Makin, Tobias, 35
Making of England, The, 283
Maleson, Diane C., 206
Mann,
    Alice Whitney, 20
    Ensign, 79, 154, 208
    George S., 208
    Helen Abbie, 20
    Samuel, Jr., 20
    Richard Baxter, 79
    Sally, 195
    Samuel, 195
    Samuel, Sr., 20
    Thomas, 20, 92
Mann Memorial, 208
Manning, Owen, 256, 260
Manorial records, 158, 190
Marbury, 162
    Anne, 160
Margaret of Wygton, 298
Maritagium, 273, 276
Mark, 269
Marmion,
    Mazera, 265
    Philip, 265
Marriages, 96, 196, 270, 272
Marshal,
    Maud, 302-03
    William, 302
    Elizabeth, 18
    George, 179
Martha's Vineyard, 60
Mary of Angouleme, 207
Matrilineal lines, 25
Mautravers, Robert, 270
Mayflower Descendant, 33, 62
Mayflower Descendants,
    General Society of, 141
Mayflower Families, 150
Mayflower Families in Progress,
    151
Mayflower genealogy, 36
Mayflower Index Numbers,
    150
Mayflower Index, The, 155
Mayflower Library, 236
Mayflower Madam, 153

Mayflower Quarterly, 12, 33,
    153, 247, 251
Mayflower Society, 44, 54, 66,
    76, 91, 113, 139, 146-47,
    153, 242, 249-252
Maynard, Ebenezer, 250
McCourt, Martha F., 73
McCracken, George E., 43, 79,
    127, 206, 232, 260
McFarlane, K. B., 273, 276, 278,
    282-83
McIntyre,
    Joseph, 99
    Mary, 99
McKisack, May, 131
McLean, MacLean W., 38-39,
    239
Medieval
    document, 285-300
    pedigrees, 253
    period, 182-83
    records, 183-89
Meinill, 163
Mensa, 204
Merovingian kings, 13
Mesne holders, 263
Messuage, 269
Metheny, W. Blake, 239
Methodology, 193
Meyer, Mary K., 238
Meyer's Directory of Genealogi-
    cal Societies in the U.S.A.
    and Canada, 238
Meyerink, Kory L., 13
Mezi'eres-Trichel-Grappe, 37
Middle Atlantic Genealogy
    and History Institute,
    235, 239
Military records, 51
Miller, Henry, 119
Mills,
    Elizabeth Shown, 1, 10,
        37-38, 191, 224,
        228, 237, 239, 258
    Gary B., 38, 206
Milsom, 280
Minors, 269
Miscelanea Heraldica et
    Genealogica, 176
Mitchell,
    Experience, 112
    Jane (Cooke), 112
    Nahum, 95, 105, 250, 252
Modena, Mary of, 1

Mohun, Lady Joan, 278
Moiety, 264, 269
Monasticon Anglicanum, 190
Moncreiffe, Iain (Sir), 37
Monette, 253
    Ora E., 92, 105
Montgomery, Roger, 264
Moore, Caroline T., 312
More, Richard, 250
Morey,
    Jonathan, 250
    Mary, 250
Moriarty, George Andrews, 6, 66, 79, 128-29, 134, 154, 168, 170-71, 175, 182, 189, 232, 244, 246, 253-54, 260, 269
Moriarty's Notebooks, 282
Morison, Samuel Eliot, 243
Mortimer, 77
    Roger, 85
Morton, Patience, 81
    Anna, 250
Moslems, 3
Moulton,
    Benjamin, 99
    Daniel, 99
    Hannah, 99
    John, 104
    Mehitabel (McIntyre), 104
    Robert, 99
    Samuel, 99
Mowbray, John 131
Mullins, 190
    Priscilla, 133
Mythical origins, 99

N

Names,
    brothers with same, 83
    interchangeable, 85
    Latin, 85
    significance in, 84
    variation in, 84-86
    after a deceased child, 84
Naming patterns, 75, 77-78
Napier, Henry A., 306
National Archives and Records Administration, 235

National Genealogical Society, 39, 226, 235, 238
National Genealogical Society Quarterly, 30, 176, 226, 241
National Genealogical Society Newsletter, 39
National Institute on Genealogical Research, 235
Natural children, 89
Nelson,
    Bathsheba, 81
    Glade I., 238
    Hannah 81
    John, 81, 103
    Lydia, 81
    Samuel, 81
    Sarah, 81
Nerford, John, 281
New Complete Peerage, 173
New England, 26
New England Historical and Genealogical Society, 5, 39, 153, 225, 237
    Library, 225, 236
New England Historical and Genealogical Register, The, 30, 176-77, 179, 225, 244
New Haven Genealogical Magazine, 30, 225
New Jersey, 4
New York Public Library, 236
New York Genealogical and Biographical Record, The, 33, 225
New York Genealogical and Biographical Society, 225, 237
New York Times, The, 155
Newberry Library, 236
Newmarch, Sir Thomas, 290
Nexus, 39
Nicholas, Nicholas Harris, 74
Nichols, 164
    Bathsheba, 81
    Elizabeth L., 13
    J., 170
Notes and Queries books, 176

O

Obscured facts, 90-91
Ogg, David, 11
Old Pretender, 2
Oldsberg, Nicholas R., 312
Olsson, Nils William, 239
Onomastics, 75-87
Outfangentheof, 269
Oxford Dictionary of English Christian Names, 87
Oxford History of England, 175

P

Page,
    David C., 208
    John, 313
    William, 12
Painter, Sidney, 182, 184, 189, 264, 280-82
Palgrave, Richard, 159
Palmer,
    Grace, 162
    Ruth (Grinnell), 82
    Walter, 82, 116
Papandreou,
    Andreas, 85
    George Andrew, 85
Parcel, 269
Parish records, 158, 181, 254
Parsons, Gerald J., 239
Paston, John, 278
Patent Rolls, 184
Paul, James Balfour (Sir), 175
Payton,
    Christopher, 71
    Francis, 71
    Robert (Sir), 71
Peabody Institute, 236
Peckham, Mary W., 129
Pedigree collapse, 18-20, *chart* 21, 22
Peerage titles, 174
Penny, 269
Pepin, 302
Percy, 77
Perkins, Mercy (Jackson), 81
Personal Ancestral File (computer program), 74, 215
Petre, Lord, 310
Petty serjeanties, 265

Peyton,
    Christopher, 72
    Edward, 72
    Elizabeth, 72
    Francis, 72
    John, 72
    Margaret (Franceys), 71, 165
    Robert (Sir), 72
    Rose, 70, 165
    Thomas (Sir), 71, 165
Phillimore Atlas and Index of Parish Registers, 168, 181
Phinney, John, 81
Pine, L. G., 12
Pipe Rolls Series, 281
Plunknett, 279
Plymouth Colony, 4, 19, 23, 30, 62, 111, 161, 193, 195
Plymouth Colony: Its History and People, 1620-1691, 105, 124, 134, 207, 211, 221
Plymouth County, 113
Poole, A. L., 270, 282
Port, Adam, 281-82
Porter,
    Gene Stratton, 78
    Roger, 35
Posey, Nehemiah, 84
Pound, 269
Powell,
    Sumner Chilton, 13, 261
    W. R., 310-11
Powicke, Sir Maurice, 132, 276, 282
Prerogative Court
    of Canterbury, 181
    of York, 181
Presidents, U.S., 30
Pride and Prejudice, 282
Primary sources, 48-52, 206, 218
Primogeniture, 158, 178
Prince, 253
Prindle, Paul W., 239
Probate
    jurisdictions, 181
    records, 51, 254
Professional genealogists, 229, 231
Professional Genealogists, Association of, 221, 231, 235, 241

Public Record Office, 185
Publishers, 236

Q

Quaker, 195
    chronology, 97
    records, 68

R

Ravens,
    Grace, 36
    Mary, 36
    Richard, 36
Reade, George, 160
Records and Collections of the College of Arms, The, 260
Redvers, Baldwin, 266
Reign of King John, The, 176, 182
Reitwiesner, William Addams, 165, 170
Reliefs, 269-70
Retford,
    Elizabeth, 306
    Henry (Sir), 307
Reversionary interest, 272
Rice Society, 138
Richards, Lysander S., 86
Richardson, Douglas, 35
Rickard,
    John, 91
    Judith, 81
Ring,
    Francis, 81
    Samuel, 81
Roberts, Gary Boyd, 169, 177
Roderick, Thomas H., 25, 207
Rogers, Thomas, 35
Roos, Thomas (Sir), 288, 293
Roots, 38
Roots (computer program), 74
Ros,
    Mary, 133
    Robert, 133
    William, 133
Rose, Christine, 239
Round, J. Horace, 5, 171, 175, 186, 191, 193, 246, 255, 260, 280-81

Royal Bastards, 42, 52, 93, 125, 131, 138-39, 142, 146, 154, 159, 170, 243, 314
Royal genealogy, 157-90
Royal lines, 178-80, 244, 259, 301
Royko, Mike, 221
Rubincam, Milton, 4, 6, 47, 171, 175, 189, 232, 239
Rumsey, Jean, 239
Russell,
    Barrett Beard, 74
    Deborah, 66
    Donna Valley, 33, 239
    George Ely, 32, 38, 134, 239
    John, 74
    Thomas, 250

S

St. Amand,
    Aumarie (Almeric), 133, 304
    Isabel, 133, 304, 315
    John, 133, 304, 315
St. Elen,
    Beatrice, 271
    John, 271
St. Haudlo,
    Elizabeth, 305
    Margaret, 305
St. John, John (Sir), 290
St. Valery, Maud, 132
Salley, A. S., Jr., 312
Salter, H. E., 135, 304
Samford University, 235
    Library, 239
Sampson,
    Abraham, 37
    Henry, 37, 54
    John, 250
    Robert, 309
Sargent, William, 164, 170
Savage, James, 127, 252
Sawin, Abijah 83
Scanners, 218
Scholarship, 191
Schulz, John H., 67
Scott, Kenneth, 239
Scrivelsby Manor, 265
Scutage, 266
Secondary sources, 52

Segar, Herald, 255
Selden, John, 41, 280
Sergeanty, 264
Sewall,
    Gilbert, 205
    Samuel, 79
Sex, premarital, 101
Shaftsbury Papers, 312
Shakespeare, 75
Sheppard, Walter Lee, Jr., 74,
    165, 170-72, 175, 189, 232,
    246
Sherman,
    Edmund Jay, 35, 90
    Frank Dempster, 90
    John, 35
    Myra Ann, 25, 90
    Robert M., 55, 87, 206
    Roy V., 104
    Ruth Wilder, 4, 34, 60,
        134, 239
Shields, William R., 202
Shilling, 269
Shurtleff,
    Benjamin, 250, 260
    Nathaniel B., 251
Siblings, 62
Silvester,
    Albert Henry, 86
    Ruth, 81
Simmons,
    Agatha A., 312
    Patience, 81
Sinclair, Guy (Sir), 291
Smallwood, Grahame Thomas,
    Jr., 139
Smith,
    Christopher, 72
    Frank, 177
    John, 72
    Sarah, 100
    William, 72
Snow, Sarah, 250
Social mobility, 158, 169, 178
Society of Genealogists in En-
    galnd, 234
Society of the Cincinnati, 142
Socrates, 18, 23
Somerby, Horatio G., 245
Sons of the American Revolu-
    tion, 153
Soule,
    George, 4, 127
    Nathaniel, 4

*Source: A Guidebook of
    American Genealogy,
    The*, 139, 153
Sources, 92-94
Southworth, Edward, 96
Southworth,
    Elizabeth, 84, 96, 102
    Mary, 96, 102
Sperry, Kip, 33, 37, 239
Spinster, 194
Spiritual tenure, 264
Spooner, William, 253
Spouses, deceased, 80
Sprague, Elizabeth, 250
Squibb, G. D., 260
Squires, 265
Standards, 41-60
Stacy, 104
Stalin, 204
Standards, 229
Standish, Myles, 77
Statute of DeDonis Con-
    ditionalibus, 273
Statute of Quia Emptores, 273
Statutes of Uses, 278
Stein, Gertrude, 75
Stenton,
    Doris M., 265, 281
    Frank (Sir), 280-81
Stern, Malcolm H., 224, 229,
    237, 239
Stetson, Ruth, 114
Stetson Society, 138
Stevenson, Noel C., 1, 11, 47,
    232, 239, 248, 252, 260
Stone,
    Anne, 20
    Esther, 20
    John, 20
    Jonas, 20
Stratton
    Abigail, 20
    Elias, 82
    Eugene A., 41, 105-06,
        133, 155, 169-70,
        180, 206, 239, 259-
        60
    Harriet Russell, 78
    Horace, 20, 25, 78
    Jabez, 20
    John, Jr., 20
    Joseph, 16, 20, 25
    Rolland, 25
    Samuel, 16
Strickland, 77

Stryker-Rodda, Kenn, 144, 239
Stuart, James Francis Edward,
    1
Sturtevant,
    Mary, 253
    Samuel, 253
Subinfeudation, 264, 272
Suffolk, Earl of, 293, 300
Surnames as first names, 78-80
Sutherland, Donald W., 285
Sutton,
    John (Sir), 291, 293
    Richard (Sir), 291
    Willie, 157
Swift,
    Elizabeth, 130
    Thomas, 130
    William, 130
Swinnerton,
    Richard (Sir), 293
    Robert (Sir), 293

T

Tamworth Castle, 265
Telecommunications, 212, 216-
    218
Tenant in capite, 263
Tenants, 263
Tenants-in-chief, 263, 269
Terence, 15
Terminology, 194
Testamenta Vetusta, 74
Tettebury Manor, *chart* 274
Textbooks, 205
Thomas of Brotherton, 281
Thompson,
    Daniel, 119
    Neil D., 32, 34, 37, 134,
        172, 189, 239, 286
    Roger, 13, 105
Thomson, Ignatius, 130
Thoreau, Henry David, 107
Thorpe, Lewis, 132
Three Crusades, Order of the,
    145
Throckmorton, 164
Tilley,
    Edward, 36
    Elizabeth, 133
    John, 36
Time Magazine, 221
Toeny, 77

Tomson,
    Elizabeth, 130
    John 130
Torrey, Clarence Almon, 232
Town of Weston - Births, Deaths and Marriages, 17077-1850, 260
Transcriptions, 53, 247
Trask, Elizabeth, 100
Trott, Nicolas, 313
Trowbridge,
    Francis Bacon, 260
    James, 18
    John, 254
    Thomas, 18-19
Trowbridge Genealogy, The, 260
Tue, Thomas, 294
Turner,
    Humphrey, 83
    John, 83
"Two nations" in genealogy, 242

U

Ufford,
    Eve, 300
    Margaret, 207, 300
    Mary, 300
    Robert, 300
Umbilical lines, 24
Understanding Genetics, 207
Undocumented sources, 116, 121, 128, 155
Unmarried mothers, 101
Uses, 278

V

Valentine,
    Comfort, 120
    John, 120
Venard, Haskell, 87
Venn, J. A., 311
Venn, John, 311
Verdon, Isabel, 197
Verdun, Eleanor, 186
    John, 186
Vere, 77, 174
    Robert, 70

Vermandois,
    Adelaide, 302
    Albert I, 302
    Gerbert IV, 302
    Herbert I, 302
    Herbert II, 302
    Herbert III, 302
    Isabel, 302
    Otho, 302
Victoria History of the Counties of England, 6
Victorian England, 26
Villein, 263
Virginia Genealogist, The, 33
Visitation Pedigrees and the Genealogist, 260
Visitations, 186, 245, 253-54
Visitations of Cambridgeshire of 1575 and 1619, The, 71
Vital records, 51
Vital statistics, 195-97

W

Wade,
    Joseph, 92
    Sarah, 92
Wagner, Anthony (Sir), 143, 169, 172, 175, 186-87, 189-90, 232, 239, 260
Wakefield, Robert S., 59, 73, 124, 134, 239
Walker, James, 142
Wall Street Journal, The, 152-53
Ward,
    Kenneth, 197
    Robert Leigh, 36, 180
Wards, 269
Wardships, 270-71
Warming-pan baby, 1-2
Warren,
    Elinor, 63
    Richard, 116, 148, 249-50
    Samuel, 63
Washburn,
    Abigail (Johnson), 114
    Benjamin, 114
    Elizabeth (Mitchell), 112-13
    George, 114
    Hannah (Latham), 110
    Hepzibah, 95, 110
    James, 112

    John, 62, 112-14, 134, 161
    Jonathan, 112
    Joseph, 110, 112
    Lydia (Billington), 114
    Lydia (Prince), 114
    Lydia, 113-14
    Philip, 112-13, 252
    Prince, 114
    Ruth, 114
    Samuel, 112
    Thomas, 112
    William, 112
Washington, George, 142
Waters,
    Henry F., 5-6, 163, 169, 177
    Robert Edmond Chester, 5, 70, 170, 285
Water's Summary, 287-88
Weis, Frederick Lewis, 70, 74, 165, 172, 246
Wentworth,
    Elder William, 285
    Lady Jane, 309
    Philip, 313
    William, 162
    Wentworth arms, 313
Western Maryland Genealogy, 33
Westfield State College, 236, 239
Weston Births, Marriages and Deaths, 247
Weston,
    Margaret, 292
    Samuel, 96
    William (Sir), 292
White,
    Elizabeth Pearson, 34, 239
    Jonathan, 93, 250
    William, 93
Whitmore,
    J. B., 179
    W. H., 6
Whitney,
    Aaron, 154
    Betsey, 119
Whole-family genealogy, 39, 61-74
Wiener, Carol Z., 206
Wilbour, Benjamin F., 87
Wilbur, Otis, 59

Wilcox, *chart* 65, 148
  Cuthbert, 129
  Daniel, 66, 154
  Edward, 66
  Elizabeth (Cooke), 154
  Herbert A., 74
  Jerry, 66
  Jireh, 66, 129, 253
  Mary (Ricketson), 67, 129
  Mary (Thomas), 67
  Mary, 68
  Micajah, 67
  Samuel, 129
  Stephen, 66-67, 129
  Susan, 25
  Tyle, 64, 79, 253
  William, 69, 129
William and Mary, 2
William the Conqueror, 5, 264
Williams,
  Alicia Crane, 33

  Elizabeth, 109
  John, 109
Willis, Elizabeth, 313
Wills, 181-82, 193, 273, 278
Wills from the Archdeaconry of Suffolk, 1629-1636, 190
Wingefeild, 309
  Alianora, 300
  John (Sir), 300
Winslow,
  Eleanor (Adams), 80
  Mary (Chilton), 110
  Susanna, 110
Winsor, Justin, 245
Wishful thinking, 134, 252
Withington, Lothrop, 5-6, 254
Withycombe, E. G., 87
Wodhull, 168
Wolfe, Nero, 104
Wood,
  Alfred, 250
  Ralph Van, Jr., 124

  Mary, 63
  Michael J., 36
  Sarah, 81
  Virginia Steele, 38
Word Processing, 211-12, 214-15
Wormall, Ichabod, 55
Wygton, Lady, 296
Wyke, John, 290, 292

Y

Young, Henry J., 164

Z

Zabriskie, George O., 239
Zimm, Louise Hasbrouck, 125

EUGENE AUBREY STRATTON is a writer and genealogist. He is a Fellow of the American Society of Genealogists; a former Historian General of the Society of Mayflower Descendants; a recipient of the Award of Merit from the National Genealogical Society; a lecturer at the conferences of the National Genealogical Society, the Federation of Genealogical Societies, and others; Faculty Coordinator of the Computers in Genealogy course at the 1988 Samford University Institute of Genealogical and Historical Research; and author of many articles and books, including the highly-acclaimed *Plymouth Colony: Its History & People, 1620-1691,* and the soon-to-be-published genealogical murder mystery, *Killing Cousins.* His writings have been especially praised for their ease of readability.